THE ENCYCLOPEDIA
OF
KNITTING

THE ENCYCLOPEDIA
— OF —
KNITTING

Pam Dawson

ORBIS·LONDON

Acknowledgments
The diagrams were drawn by Coral Mula and
the pattern pieces by Colin Salmon.
The photographs on the following pages are
by courtesy of Camera Press, London: 64, 97,
130, 137, 139 and 210. The remainder of the
photographs were taken by the following
photographers: Jan Baldwin, Tom Belshaw,
Steve Campbell, Bill Carter, Allan Grainger,
Chris Harvey, Clive Helm, Hank Kemme,
Di Lewis, Liz McAulay, Spike Powell,
Tino Tedaldi, Jerry Tubby and Nick Wright.

Cover: Allan Grainger, Tom Belshaw and Jan Baldwin
Half title page: Tino Tedaldi
Title page: Tom Belshaw
Back cover: Allan Grainger

© Eaglemoss Publications Limited 1983, 1984

First published in Great Britain
by Orbis Publishing Limited, London 1984

This material previously appeared in the
partwork *SuperStitch*

Printed in Singapore for Imago Productions (F.E.) Pte Ltd.

ISBN: 0-85613-688-3

Contents

Introduction

Knitting has a long history as a popular leisure activity and it currently enjoys tremendous fashion appeal. In fact knitting has not been out of fashion for centuries – from the black silk stockings worn by Elizabeth I of England and the elegant silk under-shirt worn by Charles I at his execution to the cashmere twin-set worn with the essential rope of pearls in the 1930s and the close-fitting jumpers worn by generously proportioned Hollywood stars which gave a new meaning to knitting in the '40s with the term 'sweater girl'. Today's preference is for big, baggy shapes, but, though the yarns may change, shapes alter slightly, the techniques remain the same.

Legends have always surrounded this beautiful and practical craft. Eve is supposed to have knitted the pattern on the serpent's back, and legend would have us believe that the robe Christ wore at his crucifixion was knitted – because it could not be divided, as would be the case with a hand-knitted fabric, the soldiers cast lots for it.

Actual evidence and samples of the craft are few and far between. It is impossible to trace how a knowledge of it spread but in all of the early cultures it is known that men were the knitters and women the spinners. It is logical, therefore, that men who travelled from one area to another would take examples of knitting with them. In the early eighth century the Arabs began a policy of territorial expansion which eventually gained them control of part of the Iberian peninsula. The Coptic arts and crafts which they had acquired in Egypt were introduced to Spain, where they developed and spread throughout the rest of Europe. In most countries in the Middle Ages knitting was established by the religious orders and in the famous altar piece known as 'The Buxtehude Altar' (popularly called 'The Knitting Madonna') painted by Meister Bertram of Minden (Germany) *c.* 1400 the Virgin Mary is depicted using a set of four needles to pick up the stitches round the neck of a simple vest.

By the fifteenth century knitting and the woollen trade in general had become the most profitable in Britain and in 1527 in France the first knitting guild, the Guild of the Hand Knitters of Stockings, received their Letters of Foundation. Knitting had become not just a profitable craft but a creative art form, requiring skills comparable to those attained in tapestry and weaving. Although by now women and children were also involved in the craft as an additional means of income, it was the men and boys who controlled the guilds and to become a master knitter a boy had to serve an apprenticeship of three years.

During the reign of Elizabeth I a modest clergyman, William Lee, invented and perfected a knitting frame to produce machine-made stockings and so set in process the establishment of a vast hosiery trade in Britain. Hand knitting gradually declined as an industry and was pushed out into the rural areas, where it continued to exist as a secondary source of income. Complete families banded together to supplement their livelihood with spinning and knitting, and regional knitting began to emerge and helped to keep alive the long traditions of the craft. Fishermen, in particular, required warm, waterproof covering, and the term 'guernsey' derives from the knitted garments originally created to fulfil this need in the Channel Island of the same name. (The island of Jersey gave its name to a more generic term now used to describe any knitted upper garment.) As the demand for this practical type of garment spread from one fishing port to another, each region developed its own traditions, incorporating different stitches which symbolized the fishermen's surroundings and working life.

The Industrial Revolution spelt the end of these country crafts. It is staggering to reflect that up to this time all yarn was still being spun by hand but the inventions of this period were soon to mechanize the whole process. The availability of machine-spun wool and the emergence of a new middle class whose women no longer had to work to earn a living led to the growth of leisure pursuits and knitting became a popular hobby. A gentlewoman from Edinburgh, Mrs Gaugain, sensed the need for information about the craft and she began writing books giving instructions and patterns. Hand knitting now revived as a fashionable hobby rather than an industry vital to survival, emerging today as an exciting, creative, practical craft with endless possibilities.

This book is a practical introduction to knitting and it can be used by a complete beginner as a basic course or as an invaluable reference book for the more experienced knitter. You can dip into it to learn a new technique, check on a particular method, or pick up hints and tips which give a professional finish to hand-knitted garments.

All the basic techniques are included – casting on and off (including several unusual and attractive methods), increasing and decreasing, tension, edge finishes, blocking, pressing and making up. These are followed by instructions for working techniques, such as buttonholes, collars, necklines and pockets. This practical knowledge is used to build up a large number of stitch samples to add variety to your knitting. Learn how to knit with two or more colours and use them in traditional Fair Isle and Scandinavian patterns or to add a personalized motif. Or use smocking or Swiss darning to add a stitched decoration after a garment is made.

Textured patterns, such as lacy or twisted stitches, bobbles or cables, add interest to plain garments and these include the traditional guernsey patterns and the delightful quilt or white knitting used for bedspreads and shawls. Most of the techniques are illustrated with a project which shows their practical application, and alternative colourways or variations in style are included so that over fifty exciting patterns for both adults and children are given in this useful collection.

Once you have mastered the basic steps you can begin to explore the tremendous scope this craft has to offer. It is inexpensive to begin and economical to pursue; you can make high-fashion garments or items of infinite beauty and skill. Whenever and wherever you choose to pick up the threads of knitting, you will find it an exciting and rewarding occupation.

Pam Dawson

Pam Dawson, 1984

The knitter's workbox

Knitting is one of the most exciting and rewarding of all the crafts. Every year new and beautiful yarns appear on the market, tools are updated, techniques are modified or rediscovered. This chapter helps you choose the best materials for the job from the wide range available.

alpaca

angora

Basic knitting techniques have remained virtually unchanged for centuries – some of the earliest known knitted items to survive include Arabian sandal socks dating from the third century BC. In Britain the Elizabethan Age was called 'The Golden Age of Knitting', and the knitters were men.

After the frame knitting machine had been invented, the handcraft was continued in Devon and Cornwall by fishermen, and in the Shetlands by sailors.

Today knitting is more popular than ever before – the only problem is choosing from the wide range of yarns and tools available.

Knitting needles are manufactured in a wide range of sizes in order to achieve various tensions. The greater the figure in millimetres, the larger the diameter of the needles. The most durable needles are made from a pale grey, lightweight, plastic-coated metal for smaller sizes. A lightweight, rigid plastic material is used for the larger sizes. These finishes make for smooth knitting and the needles will not break or chip. Almost any colour of yarn shows up against the uniform grey which makes it easier to count stitches.

Pairs of needles For working to and fro in rows to produce a flat section of knitting, needles are manufactured in pairs. Each needle has a smooth working point at one end and a knob at the other. They can be bought in standard lengths of 25/9, 30/11¾ and 35cm/13¾in.

Longer lengths are manufactured but are not so readily available. Large numbers of stitches will need longer needles but personal preference must also be taken into account. Many knitters use long needles so that the left-hand needle can be tucked under the arm to anchor it.

Pairs of colourful plastic needles are also available and children enjoy learning to knit with these. There is a limited range of sizes but they have the advantage of being available in lengths of 15/6, 20/7¾, 25/9¾, 30/11¾ and 35cm/13¾in.

Sets of needles For working in rounds to produce a tubular fabric, needles are manufactured in sets of four or five. Each needle is pointed at both ends. They come in the same size range as pairs of needles and in lengths of 20/7¾ and 30cm/11¾in.

Circular needles These can be used for knitting in rounds or in rows. They comprise two pointed needle ends joined together by a thin strip of flexible nylon. They are not made in as many sizes as pairs of needles and are available in lengths of 40/15¾, 60/23½, 80/31½ and 100cm/39½in. It is important to knit with the correct length of circular needle so that the stitches reach from one needle point to the other.

Other tools Other items in the knitter's workbox include row counters, which fit on to the end of the needle; cable needles – short needles with points at both ends for cabling; stitch holders to keep stitches to be knitted into later while you work the main body of the garment; a needle gauge; a long ruler for measuring sections of knitting; a tape measure for body measurements, a pair of sharp scissors and sewing equipment for joining seams.

Yarn used to mean any natural spun fibre such as wool, cotton or silk, but it now applies to any combination of fibres. The choice is so wide that it is possible to find something to suit all pockets and tastes.

Synthetic yarns are produced by forcing chemical solutions through metal blocks pierced with holes. The size of the holes determines the thickness (denier) of the thread. The extrusion solidifies into long, continuous filaments. Fine filaments are used for tights and stockings. For hand-knitting yarns, thicker filaments are cut into shorter lengths, which are then spun like natural fibres.

All yarns come in standard thicknesses of 2, 3 or 4 ply, double knitting, double double and chunky. The heaviest baby yarn is called quickerknit. Yarns are not spun directly into these thicknesses, but first into plys.

Ply is the term that describes individual spun threads of fibres. These can be fine or coarse and it is a mistake to think that the ply necessarily indicates the finished thickness of any yarn. A Shetland 2 ply can be just as thick as a normal 4 ply.

A yarn containing 4 plys can be made up of three threads of wool and one of nylon, or any combination of natural and man-made fibres.

Twisting the yarn in a variety of ways forms a workable thread that will not break as it is knitted. Untwisted yarn is very bulky and gives a lot of warmth, but it is difficult for the average knitter to use because it pulls apart easily.

Chemical dyeing is a complex process that produces evenly distributed colour of sufficient depth. Natural dyes rarely achieve this overall consistency of colour.

Dyeing is carried out in batches, or

2 ply   3 ply   4 ply

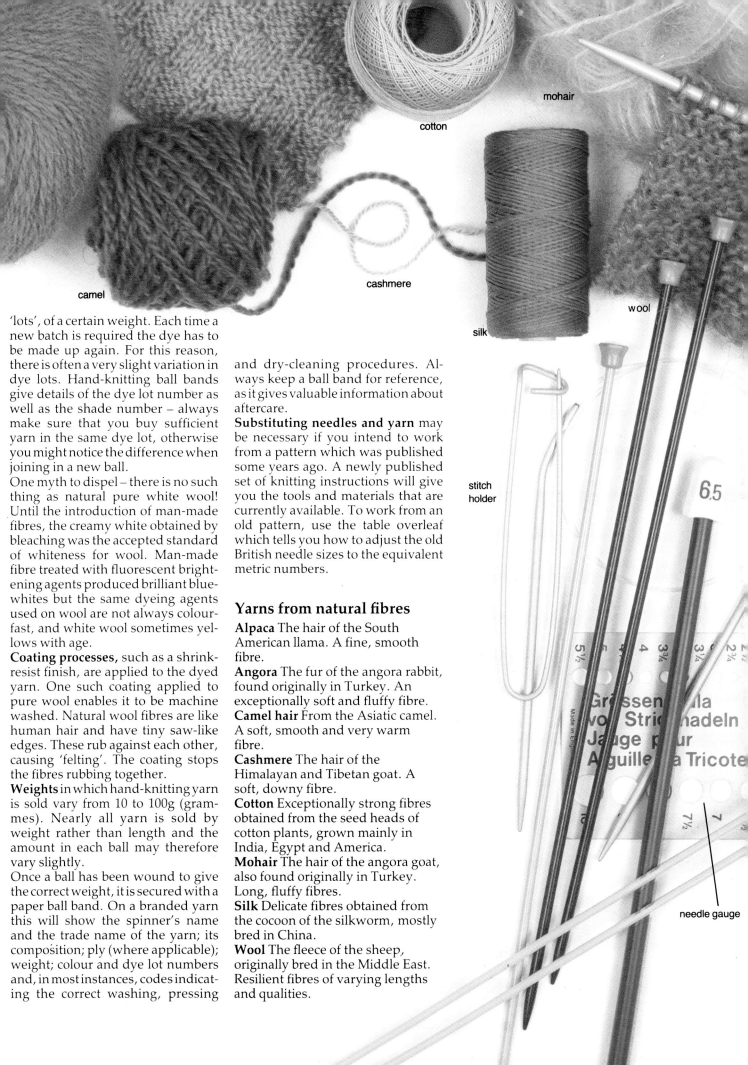

camel
cotton
mohair
cashmere
silk
wool
stitch holder
6.5
5½
4
3¾
3¾
2¾
Grössen
wol Stric nadeln
Jauge p ur
A guille a Tricote
7½
7
needle gauge

'lots', of a certain weight. Each time a new batch is required the dye has to be made up again. For this reason, there is often a very slight variation in dye lots. Hand-knitting ball bands give details of the dye lot number as well as the shade number – always make sure that you buy sufficient yarn in the same dye lot, otherwise you might notice the difference when joining in a new ball.

One myth to dispel – there is no such thing as natural pure white wool! Until the introduction of man-made fibres, the creamy white obtained by bleaching was the accepted standard of whiteness for wool. Man-made fibre treated with fluorescent brightening agents produced brilliant blue-whites but the same dyeing agents used on wool are not always colourfast, and white wool sometimes yellows with age.

Coating processes, such as a shrink-resist finish, are applied to the dyed yarn. One such coating applied to pure wool enables it to be machine washed. Natural wool fibres are like human hair and have tiny saw-like edges. These rub against each other, causing 'felting'. The coating stops the fibres rubbing together.

Weights in which hand-knitting yarn is sold vary from 10 to 100g (grammes). Nearly all yarn is sold by weight rather than length and the amount in each ball may therefore vary slightly.

Once a ball has been wound to give the correct weight, it is secured with a paper ball band. On a branded yarn this will show the spinner's name and the trade name of the yarn; its composition; ply (where applicable); weight; colour and dye lot numbers and, in most instances, codes indicating the correct washing, pressing

and dry-cleaning procedures. Always keep a ball band for reference, as it gives valuable information about aftercare.

Substituting needles and yarn may be necessary if you intend to work from a pattern which was published some years ago. A newly published set of knitting instructions will give you the tools and materials that are currently available. To work from an old pattern, use the table overleaf which tells you how to adjust the old British needle sizes to the equivalent metric numbers.

Yarns from natural fibres

Alpaca The hair of the South American llama. A fine, smooth fibre.

Angora The fur of the angora rabbit, found originally in Turkey. An exceptionally soft and fluffy fibre.

Camel hair From the Asiatic camel. A soft, smooth and very warm fibre.

Cashmere The hair of the Himalayan and Tibetan goat. A soft, downy fibre.

Cotton Exceptionally strong fibres obtained from the seed heads of cotton plants, grown mainly in India, Egypt and America.

Mohair The hair of the angora goat, also found originally in Turkey. Long, fluffy fibres.

Silk Delicate fibres obtained from the cocoon of the silkworm, mostly bred in China.

Wool The fleece of the sheep, originally bred in the Middle East. Resilient fibres of varying lengths and qualities.

Converting needle sizes

The chart below shows the old Imperial and equivalent metric sizes. A needle gauge giving both sizes will also help you to check old needles, which may not have a size stamped on them.

Imperial	Metric	Imperial	Metric
14	2mm	6	5mm
13	2¼mm	5	5½mm
—	2½mm	4	6mm
12	2¾mm	3	6½mm
11	3mm	2	7mm
10	3¼mm	1	7½mm
—	3½mm	0	8mm
9	3¾mm	00	9mm
8	4mm	000	10mm
7	4½mm		

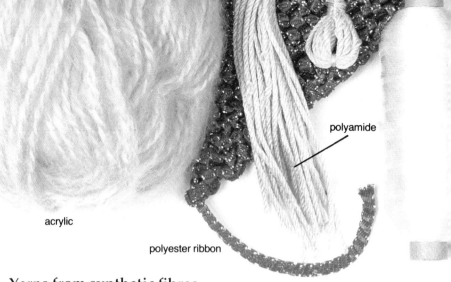

polyamide

acrylic

polyester ribbon

Yarns from synthetic fibres

Acrylics Fibres such as Courtelle and Orlon, derived from natural gas.
Yarns of high bulk and exceptional lightness. They contain pockets of air, which makes them warm to wear.

Polyamides Fibres such as nylon, produced from chemical sources. These fibres are strong yet elastic. They do not absorb moisture, so are not weakened when wet. Nylon fibres feel a little hard but are excellent strengthening agents when combined with wool or acrylics.

Polyesters Fibres such as Terylene and Crimplene, derived from petrol.
These fibres are strong yet light and do not absorb moisture. On their own, they are subject to static electricity, which attracts dirt, but they combine well with other fibres.

Viscose Regenerated fibres such as rayon obtained from the cellulose in waste cotton and wood pulp.
These fibres absorb moisture and are good conductors of heat. They are cool to touch and slippery to handle but combine well with other fibres.

Standard aftercare symbols

 A tub indicates that the yarn can be hand or machine washed.

 A hand in the tub means hand wash only.

 A figure in the water shows the correct water temperature.

 Number 1 to 9 above the water line denotes washing machine programmes.

 Where the tub is crossed through, dry-clean only.

 An iron means the yarn can be pressed – one dot means cool; two dots medium and three dots hot.

 Where the iron is crossed through do not attempt to press the yarn or you may ruin the fabric.

 An empty circle means the yarn can be dry-cleaned.

 An A inside the circle means dry-cleaning in all solvents.

 The letter P means dry-cleaning only in certain solvents.

 The letter F means dry-cleaning only in certain solvents.

 Where the circle is crossed through do *not* dry-clean.

 A triangle means that the yarn can be bleached.

 Where the triangle is crossed through do not bleach.

 Square signs denote drying instructions.

 Three vertical lines in a square means drip dry.

 One horizontal line in a square means dry flat.

 A circle in a square means tumble dry.

A loop at the top of a square means dry on a line.

glitter yarns

chenille

crepe

knop

viscose ribbon

slub

Fancy Yarns

Bouclé is a loopy textured yarn. Each ply may be of a different thickness, texture and colour.

Chenille is a velvety, tufted yarn which produces a dense fabric.

Crepe is a very highly-twisted yarn, usually 4 ply or double knitting weights.

Glitter yarn is man-made metal threads, used on its own or combined with other fibres.

Slub is an unevenly spun yarn which produces an irregularly textured fabric.

Knop is similar to slub but has small knops in place of thickened streaks.

bouclé

Converting ounces to grammes

oz balls	25g balls	oz balls	25g balls
1	1	11	13
2	3	12	14
3	4	13	15
4	5	14	16
5	6	15	17
6	7	16	18
7	8	17	19
8	9	18	21
9	10	19	22
10	12	20	23

Abbreviations

A complete list of the abbreviations used in the patterns given in this book can be found on page 234.

Right: This figure-hugging evening top with crossover straps is made from a man-made yarn with a hint of glitter for a touch of glamour.

Casting on and basic stitches

Today's knitting yarns come in a luscious choice of colours and textures. Whether you're an experienced knitter, a bit rusty, or a complete beginner, now is the time to discover how to turn a wealth of traditional stitches into fashionable designs.

Knitting is a straightforward skill that can be picked up in an evening. All you need is a pair of needles, a pattern and some yarn. From there on, learning to knit is like learning to touch-type. It takes a little patience and practice to get the action smooth, with fingers, needles and yarn working in unison. (If you knit jerkily, the knitting will be uneven and bumpy.) There are two basic stitches, knit and purl. They are bread-and-butter stitches, but they combine to produce a vast range of attractive patterns.

The following chapters are carefully planned so that skills can be easily acquired. Often techniques are married to projects so that you can make appealing garments as you practise.

How to hold the yarn and needles

1 The needle in your right hand is used to make the stitches, while the needle in your left hand holds the completed stitches.
2 Wind the yarn round the fingers of

your right hand so that it flows smoothly and freely over your fingers. This helps you to knit evenly. The main thing is to feel comfortable and relaxed.

PROFESSIONAL TOUCH

Invisible casting on with two needles

Make a slip loop, then cast on a second stitch.
1 *Insert the right-hand needle from the back to the front between these last two stitches.
2 Take the yarn round the needle as if to purl and **3**, draw the yarn through on to the right-hand needle. Put this new stitch on the left-hand needle taking care not to twist it.
4 Insert the right-hand needle from the front to the back between the last two stitches on the left-hand needle.
5 Take the yarn round the needle as if to knit and draw the yarn

through on to the right-hand needle. Put this new stitch on the left-hand needle taking care not to twist it.
Continue in this way from the point marked with an asterisk (*) until the required number of stitches are made.
With an odd number of stitches begin the next row with a purled stitch – with an even number begin with a knitted stitch.
6 Continue in single rib but on the first row work into the back loop of each knitted stitch, instead of the front.

Casting on with two needles

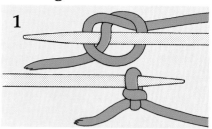

Knitting begins with a slip loop which counts as the first stitch. To make a loop take the main length of yarn across the short end.
1 Using the point of a needle, pull the main length through from the back to the front and leave this loop on the needle.
Draw up the main length to tighten the loop.

Casting on with one needle

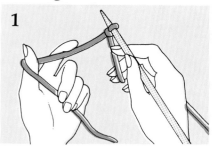

This method uses only one needle because the thumb of the left hand replaces the other needle – so it is sometimes called the thumb method. Begin by making a slip loop about 50cm/20in from end of a ball of yarn. This should be enough yarn to make about 25 stitches in double knitting yarn with 4mm/No 8 needles – leave a

The chapters are also designed to be a useful reference work for experienced knitters – to refresh their memories or unlearn any bad techniques they may have picked up.

Casting on Three methods are given here. Casting on with two needles gives a neat edging and is used with ribbing or stocking stitch. This method is also used when you need to cast on extra stitches further on in the knitting for buttonholes or to extend the shape. Casting on with one needle gives a ridged edge and so is most suitable for use with garter stitch. Experienced knitters will be interested in the invisible casting-on method (below left). This little-known technique gives a professional finish similar to that of an expensive machine-made garment. It is only used with ribbing.

A few helpful hints Hot sticky hands make knitting difficult so always wash your hands. Avoid getting your work dusty by pinning a bag over your work to keep it clean while you knit. Don't stop knitting in the middle of a row, but always continue to the end. Remember not to stick the needles into the ball of yarn as this can split the yarn. When you start to knit a piece which has been left for some weeks, it is a good idea to unpick the last row worked before continuing to knit. This overcomes any distortion of stitches by the needles and eliminates uneven fabric.

2 Hold the needle with the slip loop in your left hand and the free needle in your right hand, carrying the main length of yarn across your right hand.

3 Insert the point of the right-hand needle into the slip loop from the front to the back, take the yarn under and round the point.

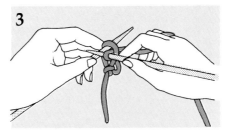

Draw the yarn through the slip loop to make a stitch. Put the new stitch on to the left-hand needle without twisting it.

4 *To make the next stitch insert the needle from the front to the back but this time *between* the two stitches. Take the yarn (as before) under and round the point and draw the yarn

through on to the right-hand needle to make another stitch. Put the new stitch on the left-hand needle without twisting it.

Continue in this way from the point marked with an asterisk (*) until you have cast on the required number of stitches.

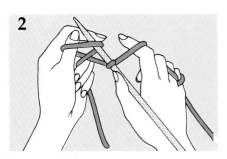

longer end if you are going to need more stitches.

1 Hold the needle with the slip loop in your right hand and wind the main length of yarn round the fingers of your right hand. With the fingers of your left hand hold the end of yarn as shown.

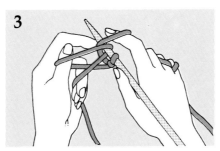

2 *Insert the needle through the loop round your thumb.

3 Take the main length of yarn under and over the point with your right hand and draw the yarn through on to the needle to make a stitch.

4 Leave this stitch on the needle and

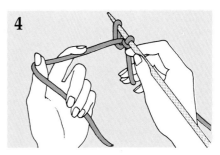

tighten the end of yarn. Wind the end of yarn round your thumb again, ready to make the next stitch.

Continue in this way from the point marked with an asterisk (*) until you have cast on the required number of stitches.

To knit stitches

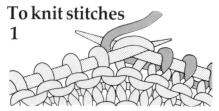

1

Hold the needle with the cast-on stitches in your left hand and the free needle and yarn in your right hand.

1 Insert the right-hand needle from the front to the back into the front loop of the first stitch of the row. *Holding the yarn at the back of the work throughout the row, take it under and round the point.

2

2 Draw the yarn through on to the right-hand needle.

3 Leave this new stitch on the right-hand needle and allow the old stitch to drop off the left-hand needle. One stitch has been knitted and is abbreviated as K1. Insert the right-hand needle from the front to the back into the front loop of the

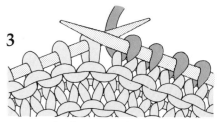

3

next stitch. Continue from the point marked with an asterisk (*) until all the cast-on stitches have been knitted on to the right-hand needle. At the end of this row transfer the needle holding the stitches to your left hand, with the yarn again at the right-hand end of the row, ready to start the next row of knitting.

To purl stitches

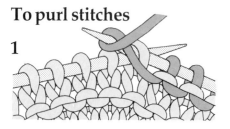

1

Hold the needle with the cast-on stitches in your left hand and the free needle and yarn in your right hand.

1 Insert the right-hand needle from right to left into the front loop of the first stitch of the row. *Holding the yarn at the front of the work throughout the row, take it over the top and round the point.

2

2 Draw the yarn through on to the right-hand needle.

3 Leave this new stitch on the right-hand needle and allow the old stitch to drop off the left-hand needle. One stitch has been purled and is abbreviated as P1. Insert the right-hand needle from right to left into the front loop of the next stitch.

3

Continue from the point marked with an asterisk (*) until all the cast-on stitches have been purled on to the right-hand needle. Transfer the needle holding the stitches to your left hand, with the yarn again at the right-hand end of the row, ready to start the next row.

To knit and purl in the same row

1

You can build up interesting reversible patterns by knitting and purling in the same row. When changing from a knit to a purl stitch remember to hold the yarn in the correct position. Bring it forward

2

between the needles to purl and take it back between the needles to knit. If you don't, the yarn will be carried across the right-hand needle and you will find you have created an extra stitch.

Stocking stitch

When the first and every following odd-numbered row is knitted and the second and every following even row is purled, it produces stocking stitch.
The right (knitted) side of this pattern is the smoothest of all knitted fabrics. The wrong (purled) side is called reversed stocking stitch. It does not look the same on both sides.

Garter stitch

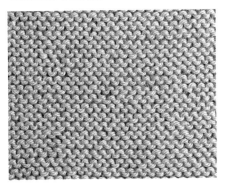

Single ribbing

Basket stitch

(The three stitches shown here are all reversible, which means they look the same on both sides.)

When each stitch in every row is knitted, this is called garter stitch. The effect is a horizontal, ridged pattern.
It can be made quickly and without too much concentration so it is ideal for a beginner. Unlike stocking stitch, a slight unevenness of stitch is acceptable.

Working single knit and purl stitches alternately across a row – K1, P1, K1, P1 – produces single ribbing, which is reversible. Remember to bring the yarn into the correct position when changing between knitting and purling.
All the stitches which were *knitted* in the previous row must be *purled* and all the purled stitches must be knitted.
It holds its shape very well and is used for cuffs and neckbands.

This reversible pattern needs a number of stitches cast on which will divide by six, eg 30.
1st row *Knit 3 stitches, called K3, purl 3 stitches, called P3, continue from the * to the end.
Repeat this row 3 times more.
5th row *P3 stitches, K3 stitches, continue from the * to the end.
Repeat the 5th row 3 times more.
These 8 rows form the pattern, which resembles woven basketwork.

Start with a mohair scarf

A mohair scarf is a welcome luxury in cold weather – better still, its fluffiness conceals the uneven fabric that some beginners may produce. The design uses two reversible stitches shown in this chapter. If you wish, the scarf can be worked entirely in garter stitch, single rib or basket stitch. It measures about 18cm×142cm/7in×56in.

You will need
5×25g balls of Jaeger Mohair Spun, plain or with glitter
One pair 5½mm/No 5 needles

Scarf
Cast on 30 stitches by the one-needle method.
Work 10 rows garter stitch.
Work 16 rows basket stitch. 26 rows in all.
Repeat these 26 rows 11 times more.
Work 10 rows garter stitch.
Page 16 shows you how to cast off and complete your scarf.

Right: Soft and fluffy, this reversible mohair scarf is easy to knit and luxurious to wear.

Casting off and simple seams

Casting off is an art in itself. Discover the different techniques used for casting off on a knitted, purled, or ribbed row and a really original way to deal with that ugly last loop which even experienced knitters sometimes get at the end of the cast off row. Knowing how to join in new yarn and seam sections together properly gives your knitting a professional finish.

Casting off is the method used for finishing off a completed section of knitting or for certain types of shaping such as armholes or shoulders.

When you are ready to cast off, continue to knit or purl the stitches in the cast-off row as the pattern dictates. If the stitches are not cast off in the correct pattern sequence, you will spoil the appearance of the work and make seaming more difficult.

Aim to keep the cast off stitches regular and even, otherwise this edge may pull the whole garment out of shape.

Some instructions emphasize that stitches must be cast off loosely, for example at a neck edge where the fabric needs to be flexible. If you find you cast off too tightly, use one size larger needle in your right hand to work the stitches, before casting off.

Three ways of casting off

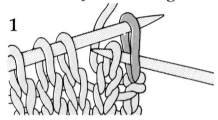 **1**

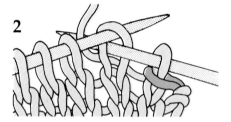 **2**

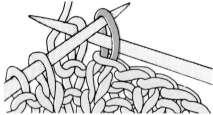

Casting off on a knitted row
Knit the first two stitches in the usual way and leave them on the right-hand needle.
1 *Insert the left-hand needle into the first of the stitches worked on to the right-hand needle. Lift this over the top of the second stitch and off the needle. One stitch has been cast off and one stitch remains on the right-hand needle.
2 Knit the next stitch and leave this on the right-hand needle. Continue from the point marked with an

asterisk (*), until all the stitches have been cast off and one stitch remains on the right-hand needle.
Fasten off this last stitch by breaking yarn, leaving an end 10cm/4in long. Draw this end through the last stitch and pull it up tightly.

Casting off on a purled row
Work this in exactly the same way as for casting off on a knitted row, but purl each stitch instead of knitting it, before casting it off.

Casting off on a ribbed row
Rib the first two stitches and leave them on the right-hand needle.
*Insert the left-hand needle into the first stitch worked on the right-hand needle. Lift this over the top of the second stitch and off the needle. Rib the next stitch and leave this on the right-hand needle. Continue from the point marked with an asterisk (*), until all the stitches have been cast off and one stitch remains on the right-hand needle. Fasten off this last stitch.

Seaming

For successful results in knitting you need to pay as much attention when sewing sections together as when knitting them.

Following chapters give full and detailed instructions for different methods of seaming and joining. Each method has a specific purpose and will help to give your garments a professional finish.

The four sections of the mohair T-top overleaf are sewn together using a flat seam, one of the two simple and effective methods given below.

Always tack the pieces together first as this will help you to ensure that you match stitches and row ends. This is important when knitting stripes.

Simple flat seaming

Flat seaming is suitable when you have been knitting with thick yarn. (Use a finer yarn of the same shade if you are sewing up mohair because it is almost impossible to sew with.) Use a blunt-ended sewing needle with a large eye.

Put the right sides of both sections of knitting together and sew from right to left.

Secure the yarn at the beginning of the seam with a few running stitches. Place the first finger of your left hand between the sections.

*Sewing one stitch in from the edge, push the needle through from the back section across to the corresponding stitch on the front section. Pull the yarn through. Move along the width of one row. Push the needle through the front section to the corresponding stitch on the back section. Pull the yarn through.

Continue in this way from the asterisk (*), along the seam. Finish off with running stitches to secure the yarn.

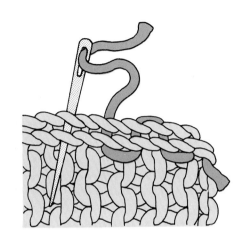

Simple oversewn seam

This method can be used to join stitches to row ends or along any edge where the minimum of bulk is required. It should also be used to join ribbing and fine fabrics.

It draws the edges together very neatly, but take care not to pull the sewing yarn up too tightly as it will form a tight ridge.

As with flat seaming, use a blunt-ended needle with a large eye. Place the two edges together with the right sides facing each other. Secure the yarn at the beginning of the seam with a few running stitches.

*Take the needle over the top of the edges and through one loop at the edge on both pieces. Pull the yarn through.

Continue in this way from the point marked with an asterisk (*), along the seam to give a lacing effect. Keep the stitches even and do not draw them up too tightly. Finish off with a few running stitches to secure the yarn.

PROFESSIONAL TOUCH

Neatening the last loop

Fastening off the last stitch in a piece of knitting can sometimes leave an ugly, loose loop, which makes seaming difficult. There is a simple way to solve this, whether the last stitch has been knitted or purled.

Cast off in the normal way until one stitch remains on the left-hand needle and one on the right-hand needle. Slip the stitch on the left-hand needle on to the right-hand needle without working it or twisting it.

Use the left-hand needle to pick up the back loop only of the last stitch on the row below from the back to the front. Leave this loop on the left-hand needle.

Put the last stitch on the right-hand needle back on to the left-hand needle and work this and the picked-up loop together as one stitch. Use the left-hand needle to lift the first stitch over the top of the second stitch and off the needle. Fasten off this last stitch.

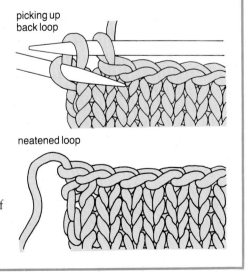

picking up back loop

neatened loop

Joining in a new ball of yarn

Whether you are knitting with just one colour of yarn or using stripes of different colours, you must always join in a new ball at the beginning of a row, never in the middle. This means you have to judge how much yarn you need to work the last row of the ball. Usually, a piece of yarn about four times the width of the knitting is enough to knit a row.

Joining with a reef knot

Where the same colour is being knitted throughout, join the new ball to the finished one with a reef knot. Take the end of the old ball of yarn from left to right over and under the end of the new ball. Take the same end from right to left over and under the other end, to form a loose reef knot.

When this piece of knitting has been completed, tighten up the reef knot. Darn in the ends along the edge of the fabric, before beginning to seam.

Joining with a slip loop

Where coloured stripes are being

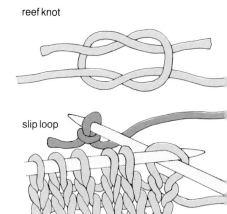

reef knot

slip loop

T-shaped mohair jersey

Often the most effective designs are the simplest. If you are working with a dramatically beautiful and textured yarn such as mohair, you want to choose stitches and shapes that let the yarn speak for itself, rather than compete. It is a beginner's bonus that the fluffy texture of mohair will disguise uneven knitting.

This T-shaped jersey is knitted in four pieces – two identical pieces for the front and the back, and two identical pieces which combine yoke and sleeves. In this simple pattern none of the pieces needs shaping.

It can be knitted in three colours, as photographed left, or all in the same colour. (If you knit it all in one colour you will need 15 balls of yarn.) As you change colour you change stitch, but you can knit the whole jersey in garter stitch or basket stitch if you prefer.

Sizes

The jersey will fit a medium bust size, 86–91cm/34–36in, loosely
Length to shoulder, 57cm/22½in

You will need

7×25g balls of plain Jaeger
  Mohair Spun (67% mohair,
  28% wool, 5% nylon) in
  colour A
5×25g balls of Jaeger Mohair
  Spun with glitter in colour B
3×25g balls of plain Jaeger
  Mohair Spun in colour C
One pair 5½mm/No 5 needles

Left: This sparkling mohair sweater is simple to knit and easy to wear.

knitted, such as with the mohair jersey left, join in each new colour with a slip loop. The first stitch will then be in the new colour. Break off the old colour, leaving an end to be darned in along the back of the last row in this colour. Form the end of the new ball into a slip loop. Insert the right-hand needle into the front of the first stitch of the row. Put the slip loop on to the right-hand needle and pull this loop through to complete the stitch in the usual way. Continue knitting with the new colour.

Dropped stitch

This is not easy for a beginner to put right as it must be picked up and worked in according to the pattern. Therefore take care to check the number of stitches at the end of every row. This may seem time-consuming, but it is easier than discovering you have dropped a stitch several rows back. As an emergency measure if you have been unlucky enough to drop a stitch in the row you have

just worked, secure it with a small safety pin. This will stop it unravelling.

On the next row, when you reach the dropped stitch put it back on to the left-hand needle and continue. This may leave an unworked thread, but is not as unsightly as a ladder.

Back and front

With plain yarn in colour A cast on 78 stitches by the one-needle method. This is the bottom of the jersey and should measure 48cm/19in across after you have knitted about 5cm/2in. If it is more than this you are knitting too loosely. Unravel this piece of knitting and start again with 5mm/No 6 needles. If it is less, you are knitting too tightly and should change to 6mm/No 4 needles.

Work 10 rows garter stitch. Break off yarn. Join in glitter yarn in colour B with a slip loop.

Work 16 rows basket stitch. Break off yarn. Join in plain yarn in colour A with a slip loop.

Work 10 rows garter stitch. Break off yarn. Join in plain yarn in colour C with a slip loop.

Work 14 rows stocking stitch. Break

off plain yarn in colour C. Join in yarn in colour A with a slip loop. 50 rows have been worked.

Repeat the first 36 rows once more. Cast off.

Make another piece in same way.

Yoke and sleeve section

With plain yarn in colour A cast on 36 stitches as given for body.

Repeat 50 pattern rows as given for body 4 times in all, then first 36 rows once more. Cast off.

Make another piece in same way.

To make up

Do not press, as this will flatten garter and basket stitch. Darn in all ends – see joining with a slip loop. Check the rows of stocking stitch to see which is the right side of each piece.

With right sides of yoke together and edges without any yarn changes (see diagram), join top arm and shoulder with flat seams, leaving 27cm/10¾in open in centre for neck. Turn in a few stitches at neck edge and lightly stitch down to neaten.

Mark centre of yoke and centre of body pieces with a contrasting coloured thread. Join cast off edge of body pieces to centre of yoke and sleeve sections (see diagram). Join side and sleeve seams.

Making up guide

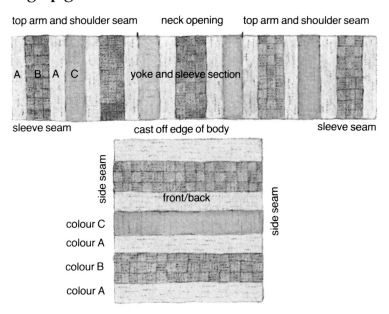

Above: Two examples of alternative colourways from the Jaeger Mohair Spun range in which to knit your jersey.

How to read knitting patterns

*The key to successful knitting lies in following the pattern
exactly – and this means knowing how to read
and carry out the instructions. Once you understand how
patterns work you will always be able
to knit a garment as attractive as the one in the picture.*

Before you begin to knit – even before you buy the yarn – always make sure to read your pattern thoroughly from beginning to end.

The designer works out tension, yarn thickness and needle size to suit the style of the garment and the pattern of the fabric, and these must be followed exactly for good results. Pay particular attention to the making-up section – even a simple shape may require intricate seaming or trimming.

Pattern writers use abbreviations and symbols in knitting instructions to save space. If in doubt, refer to the list of abbreviations given on page 234 at the end of this book.

Patterns give instructions in full for a specific stitch or technique the first time it is used, followed by its abbreviated form. From then on, only the abbreviation is given.

Symbols also denote working methods. A single asterisk, *, means

Pattern problems

1

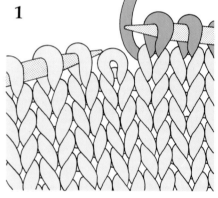

Fortunately there are ways of rectifying your mistakes if you should happen to misread a knitting pattern. If you have misread a pattern row, throwing the following rows out of sequence, follow the instructions opposite to unpick the stitches – only pull your knitting off the needles as a last resort! If you drop a stitch and it has unravelled for a number of rows it will spoil the look of your knitting. You can use a crochet hook to pick it up.

Left: The golden rule when knitting a garment from a pattern is to read the pattern thoroughly from beginning to end even before you go out to buy the yarn.

that the instructions that follow it must be repeated to the end of the row, or until a given number of stitches remains at the end of the row. Further instructions for working these remaining stitches will be given to complete the row.

An asterisk can also indicate that instructions will be repeated at a later stage in the knitting. When knitting a jersey, the pattern for back and front may well be the same to a certain point. A double asterisk, **, signals the end of the repeat.

Any instructions in round brackets, ( ), apply to all sizes. Instructions shown in square brackets [], denote larger sizes.

The instructions in knitting patterns are divided under a series of headings.

Sizes

This heading gives the finished measurements of the garment, the smallest size first, the larger sizes following in order in square brackets []. Some designs are given only in small sizes because they would not flatter a more generous figure. Some patterned designs are given only in one size because the pattern repeats are so large that one more or less would not give a standard size.

If you underline the figures that apply to your size you will be able to pick them out more quickly as you knit.

You will need

This heading lists the type and brand name of the yarn needed; the needle sizes and any additional tools such as cable needles; and trimmings, such as buttons. Make sure you have everything to hand before beginning to knit.

Tension

This heading gives the key to perfect knitting. Check your tension very carefully, especially if you are using a substitute yarn.

Note

This heading draws your attention to any unusual aspect of the pattern, such as the use of separate balls of yarn to work a coloured pattern.

Making up

This section tells you how to assemble the pieces you have knitted and add any finishing touches. Pay as much attention to these instructions as you did to the rest of the pattern for a really professional finish. Check with the ball band whether you should press the yarn, particularly if you have used a substitute. Sew the pieces together in the order given in the instructions – you may have to add edgings and trimmings before seaming. Never skimp on trimmings – it is better to buy a little too much ribbon than to find yourself short.

2

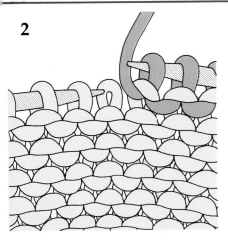

3

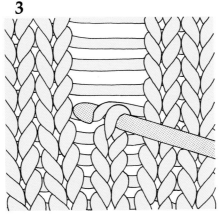

4

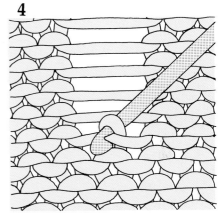

1 To unpick stitches on a knit row
Insert the left-hand needle from the front to the back into the stitch *below* the first stitch on the right-hand needle. Remove the right-hand needle and pull the yarn to unravel the stitch. Keep the yarn at the *back* of the work and repeat this process until the required number of stitches have been unpicked.

2 To unpick stitches on a purl row
Insert the left-hand needle from the front to the back into the stitch *below* the first stitch on the right-hand needle. Remove the right-hand needle and pull the yarn to unravel the stitch. Keep the yarn at the *front* of the work and repeat this process until the required number of stitches have been unpicked.

3 To pick up a dropped stitch on knitted side of stocking stitch
Insert a crochet hook from front to back through the dropped stitch. Put the hook under the thread lying between the stitches on each side of the dropped stitch. Pull this thread through the dropped stitch and leave it on the hook. Repeat this process until the dropped stitch is level with the last row worked. Put the loop on to the left-hand needle and knit it.

If the last row being worked is a purl row, turn the work to the purl side and purl the loop.

4 To pick up a dropped purl stitch in a patterned row
Insert the crochet hook from back to front through the dropped stitch. *Put the hook over the thread lying between the stitches on each side of the dropped stitch and pull this thread through the dropped stitch. Slip the loop on to a cable needle and remove the hook. Insert the hook into the loop again and continue from * until the dropped stitch is level with the last row worked. Put the loop on to the left-hand needle and purl it.

To pick up a dropped stitch in garter stitch
Alternate the knit and purl methods to keep the ridged sequence correct.

Alternative methods of casting on and off

This chapter explores the various ways of keeping your knitting neat to give your garments a professional finish. You can practise keeping in shape by knitting a clinging vest and baggy leg warmers – the ideal gear for exercising to keep yourself in shape too!

If you want to achieve a neat finish, you need to be able to keep the top and bottom edges of your knitting really straight. Depending on the garment you are knitting, you can choose methods of casting on or off to give a firm, elastic or lacy finish.

Casting on neatly

Looped casting on is a variation of the one-needle method. It forms a very loose cast-on edge, ideal for lacy patterns where a hard line would spoil the softness of the fabric. It is not suitable for ribbing or closely textured patterns.

Picot casting on forms a strip of picot loops and is a two-needle method. Instead of casting all the stitches on to one needle, you make a picot loop for each stitch. When you have the right number of stitches, you pick up the loops along one side of the strip with the free needle. The other side of the picot loops forms a dainty edge, ideal for baby garments.

Double casting on forms a very strong but flexible edge just right for husky outer garments. You use two needles, both held in your right hand, to work a variation of the thumb method of casting on.

Invisible casting on gives single ribbing a really professional finish. The ribs appear to run right round the cast-on edge, as with a ready-to-wear garment. You use the thumb method and a length of contrast coloured yarn, which is later removed. After casting on, the stitches are increased on the first row and the next four rows form a very elastic double fabric. You then continue working in single ribbing for the required length.

Casting off neatly

Single decrease casting off forms a very elastic edge and does not leave a hard ridge. It is the perfect method to use when you are working in stocking stitch.

Suspended casting off stops you casting off too tightly. You can use it to cast off in any pattern.

Eyelet hole casting off forms a row of eyelet holes as the casting off row is being worked. It makes an ideal waistband for baby garments, as you can thread ribbon or elastic through the eyelet holes. You need an odd number of stitches to work this method to cast off in any pattern.

PROFESSIONAL TOUCH

Invisible casting on

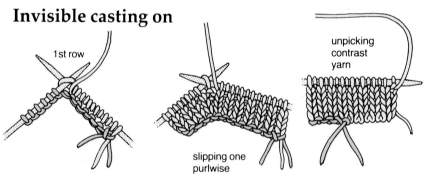

1st row

unpicking contrast yarn

slipping one purlwise

Simple invisible casting on, see page 12, is an easy way of achieving a neat edge over any number of cast-on stitches. This method is worked over an odd number of stitches. Use the thumb method and a length of contrast coloured yarn to cast on half the total number of stitches required plus one extra – 15 cast on stitches will give a final total of 29 ribbed stitches.
Change to the correct yarn and two needles. Begin the double fabric which forms this edge.

1st row K1, *yfwd to inc 1, K1, rep from * to end.
2nd row K1, *yfwd, sl 1 purlwise, ybk, K1, rep from * to end.
3rd row Sl 1 purlwise, *ybk, K1, yfwd, sl 1 purlwise, rep from * to end.
Rep the 2nd and 3rd rows once more.
6th row K1, *P1, K1, rep from * to end.
7th row P1, *K1, P1, rep from * to end.
Continue in rib for the required length. Unpick the contrast yarn used for casting on.

Above: A very neat method of casting on avoiding the common problem of a tight unsightly edge. It gives the appearance of having been cast on by machine.

Looped casting on

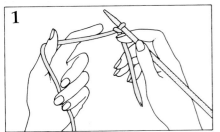

Use one needle. Make a slip loop in the end of a ball of yarn and put it on the needle.
1 *Hold the needle in your right hand and loop the yarn round the thumb of your left hand in a clockwise direction.

2 Insert the needle up under the loop just made and remove your thumb from the loop. Pull the yarn up tightly with your left hand. Continue in this way from * until the required number of stitches have been made.

Sample of catkin lace, page 165, which has been cast on by the picot method

Picot casting on

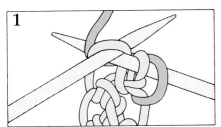

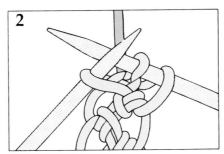

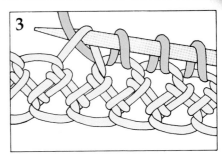

Use two needles, one in each hand. Make a slip loop and put this on the left-hand needle. Cast on one stitch by the two-needle method.
1 *Yfwd and hold at the front ready to take it across the right-hand needle to make an eyelet increase, sl the first st off the left-hand needle

on to the right-hand needle in a purlwise direction, K the second st on the left-hand needle.
2 Lift the sl st over the K st and off the right-hand needle. Turn. Continue in this way from * until the required number of loops have been made. On the last row omit

the yfwd and fasten off.
3 To begin knitting work across these loops just as though they were cast-on stitches. Rejoin the yarn with a slip loop and pick up and knit one stitch into each picot loop along one edge, then continue knitting the rows in the usual way.

Double casting on

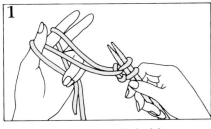

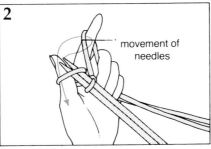

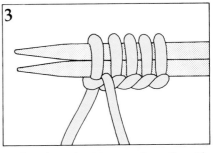

movement of needles

Use two needles, both held in your right hand. Make a slip loop in a ball of yarn as given for the thumb method. Put this loop on both needles. Take the short end of the ball of yarn from the slip loop and the main length from the ball and hold them together in the palm of your left hand.
1 *Put the slip loop end round your thumb in a clockwise direction and the main length round your forefinger in a clockwise direction.

2 Put both needles up and under the loop round your thumb, then down and under the loop round your forefinger and down and under the thumb loop again. Release the loop on your thumb and tighten the stitch on the needles with an upward movement of your right hand, without releasing the ends of yarn held in the palm of your left hand.

3 Continue in this way from * until the required number of stitches have been made. Withdraw one of the needles from the cast-on stitches then continue knitting in the usual way.

23

Single decrease casting off

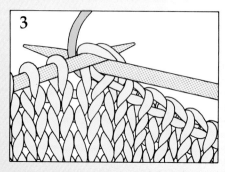

To cast off on a knit row.
1 Use the right-hand needle to knit the first two stitches on the left-hand needle together.
2 *Put this stitch back on to the left-hand needle.
3 Knit this stitch and the next stitch on the left-hand needle together. Continue in this way from * until all the stitches have been cast off. Fasten off.
To cast off on a purl row, purl the stitches together.

Suspended casting off

To cast off on a knit row, work the first two sts in the usual way.
1 *Lift the first stitch worked on to the right-hand needle over the second but instead of allowing it to drop off the right-hand needle, retain it on the point of the left-hand needle.

Camisole, vest and leg warmers

This·clinging ribbed camisole (or vest) and matching baggy leg warmers make the ideal gear for exercise classes.

Sizes

To fit 81 [86:91:97:102]cm/
32 [34:36:38:40]in bust
Camisole length to shoulder, 58cm/
24in adjustable
Vest length to shoulder, 76cm/30in adjustable
Leg warmers length 70cm/27½in adjustable

The figures in [] refer to the 86/34, 91/36, 97/38, 102cm/40in

You will need

Camisole 4 [4:5:5:5]× 25g balls of Jaeger 3 ply wool (100% botany wool) in main colour A, 1 ball of same in contrast colour B
Vest 6 [6:7:7:7] balls in main colour A, 1 ball in contrast B
One pair 2¾mm/No 12 needles
Set of four 2¾mm/No 12 needles *or* circular needle, 60cm/24in long
1.50m/1½yd ribbon, 5mm/¼in wide

Eyelet hole casting off

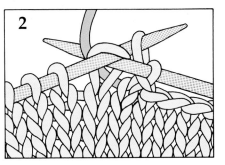

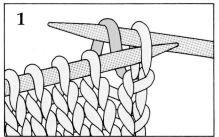

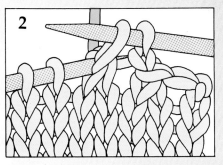

2 Pass the right-hand needle in front of the held stitch and work the next stitch, then slip this stitch and the held stitch off the left-hand needle together. Two stitches remain on the right-hand needle. Continue in this way from * until all the stitches have been cast off. Fasten off.
To cast off on a purl row, purl the stitches before casting them off.

To cast off on a knit row, knit the first stitch on the left-hand needle.
1 *Yfwd and hold across the right-hand needle to make a stitch, lift the first stitch on the right-hand needle over the made stitch and off the needle.

2 Knit the next two stitches on the left-hand needle together, lift the first stitch on the right-hand needle over the knit 2 together and off the needle.
Continue in this way from * until all the stitches have been cast off. Fasten off.
To cast off on a purl row, purl the stitches instead of knitting them and yrn to make a stitch.

Leg warmers 3×50g balls of Jaeger Luxury Spun Double Knitting (90% wool, 10% alpaca), in each of two colours, A and B
Sets of four needles in each of sizes 3mm/No 11, 3¼mm/No 10, 3¾mm/No 9, 4mm/No 8 and 4½mm/No 7

Tension

Camisole/vest 45 sts and 42 rows to 10cm/4in over *unstretched* rib worked on 2¾mm/No 12 needles; **leg warmers** 30 sts and 32 rows to 10cm/4in over *unstretched* rib worked on 3¾mm/No 9 needles

Camisole or vest

With 2¾mm/No 12 needles and separate length of contrast yarn cast on 122 [130:138:146:154] sts with the invisible method shown in this chapter. Work the first 6 rows as given.
7th row Using set of four 2¾mm/No 12 needles or circular needle, P1, *K1, P1, rep from * to last 2 sts, K1, then join work into a round by P the last st tog with the first st. 242 [258:274:290:306] sts.
Cont in rounds (see page 60) of K1, P1 rib until work measures 38cm/15in for camisole or 56cm/22in for vest, or required length to underarm. Join in B and work 4 more rows. Using B cast off by the eyelet hole method shown in this chapter.

Straps

With 2¾mm/No 12 needles and B cast on 7 sts.
1st row Sl 1, K1, (P1, K1) twice, K1.
2nd row Sl 1 knitwise, P1, (K1, P1) twice, K1.
Rep these 2 rows until strap measures 40cm/15¾in or length required. Cast off.

Leg warmers

With set of four 3mm/No 11 needles and A cast on 88 sts and arrange in a round. Cont in rounds of K1, P1 rib, working in striped patt as follows:
8 rounds A, 2 rounds B, 6 rounds A, 4 rounds B, 4 rounds A, 6 rounds B, 2 rounds A, 8 rounds B, 4 rounds A, 6 rounds B, 8 rounds A and 4 rounds B.
These 62 rounds form the patt and are rep throughout, *at the same time* when work measures 14cm/5½in from beg change to 3¼mm/No 10 needles, when work measures 28cm/11in change to 3¾mm/No 9 needles, when work measures 42cm/16½in change to 4mm/No 8 needles and when work measures 56cm/22in change to 4½mm/No 7 needles. Cont until work measures 70cm/27½in or required length. Cast off loosely.

To make up

Do not press.
Camisole or vest Take out contrast yarn from lower edge and join ends of first few rows. Sew on straps. Thread ribbon through eyelet holes at top edge to tie at centre front.

This trim camisole top and bright leg warmers keep you warm while exercising.

How to increase

Adding five ways of increasing to your basic techniques widens your knitting horizons considerably. Each of the methods described here has a different purpose. One method, decorative increasing, is used in the pattern for making a shawl for a baby or for yourself.

Whether a jersey fits well or not depends on the basic concept behind its design, and one of the most critical aspects of design is the shaping. Knitting patterns usually indicate when shaping is about to begin but do not always give details of the exact method to use. Knowing which is the best method for the job is the mark of a professional.

To increase means to add or make stitches and there are various ways of increasing the width and varying the shape of knitting. Single stitches added at regular intervals to the ends of the rows gradually change the shape of the knitting, such as when shaping a sleeve. Stitches added at intervals across the row change the shape of the knitting from within, creating panels such as those often found on matinée jackets. Large numbers of stitches added on at the ends of rows alter the outline of the knitting immediately, as with sleeves worked all in one with the body.

This chapter gives you four methods for increasing gradually and one for adding multiples of extra stitches and it gives you the necessary information to select the best method for you. **Working twice into a stitch** is the simplest way of increasing and it is used to make an extra stitch at each end of the same row, as in sleeve shaping. It is abbreviated as inc 1

Working twice into the same stitch

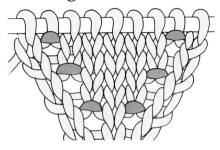 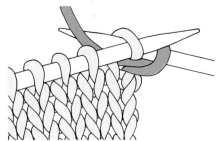 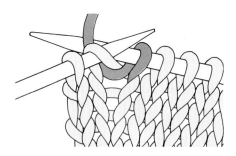

Note: When increasing at the end of a row, work the increase one stitch earlier to ensure that the position of the pip is the same on the right edge as on the left. (Because the extra stitch is formed one in from the edge seaming is easier.)

To increase a knitted stitch at the beginning of a row
Work the first stitch but do not drop it off the left-hand needle. Insert the right-hand needle into the *back* loop of the same stitch and knit it again, then drop the stitch off the left-hand needle.

To increase a knitted stitch at the end of a row
Work until two stitches remain on the left-hand needle. Knit twice into the next stitch as at the beginning of a row, then knit the last stitch.

Increasing between stitches

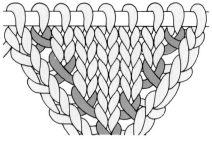 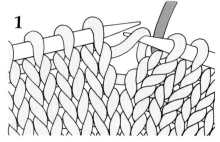 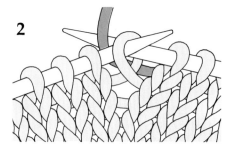

Note: If you work three stitches (for example) and increase one and on the next increasing row you work three stitches and increase one, the increase slants to the right. If you work an extra stitch each time before increasing, it slants to the left.

To make one in a knitted row
1 Work until the position for the increase is reached. Use the right-hand needle to pick up the thread lying between the stitch just worked and the next stitch on the left-hand needle. Put this loop or. the left-hand needle.

2 Knit into the *back* of the loop, this twists the stitch and avoids a hole in the fabric. (Knitting into the front leaves an open space beneath the increased stitch.)

(increase one).

The extra stitch always appears after the stitch it is worked into, making a little 'pip' in the fabric. It is ideal for use in garter stitch where the pip will not show. Do not use it in stocking stitch, particularly in the middle of a row, as it affects the smooth texture of the knitting. Never use this method to increase more than one stitch at a time.

Increasing between stitches is the method used for increasing in the middle of a row. It does not spoil the appearance of the fabric and so is the best method for increasing patterned stitches where the pip increase would spoil the sequence of the pattern. It is also suitable for stocking stitch and can be used to increase at the ends of each row. It is abbreviated as M1 (make one).

This method is particularly useful for picking up stitches on either side of a central stitch, as on v-neck shaping.

Decorative increasing (also known as eyelet hole increasing) is another method for increasing at any point in a row.

It forms an eyelet hole in the fabric and is abbreviated in various ways (see Decorative increasing overleaf), depending on whether you are knitting or purling and forms the basis of most lace patterns. This method involves putting the yarn over or round the needle which makes an extra stitch without knitting one.

Invisible increasing is a useful method of increasing, so called because it is hard to detect. It is used on stocking stitch because it is the only method which does not spoil the appearance of this stitch. It can be used at each end of a row, inside the edge stitches or in the middle of a row and so is very versatile.

This method is particularly useful for increasing three or four consecutive stitches in a row because if you keep the extra stitches fairly loose it does not affect the tension.

Multiples of extra stitches sometimes need to be added to a section of knitting, in which case extra stitches must be cast on. This can be done at the beginning and end of a row, or to replace stitches which have been cast off in a previous row, as for a buttonhole.

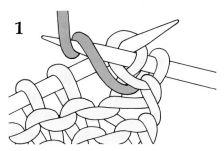

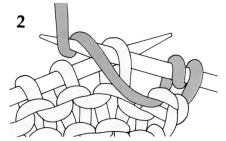

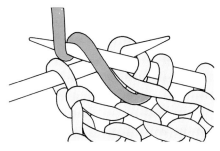

To increase a purled stitch at the beginning of a row
1 Work the first stitch but do not drop it off the left-hand needle. Insert the right-hand needle from left to right through the *back* loop of the same stitch and purl it again, then drop the stitch off the left-hand needle.

2 Purling twice into the front is not so satisfactory because it forms two loops round the right-hand needle. On the next row you must work into the front of the first loop and into the back of the second loop.

To increase a purled stitch at the end of a row
Work until two stitches remain on the left-hand needle. Purl twice into the next stitch as at the beginning of a row, then purl the last stitch.

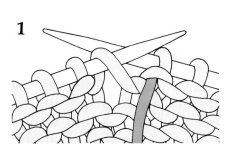

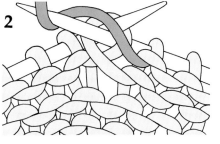

Ribbon threaded through an eyelet increase at the edge of a shawl.

To make one in a purled row
1 Work until the position for the increase is reached. Use the right-hand needle to pick up the thread lying between the stitch just worked and the next stitch on the left-hand needle. Put this loop on the left-hand needle.

2 Purl into the back of it by inserting the right-hand needle from left to right into the back loop to twist the stitch. (Purling into the front leaves an open space beneath the increased stitch.)

Decorative increasing (eyelet hole)

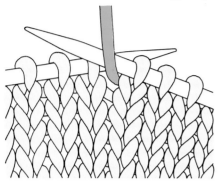

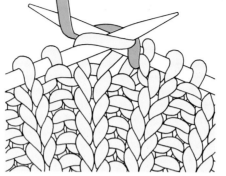

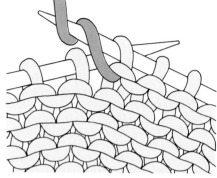

To make a stitch between two knitted stitches
Bring the yarn forward between the two needles. Take the yarn over the top of the right-hand needle ready to knit the next stitch. This is abbreviated as 'yfwd'.

To make a stitch between a purled and a knitted stitch
Carry the yarn, which is already at the front of the work, over the top of the right-hand needle ready to knit the next stitch. This is abbreviated as 'yon'.

To make a stitch between two purled stitches
Take the yarn over the top of the right-hand needle. Bring it forward between the two needles to the front again ready to purl the next stitch. This is abbreviated as 'yrn'.

PROFESSIONAL TOUCH

Invisible increasing

Note: If you work three stitches and increase one and on the next increasing row you work three stitches and increase one, the increase slants to the right. If you work an extra stitch each time before increasing, it slants to the left.

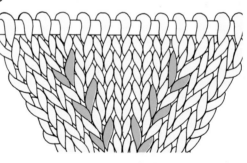

To increase one on a knitted row
Work until the position for the increase is reached. Insert the right-hand needle into the centre of the stitch on the row *below* the next stitch on the left-hand needle.
Knit an extra stitch through this stitch then knit the next stitch on the left-hand needle. The increased stitch slants to the right on the knitted side of stocking stitch.

To increase one on a purled row
Work until the position for the increase is reached. Insert the right-hand needle from the back to the front into the centre of the stitch on the row *below* the next stitch on the left-hand needle. Purl an extra stitch through this stitch then purl the next stitch on the left-hand needle. The increased stitch slants to the left when seen from the knitted side of stocking stitch.

Soft looped shawl

Simple garter stitch is used for this soft, light shawl. Use white for a baby or try a bright colour for yourself. Winding the yarn round the needle at the beginning of the row forms an eyelet increase. Use this as a decorative edging on its own or thread a coloured ribbon through for a splash of colour.

Size
Width across top edge 155cm/62in
Depth from top edge to centre point 82cm/32¼in.

You will need
9×20g balls of Patons Fairy Tale Double Knitting
One pair of 6½mm/No 3 needles
4m/4¼yd of 1cm/½in-wide ribbon

Tension
16 sts and 26 rows to 10cm/4in over garter st worked on 6½mm/No 3 needles.

Shawl
Beg at lower edge, with 6½mm/No 3 needles cast on 2 sts. K one row.
Next row Loop yarn round right-hand needle to inc 1, K to end. 3 sts.

Adding multiples of extra stitches

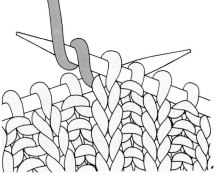

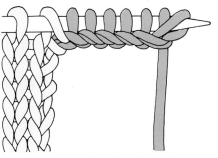

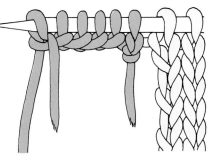

To make a stitch between a knitted and a purled stitch

Bring the yarn forward between the two needles. Carry it over the top of the right-hand needle, then between the two needles to the front again ready to purl the next stitch. This is also abbreviated as 'yrn'.

To add at the beginning of a row

Cast on the number of stitches required at the beginning of a row by the two-needle method (pages 12–13). Work across these stitches then continue along the row. (The easiest way to add stitches at each end is to cast on at the beginning of two consecutive rows.)

To add at the end of a row

After working across a row, cast on the number of stitches required by the one-needle method (pages 12-13). With a separate length of the same yarn make a slip loop on the left-hand needle. Work into this loop with the right-hand needle and the main length of yarn. Wind the short end round the thumb and use the main length to cast on the number of stitches required.

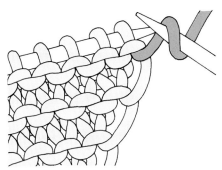

Next row Inc 1, K to end including loop on needle. 4 sts.
Rep the last row until there are 200 sts.
Cast off loosely.

To make up

Do not press. Cut ribbon into two 2m/2⅛yd lengths. Thread through side loops along edges and tie in a bow at centre point at beginning of work. Loop ribbon into bows at top corners and stitch to hold.

Right: This white shawl laced with ribbon makes a perfect christening gift. Stronger colours, such as the alternative colourway on page 27, give you a stylish coverup for chilly summer evenings.

How to decrease

Knowing how to reduce the overall width of knitted fabric is an essential part of basic techniques.
Five ways are described here and each has a different purpose.
Practise all these methods so that you
can use the correct shaping in your knitting patterns.

Decreasing the number of stitches in the width of a piece of knitting alters its size and shape. Knitting patterns usually indicate when shaping is about to begin but do not always give details of the exact method to use. Each one has a different appearance and purpose and this chapter shows

you how to choose the best method for your particular pattern. The samples are worked in stocking stitch so that you can see the angle of decrease clearly, but the methods are the same for other stitch combinations.
Depending on which method you use, the decreased stitches slant

either to the right or to the left. As a general rule, the slant should follow the line of the knitting. So when decreasing at the beginning of a row, the stitches should slant inwards to the left and at the end of a row they should slant inwards to the right. To work decreases in pairs, one at each end of a row, the decrease at the beginning of the row slants to the left and at the end, it slants to the right. This rule need not apply when the shaping serves a decorative purpose – for example when it highlights the fully-fashioned seams on a raglan-sleeved jersey. Here the decreased stitches are meant to show up and look most effective when worked against the line of the knitting – those at the beginning of the row slanting

Working stitches together

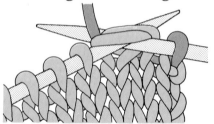

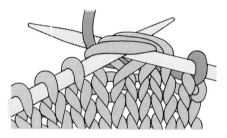

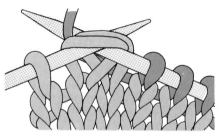

To decrease one knitted stitch at the beginning of a row
Knit the first stitch. Insert the right hand needle through the next two stitches as if to knit them. Knit them both together and drop them off the left-hand needle. The abbreviation for this is 'K2 tog'.

To decrease two knitted stitches at the beginning of a row
Knit three stitches together instead of two. The abbreviation for this is 'K3 tog'.
To decrease one or two stitches in the middle of a row, work until the position for the decrease is reached. Knit the next stitches together as for the beginning of a row.

To decrease one or two knitted stitches at the end of a row
Work until three or four stitches remain on the left-hand needle. Knit the next two or three stitches together as for the beginning of a row and knit the last stitch.

Working stitches together through the back of the loops

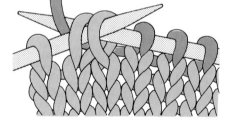

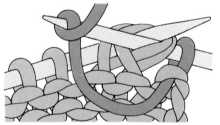

To decrease one knitted stitch at the beginning of a row
Knit the first stitch. Insert the right-hand needle through the *back* loops only of the next two stitches. Knit them both together and drop them off the left-hand needle. The abbreviation for this is 'K2 tog tbl'.

To decrease one knitted stitch at the end of a row
Work until three stitches remain on the left-hand needle. Knit the next two stitches together through the *back* loops and knit the last stitch.

To decrease one purled stitch at the beginning of a row
Purl the first stitch. Insert the right-hand needle from left to right through the *back* loops only of the next two stitches. Purl them both together and drop them off the left-hand needle. The abbreviation for this is 'P2 tog tbl'.

outwards to the right and those at the end of the row outwards to the left.

Working stitches together is the simplest way to decrease one or two knitted or purled stitches at any given point in a row. Use it when decreasing at the beginning of a purled row and at the end of a knitted row, but don't work the first or the last stitch together with its neighbour or you will create an uneven edge, difficult for seaming. When stitches are worked together in this way, the decreased stitches all slant to the *right* on the knitted side of stocking stitch.

Working stitches together through the back of the loops is a method which results in the decreased stitches slanting to the *left* on the knitted side of stocking stitch. So use this method when decreasing at the beginning of a knitted row and at the end of a purled row. However, the slip and knit or purl stitch method (detailed below) is simpler and more commonly used.

Slip and stitch decreasing is the simplest method to use at the beginning of a knitted row, using the knit two together method at the end of the same row so that the decreases form pairs, one slanting to the left and one to the right. The slip and knit stitch method results in the decreased stitch slanting to the *left* on the knitted side of stocking stitch.

Slip and purl stitch decreasing creates decreased stitches slanting to the *right* on the knitted side of stocking stitch but is less commonly used than purling stitches together.

Decreasing in a vertical line, as for a gored skirt, is achieved by using both angles of decreasing. Working across the first decreasing row all the decreased stitches should slant to the *right*. Working across the next decreasing row they should all slant to the *left*. By continuing to alternate the angle a vertical line is formed.

Casting off multiples of stitches. Use this method if you need to subtract more than one or two stitches from a section of knitting. This can be done at the beginning or the end of a row, as for the underarms of a jersey. When shaping a neck, a group of stitches is cast off in the centre of a row. Stitches also need to be cast off for details such as buttonholes.

Decreasing in a vertical line

To decrease one or two purled stitches

The methods are the same as for knitting stitches together but the stitches are purled together. Decreasing one stitch is abbreviated as 'P2 tog' and decreasing two stitches as 'P3 tog'.

To decrease two stitches in a vertical line

1 Slip one stitch, knit or purl the next two stitches together, (purling through the back of the loops).

2 Lift the slipped stitch over and off the right-hand needle. The slipped stitch and the two stitches worked together slant in towards each other. The knitted version of this method is abbreviated as 'sl 1, K2 tog, psso' and the purled version as 'sl 1, P2 tog tbl, psso'.

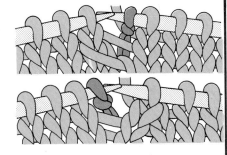

To decrease one purled stitch at the end of a row work until three stitches remain on the left-hand needle. Purl the next two stitches together through the *back* loops and purl the last stitch.

PROFESSIONAL TOUCH

Keeping slants in line

A slip loop in a length of contrast coloured yarn helps you see at a glance where the next decrease should occur in the middle of a row. Slip the loop from one needle to the other without working into it.

To keep a line slanting to the *left* on the knitted side of stocking stitch, the slip loop goes in front of stitches decreased by the 'K2 tog tbl' and 'sl 1, K1, psso' methods.

To keep a line slanting to the *right*, it goes after stitches decreased by the 'K2 tog' method.

To keep a line slanting to the *right* on the purled side, it goes in front of stitches decreased by the 'P2 tog' and 'sl 1, P1, psso' methods. To keep a line slanting to the *left* it goes after stitches decreased by the 'P2 tog tbl' method.

Slip and stitch decreasing

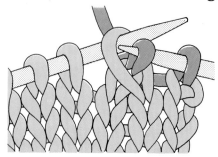
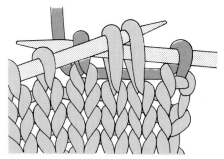
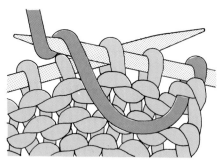

To decrease one knitted stitch at the beginning of a row
Knit the first stitch. Insert the right-hand needle into the next stitch as if to knit it. Keep the yarn at the back of the work and slip the stitch on to the right-hand needle without knitting it. Knit the next stitch on the left-hand needle. Use the left-hand needle to lift the slipped stitch over the top of the knitted stitch and off the right-hand needle. The abbreviation for this is 'sl 1, K1, psso'.

To decrease two knitted stitches at the beginning of a row
Knit the first stitch. Slip the next stitch and the following stitch on to the right-hand needle. Knit the next stitch on the left-hand needle. Lift the two slipped stitches over the top of the knitted stitch and off the right-hand needle. The abbreviation of this is 'sl 2, K1, p2sso'.

To decrease one or two purled stitches at the beginning of a row
The yarn must be kept at the front of the work throughout. Slip one or two stitches on to the right-hand needle as if to purl them. Purl the next stitch on the left-hand needle. Use the left-hand needle to lift the slipped stitches over the top of the purled stitch and off the right-hand needle. These methods are abbreviated as 'sl 1, P1, psso' and 'sl 2, P1, p2sso'.

Note: To decrease one or two knitted or purled stitches in the middle of a row, work until the position for the decrease is reached. Slip and knit or purl the next two or three stitches as for the beginning of a row.

To decrease one or two knitted or purled stitches at the end of a row, work until three or four stitches remain on the left-hand needle. Work the next two or three stitches as for the beginning of a row and knit or purl the last stitch.

Casting off multiples of stitches

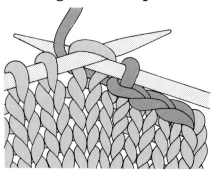
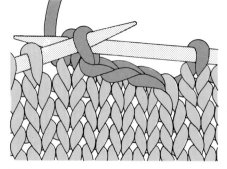
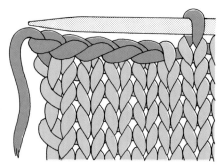

To subtract a number of stitches at the beginning of a knitted row
Cast off the number stated. One stitch remains on the right-hand needle after the casting-off has been completed. This counts as one of the remaining stitches. Continue knitting to the end of the row. The easiest way to subtract a number of stitches at each end of a piece of knitting is to cast off at the beginning of two consecutive rows.

To subtract a number of stitches in the middle of a knitted row
Work until the position for the subtraction is reached. Use the method given for the beginning of a row.

To subtract a number of stitches at the end of a knitted row
Work until the number of stitches to be cast off remains on the left-hand needle. Cast off and fasten off the last stitch. The yarn must be rejoined again at the beginning of the next row to continue knitting. These methods can be used to subtract a number of stitches at the beginning, end or in the middle of a purled row. Purl the stitches instead of knitting them before casting them off.

Tension and textures

The importance of tension cannot be underestimated. It makes the difference between knitting a garment successfully from a pattern and producing a jersey which reaches the knees. Also included in this chapter are four more reversible stitches for you to practise and perfect.

Once you can knit stitches you need to know how to obtain accurate measurements of both the length and width of your knitting, in order to follow a pattern. This is called 'tension'. Many knitters mistakenly believe that tension merely means achieving an even fabric. This is not so and you can never be a proficient knitter until you appreciate how important it is to have the correct tension.

The word tension means the number of stitches and rows to a given measurement which has been achieved by the designer, using a specific yarn and needle size. (Each spinner gives a recommended tension for its yarn on the ball band but this is only a guide and is often different from that called for by the pattern.)

A dressmaking pattern tells you how many metres of fabric are needed and this amount stays the same whether the fabric is chiffon or corduroy. However, in knitting the needle size and thickness of yarn have an effect on the number of stitches and rows needed to arrive at a given measurement. Unless you can obtain the tension called for by the pattern you will end up with a garment either too large or too small. Incorrect tension also alters the texture of the fabric.

The basic steps in knitting soon become as natural as breathing but everyone differs in the way they control the needles and yarn. There is no such thing as 'average' tension. Different people naturally knit more tightly or loosely than others. As you become more experienced your tension may alter with your progress.

Checking tension Always work a sample with the correct yarn and needle size in the stitch given before beginning any knitting. If a pattern gives 22 stitches and 30 rows to 10cm/4in worked over stocking stitch on 4mm/No 8 needles, cast on at least 26 stitches. Allow at least 4 extra stitches and 4 extra rows to enable you to measure the sample accurately. Pin the completed sample on a flat surface. Measure with a ruler and count the number of stitches and rows obtained to 10cm/4in. In this example there should be 22 stitches and 30 rows to 10cm/4in. Don't be tempted to cheat by stretching the sample. Count the stitches and rows very carefully – even half a stitch makes an overall difference.

Adjusting tension If your sample measures *more* than the tension size given you are working too loosely. Change to a size smaller needles and work another sample.

If your sample measures *less* than the tension size given you are working too tightly. Change to larger needles and work another sample.

Continue experimenting with needle sizes until you obtain the tension

Below: An incorrect tension sample which is too loose, giving 19 stitches and 27 rows to 10cm.

Above: A tension sample giving the correct tension of 22 stitches and 30 rows to 10cm.

Above: An incorrect tension sample which is too tight, giving 26 stitches and 34 rows to 10cm.

given. Most instructions give this as a number of stitches in width and a number of rows in depth. If you have to choose between obtaining one but not the other, the width tension is the most vital. If you cannot satisfactorily adapt the tension to obtain the correct width then cast on the number of stitches given for a smaller or larger size. Length can usually be adjusted by working more or less rows.

Always use new yarn for each sample. If you keep on unravelling the same length of yarn it will become stretched and will not give an accurate tension.

Each design is calculated on the tension achieved with the yarn specified in the instructions. The total amount of yarn is also based on the tension. If you choose to use a substitute it is vital to realise that the amount may vary

and you may not produce the texture of the original fabric.

Reversible patterns

The four patterns below use combinations of knit and purl stitches and form fabrics which look the same on both sides. They can be worked in separate bands or as all-over fabrics. Any of these patterns can be used to knit the bags featured in this chapter.

Moss stitch

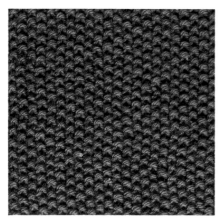

Worked over any number of stitches.
1st row *K1, P1, repeat from * to end, noting that an even number of cast-on stitches will end with P1 and an odd number with K1.
2nd row All the stitches of the previous row which were knitted must be knitted and all the purled stitches purled.
These 2 rows form the pattern.

Double moss stitch

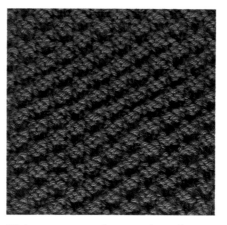

This pattern needs a number of stitches which will divide by 4.
1st row *K2, P2, repeat from * to end.
2nd row As 1st.
3rd row *P2, K2, repeat from * to end.
4th row As 3rd.
These 4 rows form the pattern.

Hurdle stitch

This pattern needs an even number of stitches.
1st and 2nd rows K to end.
3rd and 4th rows *K1, P1, repeat from * to end.
These 4 rows form the pattern.

One pattern – two useful bags

To show how tension controls the finished size and texture, this design has been made in two different yarns and needle sizes. The number of stitches and rows remain exactly the same.

Sizes

Holdall 37cm×34cm/14½in×13½in
Shoulder purse 18cm×15cm/7in×6in

You will need

Holdall 10×50g balls of Patons uncut Turkey Rug Wool
One pair 7½mm/No 1 needles
One pair cane handles

Shoulder purse 3×20g balls of Patons Beehive Double Knitting

One pair 4mm/No 8 needles
1m/1yd of cord for handle
1m/1yd decorative tape or ribbon, optional

Tension

Holdall 10 sts and 16 rows to 10cm/4in over moss st worked on 7½mm/No 1 needles
Shoulder purse 19 sts and 34 rows to 10cm/4in over moss st worked on 4mm/No 8 needles

Holdall

With 7½mm/No 1 needles cast on 36 sts by the 2 needle method.
1st row *K1, P1, rep from * to end.
2nd row *P1, K1, rep from * to end.
Work a total of 110 rows moss st. Cast off loosely.

Gussets

With 7½mm/No 1 needles cast on 8 sts. Work 44 rows moss st. Cast off loosely. Make another piece in same way.

Shoulder purse

With 4mm/No 8 needles cast on and work as given for holdall.

Gussets and handle

These are all knitted in one piece. With 4mm/No 8 needles cast on 8 sts. Work 117cm/46in moss st. Cast off loosely.

To make up

Holdall Do not press. Fold bag in half and mark centre of each side with safety pins. Mark centre of

Using up tension samples

You need not waste any of your experimental samples as the unravelled yarn can be used up in many ways. One useful tip is to wind up some of the yarn and attach it to one of the seams of the completed garment. As this will be washed with the garment it will be in the same condition and can be used for darning and repairs. If the yarn is not too thick it can be used for seaming and completing a garment.

Another way of using up yarn is to make a trimming such as a plaited tie-belt for a jersey or a pompom for a pull-on hat.

Seeded rib stitch

This pattern needs a number of stitches which will divide by 3.

1st row *K2, P1, repeat from * to end. This row forms the pattern.

cast-on edge of gussets in same way. Join gussets to bag with a flat seam matching centre markers. Turn right side out. Fold top edges of bag over cane handles and stitch down.

Shoulder purse Do not press. Mark bag and gussets and sew in gussets as given for Holdall. The remainder becomes the handle. Place cord inside the knitted handle length and firmly stitch the open edges together. Thread some decorative tape or ribbon through top edge to tie at front.

Right: Proving the point about tension – the same number of stitches and rows has been used for a sturdy knitting holdall and child's shoulder bag.

Hems, welts, borders and edges

Hems and welts are easily knitted in one with the main pattern.
Borders and neck edges are usually worked after
the pieces have been sewn together – which entails picking up
stitches along a cast-off row or on row ends.
The secret of a perfect finish is to pick them up evenly.

Hems and borders play an important part in the successful completion of knitted garments. Any unnecessary bulk must be avoided.

Once the pieces of a garment have been sewn together, it is also necessary to neaten edges, and sometimes these are worked in a different direction to the main line of the knitting. While ribbing is most commonly used where an edge which firmly hugs the contours of the figure is required – as for welts, cuffs and skirt waistbands – hems are used on the lower edge of a skirt or a shaped jacket and it is a simple matter to make provision for these.

Hems on skirts and jackets need firm edges to prevent them dropping or sagging out of shape in wearing. This chapter gives several ways of working neat hems in one with the main fabric to give a turned-under edge.

Turned-under hems are ideal for a garment knitted in stocking stitch or any textured pattern but they are not suitable for light, lacy fabrics. The turned-under section will show through an open fabric and may pull it out of shape. To give minimum bulk, the turned-under section of the hem should be worked in stocking stitch, irrespective of main pattern.

A row of eyelet holes can be added at the folding line of a hem to make a dainty picot finish on baby garments.

Front borders are needed on garments which have a centre front opening. A turned-under border in stocking stitch can be worked in one with the main fabric of a jacket but only when the pattern for the body of the jacket is of a similar texture. Garter stitch, for example, should not be worked in the same row with stocking stitch, because garter stitch stretches widthways and stocking

stitch lengthways.

A cardigan is usually best finished with separately knitted button and buttonhole borders, which are sewn on when the garment is completed.

Edges along which stitches have to be picked up are commonly used to complete garments. This method is used to pick up stitches round the curve of a neckline to work a neckband or collar.

A zip-fastened jacket also has stitches picked up along the front edges to neaten them, before the zip is sewn in place; these must be picked up evenly to avoid stretching or puckering the edge.

Right: Once you turn up the picot hem and begin to seam it, you can see how the row of eyelet holes forms a dainty edge. Inset: Detail of a neatly picked-up ribbed edge on a mohair cardigan.

Turned-under hem

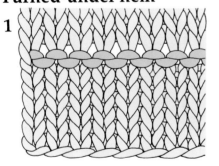

Cast on the required number of stitches with one size smaller needles than given for the main fabric. Begin with a knit row and work an odd number of rows in stocking stitch to the required depth of the turned-under hem.

1 Change to the correct needle size and, instead of purling the next row, knit all the stitches through

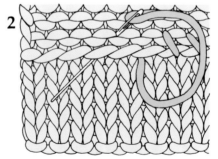

the back of the loops to form a ridge on the right side of the work which marks the hemline.**

Continue in the main pattern.

2 When the garment is completed and the side seams have been joined, turn the hem up to the wrong side of the work at the hemline ridge. Neatly slip stitch the hem in place.

Picot hem

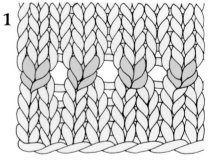

Cast on an odd number of stitches with one size smaller needles than given for the main fabric. Begin with a knit row and work an even number of rows in stocking stitch to the required depth of the turned-under hem. Change to the correct needle size.

1 Next row (eyelet hole row) *K2 tog, yfwd, rep from * to last st, K1.

Double stocking stitch hem

2

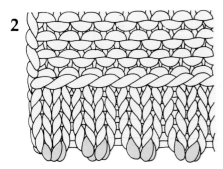

Purl one row to complete the hem. Continue in the main pattern.
2 When the garment is completed and side seams have been joined, turn the hem up to the wrong side of the work at the eyelet hole row. Neatly slip stitch the hem in place.

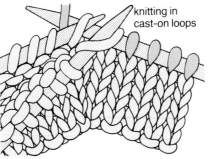

knitting in cast-on loops

Work as given for turned-under hem to **. Begin with a knit row again and work one row less in stocking stitch than the depth of the turned-under section, ending with a purl row.
With an extra needle pick up the loops from the cast-on edge from left to right, with the needle point facing the same way as the main

needle. Hold the extra needle behind the left-hand needle. Knit to the end of the row, knitting one stitch from the left-hand needle together with one stitch from the extra needle. Purl one row to complete the hem.
Continue in the main pattern. When the garment is completed join the side seams, including the top section of the hem, then join the turned-under section on the wrong side.

Turned-under front borders

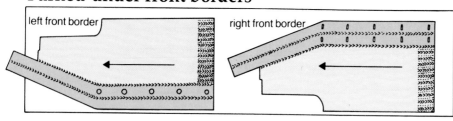

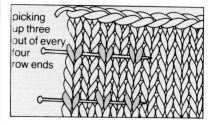

Make provision for the border before casting on. Decide on the width of the turned-under part – 3-4cm/1¼-1½in will be sufficient but it will depend on the thickness of the yarn being used. If buttonholes are to be worked, allow sufficient width for a double buttonhole, one in the top part of the border and a corresponding one in the under part.

Cast on required number of stitches. The example shown here is worked over 66 stitches. Double knitting yarn on 4mm/No 8 needles is used to give a tension of 22 stitches and 30 rows to 10cm/4in. This allows for 8 stitches to be turned under, one foldline stitch and 8 stitches for the upper part of the border, with the remaining 49 stitches being used for the body.

To work a left front border
With the right side of the work facing, work in pattern to the last 17 stitches. Work 8 stitches for the top

border, slip the next stitch in a purlwise direction to mark the foldline, knit the last 8 stitches for the turned-under part of the border. On the next row, purl the first 9 stitches, then pattern to the end of the row. Repeat these rows for the required length.

Any shaping on the front edge is worked *before* the top border stitches on a right side row.

To work a right front border
With the right side of the work facing, knit the first 8 stitches for the turned-under border section, slip the next stitch purlwise to mark the foldline, work 8 stitches for the top border then pattern to the end of the row. On the next row, pattern to the last 9 stitches then purl to the end. Repeat these rows for the required length.

Any shaping on the front edge is worked *after* the top border stitches on a right side row.

Unless picked-up stitches are evenly spaced, the edge will stretch or pucker. It is a simple matter to pick up stitches along a cast-off row but not so easy to gauge where to pick up stitches on row ends. The picked up edge needs to be very slightly shorter than the main fabric edge.
1 As a general guide, pick up a

Separate front borders

Decide on the width of the border as for turned-under borders. If buttonholes are to be worked, allow one extra stitch on the inner edge of the border so that the buttonhole is central when the border is sewn in position.

To work a border in the same pattern as the welt of the body, such as ribbing, cast on the required number of stitches for the body plus the stitches for the border. Work until the welt is completed.

Picking up edge stitches with a knitting needle

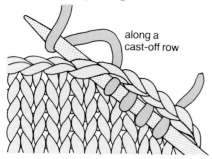

1

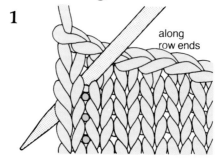

2

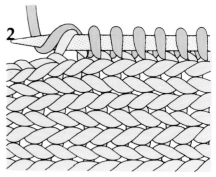

To pick up stitches along a cast-off row, have the right side of the fabric facing you, and a ball of yarn.
*Insert the needle from the front to the back under both loops at the top of the cast-off stitch, put the yarn round the needle and pull this loop through, as when working a knit stitch. Leave the stitch on the needle. Continue from the * until the required number of stitches have been picked up using the main

length of yarn to make the stitches.
To pick up stitches along row ends, have the right side of the fabric facing you, and a ball of yarn.
1 *Insert the needle from the front to the back between the first and second stitches in from the edge of the knitting.
2 Put the yarn round the needle and pull this loop through as when working a knit stitch. Leave the stitch on the needle. Insert the

needle between the first and second stitches in from the edge one row along to the left and continue from the * until the required number of stitches have been picked up using the main length of yarn to make the stitches.
To pick up stitches round a shaped edge, such as a neckline, combine the methods of picking up stitches along a cast-off row and along row ends.

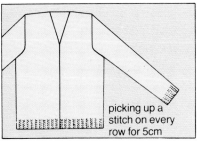

picking up a
stitch on every
row for 5cm

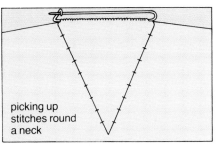

picking up
stitches round
a neck

Above: Close-up detail of a neckband,
showing how the careful spacing of picked
up stitches ensures a really snug fit.

stitch on three out of every four successive row ends.

2 If ribbing is to be worked along the edge, it tends to pull up a little from the bottom edges. To overcome this, pick up a stitch on every row end for the first 5cm/2in of the bottom edge.

Round a neck divide edge into equal sections with pins (the back neck stitches have usually been cast off or left on a holder). As an example, if a total of 180 stitches are to be picked up round the front of a V-neck, divide each front edge into nine equal sections. Pick up 10 stitches in each section. This avoids the stitches being too bunched together or too far apart.

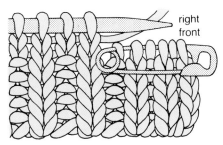

right
front

On the right front With the right side of the work facing, work across the border stitches and slip them on to a holder. Continue in pattern on the remaining stitches.

On the left front With the right side of the work facing, work until the border stitches remain and slip them on to a holder. Turn and continue in pattern on the remaining stitches.

When the main piece is completed put the border stitches back on to the same size needle as used for the welt, rejoin the yarn at the inner edge and continue in pattern. *Work about 10cm/4in and tack the border in place along the front edge, easing this in very slightly as you do so – take care not to stretch the main fabric or the border will pucker. Continue from the * until the border is the required length, then cast off. Stitch the border in place along the edge and remove the tacking stitches.

To work a border in a different pattern to the welt, cast on the border stitches separately. Work in pattern until the border is the required length. Continue from the * as given for working a border in the same pattern.

Picking up edge stitches with a crochet hook

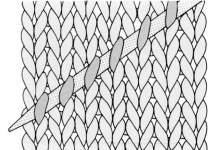

diagonally

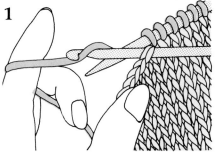

1

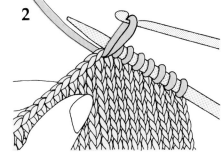

2

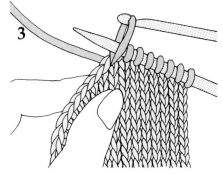

3

To pick up stitches horizontally, vertically or diagonally across a piece of knitting, have the right side of the fabric facing you. Use a double-pointed needle. You will not need any yarn at this stage as the needle is not inserted through the fabric to pull a separate loop. Instead, pick up one loop only from each of the required number of stitches. Join in the yarn and knit across the stitches picked up.

To pick up stitches along a cast-off row, or along row ends, work as given for picking up stitches with a knitting needle. Use a crochet hook to pull the loop through instead of a needle.

1 Insert the crochet hook under the top of the stitch or into the row end, and put the yarn round the hook.
2 Pull the loop through.
3 Transfer the loop from the crochet hook to a knitting needle.

Basic making up: blocking, pressing and seaming

*Care taken in the final stages of finishing the pieces of a
garment and in the actual making up will
give your knitting that professional look. Some modern yarns
need careful handling and often a garment
can be ruined by incorrect pressing or cobbled seams.*

The final preparation and making up of a garment needs as much care and skill as the knitting. The knowledge and time taken to produce a superb piece of knitting to the correct shape and proportions can be wasted if the pieces are badly seamed together or if you don't take the trouble to block and press the pieces where appropriate.

Blocking is the term given to the process of pinning out each individual piece of knitting to the correct size and shape, prior to pressing. Some patterns have a tendency to shrink in width and stretch in length. Others may have a slight bias which needs correction, or scalloped edges which must be pinned into shape. Delicate lace patterns often only need blocking out and leaving under a damp cloth for a few hours, without actually pressing them.

Diagrams of the pattern pieces give you the finished measurements of each piece and the making up instructions tell you whether or not to press the yarn. The choice of blocking out the pieces, however, will often be left to you. If you are in any doubt, *do not block* – knitting is a wonderfully pliant fabric and will eventually take its own shape.

Pressing is not always essential or even advisable. In the past, knitters did not press any pure wool garments but 'dressed' them over the steam of a kettle, then patted them into size and shape.

The ballband usually tells you if the yarn can be pressed and gives you the iron temperature setting but does not always give you exact details.

If you use a different yarn from the one specified in the pattern, don't

Blocking pattern pieces

To block out each piece you will need a firm table or ironing board. On top of this place a sheet of white carton cardboard. Over this place an ironing pad or blanket.

Place each individual piece right side down on to the prepared ironing board or table. Anchor the piece at each corner with rustless pins. Use a tape measure to check that the width and length are the same as those given in the instructions, when measured in the centre. Gently pat the piece into shape where any increasing or decreasing has been worked and check the measurements, making sure that the side edges are the same length.

Now pin the piece to the board all round the edges. Use plenty of pins evenly spaced and placed at right angles to the stitches and rows. Take great care to ensure that all the stitches and rows lie in straight lines and that the fabric does not have any bias.

If the pieces need blocking but do not require any pressing, cover them with a clean wet cloth, well wrung out. Leave for two or three hours then remove the cloth.

Right: Leave each piece in place until it is dry before removing the pins.

forget that the making up instructions may not be appropriate. The instructions may be for a yarn, such as wool, that *can* be pressed but you may have used acrylic and the ballband will tell you this *cannot* be pressed.

Many yarns are blends of man-made fibres so it is not always easy to judge whether they should be pressed. The Pressing guide (right) gives general advice; if in doubt, *do not press*.

Seaming is particularly important for a professional finish. The method you use will depend on the fabric and type of garment. Ribbing and garter stitch should be joined with oversewn and flat seams, see page 17. Backstitch seams are suitable for closely-textured fabrics, such as stocking stitch, and for all shaped edges.

The invisible seam resembles the rungs of a ladder, lacing the pieces together. It is perfect for joining straight edges in any pattern and cannot be detected on a stocking stitch seam – hence its name.

Whichever method of seaming you use, assemble all the pieces in the order given in the instructions. Make sure that stripes or patterns match exactly when pinning the edges together. Use a blunt-ended sewing needle and the original yarn. If it is very thick or textured, use a finer matching yarn.

Hemming is another important detail. Slip stitch is used on turned-under hems or facings as it produces a neat finish. Make sure you do not cast on or off too tightly when knitting an edge which has to be turned under. In hemming you will be matching one cast on or off stitch to one stitch of the main fabric. If the edge is too tight the fabric will pucker. You do not need to pick up every stitch along the edge but keep them regular and fairly loose.

Pressing guide
Pure wool Press under a damp cloth with a warm iron.
Blends of wool and nylon Provided the wool content is higher than the nylon, press as for wool.
Blends of wool and acrylic Do not press.
Nylon Press under a dry cloth with a cool iron.
Blends of nylon and acrylic If nylon content is higher than acrylic, press as for nylon.
Courtelle Do not press.
Acrylic Do not press.
Cotton Press under a damp cloth with a warm or hot iron.
Mohair Steam press very lightly with a warm iron.
Angora Steam press as for mohair.
Glitter yarn Do not press unless stated on the ballband.

Pressing

If the individual pieces have not already been blocked, lay them right side down on to an ironing board.

1 Have the iron at the correct temperature and a clean dry, or damp, pressing cloth as directed. Place the cloth over the piece. Gently but firmly press the whole area of the iron down on top of the cloth, then lift it up again. Do not move the iron over the surface of the cloth as you would when ironing normally. Press each area evenly in this way before going on to the next area.

Once a piece has been pressed, allow any steam to evaporate. Remove the pins if the piece has

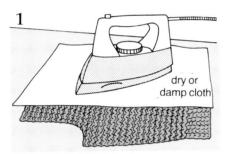

dry or damp cloth

been blocked and lay it aside ready for seaming.

2 To steam press a piece, use an iron at the correct temperature setting. Place a damp cloth over the piece. Begin at the lower edge and hold the left-hand side of the damp cloth just above the surface of the knitting with the left hand. Allow the iron to come into direct contact

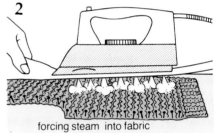

forcing steam into fabric

with the cloth but do not press down on to the knitting. This forces the steam down into the fabric. Press each area in this way.

Once a piece has been pressed allow any steam to evaporate. Remove the pins if the piece has been blocked and lay it aside ready for seaming.

SHORT CUT

An easy guide to blocking

Prepare the table or ironing board for blocking the pieces. Choose a piece of evenly-checked gingham – 2.5cm/1in or 5cm/2in squares are ideal. This material must be colour-fast.

Place the gingham over the ironing board, making sure that the checks are in straight rows, horizontally and vertically. Measure the size of the checks and use this to gauge how many stitches in width and rows in depth should cover each one. For example, using a 5cm/2in check gingham, a piece with a side seam length of 40cm/16in and a width of 40cm/16in will require an area of eight checks deep and wide for blocking out. Each check should contain the same number of stitches and rows.

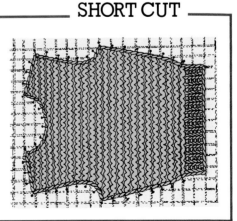

Two new methods of seaming

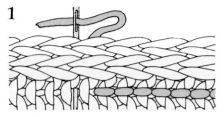

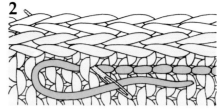

Back stitch seam

Place the right sides of the pieces together. Work along the wrong side of the fabric from right to left, one stitch in from the edge. Secure the yarn at the beginning of the seam with two or three small stitches, one on top of the other.
1 *With the sewing needle at the back of the fabric, move along to the left the width of one knitted stitch from the last stitch and push the

needle through both pieces to the front at right-angles to the edge. Pull the yarn through.
2 Take the needle across the front of the fabric from left to right and push it through both pieces at the end of the last sewing stitch to the back. Pull the yarn through.
Continue from the * until the seam is completed. Fasten off with two or three small stitches.

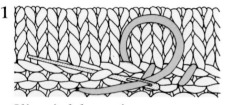

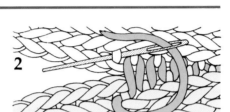

Invisible seam

With the *right side* of both pieces facing you, lay them one above the other. The seam can be joined from right to left or left to right. Secure the yarn with two or three small stitches one on top of the other on the lower piece. Pass the needle across to the first stitch on the upper piece, pick up the bar between the first and second stitch in from the edge and pull the yarn through.
1 *Pass the needle across to the

stitch on the same row on the lower piece, pick up the bar between the first and second stitch in from the edge and pull the yarn through.
2 Pass the needle across to the next stitch on the next row on the upper piece, pick up the bar between the first and second stitch in from the edge and pull the yarn through.
Continue from the * until the seam is completed, pulling each stitch up to the same tension as the fabric. Fasten off with two or three small stitches.

A neat method of hemming

Slip stitch hemming

Turn in the hem or facing and have the wrong side of the main fabric facing you. Secure the yarn to the hem or facing with two or three small stitches on top of each other.
1 *Insert the needle from right to left and lightly pick up *one thread only* of a stitch to the left on the main

fabric. Pull the yarn through fairly loosely.
2 Move along the fabric to the left, insert the needle into the hem or facing and lightly pick up *one thread only* of a stitch. Pull yarn through. Continue from the * until the hem is completed. Fasten off with two or three small stitches.

Jersey with jacquard yoke

This stylish jersey features a striking, multi-coloured jacquard yoke. The yarn used is a blend of 80% wool and 20% nylon for added strength.
Block out and press each piece as described in this chapter. Make sure the patterns on the raglans match exactly when seaming.

Sizes

To fit 86 [91:97]cm/34 [36:38]in bust
Length to shoulder, 60 [61:62]cm/ 23½ [24:24½]in
Sleeve seam, 47cm/18½in
The figures in [] refer to the 91cm/ 36in and 97cm/38in sizes respectively

You will need

9 [10:10]×50g balls of Sunbeam Trophy Double Knitting (80% wool, 20% nylon) in main colour A
1 ball of same in each of 5 contrast colours B, C, D, E and F
One pair 3mm/No 11 needles
One pair 3¾mm/No 9 needles
Set of four 3mm/No 11 needles
Set of four 3¾mm/No 9 needles

Tension

24 sts and 32 rows to 10cm/4in over plain st st worked on 3¾mm/No 9 needles

Back

With 3mm/No 11 needles and A cast on 106 [114:118] sts.
1st row (Rs) K2, *P2, K2, rep from * to end.
2nd row P2, *K2, P2, rep from * to end.
Rep these 2 rows for 6cm/2¼in, ending with a 2nd row and inc 3 [1:3] sts evenly in last row. 109 [115:121] sts.
Change to 3¾mm/No 9 needles.
Beg with a K row cont in st st until work measures 35cm/13¾in from beg, ending with a P row.
Join in colours as required and cont in st st, working first 12 rows from jacquard chart.

Note

For detailed instructions on knitting with two or more different coloured yarns at once see pages 119–135.

Jacquard chart

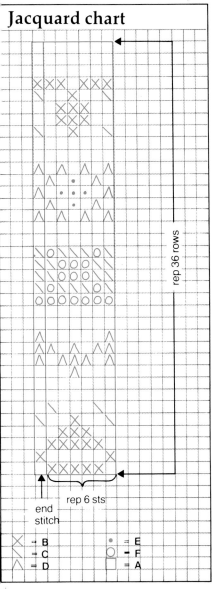

rep 36 rows

rep 6 sts

end stitch

X = B
X = C
∧ = D

⊙ = E
⊖ = F
□ = A

Shape armholes

Cont in patt from chart, cast off 4 sts at beg of next 2 rows.
Next row K1, K2 tog, patt to last 3 sts, sl 1, K1, psso, K1.
Next row Patt to end.
Working throughout in patt from chart, rep these 2 rows until 37 [39:41] sts rem, ending with a Ws row, noting that after completing the 36 rows once, the first 5 rows of next rep should be worked using F instead of B, then on foll rep go back to B.
Leave sts on holder.

Front

Work as given for back, shaping armholes until 57 [59:61] sts rem, ending with a Ws row.

Shape neck

Next row K1, K2 tog, patt 19 sts, turn and leave rem sts on holder. Complete left shoulder first.
Next row Cast off 3 sts, patt to end.
Next row K1, K2 tog, patt to end.
Next row Cast off 2 sts, patt to end.
Next row K1, K2 tog, patt to last 2 sts, K2 tog.
Next row Patt to end.
Rep last 2 rows 4 times more, then cont to dec at armhole edge only on every alt row until 2 sts rem, ending with a Ws row. Cast off.
Return to rem sts on holder, leave first 13 [15:17] sts for centre front neck, rejoin yarn to rem sts, patt to last 3 sts, sl 1, K1, psso, K1.
Next row Patt to end.

Next row Cast off 3 sts, patt to last 3 sts, sl 1, K1, psso, K1.
Complete to match first side, reversing all shapings.

Sleeves

With 3mm/No 11 needles and A cast on 50 [54:58] sts. Work 8cm/3¼in rib as given for back, ending with a 1st row.
Next row (inc row) Rib 7 [9:5] sts, *pick up loop lying between sts and K tbl – called M1, rib 3 [3:4] sts, rep from * 11 times more, M1, rib 7 [9:5] sts. 63 [67:71] sts.
Change to 3¾mm/No 9 needles.
Beg with a K row cont in st st, inc one st at each end of 9th [5th:1st] row and every foll 8th row until there are 85 [91:97] sts. Cont without shaping until sleeve measures 43cm/17in from beg, ending with a P row.
Join in colours as required and cont in st st, working first 12 rows from jacquard chart.

Shape top

Cont in patt from chart, cast off 4 sts at beg of next 2 rows.
Cont dec as given for back at each end of next and every alt row until 13 [15:17] sts rem, changing to F instead of B on first 5 rows of second patt rep and ending with a Ws row. Leave sts on holder.

Neckband

Join raglan seams with Rs facing and invisible seam, taking care to

The pattern pieces

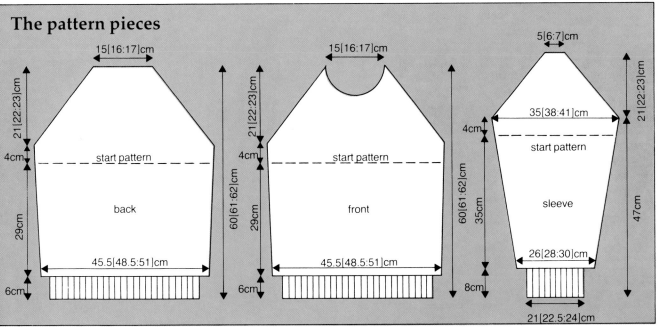

15[16:17]cm
21[22:23]cm
4cm
start pattern
back
29cm
6cm
45.5[48.5:51]cm
60[61:62]cm

15[16:17]cm
21[22:23]cm
4cm
start pattern
front
29cm
6cm
45.5[48.5:51]cm
60[61:62]cm

5[6:7]cm
21[22:23]cm
35[38:41]cm
4cm
start pattern
sleeve
35cm
47cm
8cm
26[28:30]cm
21[22.5:24]cm

match patt exactly.

With Rs of work facing, set of four 3mm/No 11 needles and A, K across sts of right sleeve, back neck and left sleeve K2 tog at each seam, pick up and K17 sts down left front neck, K across front neck sts on holder, pick up and K17 sts up right front neck. 108 [116:124] sts.

Work 8cm/3¼in in rounds of K2, P2 rib. Change to set of four 3¾mm/No 9 needles. Cont in rib until neckband measures 20cm/7¾in from beg. Cast off very loosely.

To make up

Block out each piece and press under a damp cloth with a warm iron.

Join side and sleeve seams, using oversewing for rib, invisible method for side seams and back st for sleeve seams. Press seams.

Below: Blocking and pressing the pieces of this jersey will improve the final appearance of the finished garment. Inset: Samples knitted in the same yarn as the jersey to give you an idea of some alternative colourways.

Grafting stitches to join seams or repair knitting

Two pieces of knitting can be grafted together to give the appearance of continuous stitches and to avoid an unsightly or uncomfortable seam. Grafting can be worked over stocking stitch, garter stitch or rib and gives a professional finish to a garment.

Where a hard, seamed edge will spoil the line of a garment the alternative is to graft the stitches together to form a continuous piece of knitting without a seam. Grafting works best with stocking stitch, garter stitch or single ribbing; don't use it with highly textured yarn or when you are working a complicated stitch pattern.

Below: The top seam of the hood of these coats has been grafted to give the effect of continuous knitting.

There are two ways of grafting stitches together, the first method is carried out with the stitches to be grafted still on the knitting needles, the other with the stitches off the needle.

Stitches on the needles

Use this method for joining the tops of socks and mittens, where a hard seam would be uncomfortable; for shoulders, where the shaping has been worked in steps by turning the rows rather than by casting off in stages, or for the top of a hood, where a seam would detract from the appearance when the hood is down. The hood of the child's coat featured in this chapter uses this method.

Stocking stitch or garter stitch The two pieces to be joined must have the same number of stitches on each needle and, when the right side of the knitting is facing you, one piece should have the point of the needle facing to the right and the other should have the point facing to the left. Work one row more or less on one of the two pieces to achieve this and break off the yarn, leaving an end about four times as long as the width of the stitches to be grafted together. Be generous, because although the yarn can be rejoined if you run out, the ends will have to be darned in and may show. Thread this long end into a blunt-ended sewing needle.

Break off the yarn on the other piece of knitting, leaving a short end to be darned in later.

Hold the two pieces together with the wrong side of the fabric to the inside and the piece with the long end of yarn at the back. The points of both needles are now facing to the right

and you are now ready to begin grafting at the right-hand edge.

Single ribbing requires two pairs of needles, preferably pointed at both ends. You can use four ordinary needles but you must then ensure that all the points are facing in the correct direction (see below). First the knit stitches on one side are grafted and then the fabric is turned to enable you to graft the knit stitches on the other side.

Strictly speaking, this is not true grafting but nevertheless it is easy to work and makes a satisfactory join.

Stitches off the needles

Use this method to join two pieces which have just been knitted or to repair existing garments. To achieve the best results with this method the knitted stitches should not be too small or have been worked in a yarn which will unravel easily.

The two pieces to be joined must have the same number of stitches on each needle. You need one needle point facing to the right and one to the left so work one row more or less on the last of the pieces to be joined and break off the yarn as for grafting with stitches on the needles.

Remove the needles from the stitches (or, if you prefer, remove them gradually as you work), and place the pieces flat on a table with the exposed loops pointing towards each other and the right sides uppermost.

Place the piece where the long end of yarn is still attached *above* the other piece so that you are ready to begin grafting at the right-hand edge. Work vertically across from one piece to the other.

Grafting stocking stitch edge

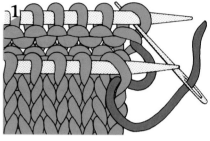

Prepare the pieces to be joined as described under Stitches on the needles and place *purl* sides together with both needles pointing to the right. Thread the long end in to a blunt-ended sewing needle.
1 Insert the sewing needle into the first stitch on the front needle as if to purl it, draw the yarn through and leave this stitch on the needle. Insert the sewing needle into the

Grafting garter stitch edge

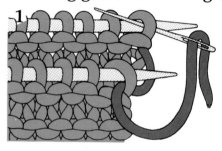

Prepare the pieces to be joined as described under Stitches off the needles and place *wrong* sides together with both needles pointing to the right. Thread the long end in to a blunt ended sewing needle.
1 Insert the sewing needle into the first stitch on the front needle as if to purl it, draw the yarn through

Grafting single ribbed edges

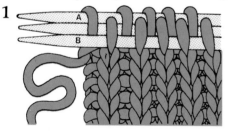

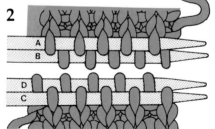

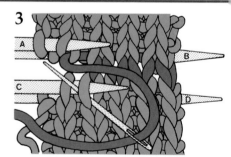

To join two pieces in single ribbing it is much easier if you use needles with points at both ends. However, if you don't have any start with the holding needle pointing to the right on both pieces. Leave a long end of yarn on one of the pieces.

Slip the point of a second needle (needle A) into all the knit stitches on the holding needle (so each knit stitch has two needles through it).
1 Turn the ribbing over so that the points face to the left and slip a third needle (needle B) into all the

remaining stitches. Remove the holding needle carefully.
Repeat for the other piece of knitting, calling the needles C and D respectively.
2 Lay the two pieces flat on a table as shown with the long end of yarn

2

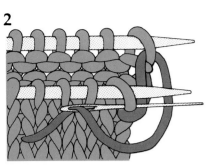

3

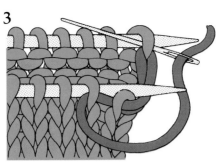

4

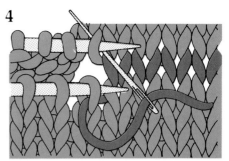

first stitch on the back needle as if to knit it, draw the yarn through and leave this stitch on the needle.
2 *Insert the sewing needle into the first stitch on the front needle again as if to knit it, draw the yarn through and slip this stitch off the needle. Insert the sewing needle into the next stitch on the front needle as if to purl it, draw the yarn through and leave stitch on needle.

3 Insert the sewing needle into the first stitch on the back needle again as if to purl it, draw the yarn through and slip this stitch off the needle. Insert the sewing needle into the next stitch on the back needle as if to knit it, draw the yarn through and leave this stitch on the needle.

4 Continue from the * until all the stitches have been worked off both needles. Darn in all the ends.

Reversed stocking stitch edges
With the *knitted* sides facing each other, work as given for stocking stitch, reading knit for purl and purl for knit.
Alternatively, use stocking stitch method, then turn fabric inside out.

2

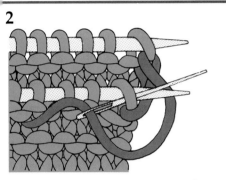

3

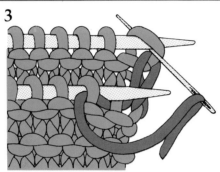

4

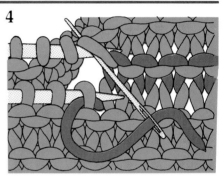

and leave this stitch on the needle. Insert the sewing needle into the first stitch on the back needle as if to purl it, draw the yarn through and leave this stitch on the needle.
2 *Insert the sewing needle into the first stitch on the front needle, again as if to knit it, draw the yarn through and slip this stitch off the

needle. Insert the sewing needle into the next stitch on the front needle as if to purl it, draw yarn through and leave this stitch on the needle.
3 Insert the sewing needle into the first stitch on the back needle, again as if to knit it, draw the yarn through and slip this stitch off the

needle. Insert the sewing needle into the next stitch on the back needle as if to purl it, draw the yarn through and leave this stitch on the needle.
4 Continue from the * until all the stitches have been worked off both needles. Darn in all ends.

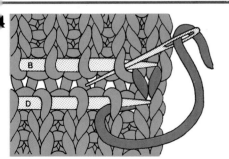

Grafting off the needles

(stocking stitch left and garter stitch right)

at the right-hand edge of top piece.
3 Graft the stitches on needles A and C together as for stocking stitch.
4 Turn the pieces over. Graft the stitches on needles B and D together as for stocking stitch. Darn in all the ends.

Single rib cannot be grafted off the needles because while joining the sets of knit stitches you would unravel the purl stitches that lie in between each of the knit stitches.
Stocking stitch is grafted as you would if it were on the needles

except that you work vertically across from the upper piece to the lower piece of knitting instead of from the back to the front needle.
Garter stitch is also grafted as you would if it were on the needles but it is worked vertically as above.

Toddler's coat for a boy or girl

This snug double-breasted coat is worked entirely in garter stitch and is trimmed with twisted rib in a contrasting colour.

The edges of the hood have been grafted together to make a neat and comfortable join.

Sizes

To fit 51 [56:61]cm/20 [22:24]in chest
Length to shoulder, 46 [50:55]cm/ 18 [19¾:21¾]in
Sleeve seam, 22 [25.5:30]cm/ 8½ [10:11½]in
The figures in [] refer to the 56/22 and 61cm/24in sizes respectively

You will need

6 [6:7] × 50g balls of Wendy
   Shetland Double Knitting (100% wool) in main colour A
1 [2:2] balls of same in contrast colour B
One pair 3¼mm/No 10 needles
One pair 4mm/No 8 needles
Eight buttons

Tension

24 sts and 48 rows to 10cm/4in over g st worked on 4mm/No 8 needles

Back

With 4mm/No 8 needles and A cast on 98 [104:110] sts. K 7 rows g st and mark first row with coloured thread to denote Ws of work.

Shape sides

Cont in g st dec one st at each end of next and every foll 8th [10th:10th] row 14 times in all. 70 [76:82] sts. Cont without shaping until work measures 34 [37:40]cm/ 13½ [14½:16]in from beg, or required length to underarm, ending with a Ws row.

Shape armholes

Cast off 3 sts at beg of next 2 rows. K one row. Dec one st at each end of next and foll 2 alt rows. 58 [64:70] sts.

Above: The contrast twisted rib bands are sewn on afterwards to give a neat tailored finish and extra buttons are added to give a double-breasted effect.

Cont without shaping until armholes measure 12 [13:15]cm/ 4½ [5:6]in from beg, ending with a Ws row.

Shape shoulders

Cast off 8 [9:10] sts at beg of next 4 rows. Cast off rem sts.

Pocket lining (make 2)

With 4mm/No 8 needles and A cast on 20 sts. Work 24 [28:30] rows g st. Leave sts on holders.

Left front

With 4mm/No 8 needles and A cast on 61 [66:70] sts. Mark first st with coloured thread to denote front edge and work 7 rows g st.
8th row K1, dec one, K to end.
Cont dec one st at beg of every foll 8th [10th:10th] row in this way 6 [5:6] times more. 54 [60:63] sts.

Work 6 rows g st, ending at front edge.

Divide for pocket

Next row K36 [38:41] sts, turn and leave rem sts on holder.
Work 7 [7.5:7.5]cm/2¾ [3:3]in g st ending at pocket opening edge. Leave sts on spare needle.
Rejoin yarn to pocket lining sts, K across these sts then K across rem sts of left front on holder. 38 [42:42] sts.
Cont dec at side edge on every 8th [10th:10th] row as before, work until this side of pocket measures same as front edge, ending at pocket lining edge.
Next row Cast off 20 pocket lining sts, K to end.
Work 14 rows g st across all sts.
Next row (buttonhole row) K3 sts, cast off 3 sts, K to end.
Next row K to end, casting on 3 sts above those cast off in previous row.
These 2 rows are rep on every foll 17th/18th [19th/20th:19th/20th] rows 3 times more, *at the same time* cont to shape side until 47 [52:56] sts rem, then work without shaping until front measures same as back to underarm, ending at side edge.

Shape armhole

Cast off 3 sts at beg of next row. Work one row. Dec one st at armhole edge on next and foll 2 alt rows. 41 [46:50] sts.
Working buttonholes as before cont without shaping until front measures 7cm/2¾in less than back to shoulder ending at front edge.

Shape neck

Next row Cast off 12 [15:15] sts, K to end.
K one row. Cast off 2 sts at beg of next and every alt row 5 times. Dec one st at same edge of every alt row until 16 [18:20] sts rem. Work without shaping until front measures same as back to shoulder, ending at armhole edge.

Shape shoulder

Cast off at beg of next and foll alt row 8 [9:10] sts twice.

Right front

With 4mm/No 8 needles and A cast on 61 [66:70] sts. Mark last st of first row with contrasting yarn to denote

front edge and work as given for left front, reversing all shaping and omitting buttonholes.

Sleeves

With 3¼mm/No 10 needles and B cast on 32 [34:38] sts.
1st row (Rs) *K1 tbl, P1, rep from * to end.
Rep this row 13 times more. Break off B. Change to 4mm/No 8 needles. Join in A.
Next row (inc row) K1 [2:1] sts, *M1, K5 [5:6] sts, rep from * to last 1 [2:1] sts, M1, K1 [2:1]. 39 [41:45] sts.
Work 6 rows g st. Inc one st at each end of next and every foll 8th row 9 [11:12] times in all. 57 [63:69] sts. Cont without shaping until work measures 22 [25.5:30]cm/ 8½ [10:11½]in from beg, ending with a Ws row.

Shape top

Cast off 3 sts at beg of next 2 rows. Dec one st at each end of next and every alt row until 37 sts rem. Cast off 2 sts at beg of next 6 rows, and 3 sts at beg of next 2 rows. Cast off rem 19 sts.

Hood

With 4mm/No 8 needles and A cast on 76 [80:84] sts. Work 18cm/7in g st.

Shape top

1st row K29 [31:33] sts, sl 1, K2 tog, psso, K12, sl 1, K2 tog, psso, K29 [31:33] sts.
2nd and every alt row K to end.
3rd row K29 [31:33] sts, sl 1, K2 tog, psso, K8, sl 1, K2 tog, psso, K29 [31:33] sts.
5th row K29 [31:33] sts, sl 1, K2 tog, psso, K4, sl 1, K2 tog, psso, K29 [31:33] sts.
7th row K29 [31:33] sts, (sl 1, K2 tog, psso) twice, K29 [31:33] sts.
9th row K30 [32:34] sts, turn. Leave

both sets of sts on needles and graft edges tog.

Pocket bands (make 2)

With 3¼mm/No 10 needles and A cast on 24 sts. Work 5 rows twisted rib as given for sleeves. Cast off with a K row.

Front bands (make 2)

With 3¼mm/No 10 needles and B cast on 100 [116:130] sts. Work as given for pocket bands.

Armhole bands (make 2)

With 3¼mm/No 10 needles and B cast on 92 [96:100] sts. Work as given for pocket bands.

Hood band

With 3¼mm/No 10 needles and B cast on 120 sts. Work as given for pocket bands.

Neck band

With 3¼mm/No 10 needles and B cast on 134 [136:138] sts. Work as given for pocket bands.

To make up

Do not press. With ridge of cast-off edge uppermost top st pocket bands to edge of pockets. Top st front bands to front edges in same way. Join shoulder seams, noting that buttonholes are on right front for a girl or left front for a boy. Sew neckband right round neck edge. Sew in sleeves. Sew on arm bands to cover seams. Join sleeve and side seams. Sew pocket linings in place. Sew hood band round front edge of hood. Sew hood to back neck just below the neckband on the outside of the coat, easing in place slightly from about 1cm/½in over shoulder seam. Make tassel with B and st to top of hood. Sew on two sets of four buttons for double breasted effect.

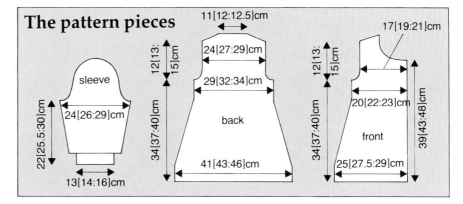

The pattern pieces

sleeve — 11[12:12.5]cm — 24[27:29]cm — 29[32:34]cm — back — 41[43:46]cm — 12[13:15]cm — 24[26:29]cm — 22[25.5:30]cm — 34[37:40]cm — 13[14:16]cm — 17[19:21]cm — 12[13:15]cm — 20[22:23]cm — front — 39[43:48]cm — 25[27.5:29]cm — 34[37:40]cm

Perky pompom toys and trims

These jolly little pompom toys can be made from oddments of yarn at a fraction of the cost of shop-bought counterparts, yet they will give hours of pleasure to a baby or toddler. And pompoms make colourful, sporty trims for all kinds of clothing and accessories, too.

Making pompoms

1

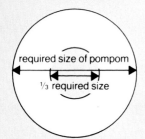

required size of pompom
⅓ required size

2 winding yarn into small ball

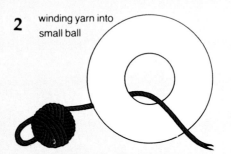

3 winding yarn round card

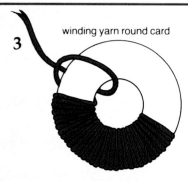

1 Mark a circle of the size required on two pieces of card, using a pair of compasses or a circular object such as the rim of a cup. In the centre of both circles mark a smaller one, with a diameter just under one-third the size of the first.
Cut out the two larger circles, then cut out the inner circles on each. Place both pieces of card together.

2 Wind a length of yarn into a tight ball, small enough to push through the central hole. To make a really full pompom you will need several balls. To achieve a multi-coloured effect, use a different colour for each ball you wind.
3 Wind the yarn round and round the pieces of card, as evenly as possible, pushing the ball of yarn

through the central hole each time. Continue winding in this way until the hole is almost completely filled and it is no longer possible to push a ball of yarn through.
Break off a long end of yarn from the ball and thread it through the eye of a blunt-ended sewing needle. Use this to continue winding, filling the hole as tightly as possible until

Pompom toys

Pompoms make ideal toys for babies and toddlers, but all additional features should be non-toxic, soft and securely stitched into place.

To make a toy duck
With yellow yarn, make two pompoms – each 10cm/4in in diameter.** Use one for the body and the second, trimmed to a slightly smaller size, for the head.

Gifts to make – a family of rabbits or a cheeky caterpillar.

Use the final ends of yarn from each pompom to tie them together securely.
Thread a blunt-ended sewing needle with black yarn and make a large knot at one end. Push the needle right through the smaller pompom at eye level and pull the yarn through so that the knot forms an eye. Knot the yarn again for the second eye and cut away the surplus.**
For the beak, cut a diamond shape from felt and stitch in place.

To make a toy rabbit
With white or grey yarn, make two pompoms – each 10cm/4in in diameter.

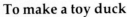

Pompoms make colourful and easy-to-change trims for hat and scarf sets, and they can be attached to each end of a twisted cord belt or a necktie for a jersey. Use one colour, multi-colours or even segments of colour.

To make pompoms all you need is a pair of sharp scissors, two pieces of firm cardboard, a blunt-ended needle and the yarn of your choice. You begin by cutting circles from the card, each with a smaller circle in the middle. The diameter of each circle determines the size and weight of the finished pompom, and the total amount of yarn needed.

As a guide to the finished size of a pompom, a circle with an outer diameter of 10cm/4in and an inner circle with a diameter of 3cm/1¼in will give a trimmed pompom size of about 10cm/4in diameter. Use double knitting yarn for a firm pompom or mohair for a fluffy one.

Right: Chirpy chickens in assorted sizes.

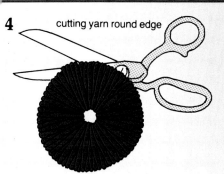
4 cutting yarn round edge

you have only sufficient space left to enable you to remove the pieces of card without cutting through them.

4 Slip one blade of a sharp pair of scissors between the two pieces of card and cut through the yarn all around the outer edges of the circles, taking care not to cut through the card.

5 tying pompom securely

5 Gently ease the two pieces of card apart without releasing the cut ends of yarn from the central hole. Break off another piece of yarn about 50cm/19¾in long, fold it in half, and wind it several times round the centre of the pompom – between the two pieces of card. Knot the ends securely.

If the pompom is going to be tied to

6 fluffing pompom into shape

another in order to make a toy, do not cut the ends but use them to tie to the next pompom. If the pompom is being used as a trim, the ends can also be used to sew it in position.

6 Remove the two pieces of card very carefully so that they can be used again another time. Fluff the pompom into shape and trim evenly.

Work as for duck from ** to **. For the ears, cut out two ear shapes from felt and stitch in place on the smaller pompom. Tie a ribbon between pompoms at neck level.

To make a caterpillar
In the colours of your choice, make one pompom 10cm/4in in diameter, three of each size 8cm/3¼in, 6cm/2¼in and 4cm/1½in in diameter and one of about 2cm/¾in. Trim ends. In graduating size, thread all the pompoms on to a piece of narrow elastic, about 65cm/25½in long, and stitch securely at each end. Cut features, as illustrated, from felt oddments and stitch in place.

Making a pompom in segments of colours

1 marking card into segments

colour A — colour B
colour D — colour C

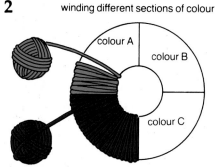
2 winding different sections of colour

colour A
colour B
colour C

1 Cut out two pieces of card as given for a pompom in one colour. Mark as many segments as you require on both pieces of card, coding each colour as A, B, C, D and so on.
2 Work as given for a pompom in one colour, winding one layer of yarn round the pieces of card in the first colour as marked on the circle. Leave this colour for the time being and join in the next colour and wind

it round the next section as marked on the circle. Continue in this way, using each colour in turn, until one layer of yarn has been wound round the card. Bring in the first colour again and continue winding each colour in turn, back across its allotted section until the hole has been almost filled.

Complete the pompom as for a plain one; tie-off with one of the colours used and trim all long ends.

The pattern for this feather-light mohair shawl is given on page 192. It is made from lace and garter stitch diamonds which are then sewn together. Add a long knotted fringing using a crochet hook as described overleaf.

Fringes and tassels

Fringes make bold and striking trimmings and bring the flavour of the Wild West to your wardrobe. Knot them directly into the fabric or knit a fringe separately and sew it on. Tassels are simple to make from oddments of coloured yarn. Use them round a shawl or to top a cheeky cap.

Colourful fringes and tassels give an individual touch to your clothes. Plan to add them to a jumper you are about to knit, or make them to match or contrast with something already in your wardrobe, whether it is hand knitted or shop bought. Fringing can also be added to lampshades, bed covers, cushions and even curtains. There are two methods of making fringing: you can knit it or knot it. Any type of yarn can be used, but take the thickness of the background fabric into account.

To gauge how much yarn you will need, see how much fringing or how many tassels you can make with one ball, then calculate how much more you will need.

Tassels are a very decorative trimming, and made in oddments of yarn they give a multi-coloured effect.

Knotted fringing is effective added to the edge of a garment, across a yoke or to trim pockets.

The fringing is attached by passing a crochet hook right through the fabric, so if you want to add it to a delicate material, first sew a row of hand or machine stitches where the fringing is required. Attach it to these stitches to avoid damaging fabric.

Eyelet holes offer another easy way

knotted fringing in eyelet holes

of attaching the fringing. They can be worked anywhere into a garment you are hand knitting so that fringes can be knotted in later. Do not use this method in a complicated pattern as the eyelet holes will make it difficult to keep track of the pattern sequence.

To make the eyelet holes, use the yarn forward, round or over the needle methods (pages 28–29) then work the next two stitches together. Along a straight edge make the eyelet holes at regular intervals two rows above the casting on or two rows below the casting off. Knot the fringing into each eyelet hole as given for working fringing along an edge.

To knot the fringing into the fabric when the eyelet holes have been worked at random, follow details given overleaf for working fringing into knitting.

Knitted fringing is made in a strip which comes out about twice as deep as the original knitted strip.

For a thicker fringe, knit with two strands of yarn. Cut through the loops or leave them uncut.

Left: Achieve an original effect by adding knotted fringing across the yoke of a sweater.

Knotted fringing

To work fringes along an edge
Cut the yarn into twice the required length of the fringe allowing an additional 2cm/¾in for the knot, and for final trimming. Work with one or more strands at a time, depending on the thickness of the yarn and the thickness of fringe required.

1 With the wrong side of the edge to be fringed facing you, insert a crochet hook from the front to the back through the edge. Fold the strands in half, put the folded loops on the hook and pull them through the fabric with the hook.

Fringing knotted along an edge.

2 Put all the ends of yarn round the hook again and pull them through the loops on the hook.
Repeat at regular intervals along the edge. The completed knot shows on the right side of the fabric.

Knitted fringing

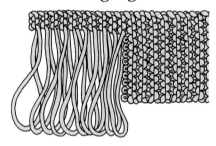

To work garter stitch fringing
The examples shown here have been worked in double knitting yarn on 4mm/No 8 needles over 12 stitches. Three stitches have been allowed for the border and nine for the fringing. Cast on and work in garter stitch on 12 stitches to the required length.

The fringe before the loops are cut.

On the last row, cast off three border stitches and fasten off. Slip the remaining nine stitches off the left-hand needle and unravel them down to the cast on row to form fringed loops. Sew the border in place on top of edge to be fringed.

To work mock double rib fringin with eyelet holes
In this example four stitches have been allowed for the eyelet hole border and eight for the fringing. Cast on 12 stitches.
1st row K to end.
2nd row P to end.
3rd row P to end.
4th row K to end.
5th row K2, yfwd, K2 tog, K to end.
6th row P to end.
7th row P to end.
8th row K to end.
These eight rows form the patt.
Cont in patt until the border is the required length.
On the last row, cast off three border stitches and fasten off the

Tassels with and without shanks

To make a tassel without a shank
Cut a strip of thin card about 10cm ×20cm/4in×8in, depending on the length and thickness of tassel required.
1 Leave a free end about 30cm/12in long and wind yarn loosely round the length of the card. Cut the yarn leaving another end 30cm/12in long.
2 Thread the last cut end of yarn into a blunt-ended needle and knot this into the last loop of yarn round the card to secure it. Insert the needle under all the strands of yarn at one edge of the card and pull the yarn through. Thread the first end of cut yarn into the needle and secure it as for the other end. Insert the needle back in the opposite

1

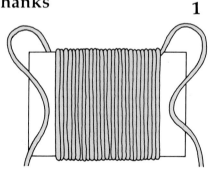

2

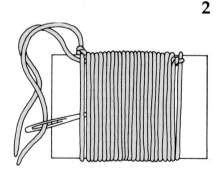

direction under all the strands of yarn at the same edge of the card. Pull both ends up tightly and knot together to secure. Remove the loops from the card. Wind one end of loose yarn round clockwise and one end anti-clockwise about 2cm/¾in from top of loops, leaving

ends about 10cm/4in long. Knot these two ends together. Thread both ends into the needle and push up through the centre of the top of the tassel. Pull the yarn through. **.
Use these ends to sew the tassel to the garment. Cut through the loops at the other end.

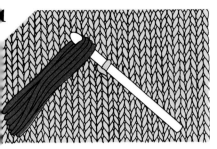

To work fringes into knitting

1 With the right side of the fabric to be fringed facing you, insert the crochet hook upwards under the central thread of the stitch to be fringed. Fold the strands in half, put the folded loops on the hook and pull them through the stitch with the hook.

2 Put all the ends of yarn round the hook again and pull them through the loops on the hook.
The completed knot shows on the right side of the fabric.

Right: Multi-coloured random fringing.

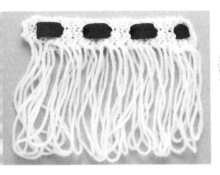

Ribbon threaded through eyelet holes.

fourth. Slip the remaining eight stitches off the left-hand needle and unravel them down to the cast on row to form fringed loops.
Thread ribbon through the eyelet holes before sewing the border in place on top of edge to be fringed.

To make a tassel with a shank

Work as given for tassel without a shank to **, leaving two ends about 50cm/20in long at beg and two ends 30cm/12in long when the tassel is completed. Make a slip loop in the ends of yarn up close to the top of the tassel. Put this loop on a crochet hook and make the required number of chains to form the shank. Fasten off and use the remaining yarn to sew on the tassel.

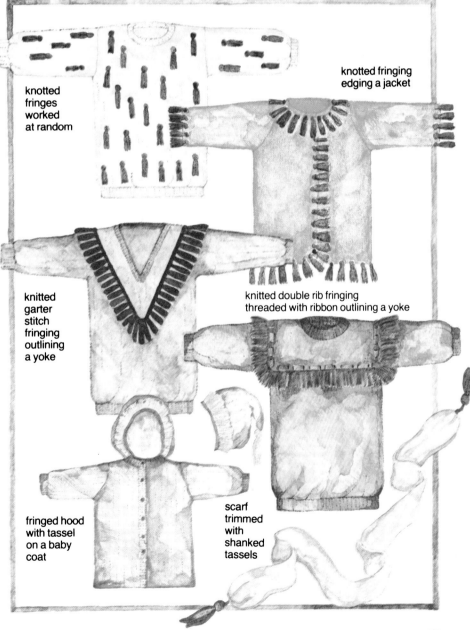

knotted fringes worked at random

knotted fringing edging a jacket

knitted garter stitch fringing outlining a yoke

knitted double rib fringing threaded with ribbon outlining a yoke

fringed hood with tassel on a baby coat

scarf trimmed with shanked tassels

Knitted cords, braids and flower trimmings

*Make these inexpensive cords, braids and flower shapes
and use them to brighten up existing garments,
or why not incorporate one of the ideas into a new project.
The thickness of the yarn and the needle
size determines the finished size of these trimmings.*

Knitted trimmings are simple to make and are far less expensive than comparable purchased trimmings. Add them to any type of garment – as suggestions, knit cords for a baby jacket instead of buying ribbon, add some braid to the front edges of a favourite jacket to give it a new look, or a posy of flowers to the pocket of a plain cardigan.

If you go through your oddments of yarn you are bound to find something in toning or contrasting colours that can be used to try out all the ideas in this chapter, without incurring any expense.

The thickness of the cords, width of the braids and size of the flower shapes can all be altered by using fine or thick yarn and needles.

Straight cord only entails casting on the number of stitches to give the length needed, then casting them off again. It is very firm, flexible and hard-wearing and is a useful way of making ties for a jacket, or as a plain narrow braid.

Ric-rac braid is worked from side to side to any length you need. It has a zig-zag appearance and needs to be worked in a firm yarn so that it lies flat.

Lace braid is worked from side to side to any length you need. It has a delicate appearance but is quite wide. It makes the ideal edging on a chunky jacket.

Faggoting braid is worked from side to side to any length you need. Ladders are formed in the centre of the braid – you can leave these as they are or use them to thread ribbon through the braid as an additional decoration.

Picot braid is very narrow and is worked by casting on the number of stitches to give the length needed, then casting them off again. This dainty braid has been added to the jersey pattern, featured in this chapter.

Plaited braid is worked from side to side to any length you need. It has a robust appearance and is a wide braid, also suitable for trimming chunky garments.

Scalloped braid has one straight and one curved edge and is worked from side to side to any length. It is ideal for trimming round a curve, such as the neck of a jersey, or Peter Pan collar.

Tubular cord is a clever way of making a rounded cord by working in rows from side to side. A pair of double-pointed needles are used for this method – as the stitches are few in number, short cable needles are ideal.

Short petal shapes can be used as flowers or leaves. Use them individually as leaves or join them together as flowers. These tiny shapes are ideal worked in a fine cotton yarn to decorate baby garments.

Long petal shapes can also be used as individual leaves or grouped together as flowers. They are worked in garter stitch and are very firm. Vary the size by using different thickness yarns and work the leaves in a contrast colour to the petals.

Knitted flowers

Long petal shape

Cast on 4 stitches and begin at bottom of petal.
Work 18 rows g st, inc one st at each end of 5th and 7th rows and dec one st at each end of 13th, 15th and 17th rows.
K2 rem sts tog and fasten off.

Make 6 petal shapes for each flower. Complete as for short petal shape.

Short petal shape

Cast on 3 stitches and begin at top of petal.
Beg with a K row work 5 rows st st, inc one st at each end of 3rd and 5th rows by picking up loop lying between sts and K tbl. 7 sts.
Work 3 more rows without shaping.
Next row Lift 2nd, 3rd, 4th, 5th, 6th and 7th sts on left-hand needle individually over first st and off needle, then K first st on left-hand needle.
Break off yarn and fasten off.
Make 5 petal shapes for each flower. Overlap one side edge of each petal to form a circle of petals and secure in centre with a few French knots in contrasting colour.

long petal

straight cord

tubular cord

Knitted cords and braids

Straight cord
Cast on stitches by the thumb method to give the full length of cord required.
Cast off knitwise, very loosely.

Ric-rac braid
Cast on 4 stitches.
1st row Cast off 2 sts knitwise, (one st on right-hand needle) K1.
2nd row Cast on 2 sts, K and cast off 2 sts, (one st on right-hand needle), K1.
Rep 2nd row for length required. Cast off 2 sts.

Lace braid
Cast on 7 stitches.
1st row (Rs) K2, (yfwd, K1) 4 times, K1. 11 sts.
2nd row (K1, P1) 5 times, K1.
3rd row K2, P1, sl 1, K1, psso, K1, K2 tog, P1, K2.
4th row K1, P1, K1, P3 tog, K1, P1, K1. 7 sts.
These 4 rows form the pattern. Cont in pattern for length required, ending with a 4th row. Cast off.

Faggoting braid
Cast on 6 stitches.
1st row (Rs) K1, K2 tog, y2rn, K2 tog tbl, K1.
2nd row K2, K into front then P into back of y2rn, K2.
Rep these 2 rows for length

required. Cast off.
If required, thread ribbon through the ladders with the right side of the braid facing, before sewing it in place.

Picot braid
Cast on an even number of stitches to give the length of braid required.
*Knit and cast off 4 sts, return st on right-hand needle to left-hand needle.
Place right-hand needle into next st on left-hand needle as if to knit it, cast on 2 sts, and rep from * to end of row. Fasten off last st.

Plaited braid
Cast on 12 stitches.
1st row (Ws) K4, P4, K4.
2nd row K1, P3, (sl 1 with yarn at back, K1, yfwd, psso the K1 and yfwd) twice, P3, K1.
3rd row As 1st.
4th row K1, P3, K1, sl 1 with yarn at back, K1, yfwd, psso the K1 and yfwd, K1, P3, K1.
These 4 rows form the pattern. Cont in pattern for length required, ending with a 1st or 3rd row. Cast off.

Scalloped braid
Cast on 2 stitches.
1st row (Ws) K1, P1, turn and cast on 3 sts.
2nd row (K next st winding yarn

twice round right-hand needle) 4 times, K1.
3rd row K1, (P next st dropping extra yarn round needle) 4 times.
4th row (K2 tog) twice, lift 2nd st on right-hand needle over first and off needle, K1.
These 4 rows form the pattern. Cont in pattern for length required, ending with a 4th row. Cast off.

Tubular cord
Use two short, double-pointed needles to cast on 3 stitches by the 2-needle method.
1st row K3 sts, *do not turn the needle but slip the sts along to the right-hand end of the same needle, leaving the yarn at the left-hand edge of the sts.
Draw the yarn firmly behind the sts from left to right and K3.
Rep from * until the cord is the required length, always knitting the sts in the same direction. Last row K3 tog and fasten off.

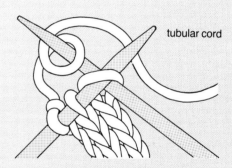

tubular cord

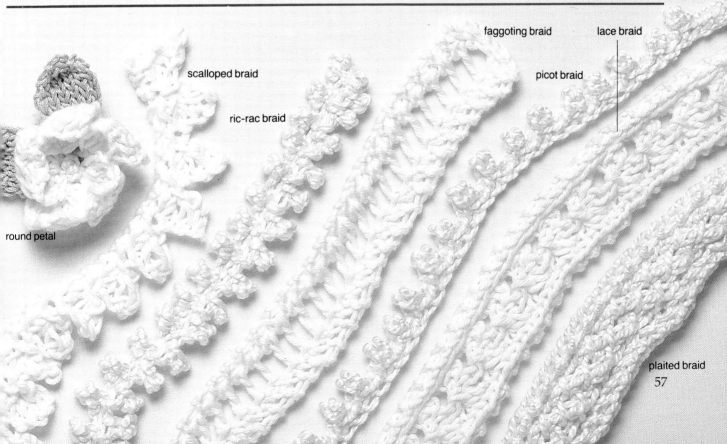

scalloped braid

ric-rac braid

faggoting braid

lace braid

picot braid

round petal

plaited braid

Braid-trimmed jersey

This simple jersey is worked in reverse stocking stitch except for a series of single knit stitches which indicate where to sew the braids.

Sizes

To fit 81 [86:91:97]cm/32 [34:36:38]in bust
Length to shoulder, 57 [58:59:60]cm/22½ [22¾:23¼:23½]in
Sleeve seam, 47cm/18½in
The figures in [] refer to the 86/34, 91/36 and 97cm/38in sizes

You will need

13 [14:14:15]×20g balls of Wendy Courtellon Double Knitting (60% Courtelle acrylic, 40% Brinylon) in main colour A
2 [2:2:2] balls of same in contrast colour B for braid, or oddments
One pair 3¼mm/No 10 needles
One pair 4mm/No 8 needles
One pair 2¾mm/No 12 needles

Tension

22 sts and 28 rows to 10cm/4in over st st worked on 4mm/No 8 needles

Back

With 3¼mm/No 10 needles and A cast on 84 [88:92:96] sts. Work 7cm/2¾in K1, P1 rib.
Next row (inc row) Rib 7 [9:4:6], (pick up loop lying between needles and K tbl – called M1, rib 7) 10 [10:12:12] times, M1, rib 7 [9:4:6]. 95 [99:105:109] sts.
Change to 4mm/No 8 needles.
1st row (Rs) P14 [14:14:15] sts, K1 to mark position for braid, P10 [11:12:12] sts, K1, P43 [45:49:51] sts, K1, P10 [11:12:12] sts, K1, P14 [14:14:15] sts.
2nd row K14 [14:14:15] sts, P1, K10 [11:12:12] sts, P1, K43 [45:49:51] sts, P1, K10 [11:12:12] sts, P1, K14 [14:14:15] sts.
Rep these 2 rows until work measures 38 [38:39:39]cm/15 [15:15¼:15¼]in from beg, ending with a Ws row.

Shape armholes

Cast off 7 sts at beg of next 2 rows.
1st row (Rs) P7 [7:7:8] sts, (K1 for position of braid, P10 [11:12:12] sts) twice, (K1, P10 [10:11:12] sts) twice, (K1, P10 [11:12:12] sts) twice, K1, P7 [7:7:8] sts.
2nd row K7 [7:7:8] sts, (P1, K10 [11:12:12] sts) twice, (P1, K10 [10:11:12] sts) twice, (P1, K10 [11:12:12] sts) twice, P1, K7 [7:7:8] sts. **
These 2 rows form yoke patt. Cont in patt until armholes measure 19 [20:20:21]cm/7½in [7¾:7¾:8¼]in from beg, ending with a Ws row.

Shape shoulders

Cast off 24 [25:28:29] sts at beg of next 2 rows. Leave rem 33 [35:35:37] sts on holder for centre back neck.

Front

Work as given for back to **.
Cont in patt until armholes measure 12 [13:13:14]cm/4¾ [5:5:5½]in from beg, ending with a Ws row.

Shape neck

Next row Patt 34 [35:38:39] sts, turn and leave rem sts on holder.
Cast off 5 sts at beg of next row, patt to end. Dec one st at neck edge on next 3 rows, then on foll 2 alt rows. 24 [25:28:29] sts.
Cont without shaping until armhole measures same as back to shoulder, ending at armhole edge. Cast off.
With Rs of work facing, leave first 13 [15:15:17] sts on holder, rejoin yarn to rem sts and complete right side to match left side, reversing shaping.

Sleeves

With 3¼mm/No 10 needles and A cast on 42 [44:44:46] sts. Work 7cm/2¾in K1, P1 rib.
Next row Rib 1 [2:2:3] sts, *inc in next st, rib 3 sts, rep from * to last 1 [2:2:3] sts, rib to end. 52 [54:54:56] sts.
Change to 4mm/No 8 needles. Beg with a P row cont in reversed st st, inc one st at each end of 5th and every foll 6th row until there are 84 [88:88:92] sts.
Cont without shaping until sleeve measures 47cm/18½in from beg, ending with a K row.
Work 10 more rows noting that these are set into armhole shaping and do not count as part of sleeve seam. Cast off loosely.

Neckband

Join left shoulder seam. With Rs of work facing, 3¼mm/No 10 needles and A, K across back neck sts on holder, dec one st in centre, pick up and K28 sts down left side of neck, K across front neck sts on holder and pick up and K28 sts up right side of neck. 101 [105:105:109] sts.
1st row (Ws) P1, *K1, P1, rep from * to end.
2nd row K1, *P1, K1, rep from * to end. Rep these 2 rows 3 times more, then 1st row again. Cast off in rib.

Picot braid

With 2¾mm/No 12 needles and B make 2 lengths of picot braid for each K st on either side of back and front body, or one length of braid of your choice, working in one piece to go over shoulder. Work braid for each K st on front and back yoke.

To make up

Do not press. Join right shoulder seam. Set in sleeves. Join side and sleeve seams.
Sew one length of picot braid to each side of every K st on back and front with picot edges to outside, or sew your chosen braid over each K st.

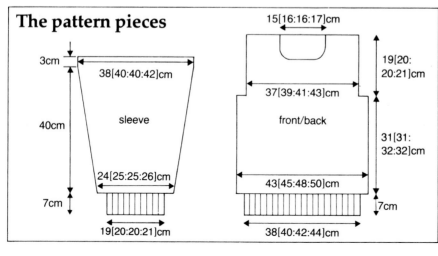

The pattern pieces

3cm

38[40:40:42]cm

40cm

sleeve

7cm

24[25:25:26]cm

19[20:20:21]cm

15[16:16:17]cm

19[20:20:21]cm

37[39:41:43]cm

front/back

31[31:32:32]cm

43[45:48:50]cm

7cm

38[40:42:44]cm

The braid is stitched to both back and front alike of these jerseys, but if you prefer, knit the back plain and make braid for the front only.

Knitting in rounds

Knitting on sets of needles pointed at each end, or on a circular needle, produces seamless, tubular fabrics. You do not turn at the end of each row as in knitting with pairs of needles, so the right side is always facing you, which affects the methods of working even basic patterns.

Knitting in rounds is the ideal way of making socks, gloves, hats, skirts, or anything that would be spoiled by a bulky seam. Jerseys can also be knitted in the round up to the underarms, then divided and continued in rows as normal – in fact this is how trad-itional Aran and Guernsey designs are knitted.

You can knit in rounds with either a set of needles – four, five or six – or a circular needle. (Circular needles can also be used to work to and fro in rows.)

When you are knitting in rounds remember that the right side of the fabric is always facing you as you do not turn to begin another row. If you are working a pattern, the method will be different from when knitting in rows, though the result will be the same.

The miniature leaf pattern, used on the bolster cushion in this chapter, is given in rounds. Using this as a guide you can adapt the other patterns given on page 165 in the same way by always knitting the second and every alternate row instead of purling it. Use your preferred method of casting on and if you need to join in a new ball, *splice* the ends of the old and new yarns together.

To cast on with a circular needle

Use the ends of the needle as a pair to cast on the number of stitches required with the method you prefer. Make sure the stitches do not become twisted round the nylon strip which joins the needle ends together. To knit in rounds use the right-hand needle point to work across all the cast-on stitches until you come to the beginning of the round again.

Alternatively, after casting on, turn and use the circular needle as a pair of needles, working the first row without joining it into a round. This is an easier method because it prevents the stitches becoming twisted round the nylon strip, but it does leave a gap in the work. Continue knitting in rounds and join the gap at the beginning with a

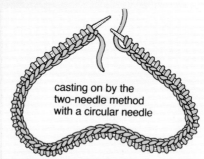

casting on by the two-needle method with a circular needle

few oversewn stitches.

Circular needles are sold in different lengths, to accommodate varying numbers of cast on stitches. The chart on the right lists the minimum number of stitches to cast on for each length of needle, to ensure that you can reach from one needle point to the other without stretching the fabric.

Minimum no of stitches required for circular needles

Tension (sts to 2.5cm/1in)	Needle length			
	40cm 16in	60cm 24in	80cm 30in	100cm 40in
5	80	117	157	196
5½	88	129	173	216
6	96	141	189	236
6½	104	153	205	255
7	112	164	220	275
7½	120	176	236	294
8	128	188	252	314
8½	136	200	268	334
9	144	212	284	353

To cast off in rounds

If you are using a set of four needles, use the free needle to cast off the stitches on the first needle of the round until one stitch remains on the right-hand needle. Put aside the left-hand needle. Use the right-hand needle to cast the stitches off the second needle, and so on. When you get to the very last stitch, fasten off.

If you are using a circular needle, use the right-hand needle point to work the stitches and the left-hand needle point to lift them over and off the needle. When one stitch remains, fasten off.

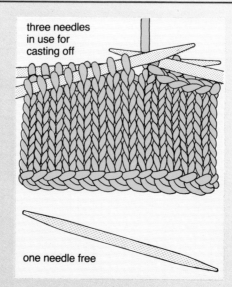

three needles in use for casting off

one needle free

To cast on with four needles

When you are knitting, the stitches will be divided more or less equally between three needles.
Using the method you prefer, you can cast the right number of stitches on to each of the three needles to start with, but be careful that they don't get twisted round the needle before you begin to knit.

An easier method for a small number of stitches is to cast them all on to one needle. Work one or two rows in your pattern, then divide and transfer them to the second and third needles. This way you avoid the stitches getting twisted round the needles, but you will have a gap at the beginning of the work. Use a

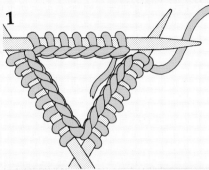

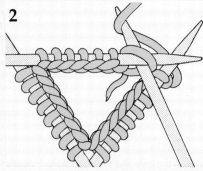

blunt-ended sewing needle and the cast-on end of yarn to join this with a few oversewn stitches.
2 Arrange the three needles in a triangle and use the fourth to begin knitting in rounds.

Work across the stitches of the first needle, then use this to work across the stitches of the second needle, and so on. Always pull the yarn tightly across to the first stitch on each needle to avoid a loose stitch.

Simple patterns knitted in the round

It is easy to convert simple patterns for knitting in the round. Here are the basic ones most often used.
Stocking stitch Work by knitting every round. This simplifies knitting multi-coloured patterns such as Fair Isle.
Garter stitch Work by knitting the first and every odd-numbered round. The second and every even-numbered round must be purled. Alternate rounds of knitting and purling form the ridged effect.
Single ribbing Work by alternately knitting and purling one stitch on the first round. If you begin a round with one knitted stitch you must end with one purled stitch to complete the round exactly. On every following round all the knitted stitches are knitted and the

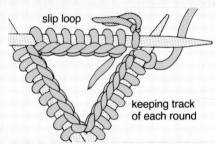

slip loop

keeping track of each round

purled stitches purled.
Single moss stitch Work by alternately knitting and purling one stitch on the first and every odd-numbered round. If you begin a round with one knitted stitch you must end with one purled stitch to complete the round exactly. In the second and every even-numbered round, the knitted stitches must be purled and purled stitches knitted.

Note:
It is easy to lose track of the beginning of each round, whether you are using sets of needles or a circular needle. Mark this point by making a slip loop in a length of different coloured yarn and put it on the needle at the beginning of the first round. Slip the loop from one needle point to the other on every round without working into it.

Splicing two ends of yarn together

1 To join in yarn when knitting in rounds unravel the ends of the old and the new ball and cut away one or two strands from each, about 5cm/2in long.
2 Overlay the remaining strands from opposite directions and firmly twist them together. The twisted ends should be of the same thickness as the original yarn. This is called splicing. Work the next few stitches very carefully with the twisted yarn. When the work is completed, neatly darn in any odd ends on the wrong side of the fabric.

Some yarns, such as mohair and

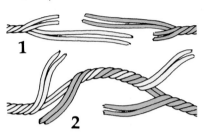

bouclé qualities, are not easy to unravel. If they cannot be spliced, use the reef knot method of joining in a new ball. When the work is completed, tighten up the reef knot so that the join is the same tension as the other stitches. Darn in the ends across the back of the work.

Bolster up your sofa

Size

57cm/22in long by 49cm/20in circumference (stretch on to pad)

You will need

6×25g balls of Sunbeam Mohair, (67% mohair, 28% wool, 5% nylon)
One 5½mm/No 5 circular needle, 40cm/16in long or set of four 5½mm/No 5 needles
Bolster cushion pad 46cm/18in long × 56cm/22in circumference

Tension

16 sts and 21 rounds to 10cm/4in worked on 5½mm/No 5 needles

To make the cover

Cast on 78 sts and join into a round. K one round. Commence miniature leaf patt.
1st round *K1, yfwd, sl 1, K1, psso, K1, K2 tog, yfwd, rep from * to end.
2nd and 4th rounds K to end.
3rd round *K2, yfwd, sl 2 tog, K1, p2sso, yfwd, K1, rep from * to end.
5th round *K1, K2 tog, yfwd, K1, yfwd, sl 1, K1, psso, rep from * to end.

Below: The lacy patterns given on page 165 can be easily converted for knitting in the round. Shown here are mesh lace (left) and arrowhead lace (right).

Above: To knit a scarf, cast on 54 sts and work as for bolster for 120cm/47in, allowing 8 balls of yarn. Gather up ends and trim with tassels.

6th round K to last st, leave last st unworked.

7th round *Sl 2 tog noting that first st is unworked st at end of last round, K1, p2sso, yfwd, K3, yfwd, rep from * to end.

8th round K to end.

These 8 rounds form the patt. Rep them 14 times more. Break off yarn, thread through sts, draw up and fasten off securely. Do not press. Place cover over cushion pad. Thread a separate length of yarn through cast on sts, draw up tightly and fasten off securely.

Make two large tassels with shanks and sew one to each end of cover, see page 55.

To make a muff

Use the same basic pattern to make a muff in mesh lace, page 165.

You will need

30cm/12in of 8oz wadding 94cm/37in wide
Materials and needles as for bolster 130cm/52in cord

Work 57cm/22in as for bolster but in mesh lace (page 165), cast off. Coil wadding twice to make a 'tube' 30cm/12in wide. Stitch down long edge. Push wadding tube into centre of knitted tube, inserting ends of knitting to meet inside muff. Catch stitch ends together. Purchase 130cm/52in of cord, thread through muff and tie ends to give desired length.

Above: The tie for this pretty muff could also be made from 30 strands of wool plaited together.

Below: Dress up your sofa with two elegant bolster cushions in soft lacy-knit covers.

Medallion knitting

Medallions are knitted in rounds, usually on sets of needles. Singly they make eye-catching table mats and coasters. Or you can join them together in a colourful geometric design for a nursery rug, or work them in fine cotton for an exquisite tablecloth.

Medallions can be knitted to any size, shape or pattern. There are two methods of knitting them in rounds. The more usual method is to knit from the centre, gradually increasing until you reach the right size. The second method is to begin with a fixed outer measurement, then decrease as you knit until you finish at the centre. Whichever method you choose, the right side of the knitting is always facing you. How many sides the medallion has determines the positions of the increasing.

Different methods of shaping suit different stitches. If you are working from the centre of a medallion in stocking stitch, you make the increases by picking up a loop between the stitches. If you are knitting from the centre in a lacy pattern, you will need an eyelet-hole method of increasing.

To work a square from the outer edge to the centre in stocking stitch, you will need to decrease at each corner in pairs of stitches (see page 30).

Casting on at the centre

Sets of needles must be used here as there will not be enough stitches to reach from one point of a circular needle to the other. Cast them all on to one needle using the thumb or two-needle method. Re-arrange them on the remaining needles, leaving one of the set free to knit the stitches.

The shape of the medallion will determine the number of needles you need. If you are knitting a square, it is obviously simpler to cast the same number of stitches on to each of four needles and use a fifth to knit with. However, all medallion shapes can be cast on to three needles so that you can use the fourth for knitting. Always knit the first round into the

back of all the stitches. This flattens the centre of the medallion. As the stitches increase in number, you can transfer them to a circular needle.

Casting off at the outer edge

The stitches must be kept very loose or the fabric will not lie flat. Use one size larger needle to cast off with the dainty picot edging opposite.

Casting on at the outer edge

Always cast on very loosely by the thumb or two-needle method. Use a circular needle or a set of needles one size larger than that given for the main pattern, or the finished shape will not lie flat.

If you use a circular needle to cast on, transfer the stitches to a set of needles as you decrease to complete the medallion, leaving one of the set free to knit the stitches. On the last round before casting off, knit into the *back* of all the stitches to flatten the centre of the medallion.

Casting off at the centre

Use the normal method of casting off and fasten off the last stitch. Leave an end about 15cm/6in long, thread this through a blunt-ended sewing needle and sew a running stitch into the back of each cast-off stitch. Draw the stitches together in the centre and secure the yarn neatly.

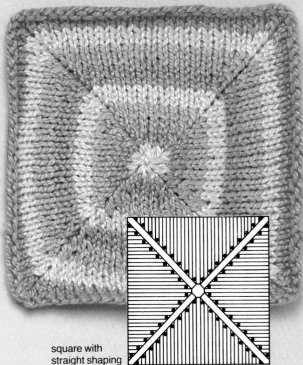

square with
straight shaping

To make a circle

This circle is in stocking stitch. The knitting begins at the centre and increases by the picked up loop method (see page 26) from the 5th round. Each increasing round adds 16 stitches to the circumference of the medallion, and is separated from the next by 3 plain rounds to keep the circle flat.
With a set of 5 needles cast on 8 stitches. Arrange 2 stitches on each of 4 needles and knit with the 5th. Form the needles into a square and begin knitting in the round.
1st round (Rs) K all sts tbl.
2nd round *K1, pick up loop lying between sts and K tbl – **called M1**, rep from * to end. 16 sts.
3rd to 5th rounds K to end.
6th round *K1, M1, rep from * to end. 32 sts.
7th to 9th rounds K to end.
10th round *K2, M1, rep from * to end. 48 sts.
11th to 13th rounds K to end.
14th round *K3, M1, rep from * to end. 64 sts.
15th to 17th rounds K to end.
18th round *K4, M1, rep from * to end. 80 sts.
Cont inc 16 sts in this way on every foll 4th round, working one more st between inc, until the circle is the required size. Cast off very loosely.

Left: By knitting larger medallions you can make useful items such as these practical and pretty cushion covers.

To make a square

This square is in striped stocking stitch. The knitting begins at the outer edge. It has straight lines of shaping at each corner and the decreased stitches are shown as black dots on the diagram above. If you use 4mm/No 8 needles and double knitting yarn it will be about 10cm/4in square. Decreasing rounds, where 2 stitches are decreased at each corner, alternate with plain rounds to keep the square flat.
With a set of 5 needles cast on 96 sts loosely. Arrange 24 sts on each of 4 needles and knit with the 5th. Form the needles into a square and begin knitting in the round.

1st round (Rs) K to end.
2nd round *K2 tog, K20, sl 1, K1, psso, rep from * 3 times more. 88 sts.
3rd and every alt round K to end.
4th round *K2 tog, K18, sl 1, K1, psso, rep from * 3 times more. 80 sts.
6th round *K2 tog, K16, sl 1, K1, psso, rep from * 3 times more. 72 sts.
Cont dec 8 sts in this way on every alt round, working 2 sts less between dec until 8 sts rem. Cast off firmly.

PROFESSIONAL TOUCH

Picot casting off

To overcome the problem of casting off too tightly on the outer edge of a medallion, use the simple picot method. It forms a single chain stitch between each cast-off stitch and can be used to cast off an odd or even number of stitches. Knit the stitches fairly loosely before casting them off.
1 Change to a size larger needle than the one you have been knitting with, K1, *yfwd and hold across the right-hand needle, use the left-hand needle to lift the K st over the yfwd and off the right-hand needle, K1 from left-hand needle, lift the yfwd over the K st and off the right-hand needle.
2 Cont from * until one st rem on right-hand needle. Fasten off.

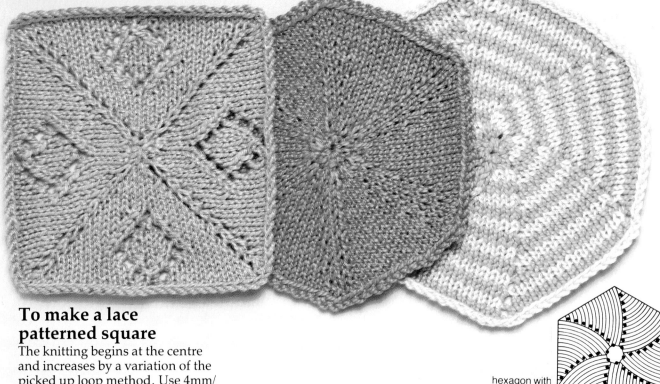

hexagon with
swirl shaping

To make a lace patterned square

The knitting begins at the centre and increases by a variation of the picked up loop method. Use 4mm/No 8 needles and double knitting yarn to make about a 11.5cm/4½in square. Increasing rounds, where 2 stitches are added at each corner, alternate with plain rounds to keep the square flat.

With a set of 5 needles cast on 8 sts. Arrange 2 sts on each of 4 needles and knit with the 5th. Form the needles into a square and begin knitting in the round.

1st round (Rs) K all sts tbl.
2nd round K twice into each st. 16 sts.
3rd and every alt round K to end.
4th round *K1, pick up loop lying between sts and K into the *front* of it – **called M1F**, K3, M1F, rep from * to end.
6th round *K1, M1F, K5, M1F, rep from * to end.
8th round *K1, M1F, K7, M1F, rep from * to end.
10th round *K1, M1F, K3, K2 tog, yfwd, K4, M1F, rep from * to end.
12th round *K1, M1F, K3, K2 tog, yfwd, K1, yfwd, sl 1, K1, psso, K3, M1F, rep from * to end.
14th round *K1, M1F, K3, K2 tog, yfwd, K3, yfwd, sl 1, K1, psso, K3, M1F, rep from * to end.
16th round *K1, M1F, K3, K2 tog, yfwd, K5, yfwd, sl 1, K1, psso, K3, M1F, rep from * to end.
18th round *K1, M1F, K6, yfwd, sl 1, K1, psso, K1, K2 tog, yfwd, K6, M1F, rep from * to end.
20th round *K1, M1F, K8, yfwd, sl 1, K2 tog, psso, yfwd, K8, M1F, rep from * to end.
22nd round *K1, M1F, K9, K2 tog, yfwd, K10, M1F, rep from * to end.
23rd round K to end.
Cast off loosely.

To make a hexagon

This hexagon is in stocking stitch. The knitting begins at the centre and increases by the picked up loop method. Six straight lines of increasing radiate from the centre. Each increasing round adds 12 stitches to the circumference of the medallion and is separated from the next by 2 plain rounds to keep the hexagon flat.

With a set of 4 needles cast on 12 sts. Arrange 4 sts on each of 3 needles and knit with the 4th. Form the needles into a triangle and begin knitting in the round.

1st round (Rs) K all sts tbl.
2nd round K twice into each st. 24 sts.
3rd round K to end.
4th round *K1, M1, (K2, M1) 3 times, K1, rep from * twice more. 36 sts.
5th and 6th rounds K to end.
7th round *K1, M1, K4, M1, K2, M1, K4, M1, K1, rep from * twice more. 48 sts.
8th and 9th rounds K to end.
10th round *K1, M1, K6, M1, K2, M1, K6, M1, K1, rep from * twice more. 60 sts.
Cont inc 12 sts in this way on every foll 3rd round until the hexagon is the required size. Cast off loosely.

To make an eyelet hole hexagon

This hexagon is in striped stocking stitch. The knitting increases by the eyelet hole method. The increases give a swirl effect and are shown as black dots on the diagram. Each increasing round adds 6 stitches to the circumference of the medallion and alternates with a plain round to keep the hexagon flat.

Cast on and work the 1st round as given for the hexagon with straight increasing.

2nd round *Yfwd to inc 1, K2, yfwd, K2, rep from * twice more. 18 sts.
3rd and every alt round K to end.
4th round *Yfwd, K3, yfwd, K3, rep from * twice more. 24 sts.
6th round *Yfwd, K4, yfwd, K4, rep from * twice more. 30 sts.
Cont inc 6 sts in this way on every alt round until the hexagon is the required size. Cast off loosely.

Octagonal place mat and coaster

This place setting is knitted in cotton yarn and can be machine washed. The attractive swirling design is very easy to work.

Sizes

Place mat, 22cm/8¾in diameter from point to point
Coaster, 13cm/5in diameter from point to point

You will need

1×50g ball of Twilleys Stalite
Set of five 3mm/No 11 needles

Tension

28 sts and 36 rows to 10cm/4in over st st worked on 3mm/No 11 needles

Place mat

With 3mm/No 11 needles cast on 8 sts. Arrange 2 sts on each of 4 needles and join into a square.

1st round K all sts tbl.
2nd round *Yfwd, K1, rep from * to end.
3rd and every alt round K to end.
4th round *Yfwd, K2, rep from * to end.
6th round *Yfwd, K3, rep from * to end.
Cont inc in this way and working one more st between inc until there are 80 sts.**
20th round *Yfwd, K1, yfwd, K7, K2 tog, rep from * to end.
22nd round *Yfwd, K3, yfwd, K6, K2 tog, rep from * to end.
24th round *Yfwd, K5, yfwd, K5, K2 tog, rep from * to end.
26th round *Yfwd, K7, yfwd, K4, K2 tog, rep from * to end.
28th round *Yfwd, K9, yfwd, K3, K2 tog, rep from * to end.
30th round *Yfwd, K11, yfwd, K2, K2 tog, rep from * to end.
32nd round *Yfwd, K13, yfwd, K1,

K2 tog, rep from * to end.
34th round *Yfwd, K15, yfwd, K2 tog, rep from * to end. 144 sts.
35th and 37th rounds P to end.
36th round *Yfwd, K17, yfwd, K1, rep from * to end.
38th round *Yfwd, K19, yfwd, K1, rep from * to end. 176 sts.
Cast off purlwise.

Coaster

Work as given for place mat to **
19th and 21st rounds P to end.
20th round *K1, yfwd, K9, yfwd, rep from * to end.
22nd round *K1, yfwd, K11, yfwd, rep from * to end. 112 sts.
Cast off purlwise.

To make up

Press under a damp cloth with a warm iron.

Below: The matching placemat and coaster can be knitted to tone with your tableware. A set would make a beautiful but inexpensive gift for a friend.

Fisherman knitting: traditional guernsey patterns

The type of fisherman's garment known as a guernsey – or gansey – originated in the Channel island of that name. As designs were adopted by one port after another, each region developed its own patterns incorporating symbols from their nautical surroundings.

Although traditional navy blue guernsey designs originated on the island of Guernsey, the patterns are also associated with many coastal areas of Britain. Ports, villages and even individual families, developed their own traditional patterns and it was said that fisherfolk could tell at a glance the port from which a sailor hailed by the designs on his jersey.

Most of the patterns have names associated with objects used by the fishermen in their daily work. Ropes of every kind, fishing nets, herring bones, anchors and ladders are all represented.

There are many similarities to Aran knitting – both use combinations of patterns such as cables and moss stitch but while Aran knitting includes relief textures and patterns featuring travelling stitches, the patterns used in fisherman's knitting do not generally stand out in relief against the background, but give the appearance of an even-textured fabric.

These everyday working garments were often knitted by the fishermen themselves – the body and sleeves in stocking stitch with a little pattern decoration on the yoke. More elaborate versions, referred to as bridal shirts, were knitted by young women for their betrothed.

The traditional square shape with a dropped shoulder-line was knitted in the round on sets of five or more needles. The sleeves were knitted from the shoulders to the cuffs which made them easy to unravel and re-knit when the elbows or cuffs wore through. The yarn, techniques and patterns used in knitting the authentic versions made them virtually wind and weatherproof.

The next chapter has a pattern for an authentic guernsey knitted in the round in the traditional navy blue worsted wool, while this chapter has a pattern for a child's jersey knitted in double knitting on two needles. The design uses four of the seven patterns given here and overleaf and experienced knitters will be able to interchange the patterns provided they make allowance for the varying multiples of stitches. The patterns included are as follows:

Ridge and furrow pattern which is made up of two rows of stocking stitch followed by two rows of reversed stocking stitch, repeated as many times as required. Used across the width of the fabric it is an effective way of separating one pattern from the next.

Anchor pattern which is one of the many nautical patterns, can be worked as a border across a row, or repeated one anchor above the other as a vertical panel.

Ridge and furrow pattern

This can be worked over any number of stitches.
1st row K to end.
2nd row P to end.
3rd row P to end.
4th row K to end.
These 4 rows form the pattern.

Ladder pattern

Cast on multiples of 6 sts plus 2 sts, eg 26.
1st row (Rs) P2, *K4, P2, rep from * to end.
2nd row K2, *P4, K2, rep from * to end.
3rd row P to end.
4th row As 2nd.
These 4 rows form the pattern.

Ladder pattern which is said to represent the ladder of life. The purl ridges form the rungs of the ladder. It is best worked as a vertical panel between purl ribs.

Flag pattern which is another nautical symbol representing the jaunty pennant on a fishing boat. It needs to be worked as a vertical panel, preferably against moss stitch.

Betty Martin's pattern which is an example of the kind of simple pattern which would have been passed from one generation to another by word of mouth, becoming known by the name of the knitter who first used it.

Diamond pattern which has a moss stitch diamond shape against a stocking stitch background and can be worked as a border or a vertical panel. There are many variations of this basic shape, some depicting windows, others fishing nets, depending on the area of origin.

Marriage lines which is made up of zigzag lines of purl stitches on a knit background. This represents difficult paths or flashes of lightning – a wry comment on daily life, showing the ups and downs of married life.

Right: The welts of these children's jerseys are knitted in rib instead of the traditional garter stitch.

Casting on for guernseys

This special way of casting on forms a very hardwearing knotted edge. Use the correct yarn and the looped method (see page 23).

Cast on 2 stitches. Use a spare needle to lift the second stitch on the main needle over the top of the first stitch and off the needle.

*Cast on 2 more stitches, then lift the second stitch over the top of the first and off the needle, leaving 2 stitches on the main needle.

Continue from the * until the correct number of stitches have been cast on.

Flag pattern

Cast on multiples of 11 sts plus 3 sts, eg 25.

1st row (Rs) *K1, P1, K1 – **called moss st 3**, K1, P7, rep from * to last 3 sts, moss st 3.

2nd row *Moss st 3, K6, P2, rep from * to last 3 sts, moss st 3.

3rd row *Moss st 3, K3, P5, rep from * to last 3 sts, moss st 3.

4th row *Moss st 3, K4, P4, rep from * to last 3 sts, moss st 3.

5th row *Moss st 3, K5, P3, rep from * to last 3 sts, moss st 3.

6th row *Moss st 3, K2, P6, rep from * to last 3 sts, moss st 3.

7th row *Moss st 3, K7, P1, rep from * to last 3 sts, moss st 3.

8th row *Moss st 3, P8, rep from * to last 3 sts, moss st 3.

These 8 rows form the pattern.

Marriage lines pattern

Cast on multiples of 13 sts plus 2 sts, eg 28.

1st row (Rs) *P2, K5, P1, K2, P1, K2, rep from * to last 2 sts, P2.

2nd row *K2, P1, K1, P2, K1, P6, rep from * to last 2 sts, K2.

3rd row As 1st.

4th row *K2, P3, K1, P2, K1, P4, rep from * to last 2 sts, K2.

5th row *P2, K3, P1, K2, P1, K4, rep from * to last 2 sts, P2.

6th row *K2, P5, K1, P2, K1, P2, rep from * to last 2 sts, K2.

7th row *P2, K1, P1, K2, P1, K6, rep from * to last 2 sts, P2.

8th row *K2, P5, K1, P2, K1, P2, rep from * to last 2 sts, K2.

9th row *P2, K3, P1, K2, P1, K4, rep from * to last 2 sts, P2.

10th row *K2, P3, K1, P2, K1, P4, rep from * to last 2 sts, K2.

These 10 rows form the pattern.

Anchor pattern

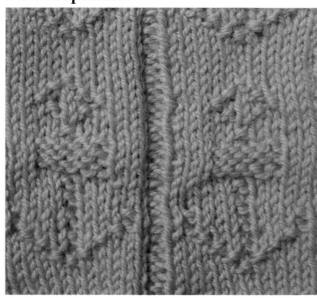

Cast on multiples of 13 sts plus 2 sts, eg 28.

1st row (Rs) *P2, K11, rep from * to last 2 sts, P2.

2nd row *K2, P11, rep from * to last 2 sts, K2.

3rd row As 1st.

4th row As 2nd.

5th row *P2, K5, P1, K5, rep from * to last 2 sts, P2.

6th row *K2, P4, K1, P1, K1, P4, rep from * to last 2 sts, K2.

7th row *P2, K3, (P1, K1) twice, P1, K3, rep from * to last 2 sts, P2.

8th row *K2, P2, K1, P5, K1, P2, rep from * to last 2 sts, K2.

9th row *P2, K1, P1, K3, P1, K3, P1, K1, rep from * to last 2 sts, P2.

10th row *K2, P1, K1, P7, K1, P1, rep from * to last 2 sts, K2.

11th row As 5th.

12th row As 2nd.

13th row As 5th.

14th row As 2nd.

Diamond pattern

Betty Martin's pattern

Cast on multiples of 13 sts plus 2 sts, eg 28.
1st row (Rs) *P2, K11, rep from * to last 2 sts, P2.
2nd row *K2, P11, rep from * to last 2 sts, K2.
3rd row As 1st.
4th row *K2, P5, K1, P5, rep from * to last 2 sts, K2.
5th row *P2, K4, P1, K1, P1, K4, rep from * to last 2 sts, P2.
6th row *K2, P3, (K1, P1) twice, K1, P3, rep from * to last 2 sts, K2.
7th row *P2, K2, (P1, K1) 3 times, P1, K2, rep from * to last 2 sts, P2.
8th row *K2, (P1, K1) 5 times, P1, rep from * to last 2 sts, K2.
9th row As 7th.
10th row As 6th.
11th row As 5th.
12th row As 4th.
These 12 rows form the pattern.

15th row *P2, K3, P5, K3, rep from * to last 2 sts, P2.
16th row *K2, P3, K5, P3, rep from * to last 2 sts, K2.
17th row As 15th.
18th row As 2nd.
19th row As 5th.
20th row As 2nd.
21st row *P2, K4, P1, K1, P1, K4, rep from * to last 2 sts, P2.
22nd row *K2, P3, K1, P3, K1, P3, rep from * to last 2 sts, K2.
23rd row As 21st.
24th row *K2, P5, K1, P5, rep from * to last 2 sts, K2.
These 24 rows form the pattern.

Right: The yoke of this child's jersey has a combination of traditional patterns. The sleeves are knitted from the sleeve head down to the cuff, so that they can be unpicked and re-knitted to lengthen or repair them.

Cast on multiples of 4 sts plus 2 sts, eg 22.
1st row (Rs) *K2, P2, rep from * to last 2 sts, K2.
2nd row *P2, K2, rep from * to last 2 sts, P2.
3rd row K.
4th row P.
These 4 rows form the pattern.

Colourful jerseys with guernsey pattern yokes

This child's version of a guernsey has been modified to suit modern knitting techniques and preferences but uses the special method of casting on.

Sizes

To fit 61[66:71:76]cm/24[26:28:30]in chest
Length to shoulder, 38[42:46:50]cm/15[16½:18:19¾]in
Sleeve seam, 30[33:36:39]cm/11¾[13:14¼:15¼]in
The figures in [] refer to the 66/26, 71/28 and 76cm/30in sizes respectively

You will need

5[6:7:8]×50g balls of Hayfield Brig Double Knitting (100% wool)
One pair 3¼mm/No 10 needles
One pair 4mm/No 8 needles
Set of four 3¼mm/No 10 needles pointed at both ends

Tension

22 sts and 30 rows to 10cm/4in over st st worked on 4mm/No 8 needles

Back

With 3¼mm/No 10 needles cast on 71[77:83:89] sts by the guernsey method.
1st row (Rs) K1, *P1, K1, rep from * to end.
2nd row P1, *K1, P1, rep from * to end.
Rep these 2 rows for 4[4:5:5]cm/1½[1½:2:2]in, ending with a 2nd row.
Change to 4mm/No 8 needles. Beg with a K row cont in st st until work measures 21[24:26:29]cm/8¼[9½:10¼:11½]in from beg, ending with a P row.
Work 14[14:18:18] rows ridge and furrow patt, ending with a 2nd row.

Yoke

1st row P1[4:3:2] sts, (**marriage lines patt** K5, P1, K2, P1, K2), P2 sts, (**Betty Martin's patt** (K2, P2) 3[3:4:5] times, K2), (**diamond patt** P2, K11, P2), (**Betty Martin's patt** (K2, P2) 3[3:4:5] times, K2,), P2 sts, (**marriage lines patt** K5, P1, K2, P1, K2), P1[4:3:2] sts.
2nd row K1[4:3:2] sts, work 11 sts as 2nd row of marriage lines patt, K2 sts, work 14[14:18:22] sts as 2nd row of Betty Martin's patt, work 15 sts as 2nd row of diamond patt, work 14[14:18:22] sts as 2nd row of Betty Martin's patt, K2 sts, work 11 sts as 2nd row of marriage lines patt, K1[4:3:2] sts.
Beg with a 3rd row of each patt, cont in patt as now set until work measures 38[42:46:50]cm/15[16½:18:19¾]in from beg, ending with a Ws row.

Shape shoulders

Cast off at beg of next and every row 7[8:8:9] sts 4 times and 7[7:9:9] sts twice. Leave rem 29[31:33:35] sts on holder for centre back neck.

Front

Work as given for back until work measures 33[37:40:44]cm/13[14½:15¾:17¼]in from beg, ending with a Ws row.

Shape neck

Next row Patt 30[32:35:37] sts, turn and leave rem sts on holder. Complete left shoulder first. Cast off at beg of next and foll alt row for neck edge 2 sts twice, then dec one

st at beg of foll 5[5:6:6] alt rows. 21[23:25:27] sts.
Cont without shaping if necessary until work measures same as back to shoulder, ending with a Ws row.

Shape shoulder

Cast off at beg of next and every alt row 7[8:8:9] sts twice and 7[7:9:9] sts once.
With Rs of work facing, leave first 11[13:13:15] sts on holder for centre front neck, rejoin yarn to rem sts and patt to end. Work one row then complete to match first side.

Sleeves

With 4mm/No 8 needles cast on 61[67:73:79] sts by the thumb method and beg at top. Work 14[14:18:18] rows ridge and furrow patt, then beg with a K row work 2 rows st st.
Cont in st st, dec one st at each end of next and every foll 6th row until 39[43:47:51] sts rem. Cont without shaping until sleeve measures 26[29:31:34]cm/10¼[11½:12¼:13½]in from beg, ending with a K row.
Next row (dec row) P1[3:0:2] sts, (P2 tog, P3) 7[7:9:9] times, P2 tog, P1[3:0:2] sts. 31[35:37:41] sts.
Change to 3¼mm/No 10 needles. Beg with a 1st row cont in rib as given for back for 4[4:5:5]cm/1½[1½:2:2]in. Cast off loosely in rib.

Neckband

Join shoulder seams. With Rs of work facing and set of 3¼mm/No 10 needles K across back neck sts on holder, pick up and K18[18:20:20] sts down left front neck, K across front neck sts on holder, pick up and K18[18:20:20] sts up right front neck. 76[80:86:90] sts.
Work 4[4:5:5]cm/1½[1½:2:2]in in rounds of K1, P1 rib. Cast off loosely in rib.

To make up

Press lightly under a damp cloth with a warm iron. Set in sleeves. Join side and sleeve seams. Fold neckband in half to Ws and sl st down. Press seams.

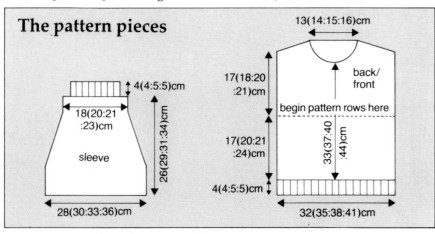

The pattern pieces

4(4:5:5)cm
18(20:21:23)cm
26(29:31:34)cm
28(30:33:36)cm
sleeve

13(14:15:16)cm
17(18:20:21)cm
back/front
begin pattern rows here
17(20:21:24)cm
33(37:40:44)cm
4(4:5:5)cm
32(35:38:41)cm

Guernseys in the round

*A true guernsey is so cleverly constructed and cunningly worked
that it pays considerable tribute to the
inventive knitters of the past. It involves the minimum of
technical problems yet creates a garment
offering maximum protection and freedom of movement*

Authentic fishermens' garments were originally knitted with a special 5 ply worsted wool similar to a double knitting weight and particularly firm and hard wearing. The traditional colour was navy blue but today guernsey wool is available in red and cream as well.

Sets of five long, double-pointed needles, about size 2mm/No 14, were used to knit the garment – four to hold the stitches and the fifth to knit with. These can be replaced by circular needles.

Scottish versions were often knitted with a 6 ply yarn. This was softer than worsted wool and tended to mat together, making the felted fabric completely weatherproof. The needles were also thicker, about 2¾mm/No 12, and shorter, sold in sets of up to eight to take all the stitches.

Knitting the body

To begin the back and front, the welts were cast on separately with two needles, using the wool double and the knotted cast-on method for greater strength (page 69). Once the welts were completed, the front and back were joined into a round for the body, leaving welt flaps open at the sides for ease of movement.

The positions for mock side seams were marked with one or two purl stitches up each side of the body and used as a guide to positioning the increased stitches for underarm gussets. The underarm gusset was incorporated about half-way up the body under the arms to give freedom of movement.

Below: The neck gusset provides extra stitches so that the loose fitting neckband stands away from the neck.

Knitting the armholes

Instead of dividing the work on to two needles at the armhole, authentic designs continued in rounds. The position of the armholes was marked on every round by winding the yarn several times round the needle, before continuing the knitting. These loops were dropped off the needle on the following round and the process repeated until the armholes were the required length. This separated back from front.

When the body was completed, a series of loose strands of yarn would mark the position of each armhole. These loops were then cut in half and the ends darned back into the main fabric. This made a rather bulky edge and nowadays most knitters prefer to divide the work at the underarm and complete back and front separately.

Knitting the sleeves

The stitches for the sleeves were picked up round the armholes, including the underarm stitches of the gusset. The sleeves were knitted from the shoulder down to the cuff – this part received the most wear and could easily be unpicked and re-knitted. Further re-inforcement was added by casting off cuffs with double yarn. The sleeves often appear to be rather short. This is because they were practical, working garments for men whose hands were often in water – and soaking wet cuffs were the last thing a fisherman would want.

Sheringham herringbone and diamond

Cast on multiples of 28 sts plus 14 sts.
1st row (Rs) *K6, P2, K12, P2, K6, rep from * to last 14 sts, K6, P2, K6.
2nd row *P6, K2, P12, K2, P6, rep from * to last 14 sts, P6, K2, P6.
3rd row *K5, P1, K2, P1, K9, P2, K2, P2, K4, rep from * to last 14 sts, K5, P1, K2, P1, K5.
4th row *P4, K1, P4, K1, P8, K2, P2, K2, P4, rep from * to last 14 sts, P4, K1, P4, K1, P4.
5th row *K3, P1, K6, P1, K5, (P2, K2) 3 times, rep from * to last 14 sts, K3, P1, K6, P1, K3.
6th row *P2, K1, P8, K1, P4, (K2, P2) 3 times, rep from * to last 14 sts, P2, K1, P8, K1, P2.
7th row *K1, P1, K10, P1, K1, (P2, K2) 3 times, P2, rep from * to last 14 sts, K1, P1, K10, P1, K1.
8th row *K1, P12, K1, (K2, P2) 3 times, K2, rep from * to last 14 sts, K1, P12, K1.
9th row *K6, P2, K8, (P2, K2) 3 times, rep from * to last 14 sts, K6, P2, K6.
10th row *P6, K2, P8, (K2, P2) 3 times, rep from * to last 14 sts, P6, K2, P6.
11th row As 3rd.
12th row As 4th.
13th row *K3, P1, K6, P1, K9, P2, K6, rep from * to last 14 sts, K3, P1, K6, P1, K3.
14th row *P2, K1, P8, K1, P8, K2, P6, rep from * to last 14 sts, P2, K1, P8, K1, P2.
15th row *K1, P1, K10, P1, K15, rep from * to last 14 sts, K1, P1, K10, P1, K1.
16th row *K1, P12, K1, P14, rep from * to last 14 sts, K1, P12, K1. These 16 rows form the pattern.

Fife heart

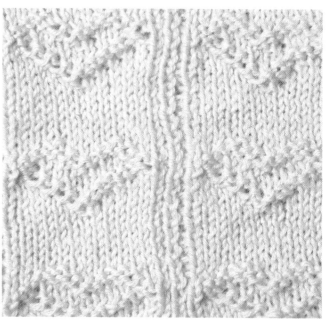

Cast on multiples of 16 sts plus 3 sts.
1st row (Rs) *P1, K1, P1, K6, P1, K6, rep from * to last 3 sts, P1, K1, P1.
2nd row *K1, P1, K1, P5, K3, P5, rep from * to last 3 sts, K1, P1, K1.
3rd row *P1, K1, P1, K4, P2, K1, P2, K4, rep from * to last 3 sts, P1, K1, P1.
4th row *K1, P1, K1, P3, K2, P3, K2, P3, rep from * to last 3 sts, K1, P1, K1.
5th row *P1, K1, P1, K2, P2, K5, P2, K2, rep from * to last 3 sts, P1, K1, P1.
6th row *(K1, P1) twice, K2, P3, K1, P3, K2, P1, rep from * to last 3 sts, K1, P1, K1.
7th row *(P1, K1) twice, P2, K2, P3, K2, P2, K1, rep from * to last 3 sts, P1, K1, P1.
8th row *K1, P1, K1, P2, K4, P1, K4, P2, rep from * to last 3 sts, K1, P1, K1.
9th row *P1, K1, P1, (K3, P2) twice, K3, rep from * to last 3 sts, P1, K1, P1.
10th row *K1, P1, K1, P13, rep from * to last 3 sts, K1, P1, K1.
11th row *P1, K1, P1, K13, rep from * to last 3 sts, P1, K1, P1.
12th row As 10th.
Rep 11th and 12th rows twice more.
These 16 rows form the pattern.

Knitting the neck

Shaped neck gussets were often included in the neckband so that it made a loose-fitting stand-up collar about 5cm/2in high.

Scottish versions had a button and buttonhole band on one shoulder and a close-fitting neckband. This makes a much neater finish and the neck does not stretch out of shape every time it is pulled over the head. Sheringham herringbone and diamond pattern and Fife heart pattern are used in the guernsey patterns given at the end of this chapter. Two other patterns are also included and can be substituted by experienced knitters.

Sheringham herringbone and diamond pattern makes an all-over pattern for a yoke. The herringbones do not have a centre spine and the diamonds are worked in double moss stitch.

Fife heart pattern is a romantic little motif and would have been worked into a bridal shirt. It makes a useful filler between larger patterns.

Filey cable and herringbone pattern is associated with this fishing port. The cable is a simple twist over six stitches and the herringbone has a centre spine.

Whitby cable and diamond pattern is one of the many patterns associated with this area. The cable is a simple twist over six stitches and the diamond is purled against a knitted background.

Filey cable and herringbone

Cast on multiples of 22 sts plus 10 sts.

1st row (Rs) *P2, K6, P2, K5, P2, K5, rep from * to last 10 sts, P2, K6, P2.

2nd row *K2, P6, K2, P4, K4, P4, rep from * to last 10 sts, K2, P6, K2.

3rd row *P2, K6, P2, K3, P1, K1, P2, K1, P1, K3, rep from * to last 10 sts, P2, K6, P2.

4th row *K2, P6, K2, P2, K1, P2, K2, P2, K1, P2, rep from * to last 10 sts, K2, P6, K2.

5th row *P2, K6, P2, K1, P1, K3, P2, K3, P1, K1, rep from * to last 10 sts, P2, K6, P2.

6th row *K2, P6, K3, P4, K2, P4, K1, rep from * to last 10 sts, K2, P6, K2.

7th row *P2, C6B (see page 206), P2, K5, P2, K5, rep from * to last 10 sts, P2, C6B, P2.

The 2nd and 7th rows inclusive form the pattern.

Whitby cable and diamond

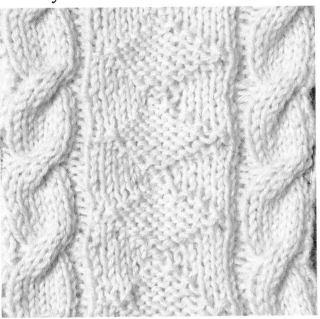

Cast on multiples of 21 sts plus 10 sts.

1st row (Rs) *P2, K6, P2, K11, rep from * to last 10 sts, P2, K6, P2.

2nd row *K2, P6, K2, P5, K1, P5, rep from * to last 10 sts, K2, P6, K2.

3rd row *P2, C6B (see page 206), P2, K4, P3, K4, rep from * to last 10 sts, P2, C6B, P2.

4th row *K2, P6, K2, P3, K5, P3, rep from * to last 10 sts, K2, P6, K2.

5th row *P2, K6, P2, K2, P7, K2, rep from * to last 10 sts, P2, K6, P2.

6th row *K2, P6, K2, P1, K9, P1, rep from * to last 10 sts, K2, P6, K2.

7th row As 5th.

8th row As 4th.

9th row *P2, K6, P2, K4, P3, K4, rep from * to last 10 sts, P2, K6, P2.

10th row As 2nd.

These 10 rows form the pattern.

Authentic guernseys for a man or woman

These jerseys include many of the traditional guernsey features, such as mock side seams and underarm and neck gussets, and the sleeves are knitted from the shoulder to the cuff. To make the garments easier to knit they have been worked on circular needles, instead of sets of needles, and divided at the armholes.

Sizes

To fit 86[91:97:102]cm/34 [36:38:40]in bust/chest loosely
Length to shoulder, 63 [65:67:69]cm/ 24¾ [25½:26½:27¼]in
Sleeve seam, 46 [47:48:49]cm/ 18 [18½:19:19¼]in, adjustable
The figures in [] refer to the 91/36, 97/38 and 102cm/40in sizes respectively.

You will need

16 [17:18:19]×50g balls of Emu guernsey (100% wool)
One pair 2¾mm/No 12 needles
One pair 3mm/No 11 needles
One 2¾mm/No 12 circular needle 100cm/40in long
One 3mm/No 11 circular needle 100cm/40in long
Set of four 2¾mm/No 12 needles pointed at both ends
Set of four 3mm/No 11 needles pointed at both ends
One cable needle

Tension

28 sts and 36 rows to 10cm/4in over st st worked on 3mm/No 11 needles

Body

With 2¾mm/No 12 needles cast on 127 [135:143:151] sts by the guernsey method
Work 7cm/2¾in g st ending with a Ws row. Break off yarn and leave these sts for time being.
Work a second piece in same way but do not break off yarn.

Join body

Change to 2¾mm/No 12 circular needle and cont working in rounds to underarm.
Next round Inc in first st, K to end across second piece, cont across first piece and inc in first st, K to end. Join into a circle taking care not to twist sts. 256 [272:288:304] sts.
Work 6 rounds K2, P2 rib.
Change to 3mm/No 11 circular needle. Commence mock side seams.
1st round *P1, K127 [135:143:151] sts, rep from * once more.
2nd round K to end.
Rep these 2 rounds until work measures 38cm/15in from beg, ending with a 1st round.

Shape underarm gusset

1st round *Pick up loop lying between sts and K tbl – **called M1**, K1, M1, K127 [135:143:151] sts, rep from * once more.
2nd round K to end.
3rd round *M1, K3, M1, K127 [135:143:151] sts, rep from * once more.
Cont inc in this way on every alt round until there are 292 [308:324:340] sts, ending with an inc round.

Divide for armholes

Next row K19 sts and sl these sts on to a thread for gusset, K127[135:143:151] sts, turn and leave rem sts on spare needle. Complete front first. K 4 rows g st, inc one st in centre of last row on 1st and 2nd sizes only, and dec one st in centre of last row on 3rd and 4th sizes only. 128 [136:142:150] sts.
Next row (Ws) K1, (K1, P1) 1 [3:1:3] times, (K2, P5) 1 [1:2:2] times, *K2, P6, K2, P13, K2, P6, K2*, P42, rep from * to *, (P5, K2) 1 [1:2:2] times, (P1, K1) 1 [3:1:3] times, K1.
Sts are now set for yoke patt. Cont in patt.

Yoke

1st row P1, (P1, K1) 1 [3:1:3] times, (P2, K5) 1 [1:2:2] times, *P2, K6, P2, (K6, P1, K6 noting that these 13 sts are 1st row of heart patt), P2, K6, P2*, (K6, P2, K12, P2, K12, P2, K6 noting that these 42 sts are 1st row of Sheringham herringbone and diamond patt), rep from * to *, (K5, P2) 1[1:2:2] times, (K1, P1) 1 [3:1:3] times, P1.
2nd row K1, (K1, P1) 1 [3:1:3] times, (on 3rd and 4th sizes only K2, P4, K1), on all sizes K3, P4, *K2, P6, K2, work 2nd row of heart patt, K2, P6, K2*, work 2nd row of Sheringham patt, rep from * to *, P4, K3, (on 3rd and 4th sizes only K1, P4, K2), on all sizes (P1, K1) 1 [3:1:3] times, K1.
3rd row P1, (P1, K1) 1 [3:1:3] times, (on 3rd and 4th sizes only P2, K3, P1, K1), on all sizes P2, K1, P1, K3, *P2, sl next 3 sts on to cable needle and hold at back of work, K3 then K3 from cable needle – **called C6B**, P2, work 3rd row of heart patt, P2, sl next 3 sts on to cable needle and hold at front of work, K3 then K3 from cable needle – **called C6F**, P2*, work 3rd row of Sheringham patt, rep from * to *, K3, P1, K1, P2, (on 3rd and 4th sizes only K1, P1, K3, P2), on all sizes (K1, P1) 1 [3:1:3] times, P1.
4th row K1, (K1, P1) 1 [3:1:3] times, (K2, P2, K1, P2) 1 [1:2:2] times, *K2, P6, K2, work 4th row of heart patt, K2, P6, K2*, work 4th row of Sheringham patt, rep from * to *, (P2, K1, P2, K2) 1 [1:2:2] times, (P1, K1) 1 [3:1:3] times, K1.
5th row P1, (P1, K1) 1 [3:1:3] times,

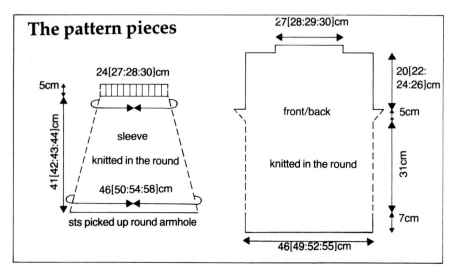

The pattern pieces

27[28:29:30]cm

24[27:28:30]cm

5cm

sleeve
knitted in the round

41[42:43:44]cm

46[50:54:58]cm

sts picked up round armhole

front/back

knitted in the round

20[22: 24:26]cm

5cm

31cm

7cm

46[49:52:55]cm

on 3rd and 4th sizes only P2, K1, P1, K3), on all sizes P2, K3, P1, K1, P2, K6, P2, work 5th row of heart patt, P2, K6, P2*, work 5th row of Sheringham patt, rep from * to *, K1, P1, K3, P2, (on 3rd and 4th sizes only K3, P1, K1, P2), on all sizes K1, P1) 1 [3:1:3] times, P1.
6th row K1, (K1, P1) 1 [3:1:3] times, on 3rd and 4th sizes only K3, P4), on all sizes K2, P4, K3, *P6, K2, work 6th row of heart patt, K2, P6*, K2, work 6th row of Sheringham patt, K2, rep from * to *, K3, P4, K2, (on 3rd and 4th sizes only P4, K3), on all sizes (P1, K1) 1 [3:1:3] times, K1.
Working 16 row rep of heart patt and Sheringham patt, rep the last 6 rows until armholes measure 20 [22:24:26]cm/7¾ [8¾:9½:10¼]in from beg, ending with a Ws row.

Shape shoulders
Cast off 26 [29:31:34] sts at beg of next 2 rows. Leave rem 76 [78:80:82] sts on holder.
Return to sts on spare needle, with Rs facing rejoin yarn, K first 19 sts of gusset and leave on a thread, K to end.
Complete back to match front.

Neckband
Join shoulder seams. Sl back and front neck sts on to 2 needles from a set of 2¾mm/No 12 needles.
With Rs of work facing and 2¾mm/ No 12 needles, pick up and K1 st from neck edge of left shoulder seam, turn and P1.
Next row K1, then K1 from needle holding front neck sts, turn.
Next row P2, then P1 from needle holding back neck sts, turn.
Next row K3, then K1 from needle holding front neck sts, turn.
Cont in this way until there are 11 sts on needle. Break off yarn and leave sts for time being.
Rep at other side of neck, reading front for back and vice versa. Do not break off yarn.
With Rs of work facing and set of four 2¾mm/No 12 needles K across all sts round neck, inc one st at centre back and centre front. 156 [160:164:168] sts.
Cont in rounds of K2, P2 rib for 5cm/2in. Cast off loosely in rib.

Sleeves
With Rs of work facing and set of

four 3mm/No 11 needles, K across 19 sts of one underarm gusset, pick up and K110 [120:132:142] sts round armhole.
1st round K19 sts, P to end.
2nd round Sl 1, K1, psso, K15, K2 tog, K to end.
3rd round K17, P to end.
4th round Sl 1, K1, psso, K13, K2 tog, K to end.
5th round K to end.
Working in st st, cont to dec in the same way at each side of gusset sts on next and every alt round until 113 [123:135:145] sts rem, ending with a plain round.
18th round Sl 1, K2 tog, psso, K to end. 111 [121:133:143] sts.
19th round K to end.
20th round P1, K to end.
Rep 19th and 20th rounds twice more.
Next round K1, sl 1, K1, psso, K to

Above: This guernsey yoke includes the Fife heart and Sheringham herringbone and diamond patterns.

last 2 sts, K2 tog.
Next round As 20th.
Keeping mock seam st correct throughout, cont to dec in this way on every 6th [6th:5th:5th] round until 67 [75:77:85] sts rem.
Cont without shaping until sleeve measures 41 [42:43:44]cm/16¼ [16½:17:17¼]in from end of gusset dec 3 [7:5:9] sts evenly in last round, or required length less 5cm/2in.
Change to set of four 2¾mm/No 12 needles. Cont in rounds of K2, P2 rib for 5cm/2in. Cast off loosely in rib.

To make up
Press very lightly under a damp cloth with a warm iron.

Simple eyelets and horizontal buttonholes

It is the attention to such simple details as buttons and buttonholes that can give your knitting a professional finish. This chapter deals with various ways of working single and double horizontal buttonholes on separate bands or turned-under facings.

Knitting patterns usually give instructions as to where to place buttonholes and how many stitches to cast off to achieve the correct width in proportion to the garment, but they rarely give the method for how to work them.

Most buttonholes are worked on a buttonhole band which can be knitted separately or as part of a garment. Separate buttonhole bands are often knitted in ribbing on finer needles than the main fabric to form a firm neat edge. Knitted-in bands are often in stocking stitch when the rest of the garment is in lace or some other pattern not suitable for buttonholes. Sometimes, when a stitch pattern extends right to the edge of a garment, extra stitches are worked along the buttonhole edge to make a facing strip which is turned back when making up.

Facing strips are usually worked in stocking stitch to give minimum bulk but remember, if you are working the main fabric in a lace pattern, the facing strip will show through.

This chapter gives methods for working eyelet and horizontal buttonholes and a way of neatening them.

Simple eyelet buttonholes This dainty method is ideal for use on baby garments with small buttons. Eyelets are suitable for buttonholes worked on a buttonhole band whether knitted separately or as part of the main fabric.

Horizontal buttonholes There are several different methods of making horizontal buttonholes all based on the same principle – that a given number of stitches are cast off on one row and replaced by stitches cast on again in the same place on the following row.

One thing to remember when working the first cast-off row for a horizontal buttonhole is that the stitch still on the right-hand needle after the casting off has been completed always counts as one of the remaining stitches of the row.

Which method you choose depends on whether your buttonhole band is knitted separately, as part of the main fabric or with a facing strip and on the size of buttonhole you need and the sort of finish you prefer.

If you are knitting a separate buttonhole band horizontally there is a choice of two methods, one for buttonholes across three or fewer stitches and one for larger buttonholes which need to be neatened at the corners.

If you are knitting a facing strip to turn back behind the opening edge of the garment, choose the method appropriate for the size of buttonhole you are making, remembering that you have to make a double buttonhole, one in the opening edge of the garment, and a corresponding one in the facing strip.

A third method, which is suitable for edges with a turned-under facing strip and for buttonhole bands knitted at the same time as the main fabric, is slightly harder to work but gives a very neat opening without any hard edges. You can use these tailored buttonholes for big and small buttons so long as you neaten the buttonhole with buttonhole stitch and ideally back it with a firm ribbon.

The fourth method, which is suitable for all types of band and size of button, is worked over one row only. You can use this hard-wearing reinforced buttonhole on stocking stitch, garter stitch, moss stitch or ribbing on a right or wrong side row.

Left: Use the method given overleaf to neaten buttonholes on a ribbed band.

Simple eyelet buttonholes

Knit the buttonhole band until the position for the buttonhole is reached. If working a separate band, always end with a wrong side row. If working the band as part of the main fabric, end at the edge where the buttonhole is required. On the next row work the given number of stitches, usually three or four, to the point where the buttonhole is needed. Take the yarn over or round the needle to make an eyelet hole, work the next two stitches together, then work to the end of the row. Work the following row across all stitches.

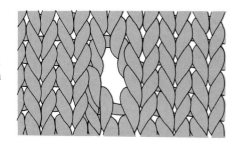

Small buttonholes for separate bands

This method is suitable for buttonholes across three or fewer stitches.
Knit the buttonhole band until the position for the buttonhole is reached, ending with a wrong side row.
On the next row work the given number of stitches in pattern to the point where the buttonhole is needed, cast off the required number of stitches, then pattern to the end of the row.
On the following row replace the cast-off stitches in the previous row with the same number of cast-on stitches, turning the needle to cast on.

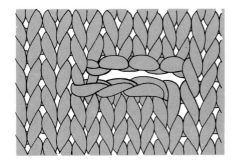

Large buttonholes for separate bands

This method is suitable for buttonholes across four or more stitches.
Knit the buttonhole band until the position for the buttonhole is reached, ending with a wrong side row.
On the next row work the given number of stitches in pattern to the point where the buttonhole is needed.
Cast off one *fewer* than the number of stitches given for the buttonhole, for example, if you are told to cast off four stitches, cast off three of these. Slip the stitch on the right-hand needle back on to the left-hand needle and knit this together with the next stitch to complete the total number of stitches required.
On the following row cast on one *more* than the number of stitches given for the buttonhole, for example, if you are told to cast on four stitches, cast on five instead.
On the next row, work to within one stitch of this extra cast-on stitch. Work the next stitch together with the extra cast-on stitch to complete the buttonhole.

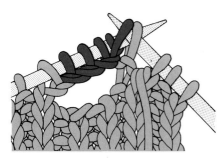

Buttonholes for edges with a facing strip

Knit the garment until the position for the buttonhole is reached, ending at the edge where the buttonhole is required.
On the next row work the given number of stitches in pattern to the point where the first buttonhole is needed in the facing strip, cast off the required number of stitches. Pattern to the point where the corresponding buttonhole is needed in the main fabric, cast off the required number of stitches, then pattern to the end of the row.
On the following row replace each set of cast-off stitches in the previous row with the same number of cast-on stitches, turning the needle to cast on.

Right: Detail of a double buttonhole – the main fabric is in moss stitch and the facing strip in stocking stitch.

Reinforced buttonholes for all types of buttonhole band

1

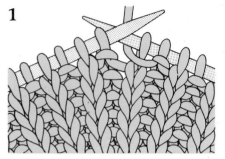

2

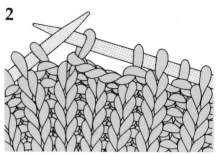

3

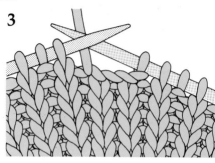

This example has been worked as a separate ribbed band over twelve stitches, with four stitches for the buttonhole.
Knit the buttonhole band in single rib until position for buttonhole is reached, ending with wrong side row.
1 (K1, P1) twice, leave the yarn at the front of the work and sl the next

st in a purlwise direction, then take the yarn back between the needles.
2 *Sl the next st on the left-hand needle in a purlwise direction, lift the 2nd st on the right-hand needle over the first st with the point of the left-hand needle and off the needle, rep from * 3 times more.

3 Sl the last st on the right-hand needle back on to the left-hand needle, turn the work, pick up the yarn and take it to the back of the work.

4

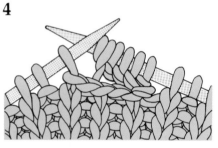

5

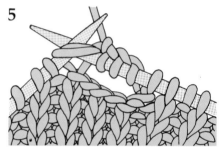

4 **Insert the right-hand needle between the last 2 sts on the left-hand needle and cast on one st, rep from ** 4 times more, turn the work, take the yarn to back of work.

5 Sl the last cast-on st on to the left-hand needle, K this st tog with the next st on the left-hand needle to complete the buttonhole, rib to end of row.

Note: When working the buttonhole row in any other stitch than rib, remember that the yarn must be taken round the first slipped st then left in its correct working position for the stitch prior to the slipped stitch, that is at the back for a knit st and at the front for a purl st.

───── PROFESSIONAL TOUCH ─────

Buttonhole stitch for neatening

Neaten eyelet and horizontal buttonholes with evenly spaced buttonhole stitches round the opening.
Do not work too many stitches round the opening or the edges will be stretched. Too few stitches and the size of the hole will be reduced and puckered out of shape.
To begin, thread a blunt-ended sewing needle with a length of matching yarn or silk. Make a knot in the other end.
For small eyelet buttonholes the straight loop of each buttonhole stitch must face towards the centre of the hole.
Insert the needle from the back to

the front the depth of one stitch in from the edge of the opening. Pull yarn through, leaving the knot at the back.
*Insert the needle again in the same way, allowing the yarn to curve round and under the needle and pull yarn through. Repeat from * all round the opening and fasten off securely.
For horizontal buttonholes the chain formed by each buttonhole stitch must lie along the opening edges.
Insert the needle from the back to the front at the top right-hand corner of the buttonhole opening. Pull the yarn through, leaving the knot at the back.

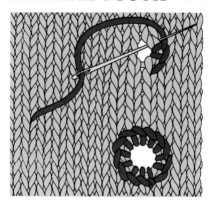

*Insert the needle again in the same way, allowing the yarn to curve round and under the needle and pull the yarn through. Repeat from * working clockwise round the opening and fasten off securely.

Tailored buttonholes for knitted-in bands and facings

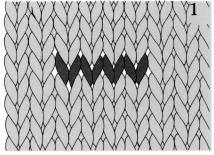

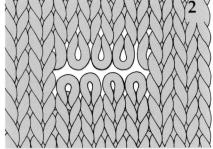

Knit the garment until the position for the buttonhole is reached, ending at the edge where the buttonhole is required.
1 On the next row work the given number of stitches in pattern to the point where the buttonhole is needed. Use a short length of contrasting coloured yarn and work in pattern across the number of

stitches given for the buttonhole. Slip these stitches back on to the left-hand needle and work them again with the correct yarn, then pattern to the end of the row.
2 When the garment section is completed, remove the contrast yarn from each buttonhole very gently, taking care not to let the stitches unravel.

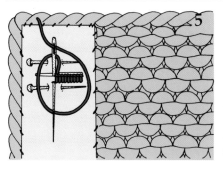

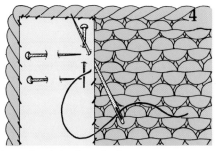

3 Complete each single or double buttonhole by threading a length of the correct yarn into a blunt-ended sewing needle, run this through all of the stitches, matching stitch for stitch on a double buttonhole. Buttonhole stitch single edge to neaten, or ideally, add a ribbon facing and then neaten.
Adding ribbon facing Carefully measure the length and width of the button and buttonhole bands, taking care not to stretch the fabric, to calculate the amount of ribbon you will require. The facing should be wide enough to cover the buttonholes and extend the full

length of the band plus extra to turn under at both ends.
It should be firm and straight grained, such as grosgrain ribbon, and without any tendency to fray.
4 Pin the ribbon in place on the wrong side of the knitting, easing it in evenly without stretching or puckering the fabric and making sure that the buttonholes are correctly spaced. Fold in the turnings at each end and pin in place. Fix a pin to each side of every buttonhole to hold it in place. Slip stitch round all the edges of the ribbon.

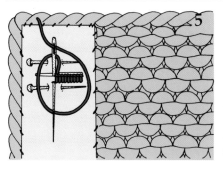

5 Cut through the ribbon for each buttonhole making sure they are the same size and taking care not to cut the knitting. Work round the ribbon and knitting in buttonhole stitch to neaten and hold the edges together.

Right: Use the tailored method for the buttonholes on a man's cardigan.

Button-through cardigan in tweed yarn

This classic button-to-the-neck cardigan is lifted into the couture class by the use of beautiful tweed yarn in a range of mouth-watering colours. All the ribbed edges are worked in a plain toning double knitting. The cardigan can be made in six sizes.

Sizes

To fit 86 [91:97:102:107:112]cm/ 34 [36:38:40:42:44]in bust
Length to shoulder, 51 [52:53.5:54.5:56:56]cm/ 20 [20½:21:21½:22:22]in, adjustable
Sleeve seam, 43 [44.5:45.5:45.5:47:47]cm/ 17 [17½:18:18:18½:18½]in adjustable
The figures in [] refer to the 91/36, 97/38, 102/40, 107/42 and 112cm/44in sizes respectively

You will need

6 [6:7:8:8:9]×50g balls of Sirdar Country Style Double Knitting Tweed (61% acrylic, 28% bri-nylon, 11% wool) in main colour A
2×50g balls of Sirdar Country Style plain Double Knitting (45% acrylic, 40% bri-nylon, 15% wool) in contrast colour B
One pair 3¼mm/No 10 needles
One pair 4mm/No 8 needles
Eight buttons

Tension

22 sts and 28 rows to 10cm/4in over st st worked on 4mm/No 8 needles

Back

With 3¼mm/No 10 needles and B cast on 101 [107:111:117:123:127] sts.
1st row (Rs) K1, *P1, K1, rep from * to end.
2nd row P1, *K1, P1, rep from * to end.
Rep these 2 rows for 6.5cm/2½in, ending with a 2nd row. Break off B. Join in A. Change to 4mm/No 8 needles. Beg with a K row cont in st st until work measures 30.5cm/12in from beg, or required length to underarm, ending with a P row.

Shape armholes

Cast off 6 sts at beg of next 2 rows.
Dec one st at each end of next 5 [5:5:5:7:7] rows, then at each end of foll 3 [4:4:5:5:6] alt rows.
73 [77:81:85:87:89] sts.
Cont without shaping until armholes measure 20.5 [21.5:23:24:25.5:25.5]cm/ 8 [8½:9:9½:10:10]in from beg, ending with a P row.

Left: This cardigan fastens neatly to the neck with eight buttons. Use the method given for separate bands.

Shape shoulders

Cast off at beg of next and every row 6 sts 6 times and 4 [5:6:7:7:7] sts twice. Leave rem 29 [31:33:35:37:39] sts on holder for centre back neck.

Left front

With 3¼mm/No 10 needles and B cast on 55 [59:61:63:67:69] sts. Work 6.5cm/2½in rib as given for back. Break off B. Join in A. Change to 4mm/No 8 needles.
Next row K to last 8 sts, leave last 8 sts on safety pin for front band.
Next row P to end.
47 [51:53:55:59:61] sts.
Beg with a K row cont in st st until work measures same as back to underarm, ending at side edge.

Shape armhole

Cast off 6 sts at beg of next row. Work one row. Dec one st at side edge on next 5 [5:5:5:7:7] rows, then at same edge on foll 3 [4:4:5:5:6] alt rows. 33 [36:38:39:41:42] sts.
Cont without shaping until armhole measures 14 rows less than back to shoulder.

Shape neck

Next row Work to last 5 [7:8:8:10:11] sts, leave last 5 [7:8:8:10:11] sts on safety pin for front neck.
Next row P to end.
28 [29:30:31:31:31] sts.
Dec one st at neck edge on next and foll 5 alt rows, ending at armhole edge. 22 [23:24:25:25:25] sts.

Shape shoulder

Cast off at beg of next and every alt row 6 sts 3 times and 4 [5:6:7:7:7] sts once.

Right front

With 3¼mm/No 10 needles and B cast on 55 [59:61:63:67:69] sts. Work 4 rows rib as given for back.
Next row (buttonhole row) Rib 3 sts, cast off 3 sts, rib to end of row.
Next row Rib to end, casting on 3 sts above those cast off in previous row.
Cont in rib until work measures same as left front to end of ribbing, ending at front edge.
Next row Rib 8 sts and leave these on safety pin for front band, change

to 4mm/No 8 needles and A, K to end.
Break off B.
Beg with a P row cont in st st and complete as given for left front, reversing all shapings.

Button band

With 3¼mm/No 10 needles and B cast on one st, then with Rs of work facing rib across 8 sts on safety pin. Cont in rib until band, when slightly stretched, fits along left front edge to neck edge, ending with a Ws row. Break off yarn and leave sts on safety pin.
Mark positions for 7 more buttons, last to come in neckband with 6 more evenly spaced between.

Buttonhole band

With 3¼mm/No 10 needles and B cast on one st, then with Ws of work facing rib across 8 sts on safety pin.
Work as given for button band, making buttonholes as before as markers are reached, ending at front edge. Do not break off yarn.

Sleeves

With 3¼mm/No 10 needles and B cast on 43 [45:49:53:55:57] sts. Work 6.5cm/2½in rib as given for back. Break off B. Join in A. Change to 4mm/No 8 needles.
Beg with a K row cont in st st inc one st at each end of 7th and every foll 6th row until there are

71 [73:75:79:81:85] sts.
Cont without shaping until work measures 43 [44.5:45.5:45.5:47:47]cm/ 17 [17½:18:18:18½:18½]in from beg, or required length to underarm, ending with a P row.

Shape top

Cast off 6 sts at beg of next 2 rows. Dec one st at each end of next 5 [5:5:5:5:7] rows, then at each end of every foll alt row until 25 [25:25:27:27:29] sts rem. Work one row.
Cast off at beg of next and every row 3 sts 6 times and 7 [7:7:9:9:11] sts once.

Neckband

Join shoulder seams. With 3¼mm/No 10 needles and Rs of work facing, pick up B and rib across sts of right front band, 5 [7:9:8:10:11] sts on safety pin, pick up and K16 sts up right front neck, K29 [31:33:35:37:39] sts on back neck holder, pick up and K16 sts down left front neck, rib across 5 [7:9:8:10:11] sts on safety pin and sts of left front band.
89 [95:99:101:107:111] sts.
Beg with a 2nd row work 2.5cm/1in rib as given for back. Cast off in rib.

To make up

Press each piece under a dry cloth with a warm iron. Sew front bands in place. Set in sleeves. Join side and sleeve seams. Sew on buttons.

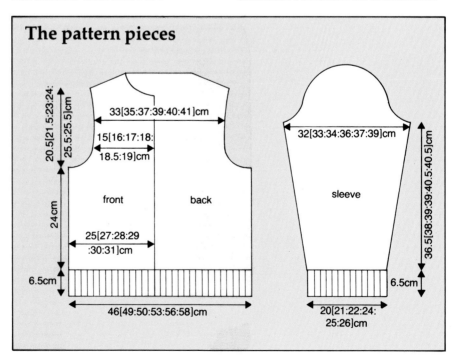

The pattern pieces

20.5[21.5:23:24: 25.5:25.5]cm
33[35:37:39:40:41]cm
15[16:17:18: 18.5:19]cm
24cm
front
back
25[27:28:29 :30:31]cm
6.5cm
46[49:50:53:56:58]cm
32[33:34:36:37:39]cm
sleeve
36.5[38:39:39:40.5:40.5]cm
6.5cm
20[21:22:24: 25:26]cm

The button and buttonhole bands on this cardigan are picked up along the edges. The buttonholes are worked horizontally.

Vertical buttonholes and hand-made buttons

This concluding buttonhole chapter shows how single and double vertical buttonholes are worked on separate bands or as turned-under facings. Learn how to position them so that the buttons do up neatly and how to cover button moulds to match a garment perfectly.

The last chapter dealt with ways of making eyelet and horizontal buttonholes. Although these are probably the best-known methods, vertical buttonholes have the advantage that they can be worked on a narrower button band and there are no loose stitches to mar the appearance.

The fabric is divided at the point where a buttonhole is needed and the two sides are worked separately. The buttonholes are worked on the buttonhole band which can be knitted separately or as part of the garment. Single buttonholes look best worked in a reversible pattern such as moss stitch or rib. If you work them in stocking stitch the edges tend to curl inwards and need to be held in place with ribbon facing.

If the stitch pattern of a garment extends to the edge, work double buttonholes. Knit the facing strip in stocking stitch which is turned back and the edges neatened with buttonhole stitch.

Choosing buttons

Choose buttons which complement the knitted fabric as well as being practical. Fun shapes look decorative but may have sharp edges that will rub and snag the buttonholes. A man's husky jacket looks best when finished with bold leather or wooden buttons; a crisp cotton cardigan is enhanced by the lustre of real pearl buttons and a lacy evening jacket needs the added sparkle of jewelled buttons.

If you are unable to find ready-made buttons suitable for your garment, the answer is to knit covers to fit over a metal or nylon button mould. Do not feel you have to stick to the same yarn as the garment.

Knit the covers using fine needles so that the mould does not show through. To knit smaller or larger covers than those given as examples simply cast on fewer or more stitches increasing and decreasing accordingly.

Consider the thickness of the knitted fabric when choosing buttons. Those with central holes will lie flat on the fabric unless you add a yarn shank but buttons with built-in shanks stand above the fabric to allow for the thickness of the buttonhole band when the buttons are fastened.

Make sure that the buttons you select are the right size to go through the buttonholes without stretching them and that they are the right weight for the fabric – if they are too heavy they will pull the band out of shape.

Positioning buttonholes

Knit the button band first and mark the position of the buttons with pins. Knit the buttonhole band, working the buttonholes to correspond with these markers. They need to be evenly spaced so that the garment does not gape or pucker so knit the same number of rows between each buttonhole.

Positioning buttons

After making up the garment, pin the buttonhole edge over the button band, matching top and bottom edges and securing these points with pins.

Horizontal buttonholes Mark the centre of the buttonholes with pins before removing the buttonhole band, leaving the pins in position.

Vertical buttonholes Mark the position of the button 3mm/⅛in below the top of the buttonhole.

Right: Sample knitted in moss stitch showing vertical buttonholes worked on a separate buttonhole band.

Buttonholes for separate bands and edges with a facing strip

separate bands

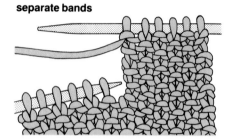

edges with a facing strip

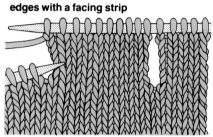

Separate bands

Knit the buttonhole band until the position for the buttonhole is reached, ending on the wrong side. On the next row work the given number of stitches in pattern to the point where the buttonhole is needed, turn the work.
Continue in pattern across these stitches only for the number of rows needed to take the size of the button, ending at the buttonhole opening edge. Break off the yarn. Leave these stitches.
Rejoin the yarn at the buttonhole edge of the remaining stitches and pattern to the end of the row. Work the same number of rows over these stitches as worked for the first part of the buttonhole, ending at the edge away from the buttonhole.
On the next row, work across all of the stitches to close the buttonhole.

Edges with a facing strip

Knit the garment until the position for the buttonhole is reached, ending at the edge where the buttonhole is required.
On the next row work the given number of stitches in pattern to the point where the first buttonhole is needed in the facing strip. Turn the work.
Continue in pattern across these stitches only for the number of rows needed to take the size of the button, ending at the buttonhole opening edge. Break off the yarn. Leave these stitches.
Rejoin the yarn at the buttonhole edge of the remaining stitches and pattern to the point where the second buttonhole is needed in the main fabric.
Repeat from ** to ** working the same number of rows.
Rejoin the yarn at the buttonhole edge of the remaining stitches and pattern to the end of the row. Work the same number of rows over these stitches, ending at the edge away from the buttonhole.
On the next row, work across all of the stitches to close the buttonhole.

Four knitted button covers

Stocking stitch button cover

This example fits a 2cm/¾in nylon button mould, using 2mm/No 14 needles and 4 ply yarn.
Cast on 4 sts. Beg with a K row work in st st, inc one st at each end of every row until there are 12 sts.
Work 6 rows without shaping.
Dec one st at each end of every row until 4 sts rem. Cast off.
Place over button mould, work a row of running stitches round outside edge, draw up and fasten off leaving end to sew on button.

Embroidered button cover

This example fits a 3cm/1¼in metal button mould, using 2mm/No 14 needles and 4 ply yarn. Lengths of 3 colours of embroidery silk.
Cast on 6 sts. Beg with a K row work in st st, inc one st at each end of every row until there are 18 sts.
Work 10 rows without shaping.
Dec one st at each end of every row until 6 sts rem. Cast off.
Embroider design in the centre of the cover and fit as for stocking stitch cover.

Bobble button cover

This example fits a 2cm/¾in nylon button mould, using 2mm/No 14 needles and 4 ply yarn.
Cast on 3 sts. Beg with a P row work in reversed st st, inc one st at each end of every row until there are 11 sts.
Work 4 rows without shaping.
Next row P5 sts, (K1, P1, K1, P1, K1) all into next st, turn and P5, turn and K5, turn and P5, turn and K5, turn and lift 2nd, 3rd, 4th and 5th sts over first and off needle, P5.
Work 4 rows.
Dec one st at each end of every row until 3 sts rem. Cast off.
Fit as for stocking stitch cover.

Moss stitch button cover

This example fits a 3cm/1¼in metal button mould, using 2¼mm/No 13 needles and double knitting yarn.
Cast on 4 sts.
1st row (Rs) *K1, P1, rep from * to end.
2nd row Inc in first st, K1, P1, inc in last st.
3rd row Inc in first st, (K1, P1) twice, inc in last st.
Keeping moss st correct as now set, cont inc one st at each end of every row until there are 14 sts.
Work 6 rows without shaping.
Cont in moss st, dec one st at each end of every row until 4 sts rem. Cast off.
Fit as for stocking stitch cover.

Double-breasted waistcoat

This low-buttoning waistcoat is knitted in a wool and silk mixture, in simple basket stitch and moss stitch. The buttonholes are worked vertically in pairs. Six sizes are given to include larger measurements.

Sizes

To fit 86[91:97:102:107:112]cm/34[36:38:40:42:44]in bust
Length to shoulder, 56[57:58:60:61:62]cm/22[22½:23:23½:24:24½]in
The figures in [] refer to the 91/36, 97/38, 102/40, 107/42 and 112cm/44in sizes respectively

You will need

11[12:12:13:13:14]×20g balls of Jaeger Wool/Silk (60% wool, 40% silk)
One pair 2¾mm/No 12 needles
One pair 3¼mm/No 10 needles
Four buttons

Tension

28 sts and 36 rows to 10cm/4in over st st worked on 3¼mm/No 10 needles

Below: The stitches are decreased for the moss stitch yoke of this waistcoat to allow for the different tensions.

Back

With 2¾mm/No 12 needles cast on 115[123:129:137:145:151] sts.
1st row (Rs) K1, *P1, K1, rep from * to end.
2nd row P1, *K1, P1, rep from * to end.
Rep these 2 rows 16 times more then first row again.
Next row (Ws) Rib 10[4:7:5:6:13] sts, pick up loop lying between needles and K tbl – **called M1**,
(rib 5[5:5:6:7:5] sts, M1) 19[23:23:21:19:25] times, rib to end. 135[147:153:159:165:177] sts.
Change to 3¼mm/No 10 needles. Commence patt.
1st row (Rs) K3, *P3, K3, rep from * to end.
2nd row P3, *K3, P3, rep from * to end.
3rd and 4th rows As 1st and 2nd.
5th row P3, *K3, P3, rep from * to end.
6th row K3, *P3, K3, rep from * to end.
7th and 8th rows As 5th and 6th.
These 8 rows form the patt. Cont in patt until work measures 34cm/13½in from beg, ending with an 8th row.

Shape armholes

Keeping patt correct, cast off 9 sts at beg of next 2 rows.
Work 14 rows without shaping, ending with an 8th row.
Next row (dec row) K8[9:8:6:5:6] sts, *K2 tog, K9[10:11:12:13:14] sts, rep from * 8 times more, K2 tog, K8[10:8:7:5:7] sts.
107[119:125:131:137:149] sts.
Commence moss st patt.
Next row K1, *P1, K1, rep from * to end.

Rep this row until work measures 22[23:24:26:27:28]cm/8¾[9:9½:10¼:10¾:11]in from cast off sts at armholes, ending with a Ws row.

Shape shoulders

Cast off at beg of next and every row 8[9:9:10:10:11] sts 6 times and 7[9:10:9:10:12] sts twice.
Cast off rem 45[47:51:53:57:59] sts.

Left front

With 2¾mm/No 12 needles cast on 77[79:83:87:91:95] sts.
Work 35 rows rib as given for back.
Next row (inc row) Rib 7[5:6:5:7:7] sts, M1, (rib 7[10:8:7:11:9] sts, M1) 9[7:9:11:7:9] times, rib to end. 87[87:93:99:99:105] sts.
Change to 3¼mm/No 10 needles.
Work 8 rows patt as given for back.

Shape front edge

Keeping patt correct throughout, dec one st at end of next and at same edge on every foll 3rd row until 60[60:66:72:72:78] sts rem. Work one row, ending with a Ws row.

Shape armhole

Cast off 9 sts, patt to end.
Cont to dec one st at front edge as before on every 3rd row until 46[46:52:58:58:64] sts rem. Work 2 rows ending with an 8th patt row.
Next row (dec row) K4[4:5:6:6:7] sts, *K2 tog, K7[7:8:9:9:10] sts, rep from * 3 times more, K2 tog, K2[2:3:4:4:5] sts, K2 tog. 40[40:46:52:52:58] sts.
Cont in moss st patt, cont to dec one st at front edge on every foll 4th row until 31[36:37:39:40:45] sts rem.
Cont without shaping until work measures same as back to shoulder, ending at armhole edge.

Shape shoulder

Cast off at beg of next and every alt row 8[9:9:10:10:11] sts 3 times and 7[9:10:9:10:12] sts once.

Right front

With 2¾mm/No 12 needles cast on 77[79:83:87:91:95] sts. Work 6 rows rib as given for back.
**Next row Rib 6 sts, turn.
Work 3 rows rib on these 6 sts.
Leave sts on safety pin.

With Rs facing and another ball of yarn, rejoin yarn to rem sts and rib 12 sts, turn.
Work 3 rows rib on these 12 sts.
Leave sts on safety pin. Break off yarn.
With Rs facing rejoin yarn to rem sts and rib to end. Work 3 rows rib on these sts. Break off yarn.
With Rs of work facing rib across first 6 sts on safety pin, then 12 sts on safety pin, rib to end.**. Work 15 rows rib across all sts.
Rep from ** to ** once more.
Work 4 rows rib across all sts.
Work inc row as given for left front and complete to match left front, reversing all shapings.

Front borders (make 2)

Join shoulder seams. With 2¾mm/No 12 needles cast on 21 sts.
1st row (Rs) K2, *P1, K1, rep from * to last st, K1.
2nd row K1, *P1, K1, rep from * to end.
Rep these 2 rows until border, when slightly stretched, fits up front neck to centre back neck, sewing in position as you go.

Armhole borders

Work as given for front borders until borders, when slightly stretched, fit round armhole, sewing in position as you go.

To make up

Do not press. Join front borders at centre back neck. Fold front border in half to Ws and sl st down.
Join side seams. Fold armhole borders in half to Ws and sl st down. Neaten at armhole shaping. Sew on buttons.

Left: Close-up showing the small vertical buttonholes worked into the welt of the waistcoat.

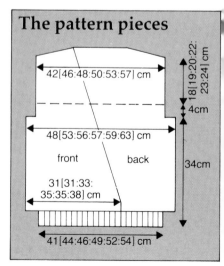

The pattern pieces

42[46:48:50:53:57] cm
18[19:20:22:23:24] cm
4cm
48[53:56:57:59:63] cm
front   back
34cm
31[31:33:35:35:38] cm
41[44:46:49:52:54] cm

88

Pleated knitting for skirts

Pleated skirts are casual and easy to wear and provide a useful addition to any wardrobe. The choice of yarn is important if they are to hold their shape and the pleats keep their swing. When knitted from the top down, the length can be adjusted according to fashion.

A knitted pleated skirt is an adaptable and comfortable garment which can form the basis of mix-and-match outfits. Team the skirt given in this chapter with the button-to-neck cardigan on page 82 – they are both knitted in the same tweedy yarn.

A knitted skirt is virtually a tube of fabric which is wider at the hem edge than it is at the waist.

Mock or ribbed pleats can start at the bottom or the top – gradually increase or decrease according to the direction of the work.

The fullness of the skirt depends on the number of stitches at the hem or the amount of increase from the waist. There is no problem of bulk at the waist using either of these methods.

Work inverted pleats from the hem to the waist where they are folded and joined to the waistband. Do not make the pleats too full as this increases the bulk at the waist.

All three methods are joined to a ribbed waistband with elastic sewn in.

Choosing suitable yarns

It is vital to use a yarn which will retain its shape. Bulky yet lightweight fashion yarns, such as mohair, are not suitable. Not only may the skirt seat and drop but the thickness of the yarn will make the skirt clumsy and unflattering. Look for a wool yarn with a nylon content for added strength – 4 ply or double knitting weights are ideal. If the yarn has a crêpe twist or tweed texture so much the better, as these give a firm fabric.

Knit in rounds or rows using finer needles than normally advised for the yarn. This gives a close, firm fabric which hangs well. Use a circular needle to knit in rows or rounds if increasing to a large number of stitches.

Do not line a knitted skirt. The pleats need to swing freely and stitching in a lining only restricts the knitting. Wear a separate waist petticoat to avoid any seating effect.

To plan a pleated skirt in one of the methods given in this chapter, first calculate the width required at the hem and waist and the finished length including the waistband. Use these measurements and the tension obtained with the yarn and needle size of your choice to arrive at the number of stitches which must be cast on at the lower edge if working from the hem up, or at the waist if working down. Remember to allow for the multiples of stitches needed to make the pattern work out correctly.

Left: Team the skirt with the matching cardigan jacket given earlier to make up this attractive outfit.

Mock pleats are the simplest of all to work. They can be knitted on two needles in two sections and joined at the side seams, or in the round.

The fabric is reversible with a knit stitch defining each pleat and separating panels of garter stitch. This method can be worked from the hem up, decreasing as required, or from the waist down, increasing as required and is ideal for a toddler's skirt.

Use waist and hem measurements to calculate the number of stitches to cast on and increase/decrease according to the tension obtained with the yarn and needle size of your choice. Cast on stitches in multiples of eight stitches plus one at hem or multiples of four stitches plus one at the waist and adjust the total accordingly. For example, a total hem width of 112cm/ 44in based on a tension of 28 stitches to 10cm/4in will require 154 stitches for the back and the same for the front. Adjust this to 153 stitches to give correct multiples.

Ribbed pleats can be knitted on two needles in two sections and joined at the side seams, or in the round. A slipped stitch defines the edge of the pleats. This method can be worked from the hem up, decreasing as required, or from the waist down, increasing as required and gives a very slimming line.

Calculate the number of stitches for waist or hem as for mock pleats.

Cast on multiples of 15 stitches at the hem or multiples of eight stitches at the waist. For example, a total hem width of 112cm/44in based on a tension of 28 stitches to 10cm/4in will require 154 stitches for the back and the same for the front. Adjust to 150 stitches to give correct multiples.

Inverted pleats can be worked on two needles or in the round. A slipped stitch defines the edge of the pleats but this method can only be worked from the hem to waist edge. Two extra needles of the same size as used to knit the skirt are needed to close the pleats at the top edge, before adding a waistband. These full pleats give an attractive swirl to a skirt and hang well. You do not need to press them into place.

Calculate the width for hem as for mock pleats and multiply by three to allow for the pleats.

Cast on multiples of 13 stitches plus two to give a pleat fold of four stitches. For example, a total hem width of 188cm/74in based on a tension of 28 stitches to 10cm/4in will require 259 stitches for the back and the same for the back. Adjust to 262 stitches to give the correct multiples.

Ribbed pleats on two needles

Cast on the stitches in multiples of 15 at the hem, or in multiples of eight stitches at the waist.

Working up from the hem
1st row (Rs) *K7, keep yarn at back of work and sl 1 in a purlwise direction – **called sl 1**, K3, P4, rep from * to end.
2nd row *K4, P11, rep from * to end.
Repeat these 2 rows for about one quarter of the length required, ending with a Rs row.
Next row (dec row) *K4, P9, P2 tog, rep from * to end. Multiples of 14 sts.
Next row (Rs) *K6, sl 1, K3, P4, rep from * to end.
Next row *K4, P10, rep from * to end.
Repeat last 2 rows for about half of the length required, ending with a Rs row.
Next row (dec row) *K4, P8, P2 tog, rep from * to end. Multiples of 13 sts.
Next row (Rs) *K5, sl 1, K3, P4, rep from * to end.
Next row *K4, P9, rep from * to end.
Repeat last 2 rows for about three-quarters of the required length, ending with a Rs row.
Next row (dec row) *K4, P7, P2 tog, rep from * to end. Multiples of 12 sts.
Next row (Rs) *K4, sl 1, K3, P4, rep from * to end.
Next row *K4, P8, rep from * to end.
Repeat last 2 rows for length required, ending with a Rs row.
Next row (dec row) *(K2 tog) twice, P2 tog, P4, P2 tog, rep from * to end. Multiples of 8 sts.
With size smaller needles work about 2.5cm/1in K2, P2 rib. Cast off. Join sides. Sew elastic inside waist edge.

Working down from the waist
Work waist ribbing, ending with a Rs row.
Next row (inc row) *Rib 1, inc in next st, rep from * to end. Multiples of 12 sts.
Change to size larger needles.
1st row (Rs) *K4, sl 1, K3, P4, rep from * to end.
2nd row *K4, P8, rep from * to end.
Repeat these 2 rows for about one quarter of the length required, ending with a Rs row.
Next row (inc row) *K4, P7, inc in next st, rep from * to end. Multiples of 13 sts.
Next row (Rs) *K5, sl 1, K3, P4, rep from * to end.
Next row *K4, P9, rep from * to end.
Repeat last 2 rows for about half of the length required, ending with a Rs row.
Next row (inc row) *K4, P8, inc in next st, rep from * to end. Multiples of 14 sts.
Next row (Rs) *K6, sl 1, K3, P4, rep from * to end.
Next row *K4, P10, rep from * to end.
Repeat last 2 rows for about three-quarters of the length required, ending with a Rs row.
Next row (inc row) *K4, P9, inc in next st, rep from * to end. Multiples of 15 sts.
Next row (Rs) *K7, sl 1, K3, P4, rep from * to end.
Next row *K4, P11, rep from * to end.
Repeat last 2 rows for length required. Cast off loosely.

Mock pleats on two needles

Cast on the stitches in multiples of eight stitches plus one at the hem, or multiples of four stitches plus one at the waist.

Working up from the hem
1st row (Rs) P1, *K7, P1, rep from * to end.
2nd row K4, *P1, K7, rep from * to last 5 sts, P1, K4.
Repeat these 2 rows for about a third of the length required, ending with a Ws row.
Next row (dec row) P1, *sl 1, K1, psso, K3, K2 tog, P1, rep from * to end. Multiples of 6 sts plus one.
Next row K3, *P1, K5, rep from * to last 4 sts, P1, K3.
Next row P1, *K5, P1, rep from * to end.
Repeat last 2 rows until work measures about two-thirds of the length required, ending with a Ws row.
Next row (dec row) P1, *sl 1, K1, psso, K1, K2 tog, P1, rep from * to end. Multiples of 4 sts plus one.
Next row K2, *P1, K3, rep from * to last 3 sts, P1, K2.
Next row P1, *K3, P1, rep from * to end.
Repeat last 2 rows for length required. With size smaller needles work about 2.5cm/1in K1, P1 rib. Cast off. Join side seams. Sew elastic inside waist edge.

Working down from the waist
Work waist ribbing. Change to size larger needles.
1st row (Rs) P1, *K3, P1, rep from * to end.
2nd row K2, *P1, K3, rep from * to last 3 sts, P1, K2.
Repeat these 2 rows for about a third of the length required, ending with a Ws row.
Next row (inc row) P1, *inc in next st, K1, inc in next st, P1, rep from * to end. Multiples of 6 sts plus one.
Next row K3, *P1, K5, rep from * to last 4 sts, P1, K3.
Next row P1, *K5, P1, rep from * to end.
Repeat last 2 rows until work measures about two-thirds of the length required, ending with a Ws row.
Next row (inc row) P1, *inc in next st, K3, inc in next st, P1, rep from * to end. Multiples of 8 sts plus one.
Next row K4, *P1, K7, rep from * to last 5 sts, P1, K4.
Next row P1, *K7, P1, rep from * to end.
Repeat last 2 rows for length required. Cast off loosely.

Inverted pleats on two needles

Cast on multiples of 13 stitches plus 2, to give a pleat fold of 4 stitches.

Working up from the hem
1st row (Rs) K5, *P1, K3, keep yarn at back and sl 1 in a purlwise direction – **called sl 1**, K8, rep from * to last 10 sts, P1, K3, sl 1, K5.
2nd row P9, *K1, P12, rep from * to last 6 sts, K1, P5.
These 2 rows form the pattern and are repeated for the length required, less about 2.5cm/1in for the waistband, ending with a Ws row.

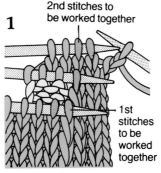

2nd stitches to be worked together

1st stitches to be worked together

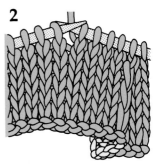

To close pleats
1 Next row K1, *sl next 4 sts on to a spare needle (A), sl next 4 sts on to 2nd spare needle (B) and *turn it round*, place needle A behind needle B and both spare needles behind the left-hand needle.
2 K the next st (the sl st) with one from needle A, K next 3 sts knitting one from all 3 needles, then K next st on left-hand needle tog with last st from needle B (the P st),

rep from * to last st, K1.
Change to size smaller needles. Work 2.5cm/1in K1, P1 rib for single waistband, or 5cm/2in for double waistband. Cast off.
Join side seams.
Sew elastic inside single waistband, or fold double waistband in half to wrong side and slip stitch in place, then thread elastic through.

Pleated skirt

To avoid bulky pleats at waist level this skirt has a well-shaped hip yoke. Extra stitches are then cast on to give the correct number to form the pleats. To complete the skirt the pleats must be closed at the top and stitched down on the wrong side. The length is adjustable.

92

Sizes
To fit 91 [97:101]cm/36 [38:40]in hips
Length from waist to hem,
65 [66:67]cm/25½ [26:26½]in, adjustable
The figures in [] refer to the 97/38 and 101cm/40in sizes respectively

You will need
15 [16:17]×50g balls of Sirdar Country Style Double Knitting

Above: This swirling pleated skirt is a flattering style for all ages. It is particularly slimming when worked in tweedy yarn with a nubbly texture.

 Tweed (61% acrylic, 28% Bri-nylon, 11% wool)
One pair 3¼mm/No 10 needles
One pair 4mm/No 8 needles
One 4mm/No 8 circular needle 100cm/40in long

Vaist length of 2cm/¾in wide elastic

Tension

24 sts and 32 rows to 10cm/4in over st st worked on 4mm/No 8 needles

Back

With 3¼mm/No 10 needles cast on 90 [96:102] sts. Work 2.5cm/1in K1, P1 rib.
Change to 4mm/No 8 needles.

Shape hip yoke

Beg with a K row work 6 rows st st.
Next row (inc row) K1, inc in next st, K22 [24:26] sts, inc in next st, K1, inc in next st, K36 [38:40] sts, inc in next st, K1, inc in next st, K22 [24:26] sts, inc in next st, K1.
96 [102:108] sts.
Beg with a P row work 9 rows st st.
Next row (inc row) K1, inc 1, K24 [26:28] sts, inc 1, K1, inc 1, K38 [40:42] sts, inc 1, K1, inc 1, K24 [26:28] sts, inc 1, K1.
102 [108:114] sts.
Beg with a P row work 9 rows st st.
Next row (inc row) K1, inc 1, K26 [28:30] sts, inc 1, K1, inc 1, K40 [42:44] sts, inc 1, K1, inc 1, K26 [28:30] sts, inc 1, K1.
108 [114:120] sts.
Beg with a P row work 9 rows st st.
Change to 4mm/No 8 circular needle and cont working in rows.

Shape pleats

Next row (inc row) *K6, turn and cast on 7 sts, rep from * to end.
234 [247:260] sts.
Next row (Ws) *K4, P9, rep from * to end.
Next row *K5, keeping yarn at back of work sl 1 in a purlwise direction – called sl 1, K3, P4, rep from * to end.
Rep last 2 rows until work measures 20cm/8in from beg, ending with a Rs row.
Next row (inc row) *K4, P8, inc in next st, rep from * to end.
252 [266:280] sts.
Next row *K6, sl 1, K3, P4, rep from * to end.
Next row *K4, P10, rep from * to end.
Rep last 2 rows until work measures 26cm/10¼in from beg, ending with a Rs row.
Next row (inc row) *K4, P9, inc in next st, rep from * to end.
270 [285:300] sts.
Next row *K7, sl 1, K3, P4, rep from * to end.
Next row *K4, P11, rep from * to end.
Rep last 2 rows until work measures 32cm/12½in from beg, ending with a Rs row.
Next row (inc row) *K4, P10, inc in next st, rep from * to end.
288 [304:320] sts.
Next row *K8, sl 1, K3, P4, rep from * to end.

Next row *K4, P12, rep from * to end.
Rep last 2 rows until work measures 38cm/15in from beg, ending with a Rs row.
Next row (inc row) *K4, P11, inc in next st, rep from * to end.
306 [323:340] sts.
Next row *K9, sl 1, K3, P4, rep from * to end.
Next row *K4, P13, rep from * to end.
Rep last 2 rows until work measures 46cm/17¾in from beg, ending with a Rs row.
Next row (inc row) *K4, P12, inc in next st, rep from * to end.
324 [342:360] sts.
Next row *K10, sl 1, K3, P4, rep from * to end.
Next row *K4, P14, rep from * to end.
Rep last 2 rows until work measures 65 [66:67]cm/25½ [26:26½]in from beg, or required length from waist to hem, ending with a Ws row.
Cast off very loosely.

Front

Work as given for back.

To make up

Do not press. Join side seams. Stitch down cast on sts at top of pleats on Ws of work.
Join elastic into a circle. Sew inside waistband with casing st.

_____ PROFESSIONAL TOUCH _____

Adding elastic to a waistband

Below: Stitching elastic into waist.

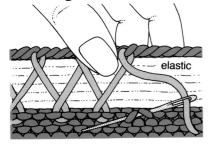

Measure your waist and cut the elastic into the required length.
For a single thickness waistband, sew elastic into a circle and mark the knitting and the elastic into four sections. Pin the elastic in place on the wrong side of the waistband. Thread a sewing needle with yarn and secure join of elastic to one seam of the knitting. Attach with casing stitch.
*Hold the waistband and elastic

over the fingers of your left hand, take the yarn over the elastic and insert the needle lightly through the knitting from right to left and pull the yarn through.
Take the yarn back over the elastic to the top edge of the waistband, insert the needle about 3 stitches along from the previous stitch from right to left and pull the yarn through.
Continue from the * in this way.
Fasten off securely at the end.

For a double thickness waistband, fold the waistband in half to the wrong side and slip stitch in place, leaving a small gap as an opening at the end.
Secure a safety pin into one end of the elastic, small enough to go through the waistband, and thread the elastic through the waistband. Make sure the elastic is not twisted, then sew the ends securely together. When the elastic is in place, sew up the gap.

Neckbands and collars for straight and round necks

Allow sufficient room at the neckline in order to get a garment comfortably over the head.
A straight across neckline is easy but where shaping rows are worked as part of the main fabric, the neck edge must be neatened with a neckband or collar.

Details for working the neck of a garment are usually given in full in the instructions but it is also a simple matter to adapt the style of a neckline or collar to suit your preference.

Basic neck shapes are straight across, round, square and V-shaped – either at back, front or both. On all of these shapes you can add front or back vertical openings.

The neatest way to complete the edge is by knitting a neckband or collar in one to avoid uncomfortable seams round the neckline. For all neck shapes except for the straight across neck stitches must be picked up round the edges (page 38), to add the neckband or collar.

To complete a straight neck without a vertical opening, work across the stitches that remain once the shoulder shaping on the back and front is completed. The shoulders and neckband seams are then joined in one, leaving an opening wide enough to pull on easily over the head.

Where a vertical opening is desired at back or front, the piece will have to be divided and each side completed separately, making provision for button and buttonhole bands if required.

To complete a round neck when working on two needles in rows, provision for turning the needles must be allowed.

On a single thickness round neck, a double thickness crew neck or polo collar, seam one shoulder before picking up the neckband stitches, leaving other shoulder unseamed until neckband is completed.

If working single rib in rows, pick up an odd number of stitches and begin and end each row with the same stitch to allow for seaming. If working variations of rib, or in a pattern, make sure you have the correct multiples, plus any edge stitches needed to make the pattern begin and end with the same stitches.

When working single rib on four needles, in rounds, pick up an even number of stitches to ensure the rounds work out exactly. If working in variations of rib or pattern, make sure you have the exact multiples of stitches.

To complete a round-necked collar a centre front or back opening must be left as part of the main fabric, to be closed with a zip or buttons. The collar is worked in rows on two needles and both shoulders can be seamed before picking up the stitches round the neck.

With a centre front overlapped placket opening, a collar is worked in one piece but with a centre back opening, a collar is usually worked in two halves unless the pattern suggests otherwise.

All the examples have been worked in double knitting yarn on 4mm/No 8 needles, using a contrast colour to show the neckline.

Straight necks

Straight neck without opening
Do not work any neck shaping on the back or front. Work the shoulder shaping as given on the back and front but do not cast off the remaining neck stitches. Work a few rows in garter stitch or ribbing across the neck stitches to give the depth of neckband required. Cast off.

Front overlapped placket opening
Complete back as for straight neck without an opening. Work the front and end with a wrong side row at the required position for the front opening.

On the next row, pattern across half of the stitches for the left side, plus about an extra four stitches for the left front band, then work the last eight stitches to match back neckband and making buttonholes as required for a man. Work as for the back. Complete the shoulder shaping and neckband.

With the right side of the work facing, rejoin the yarn and cast on eight extra stitches for the right front band and work as for left front band, making buttonholes as required for a woman and pattern to end.

Complete to match the left shoulder.

Round necks

Single round neck in rib
With the right side of the work facing, pick up and knit the required number of stitches round the neck. Work in rib for 2cm/¾in, or depth required. **
Cast off loosely.

Double crew neck in rib
Work as given for single round neck to **.
Continue in rib for a further 2cm/¾in, or same depth as first part. Cast off loosely.
Fold neckband in half to wrong side and slipstitch in place.

Polo neck in rib
Work as given for single round neck to **.
Continue in rib for a further 12cm/4¾in, or total length required. Cast off loosely.
Fold neckband in half to right side.

PROFESSIONAL TOUCH

Finishing a double crew neck

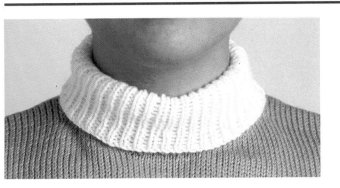

If a double width round neckband without any openings is folded in half to the inside and stitched in place too tightly, it is often difficult to pull the garment over the head – this is particularly uncomfortable for a baby.

The way to overcome this and give a really elastic neckband is to leave the stitches on a separate length of yarn once the length of neckband has been completed, instead of casting them off. The *loops* are then sewn in place and will stretch to allow the garment to be put on, reverting to the snug fit of the neckband in wear.

Thread a blunt-ended sewing needle with a length of yarn. Secure this with one or two stitches on top of each other at the base of the first of the picked-up neckband stitches.

Fold the neckband in half to the inside, insert the

sewing needle into the loop at the top of the same stitch on the separate length of thread and pull the yarn through loosely.
*Insert the sewing needle through one strand at the base of the next stitch and pull the yarn through, then insert the needle into the loop at the top of the same stitch on the separate length of thread and pull the yarn through loosely.
Repeat from * until all the loops have been secured.
Fasten off with one or two small stitches on top of each other. Remove the separate length of thread.

Round necks with collars

Single rib collar with front overlapped placket
Begin at the centre front opening with the right side of the work facing and miss half of the cast off stitches at

the top of the right front band, pick up and knit the required number of stitches round the neck then miss half of the cast off stitches at the top of the left front band, having an odd number of stitches.
If the opening is closed with a zip, pick up and knit the number of stitches round the neck, beginning and ending at the edge of the opening and having an odd number of stitches.
Work 3 rows in single rib.
Next row (Rs) K3, pick up loop lying between needles and K tbl – **called M1**, rib to last 3 sts, M1, K3.
Next row K2, P1, rib to last 3 sts as now set, P1, K2.
Repeat last 2 rows until collar is the required depth.
Cast off *very* loosely.

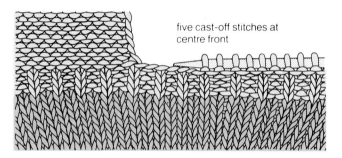

five cast-off stitches at centre front

Peter Pan collar with centre back zip opening
Begin at the centre back opening with the right side of the work facing and pick up and knit the required number of stitches round the neck, having an odd number of stitches.
Work 3 rows in single rib.
Beginning with a purl row continue in stocking stitch to allow for collar to be folded over to right side.
Next row (divide collar) Cast off 3 sts, P to centre 5 sts, cast off centre 5 sts, P to last 3 sts, cast off last 3 sts.
Complete this side first. Rejoin yarn.
** Beg with a K row work 5cm/2in st st, or length required, ending with a P row.

Next row (dec row) K1, sl 1, K1, psso, K to last 3 sts, K2 tog, K1.
Next row P to end.
Repeat last 2 rows twice more. Break off yarn.
With right side of collar facing, pick up and knit stitches evenly along side edge of half collar, knit across stitches on the needle and pick up and knit stitches along other side edge of collar. Work 2 rows single rib. Cast off loosely in rib. **
With right side of work facing, rejoin yarn to remaining stitches and work other half of collar to match first side from ** to **.
Sew down ends of rib edging at centre front and back.

Polo-necked jersey

This raglan-sleeved jersey in wide stripes of five colours can be made with a polo collar or crew neckband. To make this design in one colour only, add the quantities together.

Sizes

To fit 86 [91:97]cm/34 [36:38]in bust
Length to centre back neck,
64 [65:66]cm/25¼ [25½:26]in
Sleeve seam, 46cm/18in
The figures in [] refer to the 91/36 and 97cm/38in sizes respectively

You will need

Polo neck version 5 [5:6]×50g balls of Chat Botté Kid Mohair (80% mohair, 20% chlorofibre) in main colour A

Crew neck version 3 [4:4] balls of same in A
Both versions 2 [3:3] balls in contrast colour B
2 [2:2] balls each in contrast colours C, D and E
One pair 5mm/No 6 needles
One pair 6mm/No 4 needles
Set of four 5mm/No 6 needles pointed at both ends

Tension

15 sts and 20 rows to 10cm/4in over st st worked on 6mm/No 4 needles using 2 ends of yarn

Note

Two strands of yarn are knitted together throughout

Back

With 5mm/No 6 needles and 2 strands of A, cast on 70 [74:78] sts.
1st row (Rs) K2, *P2, K2, rep from * to end.
2nd row P2, *K2, P2, rep from * to end.
Rep these 2 rows for 9cm/3½in, ending with a 2nd row. Break off A.
Change to 6mm/No 4 needles and 2 strands of B. Beg with a K row cont in st st, working 18 rows each in B, C and D, then 14 rows with E, ending with a P row.

Right: As the yarn is used double this jersey is very quick to knit. Shown here with a generous polo collar it can also be made with a crew neckband.

alternative colourways

Shape armholes

Next row With E, K1, K2 tog, K to last 3 sts, sl 1, K1, psso, K1.
Next row With E, P to end.
Rep last 2 rows once more. Break off E.
Cont rep last 2 rows until 28 [30:32] sts rem, working 18 rows with A then cont with B to end.
Leave rem sts on holder.

Front

Work as given for back until 36 [38:40] sts rem in armhole shaping, ending with a P row.

Shape neck

Next row Keeping stripes correct throughout, K1, K2 tog, K10 sts, turn and leave rem sts on holder.
Complete left side first.
Next row Cast off 2 sts at neck edge, P to end.
Next row K1, K2 tog, K to end.
Rep last 2 rows twice more.
Next row P2 tog, P1.
Cast off rem 2 sts.
With Rs of work facing leave first 10 [12:14] sts on holder for centre front neck, rejoin yarn to rem sts, K to last 3 sts, sl 1, K1, psso, K1.
Complete to match first side, reversing shapings.

Sleeves

With 5mm/No 6 needles and 2 strands of A, cast on 34 sts. Work 9cm/3½in rib as given for back, ending with a 1st row.
Next row (inc row) Rib 4 [5:7] sts, *pick up loop lying between needles and K tbl – **called M1**, rib 26 [8:4] sts, rep from * 0 [2:4] times more, M1, rib 4 [5:7] sts. 36 [38:40] sts.
Change to 6mm/No 4 needles. Beg with a K row work 6 rows st st.
Break off A. Join in 2 strands of B.
Cont in st st, working stripes as given for back, inc one st at each end of 5th and every foll 10th row until there are 48 [50:52] sts.
Cont without shaping until 14 rows in E have been completed, thus ending with same row as back at underarms.

Shape top

Work as given for armhole shaping

on back until 6 sts rem, ending with a P row.
Leave sts on holder.

Polo neck version

Join raglan seams. With Rs of work facing, set of four 5mm/No 6 needles and 2 strands of A, K across sts of back neck and left sleeve K2 tog at seam, pick up and K12 sts down left front neck, K across front neck sts on holder, pick up and K12 sts up right front neck, then K across sts of right sleeve K last st tog with first st of back. 72 [76:80] sts.
Cont in rounds of K2, P2 rib for 24cm/9½in. Cast off very loosely in rib.

Crew neckband

Join raglan seams. With Rs of work facing, set of four 5mm/No 6 needles and 2 strands of A, K across sts of back neck and left sleeve K2 tog at seam, pick up and K8 sts down left front neck, K across front neck sts on holder, pick up and K8 sts up right front neck, then K across sts of right sleeve K last st tog with first st of back. 64 [68:72] sts.
Cont in rounds of K2, P2 rib for 5cm/2in. Leave sts on a separate length of thread.

To make up

Do not press. Join side and sleeve seams. Fold polo neck over to outside.
Fold crew neckband in half to Ws and sl st in place, sewing the loops on the thread to picked up sts of neck and removing the thread as you go.

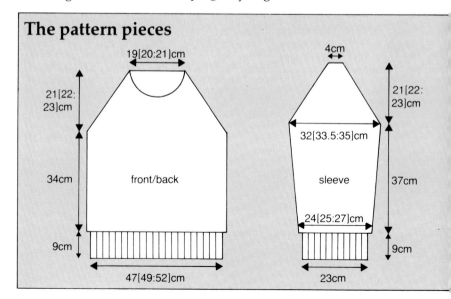

The pattern pieces

19[20:21]cm

21[22:23]cm

34cm

front/back

9cm

47[49:52]cm

4cm

21[22:23]cm

32[33.5:35]cm

sleeve

37cm

24[25:27]cm

9cm

23cm

Polo-neck inset

For extra warmth and comfort knit this simple polo-neck inset to wear under a V-neck jersey, your favourite casual dress or track suit.

Two straight pieces are joined at the shoulders and completed with a polo collar – simply pull it on over your head.

Sizes

To fit 81–91cm/32–36in bust
Length to shoulder, 30cm/11¾in

You will need

3×50g balls of Sirdar Country Style Double Knitting (45% acrylic, 40% Bri-nylon, 15% wool)
One pair 3¾mm/No 9 needles
Set of four 3mm/No 11 needles pointed at both ends

Tension

24 sts and 32 rows to 10cm/4in over st st worked on 3¾mm/No 9 needles

Back

With 3¾mm/No 9 needles cast on 72 sts. K 4 rows g st.
Next row (Rs) K to end.
Next row K2, P to last 2 sts, K2.**
Rep these 2 rows until work measures 30cm/11¾in from beg, ending with a Ws row.

Shape shoulders

Cast off at beg of next and every row 5 sts 4 times and 7 sts twice. Leave rem 48 sts on holder for centre back neck.

Front

Work as given for back to **.
Rep last 2 rows until work measures 24cm/9½in from beg, ending with a Ws row.

Shape neck

Next row K29 sts, turn and leave rem sts on spare needle.
Complete left shoulder first.
Keeping 2 sts at outer edge in g st, cast off 2 sts at beg of next and foll 3 alt rows.
Next row K to last 3 sts, sl 1, K1, psso, K1.
Next row P to last 2 sts, K2.
Rep last 2 rows 3 times more. 17 sts.
Cont without shaping until work measures same as back to shoulder, ending at armhole edge.

Shape shoulder

Cast off at beg of next and every alt row 5 sts twice and 7 sts once. With Rs of work facing, sl first 14 sts on to holder for centre front neck, rejoin yarn to rem sts and K to end.
Next row K2, P to end.
Complete to match first side reversing all shapings.

Polo Neck

Join shoulder seams. With Rs of work facing and set of four 3mm/No 11 needles, K across 38 back neck sts, pick up and K30 sts down left front neck, K across 14 front neck sts, pick up and K30 sts up right front neck. 112 sts.
Cont in rounds of K1, P1 rib for 18cm/7in. Cast off loosely in rib.

Neckband variations for square and V necks

Square and V necklines have fewer styles than round necks and, as there is plenty of room to go over the head, they do not usually need a front or back opening. Finish them with a neat ribbed edging worked in rounds, or a picot hem in stocking stitch.

For a better finish work these neckbands in rounds on a set of four needles pointed at both ends or on a circular needle.

These necklines do not usually need front or back vertical openings, except as a decorative feature, as they are wide enough for the average person to get over the head.

To complete a square neckband on a jersey, seam both shoulders before picking up stitches round the neck.

To ensure that the neckband sits neatly, all four corners of the square must be mitred.

With a single thickness of ribbing, decrease at each corner to form the mitres. With a double thickness of fabric when the neckband is folded over to form a hem, decrease at each corner on the upper side of the neckband and increase to the original number on the under side.

A heart-shaped neckline is a variation of square with the main fabric at centre front gathered up for about 10cm/4in, pulling the neckband down in the centre. Complete by sewing a separate tab over the gathers.

To complete a V-neckband on two needles, join one shoulder seam only, before picking up the stitches. This enables the work to be turned after each row.

If working single rib in rows, pick up an odd number of stitches and begin and end each row with the same stitch to allow for seaming. If working in a pattern, make sure you have the correct multiples plus any edge stitches needed to ensure that the pattern begins and ends with the same stitches.

When working single rib in rounds pick up an even number of stitches or exact multiples if working a pattern to ensure the rounds work out correctly.

To ensure that the neckband sits correctly, decrease stitches on each side of the centre point of the V. Mark the centre front stitch with a length of contrasting coloured yarn as a guide to shaping.

For a variation work the neckband without any shaping and complete by overlapping one centre front edge over the other depending whether it is for a man or a woman.

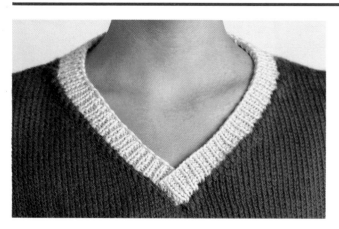

Overlapped V-neck in single rib
With the right side facing pick up and knit the required number of stitches round the neck, beginning and ending at the centre point. Do not pick up a centre stitch.
Work 2.5cm/1in single rib, or required depth. Cast off firmly.
Overlap edges of neckband and sew down row ends along edge where stitches were picked up.

Double V-neck in single rib
With the right side facing pick up and knit the required number of stitches round the neck having an even number and one stitch from the exact centre of the point.
Work in rounds of single rib.
Next round Rib to within 2 sts of centre front st, sl 1, K1, psso, K centre st, K2 tog, rib to end.
Keeping rib correct repeat this round for about 2.5cm/1in, or required depth.
Next round Rib to centre front st, pick up loop lying between needles and K tbl – **called M1**, K centre front st, M1, rib to end.
Keeping rib correct repeat last round for about 2.5cm/1in, or required depth to match first side. Cast off firmly, still increasing at centre front. Fold neckband in half to inside and slipstitch in place.

Square neck in single rib
With the right side facing, begin at the back neck and pick up and knit the required number of stitches round the neck.

Work in rounds making sure that you have an odd number of stitches across the back, any number of stitches down the side of the neck, a corner stitch, the same odd number of stitches across the front as for the back, a corner stitch, the same number of stitches up the other side of the neck as for the first side. **

Next round *Rib to within 2 sts of marked corner st, K2 tog, P corner st, sl 1, K1, psso, rep from * once more, rib to end.

Next round Keeping rib correct over dec, rib to end.
Repeat these 2 rounds until neckband measures 2.5cm/1in, or required depth ending with a 2nd round. Cast off in rib dec as before. ***

A selection of necklines showing a heart-shaped, a V, and a square neck

Heart-shaped neck in single rib
Work as given for square neck in single rib to ***.
Tab
Cast on 2 sts. P one row.
Next row K1, pick up loop lying between needles and K tbl, **called M1**, K1.
Next row P1, K1, P1.
Next row K1, M1, K1, M1, K1.
Next row P1, K1, P1, K1, P1.
Next row K1, M1, rib to last st, M1, K1.
Continue in single rib without shaping for about 7.5cm/3in, or required length to cover gathers less about 2.5cm/1in.
Gather up 10cm/4in of main fabric below neckline at centre front. Sew straight edge of tab to lower edge of neckline. Sew shaped edge of tab at bottom of gathers or fasten down with a button.

Square neck with picot hem
Work as given for square neck in single rib to **.
Next round *K to within 2 sts of corner st, K2 tog, K corner st, K2 tog tbl, rep from * once more, K to end.
Next round K to end.
Repeat last 2 rounds until neckband measures 2.5cm/1in, or required depth ending with a dec round.
Next round (picot round) *K2 tog, yfwd, rep from * to end.
Next round *K to within one st of corner st, inc in each of next 2 sts, rep from * once more, K to end.
Next round K to end.
Repeat last 2 rounds until neckband measures 2.5cm/1in from picot round, or required depth to match first side. Cast off.

Square-necked jersey

This stylish jersey is shown here with either a high, square neckline or a lower one, which you can make into a heart-shape.

The dropped shoulder line and straight set-in sleeves do not detract from the square neckline and all the edges are worked in single ribbing.

Above: This jersey is worked in a stitch which produces a zig-zag pattern all over the surface of the fabric.
Inset: The high neckline cannot be adapted; if you prefer a heart-shape, knit the lower square neck.

102

Sizes

To fit 86–91 [97–102]cm/34–36 [38–40]in bust
Length to shoulder, 57cm/22½in
Sleeve seam, 47cm/18½in
The figures in [] refer to the 97–102cm/38–40in size only

You will need

12 [13]×50g balls of Scheepjeswol Superwash Zermatt (100% wool)
One pair 3¼mm/No 10 needles
One pair 4mm/No 8 needles
Set of four 3¼mm/No 10 needles pointed at both ends

Tension

21 sts and 29 rows to 10cm/4in over patt worked on 4mm/No 8 needles

Back

With 3¼mm/No 10 needles cast on 101 [111] sts.
1st row (Rs) K1, *P1, K1, rep from * to end.
2nd row P1, *K1, P1, rep from * to end.
Rep these 2 rows for 5cm/2in, ending with a 2nd row and inc one st at end of last row on 2nd size only. 101 [112] sts.
Change to 4mm/No 8 needles.
Commence patt.
1st row (Rs) K1, *P1, K10, rep from * to last st, K1.
2nd row K1, *P9, K2, rep from * to last st, K1.
3rd row K1, *P3, K8, rep from * to last st, K1.
4th row K1, *P7, K4, rep from * to last st, K1.
5th row K1, *P5, K6, rep from * to last st, K1.
6th and 7th rows As 5th row.
8th row As 4th.
9th row As 3rd.
10th row As 2nd.
11th row As 1st.
12th row K1, *K1, P10, rep from * to last st, K1.
13th row K1, *K9, P2, rep from * to last st, K1.
14th row K1, *K3, P8, rep from * to last st, K1.
15th row K1, *K7, P4, rep from * to last st, K1.
16th row K1, *K5, P6, rep from * to last st, K1.
17th and 18th rows As 16th row.
19th row As 15th.
20th row As 14th.
21st row As 13th.
22nd row As 12th.

These 22 rows form the patt and are rep throughout.
Cont in patt until work measures 53cm/20¾in from beg for high neck, or 45cm/17¾in for low neck, ending with a Ws row.

Shape neck
**Next row Patt 30 [35] sts, turn and leave rem sts on holder.
Complete right back shoulder first.
Cont without shaping until work measures 57cm/22½in from beg, ending with a Ws row. Cast off.
With Rs of work facing return to rem sts on holder, leave first 41 [42] sts for centre back neck, rejoin yarn to rem sts and patt to end.
Complete to match first side.

Front

Work as given for back.

Sleeves

With 3¼mm/No 10 needles cast on 43 sts. Work 5cm/2in rib as given for back, ending with a 1st row.
Next row (inc row) P1, *inc in next st, rib 2 sts, rep from * to end. 57 sts.
Change to 4mm/No 8 needles. Cont in patt as given for back, inc one st at each end of 5th and every foll 6th [5th] row, working extra sts into patt, until there are 91 [101] sts.
Cont without shaping until sleeve measures 47cm/18½in from beg, ending with a Ws row.
Cast off loosely.

High neckband

Join shoulder seams.
With Rs of work facing and set of four 3¼mm/No 10 needles, *K across back neck sts on holder inc 2

[1] sts evenly, pick up and K19 sts evenly along side edge of neck, rep from * round front neck and along other side. 124 sts.
Next round *K1, P1, rep from * to end.
Next round (shape corners) K1, P2 tog, rib 37 sts, *P2 tog, K1, P2 tog *, rib 15 sts, rep from * to *, rib 37 sts, rep from * to *, rib 15 sts, P2 tog.
Next round (K1, rib 39 sts, K1, rib 17 sts) twice.
Work 4 more rounds in rib, dec at corners as before on next and foll alt round.
Cast off in rib still dec at corners.

Low neckband

Join shoulder seams.
With Rs of work facing and set of four 3¼mm/No 10 needles, *K across back neck sts on holder inc 2 [1] sts evenly, pick up and K57 sts along side edge of neck, rep from * round front neck and along other side. 200 sts.
Next round *K1, P1, rep from * to end.
Next round (shape corners) K1, P2 tog, rib 37 sts, *P2 tog, K1, P2 tog *, rib 53 sts, rep from * to *, rib 37 sts, rep from * to *, rib 53 sts, P2 tog, K1.
Next round (K1, rib 39 sts, K1, rib 55 sts) twice.
Complete as given for high neckband.

To make up

Do not press. Set in sleeves with centre to shoulder seams. Join side and sleeve seams. Press seams lightly under a wet cloth with a warm iron, taking care not to flatten the pattern.

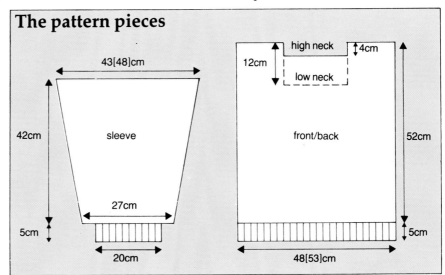

The pattern pieces

43[48]cm
42cm
sleeve
27cm
5cm
20cm

high neck
4cm
12cm
low neck
front/back
52cm
5cm
48[53]cm

Inserted pocket techniques

Pockets are a practical and useful addition to a garment and it is easy to add them to a pattern or to change the style to suit your requirements. These inserted pockets can be horizontal, vertical or diagonal and knitted to match the garment fabric.

If you want to use a pattern that does not include inserted pockets, it is a simple matter to add them. A little pre-planning is necessary and you will also need an extra ball of the yarn.

Choose the style of pocket to fit in with the structure of the main fabric and the shape of the garment. Make sure the fabric is suitable so that it will hold the shape of a pocket without sagging. For example, pockets on very lacy fabrics tend to pull out of shape.

The size of the pocket must also be taken into account at the planning stage. A small pocket on a chunky jacket will look out of proportion while a large pocket on a dainty cardigan would look clumsy and sag out of shape.

Horizontal stocking stitch pocket

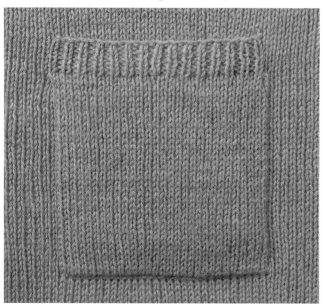

Check the number of stitches and rows needed to give the correct size. This example is worked over 30 stitches in double knitting yarn on 4mm/No 8 needles on the right front of the cardigan. For any other pattern, make sure the multiples of stitches for the upper side of the pocket will work out exactly. Adjust the number left for the pocket opening and cast on for the lining, as required.

Cast on 30 sts for the inner pocket lining. Beg with a K row cont in st st for the depth of pocket required, ending with a P row. Break off yarn and leave these sts on a holder.

Work the welt or hem as given in the instructions. Cont in the patt for the main fabric to the same depth as the lining, ending with a Ws row.

Next row Work to the position for the opening, sl 30 sts for the pocket opening on to a holder, with Rs of pocket lining sts to the Ws of the main fabric, work across lining sts on holder, then work to end of row. Complete the right front as given in the instructions. With the Rs of the work facing and a size smaller needles, rejoin yarn to the pocket opening sts on holder. Work 2.5cm/1in ribbing. Cast off loosely. Stitch pocket lining in place.

Vertical basket stitch pocket

This example is worked over 32 stitches and 40 rows in double knitting yarn on 4mm/No 8 needles on the left front of a jacket. For any other pattern, check that the position for the pocket opening comes at the end of a repeat of the multiples of stitches.

Work in basket stitch pattern of K4, P4 until lower edge of opening is reached, ending at the side edge.

Next row Patt multiples of 4 sts to the position for the opening, turn and leave rem sts on holder.

Next row Cast on 32 sts for pocket lining, P32 then patt to end.

Keeping pocket lining in st st, work the number of rows over these sts to give the depth of pocket, ending at lining edge.

Next row Cast off 32 sts, patt to end. Do not break off yarn. Return to where the work was divided, join in a separate ball of yarn to rem sts and patt to end. Work the same number of rows as for the first side, ending at pocket opening edge. Break off yarn.

Return to the first section, work across all sts in patt to close the opening. Complete the left front as given in the instructions. Stitch lining in place. With Rs facing and a smaller needle size, pick up and knit sts along edge of pocket. Work 2cm/¾in rib. Cast off in rib.

Inserted pockets can be horizontal or vertical. If they are not included in the instructions you must work out the position for each pocket before beginning to knit.

Calculate the width and depth of pocket needed – on a woman's cardigan in double knitting, 12.5cm/5in square is a good size. The opening must be clear of any shaping and front edges.

If a horizontal pocket is to be placed above a ribbed welt you must work sufficient depth in the main fabric to allow the lower edge of the pocket lining to come at the top of the ribbing. The pocket opening edge looks best neatened with the type of ribbing used on the other edges.

If vertical pockets are to be positioned on the fronts of a jacket, you must allow sufficient width in the main fabric from the pocket opening to ensure that the edges of the lining do not overlap the front edges.

A vertical pouch pocket can be placed on the front of a jersey. The pocket opening edges look best neatened with ribbing, as used on the other edges.

Diagonal inserted pockets Before beginning to knit, decide where the pocket opening is to begin and the direction in which it must slant for the right or left front. The opening must be clear of any shaping and allow for a lining to be sewn above the welt, also without overlapping front edges. The slanting edge of the pocket can be neatened with ribbing, as used on the other garment edges.

On all of the inserted pocket techniques, the pocket lining is slipstitched into place on completion of the garment.

Vertical stocking stitch pocket

Check the number of stitches and rows needed to give the correct size. This example is worked over 59 stitches and 46 rows in double knitting yarn on 4mm/No 8 needles across the centre front of a jersey.

Cast on 59 sts for the inner pocket lining. Beg with a K row work 10 rows st st, or the depth required to reach from the top of the welt to the lower edge of the pocket opening, ending with a P row. Leave sts on a holder. Work the welt as given in the instructions, then beg with a K row and work the same number of rows as worked for the pocket lining.

Next row K to the position for the left-hand pocket opening, sl the next 59 sts on to a thread and leave for the time being, K across the pocket lining sts then K to the end of the row.

Beg with a P row cont in st st for 45 rows, or the required depth of pocket, ending with a P row. Leave sts for time being. Do not break off yarn.

Complete the pocket front by joining in a separate ball of yarn to the sts left on the thread and work the same number of rows as for the first piece. Break off the yarn.

Return to where the yarn was left and join the pocket front and lining.

Next row K to the pocket opening, place the sts of the pocket front in front of the main fabric and K together one st from each needle until all the sts have been worked, then K to end.

Complete the front as given in the instructions.

With the Rs of the work facing and a smaller needle size, pick up and knit the required number of stitches along the left-hand edge of the pocket front. Work 2cm/¾in ribbing. Cast off.

Work along the right-hand edge of the pocket front in the same way.

Stitch base of pocket lining in place.

Below: A close-up view of the vertical pouch pocket on the front of the raglan jersey featured in this chapter. The pocket lining is carefully slipstitched in place at the back.

Diagonal stocking stitch pocket

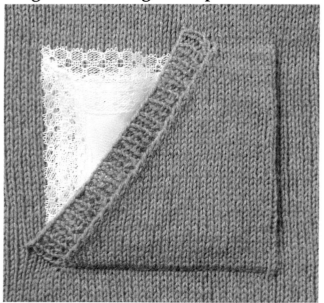

Check where the lower edge of the pocket opening is to begin and the way in which it must slant. This example is worked over 30 stitches in double knitting yarn on 4mm/No 8 needles on the right front of a jacket and slants from left to right.

Work the welt or hem as given in the instructions. Beg with a K row cont in st st until the lower edge of the opening has been reached, ending with a P row.
Next row Work to the position for the opening, turn. Leave remaining stitches on holder.
Dec one st at beg of next row and at same edge on every alt row 30 times in all, ending at front edge. Do not break off yarn.
With separate ball of yarn cast on 30 sts for pocket lining and use this yarn to complete other side of pocket opening.
Beg with a K row cont in st st to give depth of pocket from top edge of welt to lower edge of opening, ending with a K row.
Continue to knit across stitches on holder to end of row. Cont in st st until same number of rows have been worked as for first side, omitting dec, ending with a P row. Break off yarn.
Return to the first section, work across stitches, knitting together one stitch from each needle to join pocket top to main fabric. Complete the right front as given in the instructions.
Complete as given for basket st vertical pocket.
Stitch pocket lining in place.

DESIGN EXTRA

Patch pockets

This quick and simple method can add pockets to an existing garment as well as to the jersey you are knitting. Buy a ball of yarn in a toning or contrasting colour, or use up oddments of yarn of the same thickness to work jazzy stripes or a Fair Isle motif.
Calculate the width and depth of the pocket using an oddment of fabric pinned to the garment. Make sure the pocket does not interfere with any shaping or overlap edges. Large patch pockets are usually positioned with the lower edge just above the ribbing or hem. Smaller pockets look effective as breast

selection of design ideas for patch pockets

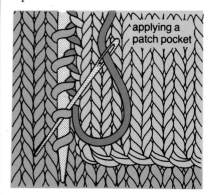

pockets or as a decorative feature on a sleeve.
Knit them in a textured pattern or add cables against a reversed stocking stitch background. Finish the top edge with a few rows of ribbing to match the garment edges or reverse the pattern at the top of the pocket to make a turned down flap.
Apply patch pockets directly on to the garment. Use a fine knitting needle, pointed at both ends, to keep the pocket side edges in line with the main fabric. Pick up every alternate stitch along the line of the main fabric with the needle. Catch one stitch from pocket edge and one from needle alternately.
Work across the row of the main fabric corresponding with the lower edge of pocket in the same way.

Raglan-sleeve jersey with pouch pocket

This classic crew-neck jersey in stocking stitch, is quick and easy to knit. The pouch pocket is ideal for keeping hands warm on cold winter days and adds an attractive feature to an otherwise plain garment. All the ribbing is knitted in a contrast colour.

Sizes

To fit 81 [86:91:97:102:107]cm/
32 [34:36:38:40:42]in bust/chest
Length to centre back neck,
56 [57:58:59:60:61]cm/
22 [22½:22¾:23¼:23½:24]in
Sleeve seam, 43 [44:45:46:47:48]cm/
17 [17¼:17¾:18:18½:19]in
The figures in [] refer to the 86/34, 91/36, 97/38, 102/40 and 107cm/42in sizes respectively

You will need

6 [7:7:8:8:9]×50g balls of Hayfield Grampian Double Knitting (45% acrylic, 40% Bri-nylon, 15% wool) in main colour A
1 [1:1:1:2:2] balls of same in contrast colour B
One pair 3¼mm/No 10 needles
One pair 4mm/No 8 needles
Set of four 3¼mm/No 10 needles pointed at both ends

Tension

22 sts and 30 rows to 10cm/4in over st st worked on 4mm/No 8 needles

Back

With 3¼mm/No 10 needles and B cast on 99 [105:111:117:123:129] sts.
1st row (Rs) K1, *P1, K1, rep from * to end.
2nd row P1, *K1, P1, rep from * to end.
Rep these 2 rows for 5cm/2in, ending with a 2nd row. Break off B. **
Change to 4mm/No 8 needles. Join in A. Beg with a K row cont in st st until work measures 36cm/14¼in from beg, ending with a P row.

Shape raglan armholes

Cast off 5 sts at beg of next 2 rows.
Next row K1, sl 1, K1, psso, K to last 3 sts, K2 tog, K1.
Next row P to end.

Right: Use a plain or tweedy yarn as the main fabric and a toning colour for the ribbing on this stylish jersey.

Above: detail of pocket edgings.

Rep last 2 rows until
31 [33:35:37:39:41] sts rem, ending
with a P row.
Leave sts on holder for centre back
neck.

Front

With 4mm/No 8 needles and A cast
on 55 [55:57:57:59:59] sts for pocket
lining. Beg with a K row work 10
rows st st. Leave sts on holder.
Work front as given for back to **.
Change to 4mm/No 8 needles. Join
in A. Beg with a K row work 10
rows st st.

Place pocket

Next row K22 [25:27:30:32:35] sts, sl
next 55 [55:57:57:59:59] sts on to a
thread and leave for time being, K
across pocket lining sts, K to end.
Beg with a P row cont in st st for
13 [13:14:14:15:15]cm/
5 [5:5½:5½:6:6]in, ending with a
P row. Leave sts for time being.
Do not break off yarn.

Complete pocket front

With Rs of work facing and 4mm/
No 8 needles, join in another ball of
yarn to sts on thread and work to
match length of first piece, ending
with a P row.
Break off yarn. Leave sts on needle.

Join pocket front and lining

Next row With Rs facing return to
where yarn was left,
K22 [25:27:30:32:35] sts, place sts of
pocket front in front of work and K
tog one st from each needle until all
sts are worked, then K rem
22 [25:27:30:32:35] sts.
Cont as given for back until
49 [51:53:55:57:59] sts rem in raglan
armhole shaping, ending with a P
row.

Shape neck

Next row K1, sl 1, K1, psso, K14 sts,

turn and leave rem sts on spare
needle.
Next row P to end.
Next row K1, sl 1, K1, psso, K to last
3 sts, sl 1, K1, psso, K1.
Rep last 2 rows 5 times more, then
dec at armhole edge only on foll 2
alt rows.
Cast off rem 2 sts.
With Rs of work facing, sl first
15 [17:19:21:23:25] sts on to holder,
rejoin yarn to rem sts, K to last 3 sts,
K2 tog, K1.
Next row P to end.
Next row K1, K2 tog, K to last 3 sts,
K2 tog, K1.
Complete to match first side.

Sleeves

With 3¼mm/No 10 needles and B
cast on 41 [43:45:47:49:51] sts. Work
5cm/2in rib as given for back,
ending with a 1st row.
Next row (inc row) Rib
5 [6:5:6:3:4] sts, *pick up loop lying
between needles and K tbl – **called
M1**, rib 10 [10:7:7:6:6] sts, rep from
* to last 6 [7:5:6:4:5] sts, M1, rib to
end. 45 [47:51:53:57:59] sts.
Break off B. Join in A. Change to
4mm/No 8 needles. Beg with a K
row cont in st st inc one st at each
end of 5th and every foll 8th row
until there are 71 [75:79:83:87:91] sts.
Cont without shaping until sleeve
measures 43 [44:45:46:47:48]cm/
17 [17¼:17¾:18:18½:19]in from
beg, ending with a P row. Place a
marker at each end of last row then
work a further 6 rows.

Shape top

Next row K1, sl 1, K1, psso, K to last

3 sts, K2 tog, K1.
Next row P to end.
Rep last 2 rows until 13 sts rem,
ending with a P row. Leave sts on
holder.

Neckband

Join raglan seams, sewing the last 6
rows of sleeves from markers to cast
off sts at armholes.
With Rs of work facing, set of four
3¼mm/No 10 needles and B, K
across sts of back neck and left
sleeve K2 tog at seam, pick up and
K10 sts down left front neck, K
across front neck sts, pick up and
K10 sts up right front neck, then K
across sts of right sleeve K last st of
sleeve tog with first st of back neck.
90 [94:98:102:106:110] sts.
Cont in rounds of K1, P1 rib for
5cm/2in. Cast off loosely in rib.

Pocket edges

With Rs of work facing, 3¼mm/No
10 needles and B, pick up and
K31 [31:35:35:39:39] sts along edge
of pocket.
1st row (Ws) K1, *P1, K1, rep from *
to end.
2nd row P1, *K1, P1, rep from * to
end.
Rep these 2 rows for 2cm/¾in. Cast
off in rib.

To make up

Press lightly under a dry cloth with
a warm iron. Join side and sleeve
seams. Sew cast-on edge of pocket
lining to top of ribbed welt. Sew
down ends of pocket edges. Fold
neckband in half to Ws and sl st in
place. Press seams.

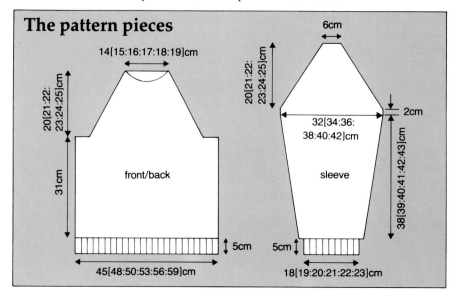

The pattern pieces

14[15:16:17:18:19]cm

20[21:22:23:24:25]cm

31cm

front/back

45[48:50:53:56:59]cm

5cm

6cm

20[21:22:23:24:25]cm

32[34:36:38:40:42]cm

2cm

38[39:40:41:42:43]cm

sleeve

5cm

18[19:20:21:22:23]cm

MULTI-COLOURED KNITTING

Practise knitting with several different coloured yarns by making this collection of eye-catching cushion covers.

Colouring-book stripes and checks

Incredible it may seem, but every one of the exciting striped and checked patterns in this chapter was created simply by using two or more colours and basic knit or purl stitches. So cue yourself in to colour and transform a basic jersey into a unique design.

Random horizontal stripe

Working striped (or checked) patterns is a most enjoyable way of experimenting with colour and, at the same time, using up oddments of the same thickness of yarn.

Horizontal and chevron stripes are particularly easy, as only one colour at a time is used in a row. These patterns produce fabrics of a *single* thickness.

Narrow vertical or diagonal stripes use two colours at a time in a row, and produce fabrics of *double* thickness.

The colours used in all patterns of this type are coded for ease of identification, the first colour as A, the second B, the third C and so on.

Horizontal stripes

In stocking stitch, the knitted side will show an unbroken line of colour and the purl side a broken line.

In garter stitch, if an even number of rows is worked in each colour the right side shows an unbroken line of colour and the wrong side a broken one.

All ribbed stitches can be worked in stripes, but if you wish to keep an unbroken line of colour on the right side, the first row of each new colour must be knitted instead of ribbed. If you work in ribbing throughout, a broken line of colour will show on the right side.

When horizontal stripes are worked over an even number of rows, it is a simple matter to change colours. Whatever the pattern, each new colour is brought into use at the beginning of a row and at the same edge. When working narrow stripes with no more than three colours, the two colours not in use can be carried loosely up the side of the work and twisted round the last colour used before you continue to knit with the next colour.

However, to work more than eight rows in any colour – or in more than three colours – do not carry yarns up the side, as this will pull the side edge out of shape. Instead, break off the yarn at the end of each stripe and rejoin it when it is needed again.

To work horizontal stripes over a random number of rows, use a pair of needles pointed at both ends. Each new colour will not necessarily be joined in at the same edge and working an odd number of rows will leave the yarn at the opposite end of the row.

Chevron stripes

Whether regular or random, these are worked in the same way as horizontal stripes. The scalloped effect is achieved by increasing and decreasing at regular points in each row.

Narrow vertical stripes

Two-colour stripes of this type look best worked in stocking stitch as this defines the edge of each stripe. Stitches are worked with the first and second colours alternately, changing at regular points across each row.

The yarn not in use is carried loosely across the back of the work each time it is needed. On a knit row carry the yarn across the back and on a purl row across the front of the work. Take the yarn not in use across in the same position each time – the second colour over the top of the first and the first colour under the second. Do not pull the yarn across tightly or you will pucker the fabric.

Narrow diagonal stripes

These are also best in stocking stitch. The method is the same as for vertical stripes but the position of each stripe is changed by one stitch on every row.

Stocking stitch stripes

Using A cast on any number of sts. Work in st st, 2 rows A, 1 row B, 3 rows C, 1 row D, 4 rows E, 1 row B, 2 rows A, 1 row E and 3 rows D. These 18 rows form the pattern.

Regular chevron stripes

Using A cast on multiples of 20 sts plus 3, eg 43. Work in g st.
1st row (Rs) Using A, K1, K2 tog, *K8, yfwd, K1, yfwd, K8, sl 1 knitwise, K2 tog, psso, rep from * to last 20 sts, K8, yfwd, K1, yfwd, K8, sl 1, K1, psso, K1.
2nd row Using A, K1, P1, *K8, K1 tb1, K1, K1 tb1, K8, P1, rep from * to last st, K1.
These 2 rows form the chevron patt. Work 2 rows each in B, C, D, E, F & A. These 12 rows form the striped patt.

Regular horizontal stripes

Random chevron stripes

Garter stitch stripes
Using A cast on any number of sts.
Work in g st, 3 rows A, 3 rows B,
3 rows C and 3 rows D.
These 12 rows form the pattern.

Using A cast on multiples of 4 sts
plus 2, eg, 18.
1st row (Rs) Using A, K2, *P2, K2,
rep from * to end.
2nd row Using A, P2, *K2, P2, rep
from * to end.
These 2 rows form the rib pattern.
Rep them once more. Join in B. K
one row then rib 3 rows. Join in C.
K one row then rib 3 rows. Join in
D. K one row then rib 3 rows.
These 16 rows form the striped
pattern.

Using A cast on multiples of 13 sts
plus 2, eg 41. Beg with a K row work
2 rows st st. Commence patt.
1st row (Rs) Using A, *K2, pick up
loop lying between sts and K tbl –
called M1, K4, sl 1 knitwise, K2 tog,
psso, K4, M1, rep from * to last
2 sts, K2.
2nd row Using A, P to end.
These 2 rows form the chevron patt.
Work 2 more rows A, 3 rows B,
6 rows C, 1 row D and 2 rows E.
These 16 rows form the striped patt.

Narrow vertical stripes

Narrow diagonal stripes

Small checked pattern

Using A cast on multiples of 6 sts
plus 3, eg 27. Work in st st.
1st row (Rs) Keeping yarn at back,
K3 A, *K3 B, K3 A, rep from * to
end.
2nd row Keep yarn at front, P3 A,
*P3 B, P3 A, rep from * to end.
These 2 rows form the pattern.

Using A cast on multiples of 4 sts
plus 2, eg 26. Work in st st.
1st row (Rs) Keep yarn at back, K2
A, *K2 B, K2 A, rep from * to end.
2nd row Keep yarn at front, P1 B,
*P2 A, P2 B, rep from * to last st,
P1 A.
3rd row K2 B, *K2 A, K2 B, rep from
* to end.
4th row P1 A, *P2 B, P2 A, rep from
* to last st, P1 B.
These 4 rows form the pattern.

Using A cast on multiples of 4 sts.
Work in st st.
1st row (Rs) Keep yarn at back, *K2
A, K2 B, rep from * to end.
2nd row Keep yarn at front, *P2 B,
P2 A, rep from * to end.
3rd row *K2 B, K2 A, rep from * to
end.
4th row *P2 A, P2 B, rep from * to
end.
These 4 rows form the pattern.

111

Judo-style dressing gown for toddlers

Wrap-over style dressing gowns are popular for toddlers, especially as the crossover fronts with tie belt help it to fit more snugly for extra warmth. The back and fronts have been knitted sideways to enable the stripes to run vertically without the need for making a double fabric by carrying the yarn across the back of the work.

Sizes

To fit 56-61cm/22-24in chest loosely
Length to shoulder 55cm/21¾in
Sleeve seam 22cm/8¾in

You will need

3×50g balls of Sirdar Terry Look (90% acrylic, 10% nylon), in main colour A

2 balls each of 3 contrast colours, B, C and D
One pair 3mm/No 11 needles
One pair 3¼mm/No 10 needles

Below: No more tears at bed-time if you make this cuddly dressing gown for a boy or girl. The yarn knits up like terry-towelling and is machine washable.

Tension

26 sts and 38 rows to 10cm/4in over st st worked on 3¼mm/No 10 needles

Back

With 3¼mm/No 10 needles and A, cast on 150 sts and beg at side seam. Beg with a K row work 6 rows st st.
Next row K7 A, join in B, K143 B.
Next row P143 B, P7 A.
Rep last 2 rows 4 times more.
Keeping 7 sts at right-hand edge in A throughout for hem at lower edge, work 10 rows each in C, D and A. **. Cont working 10 rows each in B, C, D, A, D, C, B, A, D, C, B and 6 rows A. Cast off.

Right front

Work as given for back to **

Shape front edge

Next row K7 A, K in B to last 3 sts, K2 tog, K1.
Next row Using B, P1, P2 tog, P to last 7 sts, P7 A.
Rep last 2 rows once more, then K one row without shaping.
Cont dec in this way, working dec on 4 rows then one row without shaping, *at the same time* work 5 more rows in B, then 10 rows each in C, D, A, B, C and D. 94 sts. Cast off.

Left front

Work first 6 rows as given for back.
Next row K in B to last 7 sts, K7 A.
Reversing position of hem as set,

The pattern pieces

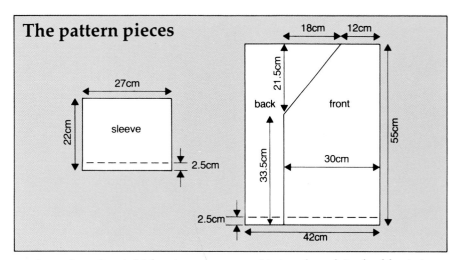

work as given for right front, working shaping at opposite end to hem.

Sleeves

With 3mm/No 11 needles and A cast on 70 sts. Beg with a K row work 10 rows in st st.
Change to 3¼mm/No 10 needles.
Cont in st st working 10 rows each in A, B, C, D, A, B, C, D and 6 rows A. Cast off.

Front band

With 3mm/No 11 needles and A cast on 15 sts. Beg with a K row work in st st until band is long enough to go up front, round back neck and down other front. Cast off.

Ties (make 2)

With 3mm/No 11 needles and A, cast on 14 st and work in double st st as foll:
1st row *K1, yfwd, sl 1, ybk, rep from * to end.
Rep this row for 65cm/25½in or length required. Cast off K2 tog along the row.

To make up

Do not press. Join shoulder seams. Set in sleeves. Join side and sleeve seams, leaving an opening in right seam for tie to go through for a girl, or left seam for a boy. Turn up hem at lower edge and sl st in place. Turn up hem of 10 rows on sleeve and sl st in place. Sew on front band, fold in half to inside and sl st in place. Sew on ties.

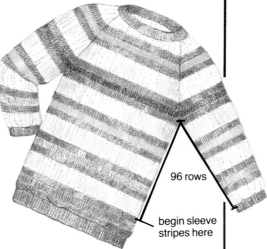

Mosaic patterns in two or more colours

These sophisticated coloured patterns in combinations of horizontal stripes and slipped stitches could not be easier, but they have tremendous impact. Some look best in only two colours, others in as many colours as you wish. Try them out on the cushions overleaf.

Mosaic patterns can be used to create a wonderful variety of coloured fabrics, so don't be put off by their apparent intricacy – they are easy to work. Only one colour is used in any row, some of the stitches being knitted and others simply slipped from one needle to the other. Two rows are worked with the first colour. Then the next two rows are worked with a second colour – again, some of the stitches being knitted and others slipped, but in a different sequence.

Working mosaic patterns

The right side rows are always knitted. Every slipped stitch is slipped with the yarn at the *back* on right-side rows and the same stitch is slipped again with the yarn at the *front* on following wrong side rows. The colours are alternated after every two rows and each slipped stitch – spanning two rows – is caught in again with its own, or an additional colour, on the third row. To begin, cast on with colour A and work the number of rows given.

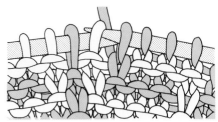

Knitting a right side row
Join in B. Keep the yarn at the *back* of the work, *K the number of stitches given, slip the number of stitches given in a purlwise direction, repeat from * to end.

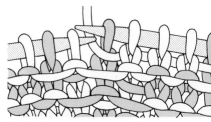

Knitting a wrong side row
Using same colour as previous row, keep the yarn at the back and knit all knitted stitches and bring the yarn forward to the front to slip all slipped stitches of the previous row.

Turret pattern

Using A cast on multiples of 4 sts plus 3, eg 23.
1st row (Rs) Using A, K to end.
2nd row Using A, P to end.
3rd row Using B, K3, *sl 1, K3, rep from * to end.
4th row Using B, K3, *yfwd, sl 1, ybk, K3, rep from * to end.
5th row Using A, K2, *sl 1, K1, rep from * to last st, K1.
6th row Using A, P2, *sl 1, P1, rep from * to last st, P1.
7th row Using B, K1, *sl 1, K3, rep from * to last 2 sts, sl 1, K1.
8th row Using B, K1, *yfwd, sl 1, ybk, K3, rep from * to last 2 sts, yfwd, sl 1, ybk, K1.
9th and 10th rows Using A, as 1st and 2nd.
11th and 12th rows Using B, as 7th and 8th.
13th and 14th rows Using A, as 5th and 6th.
15th and 16th rows Using B, as 3rd and 4th.
These 16 rows form the pattern. To work in more than two colours use different colours for next repeat.

Tricolour pattern

Using A cast on multiples of 4 sts plus 3, eg 23.
1st row (Rs) Using A, *K3, sl 1, rep from * to last 3 sts, K3.
2nd row Using A, K3, *yfwd, sl 1, ybk, K3, rep from * to end.
3rd row Using B, K1, *sl 1, K3, rep from * to last 2 sts, sl 1, K1.
4th row Using B, K1, *yfwd, sl 1, ybk, K3, rep from * to last 2 sts, yfwd, sl 1, ybk, K1.
5th and 6th rows Using C, as 1st and 2nd.
7th and 8th rows Using A, as 3rd and 4th.
9th and 10th rows Using B, as 1st and 2nd.
11th and 12th rows Using C, as 3rd and 4th.
These 12 rows form the pattern. To work in two colours only repeat first 4 rows.

Altering the sequence of knitted and slipped stitches causes parts of each pair of rows to be concealed by slipped stitches in a different colour carried up from the previous row. This way the slipped stitches form a superimposed pattern.

You can use only two colours throughout or introduce more colours in the following rows. In printed patterns the colours are coded as A, B, C and so on, for ease of reference and to allow you to substitute colours

of your own choice, if you wish. If you are creating your own mosaic design, it is well worth coding your colours in this way so that you have a handy record of the sequence worked.

Purl or plain All mosaic patterns can be worked in either stocking stitch or garter stitch. If the instructions are for garter stitch and you want to work stocking stitch, simply purl all the wrong-side rows instead of knitting them. To work garter stitch instead of stocking stitch, knit the wrong side rows instead of purling them. If you are using a printed pattern, you may find it helpful to write in these adjustments, to save confusion.

The type of yarn you choose should relate to the effect you wish to achieve. The smooth surface of stocking stitch is complemented by bouclé or fluffy yarns, while the knobbly texture of garter stitch looks best worked in a plain yarn. Both fabrics look stunning when a glitter yarn is introduced as one of the colours. Because stitches are slipped on every row the fabric is very dense.

Stitch requirements The fascinating thing about mosaics is that they can be worked over any number of stitches, so you are not tied to exact multiples of stitches.

Each example given here has an exact multiple of stitches shown but don't let this put you off if you want to experiment. Simply begin each right-side pattern row at the right-hand edge, as given, and work across the row until you run out of stitches, irrespective of what point you have reached in the pattern. Work the return row by knitting (or purling) all the knitted stitches of the previous row and slipping all the slipped stitches. The ends of the rows may not match exactly but these patterns are easy to incorporate into a basic design whether for a garment or household items such as bedcovers or cushion covers.

The easiest mosaic pattern to practise if you are a beginner is the tricolour pattern as this has a pattern repeat of only four rows with the effect being formed by changes in the colour of the yarn.

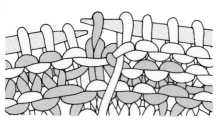

Purling a wrong side row
Using same colour as for previous row, keep the yarn at the front and purl all the knitted stitches and slip all the slipped stitches of the previous row.

Overcheck pattern

Using A cast on multiples of 6 sts, eg 24. P one row.
1st row (Rs) Using B, K5, *sl 2, K4, rep from * to last st, K1.
2nd row Using B, K5, *yfwd, sl 2, ybk, K4, rep from * to last st, K1.
3rd row Using A, K1, *sl 1, K2, rep from * to last 2 sts, sl 1, K1.
4th row Using A, P1, *sl 1, P2, rep from * to last 2 sts, sl 1, P1.
5th row Using B, K2, *sl 2, K4, rep from * to last 4 sts, sl 2, K2.
6th row Using B, K2, *yfwd, sl 2, ybk, K4, rep from * to last 4 sts, yfwd, sl 2, ybk, K2.
7th and 8th rows Using A, as 3rd and 4th.
These 8 rows form the pattern. This pattern is best worked in two colours only.

Zigzag pattern

Using A cast on multiples of 5 sts plus 1, eg 21. K one row.
1st row (Rs) Using B, *K4, sl 1, rep from * to last st, K1.
2nd row Using B, P1, *sl 1, P4, rep from * to end.
3rd row Using A, K5, *sl 1, K4, rep from * to last st, K1.
4th row Using A, K5, *yfwd, sl 1, ybk, K4, rep from * to last st, K1.
5th row Using B, K1, *sl 1, K4, rep from * to end.
6th row Using B, *P4, sl 1, rep from * to last st, P1.
7th and 8th rows Using A, as 3rd and 4th.
These 8 rows form the pattern. This pattern is best worked in two colours only.

Greek key pattern

Using A cast on multiples of 6 sts plus 2, eg 26.
1st row (Rs) Using A, K to end.
2nd row Using A, K to end.
3rd row Using B, K1, *sl 1, K5, rep from * to last st, K1.
4th and every alt row Using same colour as previous row keep yarn at front of work to sl all sl sts of previous row and take it back to K all K sts.
5th row Using A, K2, *sl 1, K3, sl 1, K1, rep from * to end.
7th row Using B, K1, *sl 1, K3, sl 1, K1, rep from * to last st, K1.
9th row Using A, K6, *sl 1, K5, rep from * to last 2 sts, sl 1, K1.
11th and 12th rows Using B, as 1st and 2nd.
13th row Using A, K4, *sl 1, K5, rep from * to last 4 sts, sl 1, K3.
15th row Using B, *K3, sl 1, K1, sl 1, rep from * to last 2 sts, K2.
17th row Using A, K2, *sl 1, K1, sl 1, K3, rep from * to end.
19th row Using B, K3, *sl 1, K5, rep from * to last 5 sts, sl 1, K4.
20th row As 4th.
These 20 rows form the pattern. To work in more than two colours use different colours for next repeat.

Pyramid pattern

Using A cast on multiples of 14 sts plus 3, eg 31. K one row.
1st row (Rs) Using B, K8, *sl 1, K13, rep from * to last 9 sts, sl 1, K8.
2nd and every alt row Using same colour as previous row keep yarn at front of work to sl all sl sts of previous row and take it back to K all K sts.
3rd row Using A, K2, *(sl 1, K1) twice, sl 1, K3, (sl 1, K1) 3 times, rep from * to last st, K1.
5th row Using B, K7, *sl 1, K1, sl 1, K11, rep from * to last 10 sts, sl 1, K1, sl 1, K7.
7th row Using A, K2, *sl 1, K1, sl 1, K7, (sl 1, K1) twice, rep from * to last st, K1.
9th row Using B, K5, *(sl 1, K1) 3 times, sl 1, K7, rep from * to last 12 sts, (sl 1, K1) 3 times, sl 1, K5.
11th row Using A, K2, *sl 1, K11, sl 1, K1, rep from * to last st, K1.
13th row Using B, K3, *(sl 1, K1) 5 times, sl 1, K3, rep from * to end.
15th row Using A, K1, *sl 1, K13, rep from * to last 2 sts, sl 1, K1.
16th row As 2nd.
These 16 rows form the pattern. To work in more than two colours use different colours for next repeat.

Razzle-dazzle cushion covers

The attractive cushion covers shown earlier on page 109, can be made in the colours and patterns of your choice. For all three versions shown, the backs and the front 'frames' with their mitred corners are worked as one piece, in garter stitch.
One front cover is worked in Greek key mosaic pattern, one in random stripes and one in square patches – each with a different pattern.
Instructions are given for 40cm/15¾in covers but, if you wish to use one of these designs for a cushion of a different size, it is a simple matter to scale them up or down.

Size

To fit a 40cm/15¾in cushion

You will need

Cushion back all versions, 6×20g balls of Wendy Courtellon Double Knitting (60% Courtelle, 40% Bri-Nylon) in main colour A
Greek key cushion front 1 ball each of same in contrast colours B and C
Striped cushion front Oddments of same in 6 contrast colours
Patchwork cushion front Oddments of same in 6 contrast colours
One pair 4mm/No 8 needles
30cm/12in zip fastener
40cm/15¾in cushion pad

Tension

20 sts and 28 rows to 10cm/4in over st st (20 sts and 40 rows for g st) worked on 4mm/No 8 needles

Cushion back

With 4mm/No 8 needles and A cast on 62 sts. K 2 rows.
3rd row K into front and back of first st – called inc 1, K to last 2 sts, inc 1, K1. **4th row** K to end.
Rep 3rd and 4th rows 7 times more, then 3rd row again. 80 sts.
20th row (opening for zip) K10, cast off 60 sts, K to end.
21st row Inc 1, K9, cast on 60 sts, K to last 2 sts, inc 1, K1.**22nd row** As 4th.
Rep 3rd and 4th rows 9 times more. 100 sts.
Cont without shaping until work measures 40cm/15¾in from beg, ending with a Ws row.
Next row K2 tog tbl, K to last 2 sts, K2 tog.

The pattern pieces

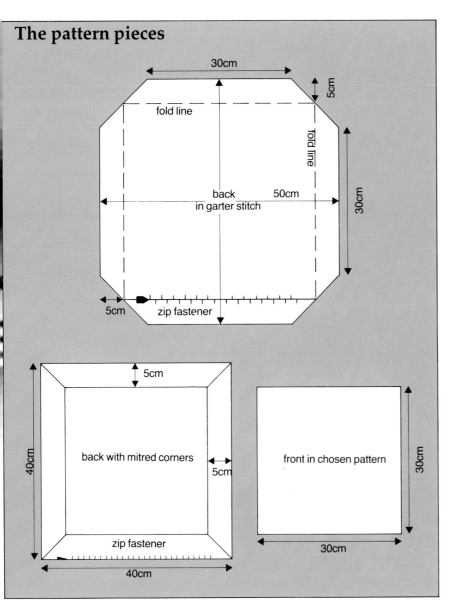

Next row K to end.
Rep last 2 rows 18 times more, then K one row. Cast off loosely.

Greek key cushion front

With 4mm/No 8 needles and B cast on 62 sts. Work 30cm/11¾in in Greek key pattern ending with a 20th patt row. K one row. Cast off.

Striped cushion front

With 4mm/No 8 needles and any colour cast on 62 sts. Work in st st and random stripes, see page 110, for 30cm/11¾in. Cast off.

Patchwork cushion front

This is made up of 9 squares, each in a different pattern, shown here in random stripes, basket st, vertical stripes, small check, diagonal stripes, moss st, double moss st, and overcheck and turret mosaic patt.
For each square cast on 22 sts or the nearest multiple of sts for the patt of your choice.
Work 10cm/4in patt. Cast off.

To make up

Join 9 patches to make a square. Press all cushion fronts lightly under dry cloth with a warm iron. Do not press backs.
Join mitred corners of cushion back. Turn to Ws. Join edges of front to back. Turn Rs out. Sew in zip. Insert cushion pad.

Sizing the cushions up or down

If you have an existing cushion in a different size and would like to make one of these covers, this is how to scale the designs up or down. Use the tension given to calculate how many stitches and rows you must work to give the size required.
Cover back For a width of 30cm/11¾in the instructions were to cast on 62 stitches. To take a size down to 25cm/9¾in, cast on 52 stitches. To take it up to 35cm/13¾in, cast on 72 stitches. Increase at each end of every row as given in the instructions to give a width of 45cm/17¾in (smaller size) or 55cm/21¾in (larger size).

(Both measurements allow for mitred corners.) Adjust the number of rows for the length, then decrease as given in the instructions down to the original number of stitches. When the corners are turned in and mitred the finished size of the back will be 35cm/13¾in (smaller size) or 45cm/17¾in (larger size).
Cover front This is adjusted up or down in the same way by subtracting or adding 10 stitches for every 5cm/2in.
Patchwork cushion front Each patch for this design needs to be 8cm/3¼in square (smaller size), 12cm/4¾in square (larger size).

Above: An example of the cushion covers sized up and down from the original measurements given in the pattern.

117

Timeless and true Fair Isle

*Fair Isle is the original multi-coloured, patterned knitting
from the Shetland Island of that name. There
are many pale imitations, but it is the colour sequence that
sets the true Fair Isle in a class on its
own. Knit a tam-o-shanter and judge for yourself.*

Authentic Fair Isle patterns are
Spanish in origin, probably introduced to the island by shipwrecked
sailors of the Armada.

The original Fair Isle knitters worked
all their garments in the round. This
is an ideal method for coloured knitting because the front of the knitting
is always facing you and all rounds
are knitted. When the knitting had to
be divided, as at the underarm, the
yarns were broken off at the end of
each row and rejoined at the beginning of the next. Flat knitting can also
be used for these patterns which are

always worked in stocking stitch.
Fair Isle designs are different from
other coloured knitting in the particular way that the colours are
changed on every row.

The number of stitches worked in
any colour is never so great that the
yarn cannot easily be stranded across
the back of the fabric.

In a traditional pattern sequence, a
broad band is worked in a number of
colours followed by a narrow band
worked in just two or three colours.
The backgrounds are in natural
colours – cream, beige or grey – to set

off the strong, bright colours in the
designs.

To achieve a different look, while
using the same patterns, the colour
emphasis can be reversed so that the
bright colours form the background
and the natural shades the design.
The main aim is to keep the level of
contrast between the background
and the design constant.

No more than two colours at a time
are used in a row, a method that
produces an even fabric of double
thickness as the yarns are carried
across the back of the work when not
being used. The multi-coloured
effect is achieved simply by changing
the background colour on one row
and the contrast colour on the next
row, continuing this sequence
throughout all the patterns.

Abstract or pictorial

In an abstract design the sequence is
two rows in each background colour
and two rows in each contrast colour
to the centre of the chart. The centre
row is worked in the main colours
chosen for the design, to emphasize
them, then the original colours and

attern rows are reversed back down
he chart to the beginning again.
'ictorial designs carry on altering the
olour sequence to the end of the
hart.

Here is just one colour sequence used
or a narrow band of pattern in four
olours.
st row Background A, pattern B.
nd row Background A, pattern C.
rd row Background D, pattern C.
th row As 1st.
th row As 3rd.
th row As 2nd.
'th row As 1st.

air Isle patterns can be knitted
simultaneously with both hands.
The right hand is used throughout to
knit with one colour and the left hand
o knit with the other. This may be
complicated at first glance but once
you have tried it and discovered how
simple it is, knitting coloured pat-
erns in any other way will seem
strange.

*Below: These lovely examples of
uthentic Fair Isle knitting show what
an be achieved once you have mastered
he basic techniques of this ancient art.*

Knitting with yarn in both hands

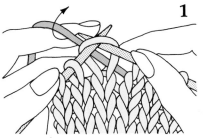

To knit in the continental way
hold the yarn in the left hand, as
for crochet.

To knit with the left hand
1 Insert the right-hand needle

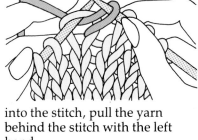

into the stitch, pull the yarn
behind the stitch with the left
hand.
2 Use the right-hand needle to
pull a loop through on to the
needle, where it remains.

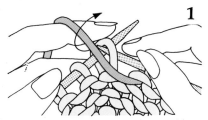

To purl with the left hand
1 Insert the right-hand needle
into the stitch, pull the yarn
across in front of the stitch with
the left hand.

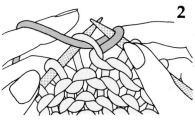

2 Use the right-hand needle to
pull a loop through on to the
needle, where it remains.

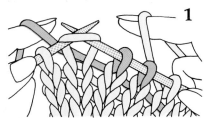

To change colours in a knit row
1 Knit the required number of
stitches in the usual way with the
right hand, stranding the yarn
across the back of the work with
the left hand.

2 Knit the required number of
stitches in the continental way
with the left hand, stranding the
yarn across the back of the work
with the right hand.

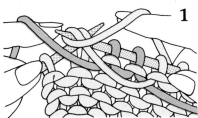

To change colours in a purl row
1 Purl the required number of
stitches in the usual way with the
right hand, stranding the yarn
across the front of the work with
the left hand.

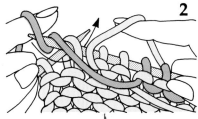

2 Purl the required number of
stitches in the continental way
with the left hand, stranding the
yarn across the front of the work
with the right hand.

Reading a Fair Isle chart

Reading a Fair Isle chart is by no means as daunting as you might suppose. Each square represents one stitch horizontally and one row vertically. The chart shows the multiples of stitches needed for each pattern repeat, plus any edge stitches required to make the pattern match at side seams.

Each colour is coded with a different letter in the instructions, the first colour used as A, the second as B and so on. Each of these letters is represented by a symbol on the chart.

In flat knitting

Right side rows are knitted and wrong side rows are purled.

Begin the first row at the lower right-hand corner of the chart and knit across the row, working any edge stitches shown only at the beginning and end of the row and repeating the multiples of stitches across the row. Begin the second row at the left-hand side of the chart and purl across the row to the end, working the edge stitches as before.

Alternate the rows from right to left on the knit rows and from left to right on the purl rows.

In circular knitting

All the rounds are knitted and the right side of the work is always facing you.

Begin each round at the right-hand edge of the chart and work across to the left-hand edge. Only the multiples of stitches needed for each pattern repeat are worked and any edge stitches are omitted, as in the charts for the tam-o-shanter.

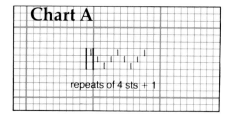

Chart A

repeats of 4 sts + 1

□ = A natural

I = contrast colour

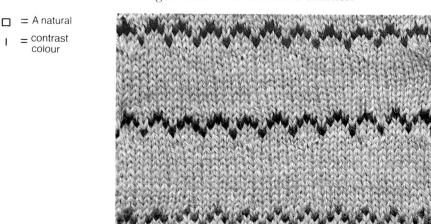

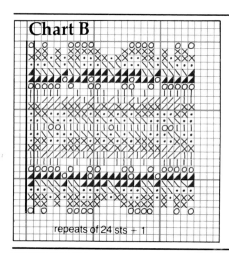

Chart B

repeats of 24 sts + 1

□ = A natural
• = C yellow
× = B brown
O = D blue
\ = F red
▲ = G camel
I = H green
/ = E cream

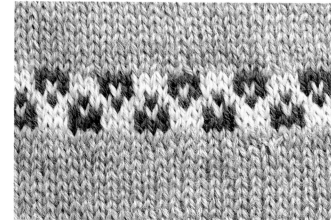

Chart C

repeats of 6 sts + 1

• = C yellow
O = D blue

Chart D

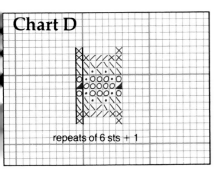

□ = A natural
✕ = B brown
╲ = F red
╱ = E cream
• = C yellow
○ = D blue
◢ = G camel

repeats of 6 sts + 1

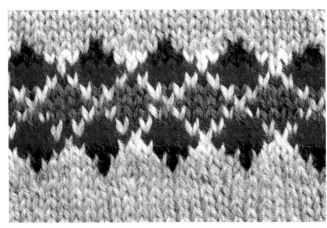

Chart E

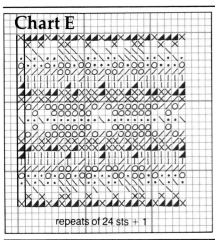

□ = A natural
◢ = G camel
✕ = B brown
╲ = F red
• = C yellow
○ = D blue
╱ = E cream
| = H green

repeats of 24 sts + 1

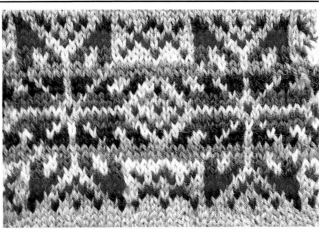

Chart F

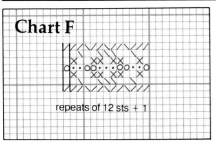

╱ = E cream
╲ = F red
□ = A natural
✕ = B brown
• = C yellow
○ = D blue

repeats of 12 sts + 1

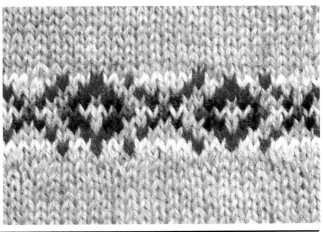

Chart G

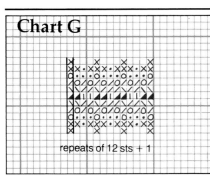

□ = A natural
✕ = B brown
• = C yellow
○ = D blue
╱ = E cream
╲ = F red
◢ = G camel
| = H green

repeats of 12 sts + 1

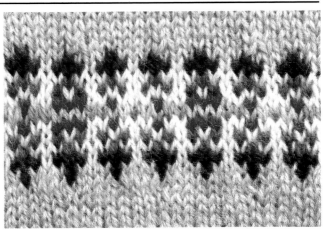

121

Traditional tam-o-shanter

Robert Burns' famous character, Tam o'Shanter, gives his name to the type of beret known as a tammy. The ribbed headband is in the main background colour and the bands of coloured patterns are introduced as you increase stitches towards the widest part. Then the stitches are gradually decreased again to form the crown. You can knit yourself a jaunty tam-o-shanter while trying out one of these lovely traditional Fair Isle patterns. If you want a different pattern from the one illustrated, you could use one of the other charts for the first 32 rounds, filling in with plain rounds if necessary.

Size

Diameter at widest point about 27cm/10¾in
To fit an average adult head

You will need

1×50g ball of Patons Clansman 4 ply (100% wool) in main colour A
1 ball each of same in contrast colours, B, C, D, E, F and G
Set of four 2¾mm/No 12 needles
Set of four 3¼mm/ No 10 needles

Tension

28 st and 36 rows to 10cm/4in over st st and 32 st and 32 rows to 10cm/4in over Fair Isle patt worked on 3¼mm/No 10 needles

Note

To work tam-o-shanter from charts H and I read all rounds from right to left.

Tam-o-shanter

With set of four 2¾mm/No 12 needles and A cast on 144 sts, 48 on each of 3 needles. Work 10 rounds K1, P1 rib.
Next round (inc round) *Rib 2 sts, pick up loop lying between sts and K tbl, rep from * to end. 216 sts.
Change to set of four 3¼mm/No 10 needles. K 3 rounds st st.
Commence Fair Isle patt.
Join in and break off colours as required. Work in patt from Chart H, rep the 6 patt sts 36 times, until 16 rounds have been completed.
Rep these 16 rounds once more.

Shape crown

Next round Using A, *K2 tog, K4, rep from * to end. 180 sts.
Next round Using A, K to end.
Next round Using A, *K2 tog, K7, rep from * to end. 160 sts.
Commence Fair Isle patt. Join in and break off colours as required. Work in patt from Chart I, rep the 20 patt sts 8 times, then dec as indicated on 5th, 7th, 9th, 11th, 12th, 13th, 14th, 15th and 16th rounds, until 16 sts rem.
Break off yarn, thread through rem sts, draw up tightly and fasten off securely.

To make up

Tam-o-shanter requires pressing only. Cut a circle of card 27cm/10¾in in diameter. Insert into tammy and press lightly under a damp cloth with a warm iron, omitting ribbing.

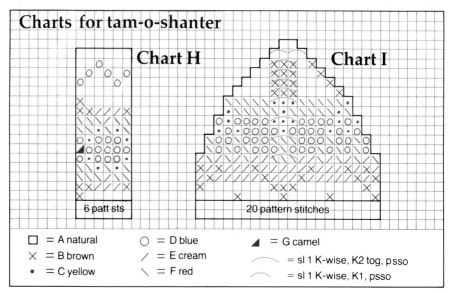

Charts for tam-o-shanter

Chart H — 6 patt sts

Chart I — 20 pattern stitches

☐ = A natural
✕ = B brown
• = C yellow
○ = D blue
╱ = E cream
╲ = F red
◢ = G camel
⌒ = sl 1 K-wise, K2 tog, psso
⌒ = sl 1 K-wise, K1, psso

MULTI-COLOURED KNITTING

Fair Isle effect yarns for a unique pattern

*Mock Fair Isle yarns give a new look to traditional designs.
Knit the pattern in the multi-coloured
wool to achieve a Fair Isle effect without having to change
yarns continuously. Work them in borders
or all-over patterns and get a different result each time!*

Multi-coloured patterns are as old as the history of knitting and although often wrongly referred to as Fair Isle – a term which specifically describes one technique – their origins are world-wide. Arabia, Peru, Spain, France, Scandinavia as well as the Shetlands have all influenced this type of knitting.

Mock Fair Isle knitting, on the other hand, is as new as the technology which made random-dyed yarn possible. The use of one random-coloured yarn to replace several yarns in contrasting colours is an exciting way of adapting old methods to create new effects.

You can use any knitting pattern given in chart form which involves knitting with at least two colours in a row to form a double fabric, with the yarn stranded across the back, see page 119. Only two yarns are used throughout to achieve mock Fair Isle patterns – one plain and one in random colours. Because you do not control the point where a change of colour takes place, as you would with authentic Fair Isle knitting, the effect will vary from row to row.

The charts given overleaf can all be used for mock Fair Isle knitting. Six of them are border patterns, two of which have been incorporated into the combination of border patterns used to form the design on the yoke of the cardigans.

The other six charts are for all-over patterns which can be used for any classic stocking stitch design, working the pattern all over the fabric. All the patterns use the same multiples of stitches so any of them can be used for the yoke of the cardigan, either in a combination of border patterns or as an all-over pattern for the yoke section only. You could use them on just the front of a man's slipover.

For those of you who prefer to control the pattern, all of these charts can be used bringing in the colours of your choice as and when you wish.

Above: Sample showing different colourway. Below: Close up view of cardigan showing the unusual effect mock Fair Isle can achieve.

123

Mock Fair Isle border patterns

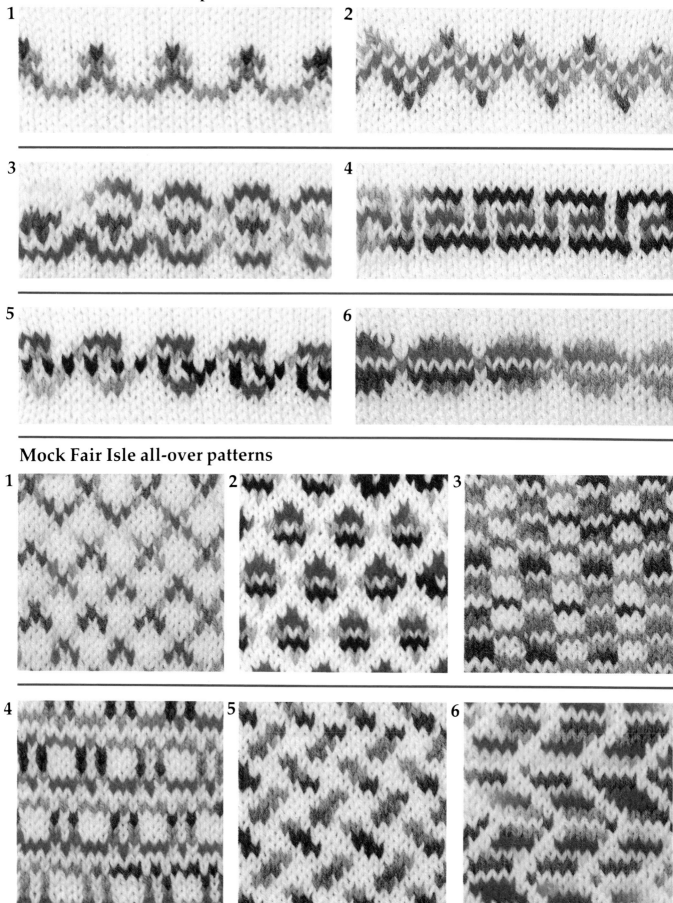

Mock Fair Isle all-over patterns

all patterns multiples of 6sts plus 1

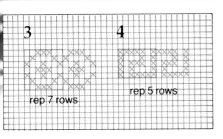

rep 5 rows   rep 6 rows

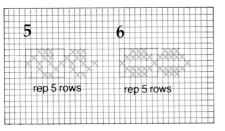

rep 7 rows   rep 5 rows

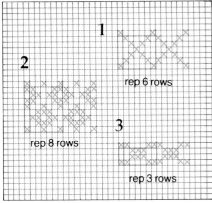

rep 5 rows   rep 5 rows

all patterns multiples of 6sts plus 1

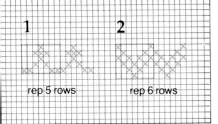

rep 6 rows

rep 8 rows

rep 3 rows

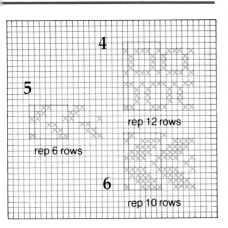

rep 12 rows

rep 6 rows

rep 10 rows

Classic cardigans with mock Fair Isle

This stylish V-neck design shows just how effective mock Fair Isle can look.

The back and fronts, are worked in one piece to avoid shoulder seams spoiling the pattern sequence of the multi-coloured yoke. The sleeves are knitted from underarm seam to underarm seam with a central panel worked in the same direction to match the yoke. Neat patch pockets complete the theme.

Sizes

To fit 81 [86:91:97:102:107]cm/
32 [34:36:38:40:42]in bust
Length to shoulder,
64 [66:66:69:69:69]cm/
25 [26:26:27:27:27]in
Sleeve seam, 47 [47:47:49:49:49]cm/
18½ [18½:18½:19¼:19¼:19¼]in
The figures in [] refer to the 86/34, 91/36, 97/38, 102/40 and 107cm/42in sizes respectively

You will need

7 [8:8:9:9:10]×50g balls of Lister-Lee
  Richmond Double Knitting
  (45% nylon, 40% acrylic,
  15% wool) in main colour A
1 [2:2:2:2:2]×50g balls of Lister-Lee
  Richmond Fair Isle Effect
  (45% nylon, 40% acrylic,
  15% wool) in contrast colour B
One pair 3¼mm/No 10 needles
One pair 4mm/No 8 needles
Five buttons

Tension

22 sts and 28 rows to 10cm over st st worked on 4mm/No 8 needles

Back and fronts

With 3¼mm/No 10 needles and A cast on 97 [103:109:115:121:127] sts and beg at lower edge of back.
1st row (Rs) P1, *K1, P1, rep from * to end.
2nd row K1, *P1, K1, rep from * to end.
Rep these 2 rows for 5cm/2in ending with a Ws row.
Change to 4mm/No 8 needles.
Beg with a K row cont in st st until work measures 48 [50:50:53:53:53]cm/
19 [19¾:19¾:20¾:20¾:20¾] in from beg, ending with a P row.
Join in B. Work first 42 rows of patt from chart.
Border patterns 1 and 3 from this page are used as part of the mock Fair Isle yoke of the cardigan.
The chart overleaf incorporates four more border patterns, all of them worked over the same number of stitches, so that you can choose your own pattern combinations to create a different Fair Isle effect.

Divide for right front

43rd row Working in patt from chart, K36 [39:42:45:48:51] sts for right shoulder, leave rem sts on spare length of thread for back neck and left shoulder.
Complete right shoulder first. Cont in patt from chart until the 84th row has been completed, then with A only inc one st at front edge at beg of next and every foll 6th row until there are 48 [51:54:57:60:63] sts.
Cont with A only in st st until work measures same as back down to top of ribbing ending with a P row and inc one st at end of last row on 1st, 3rd and 5th sizes only.
49 [51:55:57:61:63] sts. Change to 3¼mm/No 10 needles.
Beg with a 2nd row work 5cm/2in rib as given at beg of back. Cast off in rib.

Below: The back and fronts are knitted in one continuous piece to avoid shoulder seams spoiling the pattern.

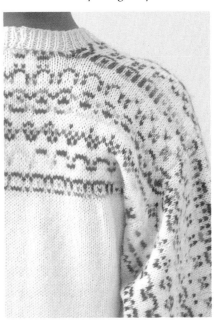

Chart for mock Fair Isle

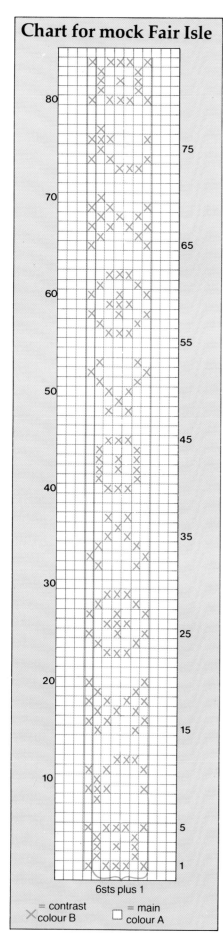

6sts plus 1

✕ = contrast colour B   ☐ = main colour A

With Rs of work facing, 4mm/No 8 needles and A, rejoin yarn to rem sts on thread, cast off first 25 sts for back neck, join in B and keeping 43rd row of chart correct, patt to end. Complete left front to match right front, reversing all shaping.

Sleeves

With 4mm/No 8 needles and A cast on 85 [85:85:91:91:91] sts and work from side edge to side edge. Beg with a K row work 9cm/3½in st st, ending with a P row.
Join in B. Patt 84 rows from chart. Break off B.
Using A only work a further 9cm/3½in st st. Cast off loosely.

Cuffs

With Rs of sleeve facing, 3¼mm/No 10 needles and A, pick up and K122 sts along one side edge of sleeve.
Next row (dec row) *K2 tog, P2 tog, rep from * to last 2 sts, K2 tog. 61 sts.
Beg with a 1st row work 8cm/3in rib as given for back. Cast off in rib.

Pockets (make 2)

With 4mm/No 8 needles and A cast on 37 sts. Join in B. Work 1st to 30th patt rows from chart inc one st at each end of last row. Break off B. Change to 3¼mm/No 10 needles. Beg with a 1st row work 6 rows rib as given for back. Cast off in rib.

Button band

With Rs of work facing, 3¼mm/No 10 needles and A, pick up

evenly and K188 [192:192:196:196:196] sts from centre back neck and down left front edge. Beg with a 2nd row work 9 rows rib as given for back, inc one st at centre back neck on first row. Cast off in rib.

Buttonhole band

With Rs of work facing, 3¼mm/No 10 needles and A, pick up evenly and K188 [192:192:196:196:196] sts up right front edge to centre back neck. Beg with a 2nd row work 3 rows rib as given for back, inc one st at centre back neck on first row.
4th row (buttonhole row) Rib 4 sts, cast off 2 sts, *rib 25 [26:26:27:27:27] sts, cast off 2 sts, rep from * 3 times more, rib to end.
5th row Rib to end, casting on 2 sts above those cast off in previous row. Work 4 more rows rib. Cast off in rib.

To make up

Press under a dry cloth with a cool iron. Sew other side edge of sleeves to back and front edges of cardigan, taking care to match patt exactly. Join side and sleeve seams. Join button and buttonhole bands at centre back neck. Sew on pockets, lower edge to come at top of ribbing. Sew on buttons.

Note: The patterns take on a totally different look simply by using a different combination of background colour and mock Fair Isle yarn as seen on page 123.

The pattern pieces

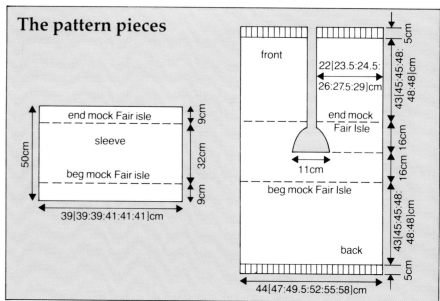

Traditional Scandinavian coloured knitting

Patterns from Norway, Finland, Sweden and Denmark are grouped together under this heading. The authentic designs used only two colours in a row and were inspired by regional flora and fauna. Use them in bands across the yoke and sleeves against a seeded background pattern.

Centuries ago knitting was a very important peasant activity in the remote Scandinavian communities. The traditional garments were mittens, socks, pull-on hats and jerseys, practical with very little scope for frivolities, they all had to serve the same purpose – warmth and comfort to off-set harsh weather conditions. To compensate, the designs were lively using boldly contrasting colours.

Each country in the region has adapted and developed designs from the same source, so ideas overlap. These themes are easily recognizable and distinguish the patterns from Fair Isle knitting.

Snowflake motifs, reindeer and pine trees are common to all regions, also small, all-over patterns, known as 'seedings'. Other designs feature gaily-coloured peasant figures, birds, flowers and geometric repeating patterns.

Below: Your fingers will itch to begin knitting these beautiful, traditional Scandinavian patterns. Experiment by knitting up squares from the charts.

In authentic patterns, only two colours are used in a row on a stocking stitch fabric, working the design from a chart (see page 120), stranding or weaving the yarn not in use across the back of the work (see page 132). The background colour can be pale with a darker colour picking out the pattern, or vice versa. Norwegian designs in black on white are particularly striking. All the regions introduced bright colours which originally depended upon what natural dye materials were available. Modern versions of these patterns use a range of paintbox colours, or soft pastels as chosen for the jersey in this chapter. **Stag designs** vary from magnificent reindeer with full antlers to gentle does and fauns. They make suitable motifs on the front or back of a man's jersey.

Snowflake designs are as numerous as the crystals themselves. They can be worked as a single motif or as all-over patterns, depending on their size. Use them to highlight the yoke of a jersey.

Peasant figures can be used one or two at a time as a motif, or linking

Stag design

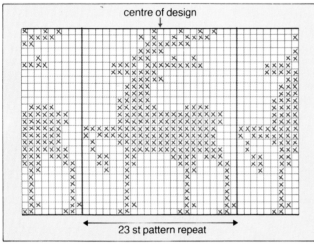

23 st pattern repeat

With A cast on multiples of 23 sts plus two, eg 48, or position 25 sts as a single motif.
1st row (Rs) K1 A, *K1 A, join in B, K2 B, K4 A, K2 B, K7 A, K2 B, K5 A, rep from * to last st, K1 A.
Beg with a P row and 2nd row of chart, cont in patt until 27 rows have been completed.

Snowflake design

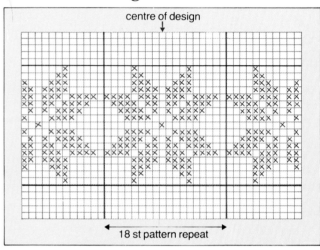

18 st pattern repeat

With A cast on multiples of 18 sts plus one, eg 37, or position 19 sts as a single motif.
1st row (Rs) *K5 A, join in B, K1 B, K7 A, K1 B, K4 A, rep from * to last st, K1 A.
Beg with a P row and 2nd row of chart, cont in patt until 18 rows have been completed.

Peasant figures

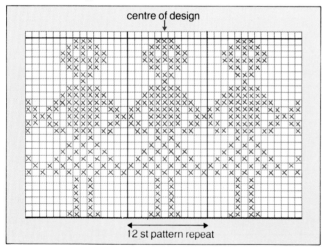

12 st pattern repeat

With A cast on multiples of 12 sts plus one, eg 25, or position 13 sts as a single motif.
1st row (Rs) *K4 A, join in B, K2 B, K1 A, K2 B, K3 A, rep from * to last st, K1 A.
Beg with a P row and 2nd row of chart, cont in patt until 26 rows have been completed.

Geometric design

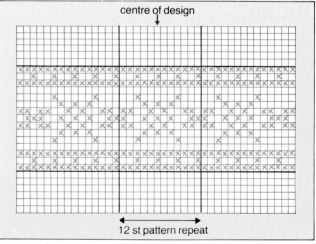

12 st pattern repeat

With B cast multiples of 12 sts plus one, eg 25.
1st row (Rs) With B, K to end.
2nd row With B, P1, join in A, *P2A, P1B, rep from * to end.
3rd row With B, K to end. Beg with a P row and 4th row of chart, cont in patt until 16 rows are completed.

hands as a border, similar to a string of paper dolls – great fun on a child's garment!
Geometric designs of all shapes and sizes are used one above the other in bands as all-over fabrics, or as borders separating one type of motif from another. They are not suitable as single motifs.
Pine tree designs vary from simplis-tic outlines to full Christmas tree shapes. Work them as a border or combine them with other motifs on the yoke of a jersey or cardigan.
Seeding patterns are very tiny and are used specifically as all-over patterns, particularly at points where shaping is required. Use them on the body and sleeves of a jersey to draw attention to the yoke featuring an impressive stag motif.
The jersey given in this chapter has a simple all-over seeding pattern and a snowflake design across the yoke and sleeve tops. The method for positioning other motifs is given in the Professional Touch using the reindeer as an example. You could, of course, choose your own motif to use instead of either of these.

Pine tree design

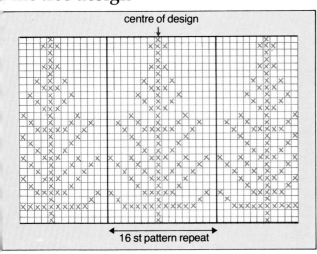

centre of design

16 st pattern repeat

With A cast on multiples of 16 sts plus one, eg 33, or position 17 sts as a single motif.
1st row (Rs) *K8 A, join in B, K1 B, K7 A, rep from * to last st, K1 A.
Beg with a P row and 2nd row of chart, cont in patt until 27 rows have been completed.

Seeding pattern

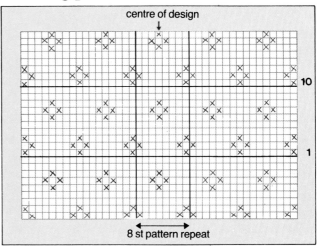

centre of design

8 st pattern repeat

With A cast on multiples of 8 sts plus one, eg 25.
1st row (Rs) Join in B, *K1 B, K7 A, rep from * to last st, K1 B.
Beg with a P row and 2nd row of chart, cont in patt until 10 rows have been completed. Repeat these 10 rows for an all-over pattern.

PROFESSIONAL TOUCH

Positioning a motif accurately

Determine the exact centre of the motif you wish to use and the centre of the background fabric. Check that sufficient rows remain to complete the motif and that it is positioned clear of any shaping.
For example, you can feature the stag motif in this chapter on either side of the yoke and head of the sleeves of the jersey, instead of the band of snowflakes. (You cannot work this as a central motif as the front neck shaping will interfere.)
Complete the armhole shaping on the body. The centre stitch on the motif is the 12th, as marked.

Working from chart

Work the first four rows from the jersey chart and begin the stag on the 5th row. The centre stitch of the body is the 45th stitch so a stag is positioned, to the nearest stitch, centrally on the 44 stitches on either side of the yoke, as follows:
5th row (Rs) K10 A, K2 B, K4 A, K2 B, K7 A, K2 B, K17 A, K1 A for centre st, now work back across the chart from the 44th st from left to right to reverse the position of the stag on the other side of the yoke.
6th row Beg at the right-hand edge of the stag chart, P9 A, P2 B, P4 A, P2 B, P7 A, P2 B, P18 A, P1 A for centre st, now work back across the chart from the 44th st from left to right to reverse the position.
Continue working the 27 rows of the stag in this way, then purl

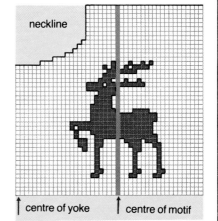

neckline

centre of yoke   centre of motif

one row with A.
Work from the 31st row of the jersey chart to complete the yoke, noting that 2 extra rows have been worked.
Work the head of the sleeves in the same way, noting that 2 extra rows have been worked.

Norwegian-style jersey

The crew-necked jersey features the traditional dropped shoulder line of a Norwegian design.

A small seeding design is used as an all-over pattern on the body and sleeves. At the yoke level and the top of the sleeves a geometric border is worked and the garment is completed with a broad band of snowflake motifs.

Sizes

To fit 86–91cm/34–36in bust
Length to shoulder, 61cm/24in
Sleeve seam, 49cm/19¼in

You will need

8 × 50g balls of Scheepjeswol Luzern (55% wool, 45% acrylic) in main colour A
4 balls of same in contrast colour B
One pair 4mm/No 8 needles
One pair 5mm/No 6 needles
Set of four 4mm/No 8 needles pointed at both ends

Tension

20 sts and 24 rows to 10cm/4in over patt worked on 5mm/No 6 needles

Back

With 4mm/No 8 needles and B cast on 101 sts.
1st row (Rs) K1, *P1, K1, rep from * to end.
2nd row P1, *K1, P1, rep from * to end.
Rep these 2 rows for 5cm/2in, ending with a 2nd row. Change to 5mm/No 6 needles. Commence border and seeding patt.
1st row (Rs) With B, K to end.
2nd row With B, P to end. Join in A.
3rd row K1 A, *K3 B, K1 A, rep from * to end.
4th row P2 A, *P1 B, P3 A, rep from * to last 3 sts, P1 B, P2 A.
5th row With A, inc in first st, K to last 2 sts, inc in next st, K1. 103 sts.
6th row With A, P to end.
7th row K1 B, *K5 A, K1 B, rep from * to end.
8th row With A, P to end.
9th row With A, K to end.
10th row P3 A, *P1 B, P5 A, rep from * to last 4 sts, P1 B, P3 A.
11th row With A, K to end.
Rep the 6th to 11th rows until work

Left: A typical Scandinavian design.

measures 39cm/15¼in from beg, ending with a Ws row.

Shape armholes

Keeping patt correct as set, cast off 7 sts at beg of next 2 rows. 89 sts. Cont without shaping until work measures about 41cm/16¼in from beg, ending with a 6th patt row. Beg with a K row cont in st st, working yoke patt from chart to end. Cast off with B.

Front

Work as given for back, shaping neck as shown on chart.

Sleeves

With 4mm/No 8 needles and B cast on 37 sts. Work 5cm/2in K1, P1 rib as given for back, ending with a 1st row.
Next row (inc row) Rib 3 sts, *K1, P twice into next st, rep from * to last 2 sts, rib 2. 53 sts.
Change to 5mm/No 6 needles.

Work in border and seeding patt as given for back, inc one st at each end of 5th row as given and every foll 4th row, working extra sts into patt, until there are 89 sts and work measures about 37cm/14½in, ending with a 6th patt row. Beg with a K row cont in st st without shaping, working in patt from chart until 30 rows have been completed, then work first 3 rows of chart again. Cast off loosely with B.

Neckband

Join shoulder seams. With Rs of work facing, set of four 4mm/No 8 needles and B, pick up and K33 sts across back neck, 22 sts down left front neck, 11 sts across front neck and 22 sts up right front neck. 88 sts. Cont in rounds of K1, P1 rib for 8cm/3¼in. Cast off loosely in rib with B.

To make up

Do not press. Sew in sleeves, setting in last 8 rows to cast off sts at armholes. Join side and sleeve seams. Fold neckband in half to Ws and sl st down.

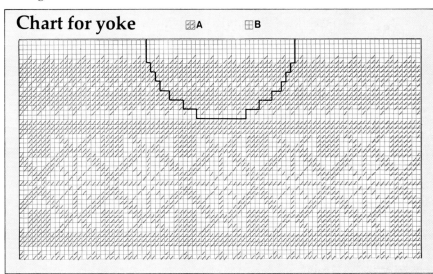

Chart for yoke ▨A ⊞B

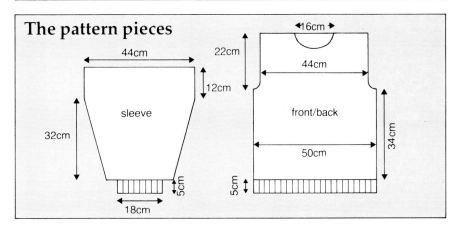

The pattern pieces

44cm — sleeve — 32cm — 18cm — 5cm
22cm — 16cm — 44cm — front/back — 50cm — 34cm — 12cm — 5cm

More Multi-Coloured Patterns

*In jacquard knitting a single, multi-coloured motif or repeats
of the motif forming a pattern are used to highlight
basic garments. Random pictorial and regular geometric
collage patterns produce all-over fabrics.
These techniques use many colours in any one row.*

Jacquard, random pictorial and regular geometric collage patterns (also called intarsia knitting), use any number of colours in the same row and are worked in stocking stitch.

It is possible to work a small jacquard design using only three colours in any row, by stranding the yarns across the back of the fabric. To strand more than three colours makes the fabric clumsy and untidy. In a random pictorial pattern small areas may have the yarn stranded or woven in across the back, while larger areas need to be worked with

Weaving in yarns across the fabric

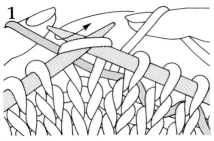 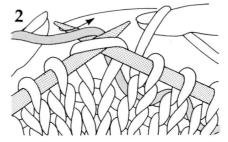 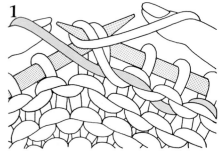

Working a knit row
Keep the yarns at the back of the work throughout and repeat the following action each time a new colour is brought into use.
1 Knit the first stitch with the first colour in the right hand.

2 On the second and every following *alternate* stitch in the first colour, insert the right-hand needle from front to back into the stitch. Use the left hand to place the contrast yarn not being used over the top of the right-hand needle, then knit the stitch with the first colour. The stitches in between are knitted in the usual way.

Working a purl row
Keep the yarns at the front of the work throughout, and repeat the following action each time a new colour is brought into use.
1 To alternate the position of the weaving, purl the first two stitches with the first colour in the right hand.

Working jacquard patterns from charts

Jacquard motifs or repeating patterns use more than two colours in a row. Working from charts, the first and odd-numbered rows read from right to left and the second and even-numbered rows from left to right.

Below: A sample showing a rose motif in double knitting yarn. Embroider the stem afterwards in stem stitch.

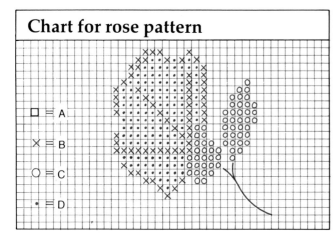

Chart for rose pattern

□ = A
× = B
O = C
• = D

separate balls of colour. In consequence some areas of the fabric will be of double thickness and others of single thickness so it is particularly important to keep the tension regular and even – otherwise you will emphasize the irregularities already inherent in the design.

The correct method for working all large jacquard motifs, all-over-pictorial or geometric collage patterns and wide vertical stripes is to use small, separate balls of yarn for each colour. As each new colour is brought into use loop it round the previous one to avoid leaving a gap in the fabric. Work with short lengths of each contrast colour or the yarns will become very tangled and difficult to unravel. An alternative is to use bobbins – see Professional Touch overleaf. These patterns form fabrics of single thickness as the yarns are not stranded across the back of the work.

Joining in new colours

On jacquard and pictorial patterns when more than four stitches have to be worked in one colour, weave in the yarn on every alternate stitch. This avoids long, loose strands of yarn on the back of the fabric which catch and snag in wear.

On wide vertical stripes and regular geometric collage patterns, loop each new colour round the last stitch in the previous colour on every row. If you do not, you will produce unjoined stripes or shapes of each colour.

On large motifs and random pictorial patterns, loop the new colour yarn round the last stitch in the previous yarn in any row where the same number of stitches have been worked in one colour, to avoid a gap in the fabric. With such patterns and motifs, however, some stitches will inevitably overlap other areas of colour – in which event the yarn will automatically be looped and the fabric closed.

Changing colours in wide vertical stripes

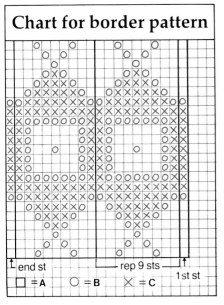

2 On the third and every following *alternate* stitch in the first colour, insert the right-hand needle from right to left into the stitch. Use the left hand to place the contrast yarn not in use across the top of the right-hand needle, then purl the stitch with the first colour. The stitches in between are purled in the usual way.

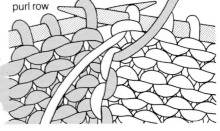

knit row   purl row

Working a knit row
Keep the yarns at the back of the work throughout and repeat the following for each new colour.
Knit across the stitches in the first colour. Take this end of yarn over the top of the next colour to be used and drop it. Pick up the next colour under this strand of yarn and take it over the strand ready to knit the next stitch.

Working a purl row
Keep the yarns at the front of the work throughout and repeat the following for each new colour.
Purl across the stitches in the first colour. Take this end of yarn over the top of the next colour to be used and drop it. Pick up the next colour under this strand of yarn and take it over the strand ready to purl the next stitch.

Chart for border pattern

end st — rep 9 sts — 1st st

□ = A   O = B   X = C

Baby-size jerseys in hexagons and stripes

This pattern is very simple, with no shaping at all – a very good one on which to start collage knitting. Each jersey sports six colours in every row, so wind the yarns on to bobbins first to avoid getting into a tangle when changing colours.

If you cannot decide between the hexagons and the stripes, why not treat baby and knit them both.

Sizes

To fit 46cm/18in chest
Length to shoulder, 28cm/11in
Sleeve seam, 19cm/7½in

You will need

Striped jersey 1×50g ball of Robin Columbine Double Knitting (60% acrylic, 40% nylon) in main colour A
1 ball of same in each of 6 contrast colours B, C, D, E, F and G

Hexagon jersey 1×50g ball of Robin Columbine Double Knitting (60% acrylic, 40% nylon) in main colour A
1 ball of same in each of 6 contrast colours B, C, D, E, F and G
One pair 3mm/No 11 needles
One pair 3¾mm/No 9 needles
Four buttons

Tension

24 sts and 32 rows to 10cm/4in over st st worked on 3¾mm/No 9 needles

Striped jersey front

With 3mm/No 11 needles and A cast on 62 sts.
1st row (Rs) K2, *P2, K2, rep from * to end.
2nd row P2, *K2, P2, rep from * to end.
Rep these 2 rows 5 times more.
Break off A.**

Above: The back and front are knitted exactly the same on these simple jerseys.

Change to 3¾mm/No 9 needles.
Beg with a K row cont in st st and vertical stripes as foll, twisting colours where they join on every row:
Next row K11 B, 10 C, 10 D, 10 E, 10 F, 11 G.
Next row P11 G, 10 F, 10 E, 10 D, 10 C, 11 B.
Rep these 2 rows until work measures 26cm/10¼in from beg, ending with a Ws row. Break off contrast colours. Join in A. K one row.
Beg with a 2nd row work 5 rows rib as given for welt.
***Next row** (buttonhole row) (K2, P2, K2, P2 tog, yon) twice, rib to last 16 sts, (yrn, P2 tog, K2, P2, K2) twice.

Knitting with bobbins

Small bobbins can be used to keep the various colours free of tangles. Wind each colour round a separate bobbin. As each one needs to be brought into use it hangs ready at the back of the work and tangle-free.
1 To make a bobbin, simply cut the shape from stiff cardboard, making a narrow opening at the top of each, as shown, to allow the yarn to unravel. Cut one bobbin for each colour used.

2 Wind a small amount of yarn round the bobbin, passing the working end of the yarn through the slit.
As each new colour is required, join it in with a slip loop. Work the number of stitches with each colour after first twisting it round the last stitch in the previous colour. When a colour is not in use, leave the bobbin hanging at the back of the work in readiness for when it is required again.

bobbin made from card

Work 2 more rows in rib. Cast off in rib.

Striped jersey back

Work as given for front, omitting buttonholes.

Striped jersey sleeves

With 3mm/No 11 needles and A cast on 30 sts. Work 11 rows rib as given for back.
Next row (inc row) Rib 4, *pick up loop lying between needles and K tbl – **called M1**, rib 2, rep from * 10 times more, M1, rib 4. 42 sts. Break off A.****
Change to 3¾mm/No 9 needles. Beg with a K row cont in st st and vertical stripes as foll, twisting colours where they join on every row:
Next row K11 B, 10 C, 10 D, 11 E.
Next row P11 E, 10 D, 10 C, 11 B. Rep these 2 rows until sleeve measures 19cm/7½in from beg, ending with a Ws row. Cast off loosely.

Hexagon jersey front

Work as given for striped jersey front to **.
Change to 3¾mm/No 9 needles. Beg with a K row cont in st st and hexagon patt as foll, using separate small balls of each colour and twisting colours where they join on every row:
1st row K11 B, 10 C, 10 D, 10 E, 10 F 11 G.
Beg with a P row work 3 rows st st in colours as now set.
5th row K2 E, 8 B, 2 F, 8 C, 2 G, 8 D, 2 B, 8 E, 2 C, 8 F, 2 D, 8 G, 2 E.
Cont in this way working in patt from chart until 72 rows have been completed. Break off contrast colours.

Join in A. K one row. Complete as given for striped jersey front from *** to end.

Hexagon jersey back

Work as given for front, omitting buttonholes.

Hexagon jersey sleeves

Work as given for striped jersey sleeves to ****.
Change to 3¾mm/No 9 needles.

Beg with a K row cont in st st, working in patt as given on chart until 48 rows have been completed. Cast off loosely.

To make up
Press each piece under a dry cloth with a warm iron.
Both versions Lap front shoulder over back and st down at armhole edge. Sew in sleeves. Join side and sleeve seams. Sew on buttons.

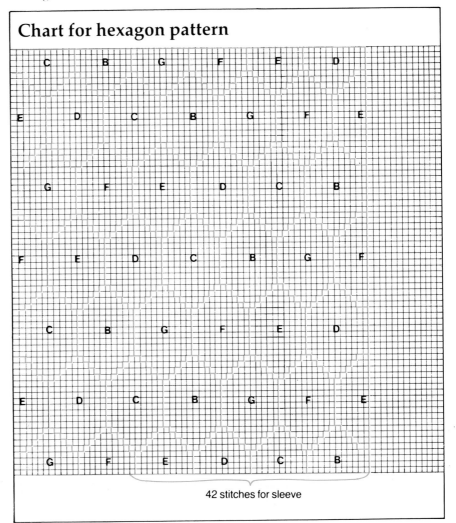

Chart for hexagon pattern

42 stitches for sleeve

APPLIED EMBROIDERY AND BEADS
Swiss darning

*This charming embroidery exactly duplicates the outline of the knitted stitches in plain stocking stitch.
Any motif given in chart form may be used for a design, or you can have fun creating your own. Delicate flowering herbs inspired the lovely motifs on the jersey overleaf.*

Swiss darning can be used to embroider any area of stocking stitch, matching stitch for stitch. Any embroidery, tapestry or coloured knitting design shown in chart form can be adapted but, for the best results, choose a design with clear outline and not too many colours – say, four or five at most.

It is also important to bear in mind that an embroidery or tapestry chart (not a transfer) will show the number of stitches in width and rows in depth but will not give the correct scale of a knitted motif. The reason for this is that knitting takes fewer stitches than rows to work a given measurement. A 10cm/4in square using double knitting yarn will need about 24 stitches and 30 rows, so the chart of a square embroidery or tapestry motif will appear to be squashed down. A tall, rectangular embroidery or tapestry motif will be a square.

Swiss darning forms a double fabric, so it is also a useful way of re-inforcing areas of a garment which receive extra wear. Use a contrasting colour as a patch to strengthen the knees of a pair of trousers for a toddler, or some of the original colour to re-inforce the elbows of a favourite jersey.

When planning a motif work out a suitable position on an existing garment or, if you are about to knit a garment, decide in advance where a motif would be most effective. For example,. you could add a colourful and practical touch to a plain cardigan by knitting and embroidering patch pockets. A rose motif at armhole level would look elegant on a classic jersey and you could work a fun motif on a child's jacket.

Use short lengths of yarn for the embroidery, completing one colour area and fastening off neatly before beginning another colour. In this way you will avoid a daunting tangle of ends to be finished off at the end of the work. Keep the embroidered stitches to the same tension as the knitted stitches and take care not to pull the yarn across the back of the work too tightly or you will pucker the fabric.

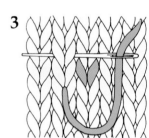

Planning Swiss darning
On a stocking stitch background decide the size and the position for the embroidered design.
Choose a suitable embroidery, tapestry or knitting chart, drawn up on graph paper. If the chart does not already show them, it may help to add the number of stitches in width across the bottom and the

Above: Embroider one of these motifs on to a plain stocking stitch tea cosy in colours to match your china.

How to work Swiss darning

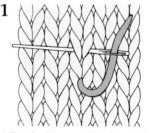

1 Push the needle through from the back to the front at the base of the first stitch to be embroidered and draw the yarn through. *Insert the needle from *right to left* behind the two loops of the same stitch one row above.

2 Draw the yarn through. Insert the needle back into the base of the same stitch and draw the yarn through to the back.

3 Push the needle through from the back to the front at the base of the next stitch to be worked in this colour and to the left of the last stitch. Draw the yarn through. Continue from the * all along the row.

4 At the end of the row insert the needle back into the base of the last stitch worked, then up into the centre of the same stitch and draw

Above: Assortment of equipment needed to draw up and embroider your motifs.

number of rows in depth along the side. Check that these will fit into the area chosen, then mark this out with pins.
For this type of embroidery always use oddments of yarn of the same thickness as the knitted fabric. If the yarn used for embroidery is too thin the knitted stitches will show through; if it is too thick the embroidered design will look clumsy. Check that you have sufficient colours to work the motif. The colours will be coded on the chart, each with a different symbol.

Preparing to embroider
Have the knitted side of the fabric to be embroidered facing you.
Thread a blunt-ended sewing needle with a short length of yarn and make a knot in one end.
Begin at the lower right-hand corner of the motif and work across the knitting from right to left in this colour. Join in a new colour as each area is completed.

4

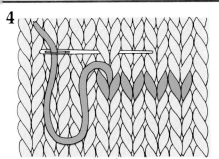

the yarn through. This now becomes the base of the same stitch on the next row above. Insert the needle from *left to right* behind the two loops of this stitch one row above and draw the yarn through. Insert the needle back into the base of the same stitch. Push the needle through at the base of the next stitch to be worked in this colour and to the right of the last stitch.

5

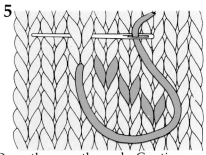

Draw the yarn through. Continue in this way back along the row.
5 To work diagonally in any direction across the fabric, after completing the first stitch, push the needle through from the back to the front at the base of the next stitch one row above and complete this stitch. Continue in this way working one stitch above the next, either to the right or left of the

6

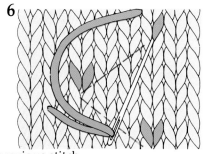

previous stitch.
6 To work at random across the fabric, after completing the first stitch carry the yarn across the back of the fabric and insert the needle into the base of the next stitch to be worked. Complete this stitch, then carry the yarn across the back of the fabric to the next stitch.

137

Tyrolean-style jersey

This stunning design is knitted in separate sections, embroidered with floral motifs worked in Swiss darning and then sewn together. The only shaping is in the sleeves.

Sizes

To fit 86-97cm/34-38in bust loosely
Length to shoulder, 62.5cm/25in
Sleeve seam, 50cm/19¾in

You will need

8×50g balls of DMC Pearl Cotton No 4, (100% cotton)
Embroidery wools or cottons in 13 colours as shown in key overleaf
One pair 3¾mm/No 9 needles
One pair 3mm/No 11 needles

Tension

24 sts and 32 rows to 10cm/4in over st st worked on 3¾mm/No 9 needles

Back and front

Make 9 sections for back and 9 for front. (18 in all).
Body section With 3¾mm/No 9 needles cast on 42 sts. Beg with a K row 58 rows st st. Cast off.

Sleeves

Make 2 each of sections A, B, C, D, E and F. (One for each sleeve).
Section A
With 3¾mm/No 9 needles cast on 36 sts.
Beg with a K row work in st st, inc on st at end of 5th and every foll 8th row until there are 43 sts. Cont without shaping until 58 rows in all have been completed. Cast off.
Section B
Work as given for section A, inc one st at beg of rows, instead of at end.
Section C
With 3¾mm/No 9 needles cast on 43 sts.
Beg with a K row work in st st, inc one st at end of 5th and every foll 8th row until there are 50 sts. Cont without shaping until 58 rows in all have been completed. Cast off.
Section D
Work as given for section C, inc one st at beg of rows, instead of at end.
Section E
With 3¾mm/No 9 needles cast on 50 sts.
Beg with a K row work in st st, inc one st at end of 5th, 13th and 21st rows. Cont without shaping until

28 rows in all have been completed. Cast off.
Section F
Work as given for section E, inc one st at beg of rows, instead of at end.

To make up

Embroider each section from the charts, using colours as coded.

Front

Working from left to right, as illustrated.
Top row dandelion, sage, mint.
Middle row basil, clover, plantain.
Bottom row thyme, ragwort, forget-me-not.

Back

Top row ragwort, mint, plantain.
Middle row forget-me-not, basil, clover.
Bottom row thyme, dandelion, sage.

Left sleeve

Section A sage.
Section B dandelion.
Section C plantain.
Section D thyme.
Section E motifs 4 and 5.
Section F motifs 2 and 3.

Right sleeve

Section A forget-me-not.
Section B clover.
Section C basil.
Section D ragwort.
Section E motifs 2 and 3.
Section F motifs 1 and 5.
Press all pieces lightly under a damp cloth with a cool iron.
Join back and front sections. Join

sleeve sections as shown in diagram.

Ribbed welts

With 3mm/No 11 needles and Rs of work facing, pick up and K111 sts along lower edge of front.
1st row P1, *K1, P1, rep from * to end.
2nd row K1, *P1, K1, rep from * to end.
Rep these two rows for 6cm/2¼in. Cast off loosely in rib.
Work along lower edge of back in same way.

Ribbed top edge

With 3mm/No 11 needles and Rs of work facing, pick up and K125 sts along top edge of front. Work 2.5cm/1in rib as given for welts. Cast off in rib. Work along top edge of back in same way.

Ribbed cuffs

With 3mm/No 11 needles and Rs of work facing, pick up and K47 sts along lower edge of sleeve. Work 5cm/2in rib as given for welts. Cast off in rib. Join cast off edges of back and front top edge for shoulders, leaving about 30cm/12in open in centre for neck. Set in sleeves. Join side and sleeve seams. Press seams, omitting ribbing.

Embroider over seams

With any colour work optional embroidery over all seams, using a slanting st from left to right and back from right to left, feather st or herringbone st.

Right: Work embroidery over all the seams to enhance the individual motifs.

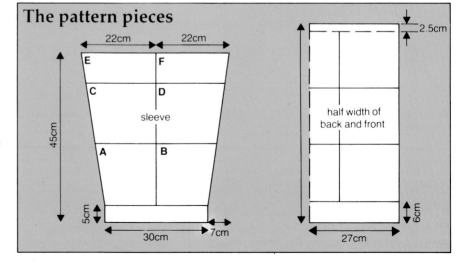

The pattern pieces

Motifs for Swiss darning

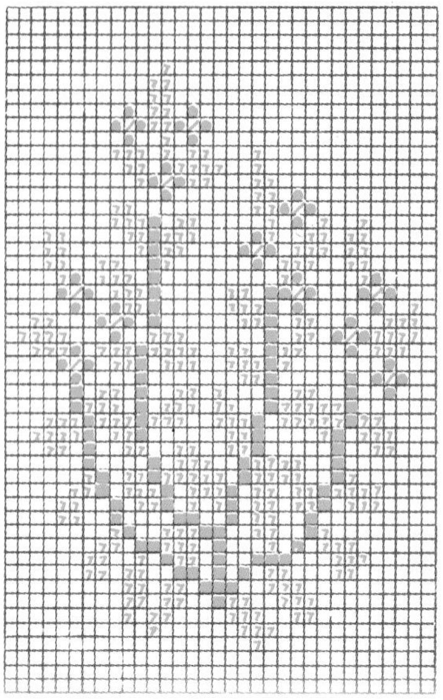

Forget-me-not

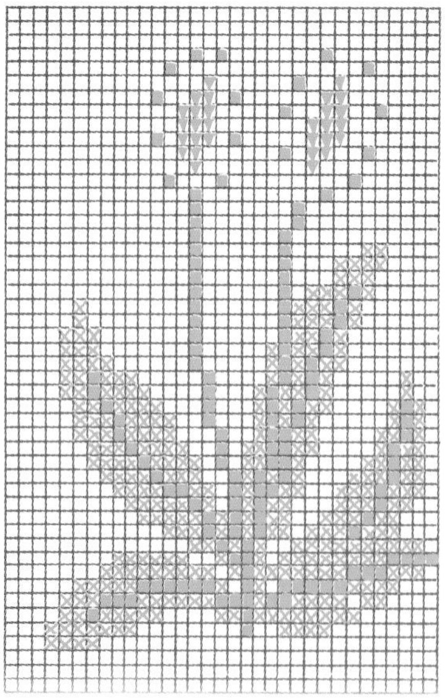

Plantain

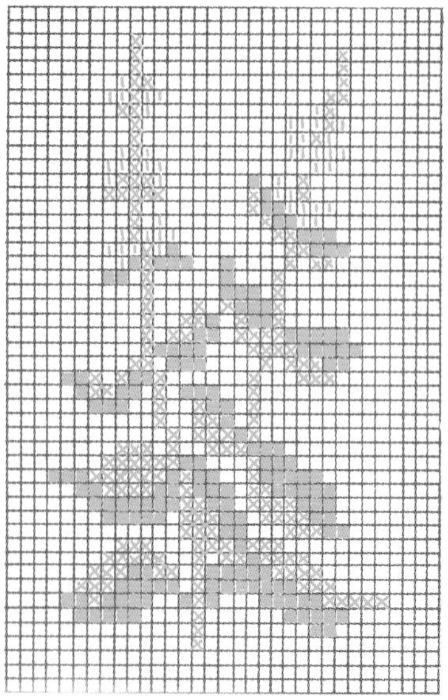

Basil

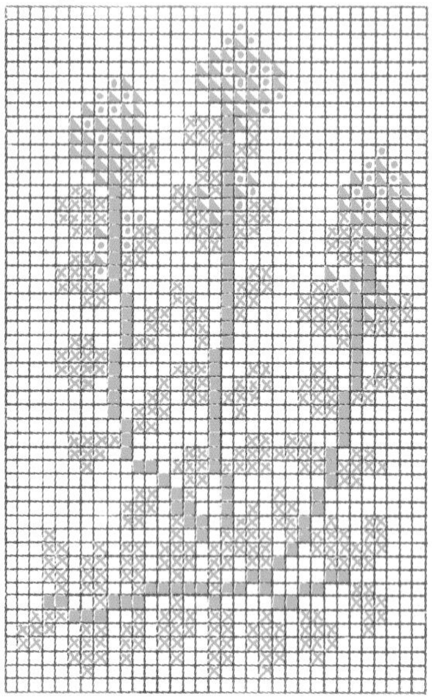

Thyme

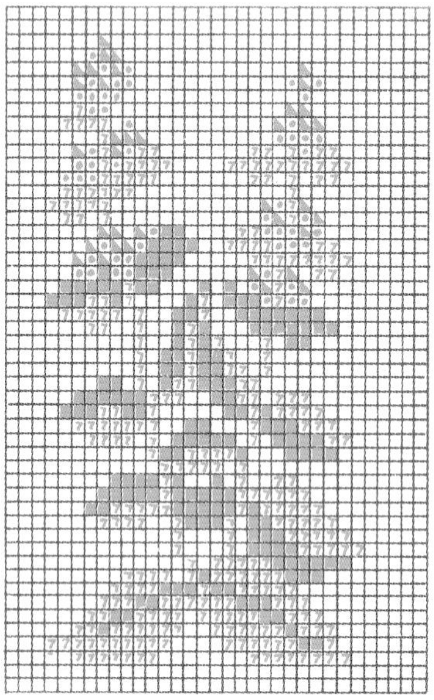

Mint

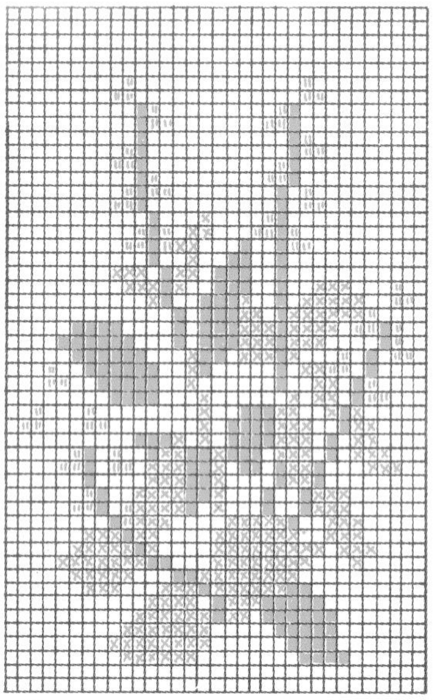

Sage

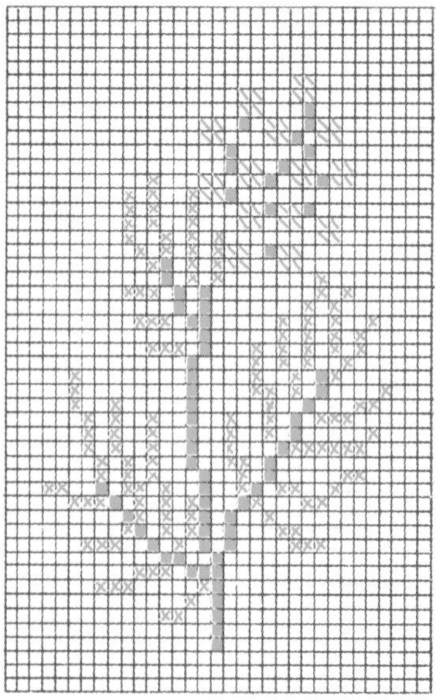

Ragwort

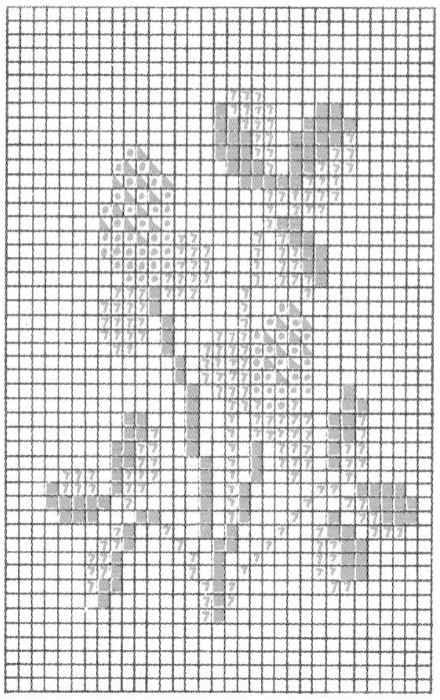

Clover

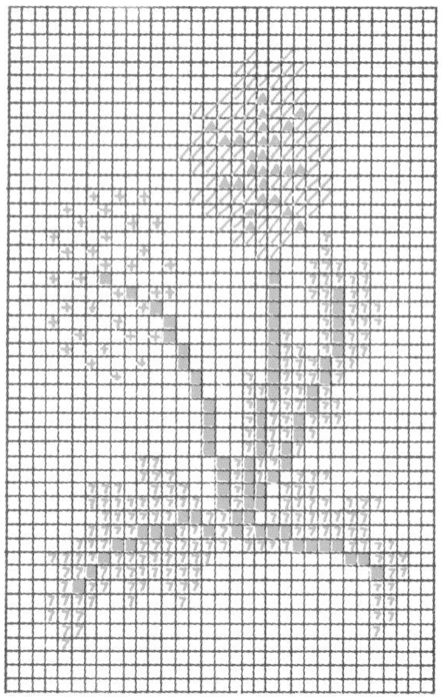

Dandelion

1

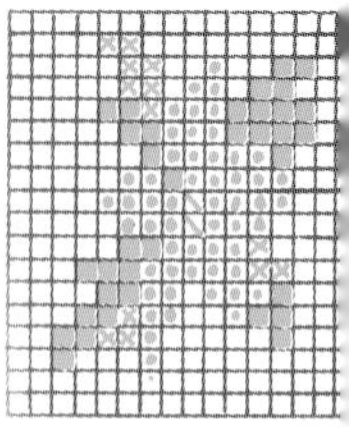

2

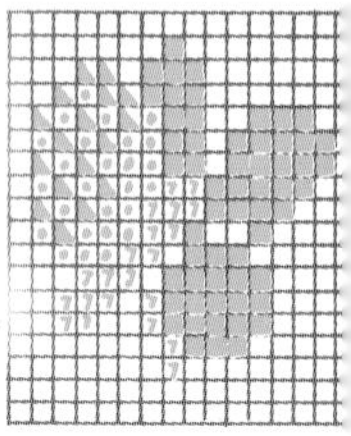

3

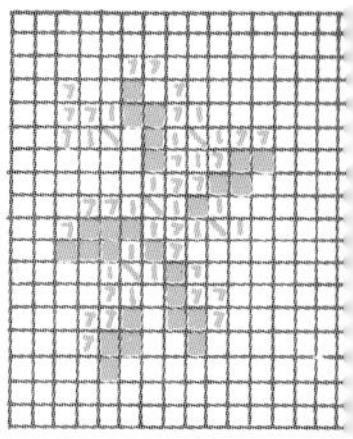

4

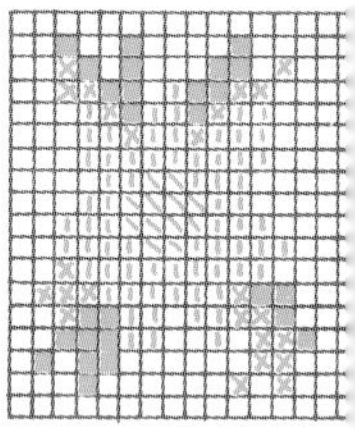

5

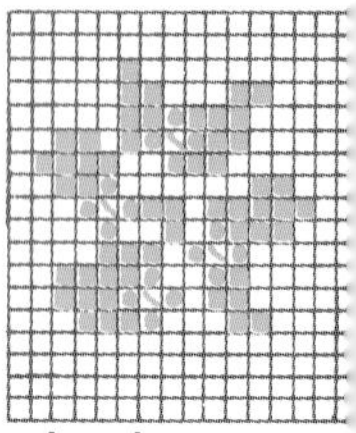

colour key

= lime green

= dark green

= yellow

= pale yellow

= lilac-pink

= silver grey

= mid green

= white

= light brown

= pale pink

= dark brown

= mid pink

= turquoise

140

Experiment with Swiss darning by applying colour to an existing garment. Six stitches have been Swiss darned at random on the paler coloured stripes on this jersey.

Applied embroidery stitches to add patterns to knitted fabrics

Stitching directly on to a knitted background adds decoration without the use of complicated charts or the need to carry yarns across the back of the work. Smocking and checks need some advance planning but the other stitches can be added to existing garments.

In the 18th century fine cotton lace knitting was used to imitate needlepoint lace which was a prized possession. To create the texture of the needlepoint, solid parts of the knitting were embroidered with self-coloured bullion knots. The technique of adding self-coloured embroidery to knitting developed in the 19th century when a much coarser thread was used to knit bedspreads.

Today, we tend to use embroidery on knitting as a way of applying colour to a background fabric. It is a simple way of adding colour in a striking way without actually knitting with several different coloured yarns.

The most popular form of applied embroidery on stocking stitch is the Swiss darning method (see page 136). This chapter gives other variations of background fabrics and embroidery stitches which will give any basic garment added interest.

Applying the embroidery

Work the embroidery after the knitted pieces are completed or apply to an existing garment. If you use the same weight of yarn to embroider on to the knitted fabric, the stitches will look as though they have been knitted in. Work from the right side of the garment and use a blunt-ended sewing needle threaded with your chosen yarn.

Make a knot in the end of the yarn to

Applying honeycomb smocking 1

This example is worked in two colours, one for the knitting and the other for the embroidery. To make the background rib of three purl stitches followed by one knit stitch, cast on multiples of eight stitches plus 3, eg 27. Remember that the width of the fabric will be reduced by about a third

once the smocking has been applied.

To keep the fabric elastic two rows of smocking are worked at a time. Miss the first 8 stitches, insert the needle from back to front through the fabric to the left of the second knit stitch of the row where the smocking is to commence.

1 *Pass the needle across in front of this stitch, the next 3 purl stitches and the next knit stitch from left to right, insert the needle from the front to the back to the right of the last of these stitches and pull the yarn through.** Carry the yarn across the back of the fabric, push the needle through from the back to the front and across the same 5 stitches again, through to the back of the fabric. Draw the stitches together to complete one smocking stitch.

2 Carry the yarn across the back of the fabric to the next knitted rib stitch to the left, 6 rows *above*,

push the needle through from the back to the front *after* the last knit stitch and pull the yarn through.

Repeat steps 1 and 2. Carry the yarn to the next knitted rib stitch to the left, 6 rows *below*, ie the 1st row again, push the needle through from the back to the front *after* the last knit stitch and pull the yarn through. Continue from the * in this way to complete 2 rows of smocking. Miss the next 5 rows above the last rows of smocking and repeat the 2 rows as required.

ensure that it will not pull out. Pull the yarn through leaving about 5cm/2in free above the knot. When the embroidery is completed, secure the final end, unpick the knot and secure this end.

Six embroidery stitches are given in this chapter and the first of the two variations of honeycomb smocking is used to decorate the bodice and sleeves of the child's dress pattern.

Honeycomb smocking is a popular decoration on a knitted rib background. It is used to reduce the width of a fabric, usually at the yoke or cuffs. Extra width must be included in the pattern and for this reason it is not advisable to use this method on an existing garment.

In dressmaking, the fabric required for smocking is about three times the finished width. If this was applied to knitting it would give far too much bulk and so you need only allow about one and a half times the finished width of the smocking.

There are two methods of applying honeycomb smocking to knitting. With the first the embroidery yarn only shows where the stitches are caught together. On the second, the embroidery yarn travels from one group of stitches to another across the surface of the fabric, for added interest.

Open check patterns are easy to incorporate into any basic stocking stitch garment. The horizontal stripes are knitted with the garment and the vertical stripes are embroidered when the pieces are complete.

Cross stitches are most effective as an all-over pattern when worked on a stocking stitch background for a new or existing garment. You can also work individual stitches separately, for example into the centre of every alternate square of a basket stitch pattern, or use them to build up embroidered motifs for a border pattern. To work a long horizontal border of cross stitches in one colour it is easier to make a line of half cross stitches in one direction, then return in the other direction, filling in the other half of each stitch.

Take care not to pull the cross stitches up too tightly or you will pucker the fabric.

Woven bows should be embroidered on to a stocking stitch background. They look most effective worked completely at random, using a different colour for each bow – this is the ideal way of up-dating an existing garment. If the bows are worked closely together they form a fabric with areas of double thickness. Do not pull the bows up too tightly or you will distort the fabric.

Ladder hemstitch is a particularly beautiful way of decorating a lace ladder pattern, where threads of yarn in the fabric link up one group of stitches to the next. It can only be worked in vertical panels and cannot be used on an existing garment.

This is one embroidery stitch which looks more effective worked in a yarn of the same colour as the background fabric.

Applying honeycomb smocking 2

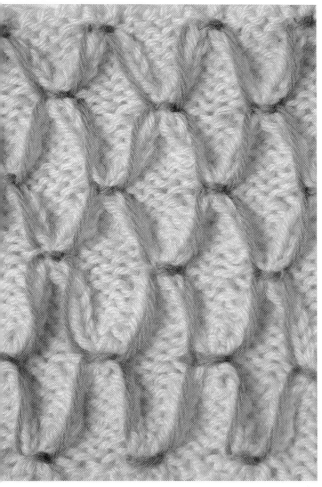

Begin to apply the smocking as for honeycomb smocking 1 to **.

1 Carry the yarn across the back of the fabric, push the needle through from the back to the front in the same place as before, after the knit stitch, draw the stitches together.

Insert the needle from the front to the back to the right of the same knit stitch 6 rows *above* and pull the yarn through.

2 Carry the yarn across the back of the fabric on this row, miss knit one, purl 3, knit one, push the needle through from the back to the front, round these 5 stitches and through to the back of the fabric. Draw the stitches together. Carry the yarn across the back of the fabric on the same row and push the needle through from the back to the front in the same place as before on this stitch.

Insert the needle from the front to the back and to the right of the same knit stitch 6 rows *below* and pull the yarn through.

Continue from the * to the end of the row. Begin again at the right-hand edge of the last row of smocking and work the next 2 rows in the same way, alternating the position of the smocking.

Working open check pattern

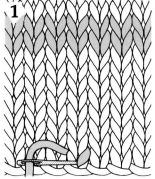

This example is worked on a stocking stitch background of stripes in two colours.
To make the background cast on multiples of 7 stitches plus 6, eg 34, and work 8 rows in main colour and 2 rows in contrast colour.

Applying vertical stripes
Begin at the lower right-hand edge of the fabric, miss the first 6 stitches, insert the needle from back to front at the base of the next stitch and pull the yarn through.

1 *Hold the yarn down with the thumb of the left hand, insert the needle from right to left behind the two loops of the same stitch one row above and pull the yarn through.
2 Insert the needle back into the base of the first stitch and pull the yarn through. Insert the needle from the back to the front at the base of the stitch in the row above and pull the yarn through.

Continue from the * forming a line of chain stitches to the top of the piece.
Miss the next 6 stitches along the lower edge of the fabric, insert the needle from the back to the front at the base of the next stitch and pull the yarn through.
Repeat from * to form another line and continue in this way until the over-checking has been completed.

Working cross stitches

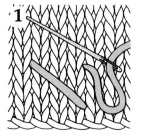

This example is worked in two colours, using one colour for the knitting and a contrast colour for the embroidery.
To make the background cast on multiples of 6 stitches plus 3, eg 27, and work in stocking stitch. Begin at the lower right-hand edge of the fabric, miss the first 3 stitches, insert the needle from back to front to the right of the next stitch and pull the yarn through.**

1 *Working from right to left carry the yarn across the front of the work and insert the needle from the front to the back to the left of the following 3rd stitch on the 4th row *above* and pull the yarn through.
Working from left to right carry the yarn across the back of the fabric, insert the needle from the back to the front to the right of the 3rd stitch along on the same row and pull the yarn through.

2 Working from right to left carry the yarn across the front of the fabric, insert the needle from the front to the back to the left of the 3rd stitch along on the first row and pull the yarn through, miss the next 3 stitches on the same row, insert the needle from the back to the front at the side of the next stitch and pull the yarn through.
Continue from the * to the end of the row. Begin again on the next row above and continue in this way until the required number of rows of cross stitches have been completed.

144

Working ladder hemstitch

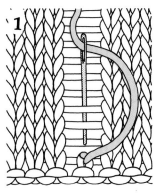

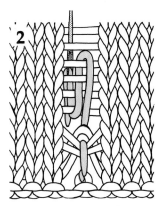

This example is worked in stocking stitch to any shape and size.
To achieve a ladder, cast off the number of stitches to the position for the ladder, allow the next stitch to drop off the left-hand needle.
Unravel the stitch down to the last row, catch the loop of this stitch with a sewing needle threaded with the yarn to be used for embroidery and secure the stitch.
Complete this line of ladder hemstitch before casting off the required number of stitches to the position for the next ladder, or cast off the remaining stitches to complete the piece.

1 *Take the needle across the front of 4 rows of the ladder, push the needle through from the front to the back and out to the front again between the 2nd and 3rd of these threads and pull the yarn through.

2 Push the needle through from the front to the back before the first of the same 4 threads, then out again after the same 4 and pull the yarn through, twisting the pairs of threads.
Continue from the * until all the threads have been hemstitched. Fasten off securely at the top.

Working the woven bows

This example is worked in two colours, using one colour for the knitting and a contrast colour for the embroidery. To make the background cast on multiples of 10 stitches plus 5, eg 25, and work in stocking stitch.
Begin at lower right-hand edge of fabric, miss first 5 stitches, insert the needle from back to front to the right of the next stitch and pull through.

1 *Working from right to left, insert the needle under the two loops of the following 3rd stitch of the 3rd row above and pull the yarn through, miss 2 stitches, insert the needle from the front to the back to the left of the stitch in the first row and pull the yarn through.

2 Carry the yarn across the back of the fabric, push the needle through from the back to the front to the right of the first stitch but one row above, insert the needle under the same 3rd stitch of the 3rd row and pull the yarn through, miss two stitches and insert the needle from the front to the back to the left of the stitch of the 2nd row and pull the yarn through.
Work as step 2 on the 3rd, 4th and 5th rows to complete one bow.
Carry the yarn across the back of the fabric, miss the next 5 stitches, insert the needle from the back to the front to the right of the next stitch on the first row and pull the yarn through.
Continue from the * to complete the row of bows. Miss 3 rows then begin again on the next row above, working the bow over the *first* 5 stitches to alternate the position and continue in this way until the required number of rows have been completed.

Smocked dress for a little girl

Knit this pretty little dress with honeycomb smocking on the bodice and round the sleeves. Choose a colour for the applied smocking that will tone with accessories for a special occasion.

The hem, neck and sleeves have a dainty picot edging and the centre back opening on the bodice is edged with garter stitch and fastens with buttons.

Sizes

To fit 46 [51:56]cm/18 [20:22]in chest
Length to shoulder, 34 [45:51]cm/ 13½ [17¾:20]in
Sleeve seam, 3 [4:5]cm/1¼ [1½:2]in
The figures in [] refer to the 51/20 and 56cm/22in sizes respectively

You will need

5 [6:7] × 50g balls of Twilleys Stalite (100% cotton) in main colour A
1 [1:1] ball of same in contrast colour B for smocking
One pair 2mm/No 14 needles
One pair 3mm/No 11 needles
Three buttons

Tension

30 sts and 36 rows to 10cm/4in over st st worked on 3mm/No 11 needles

Back

With 2mm/No 14 needles and A cast on 128 [146:154] sts. Beg with a K row work 4 rows st st.
Next row (picot hem) K1, *yfwd, K2 tog, rep from * to last st, K1.
Beg with a P row work 5 rows st st. Change to 3mm/No 11 needles. Beg with a K row cont in st st until work measures 24 [32:36]cm/

9½ [12½:14¼]in from picot hem, ending with a P row.
Next row (dec row) K15 [14:18] sts, (K2 tog) 49 [59:59] times, K to end. 79 [87:95] sts.**

Divide for back opening

Next row P39 [43:47] sts, turn and leave rem sts on holder.
Complete left side first.
Next row (Rs) P3, *K1, P3, rep from * to end.
Next row K3, *P1, K3, rep from * to end.
Rep last 2 rows until rib measures 2cm/¾in, ending with a Rs row.

Shape armhole

Cast off 8 sts, patt to end. Cont in rib without shaping until armhole measures 8 [11:13]cm/3¼ [4¼:5]in from beg, ending with a Rs row.

Shape shoulder

Cast off at beg of next and every alt row 6 sts once, 7 [9:11] sts once, then leave rem 18 [20:22] sts on holder.
With Ws of work facing, rejoin yarn to rem sts, cast off first st, P to end.
Complete as given for left side, reversing all shapings.

Front

Work as given for back to **.
P one row, then rep 2 row rib patt as given for back for 2cm/¾in, ending with a Ws row.

Shape armholes

Cast off 8 sts at beg of next 2 rows. 63 [71:79] sts.
Cont in rib without shaping until armholes measure 4 [7:9]cm/

1½ [2¾:3½]in from beg, ending with a Ws row.

Shape neck

Next row Patt 28 [31:34] sts, turn and leave rem sts on holder.
Complete left side first. Cast off at beg of next and every alt row for neck edge 3 sts 3 times, 2 sts 2 [2:3] times, then dec one st at same edge on every row until 13 [15:17] sts rem. Cont without shaping until armhole measures same as back to shoulder, ending at armhole edge.

Shape shoulder

Cast off at beg of next and foll alt row 6 sts once and 7 [9:11] sts once.
With Rs of work facing, rejoin yarn to rem sts, cast off first 7 [9:11] sts for centre front neck, patt to end. Complete to match left side reversing all shapings.

Sleeves

With 2mm/No 14 needles and A cast on 67 [71:75] sts.
Work first 10 rows for picot hem as given for back.
Change to 3mm/No 11 needles.
Work 2cm/¾in rib patt as given for back, ending with a Rs row.
Next row (inc row) Rib 0 [2:4] sts, *inc in next st, rib 4 sts, rep from * 12 times more, inc in next st, rib 1 [3:5] sts. 81 [85:89] sts.
Beg with a K row work in st st until sleeve measures 3 [4:5]cm/ 1¼ [1½:2]in from picot edge, ending with a Ws row.

Shape top

Cast off at beg of next and every row 3 sts twice and 2 sts 18 times.
Next row K1, *K2 tog, rep from * to end.
Cast off rem sts.

Smocking

Work smocking with B on front and back yoke rib and sleeve rib, as given in this chapter.

Neckband

Join shoulder seams. With Rs of work facing, 2mm/No 14 needles and A, K across 18 [20:22] sts of left back from holder, pick up and K39 [41:43] sts round front neck edge and K across 18 [20:22] sts of right back from holder. 75 [81:87] sts.
Beg with a P row work 3 rows st st.
Next row (picot hem) K1, *yfwd, K2

The pattern pieces

sleeve
3[4:5]cm
22[24:25]cm

8[11:13]cm
21[24:26]cm
4[7:9]cm
2cm
26[29:32]cm

front/back
24[32:36]cm
43[49:51]cm

tog, rep from * to end.
Beg with a P row work 3 rows st st.
Cast off.

Back buttonhole border
With Rs of work facing, 2mm/No 14
needles and A, pick up and K24

*Below: The skirt of this dress is knitted
in plain stocking stitch, without any
shaping, so it is easy to adjust the length
to suit the height of the child.*

[30:36] sts along right back opening
edge. K one row.
Next row (buttonhole row) K2,
*yfwd, K2 tog, K7 [10:13] sts, rep
from * once more, yfwd, K2 tog, K2.
K2 rows. Cast off.

Back button border
Work as given for buttonhole
border, omitting buttonholes.

To make up
Press under a damp cloth with a
warm iron. Join side and sleeve
seams. Sew in sleeves. Fold hems of
skirt and sleeves to Ws at picot row
and sl st in place. Fold neckband to
Ws at picot row and sl st in place.
Sew down lower edge of back
borders. Press seams. Sew on
buttons.

Techniques for knitting with beads and sequins

Beads and sequins can be knitted in as sparsely or lavishly as you like – to add a hint of sparkle at each crossover point in diamond lace, or as encrusted all-over fabrics. Learn how to thread them on to the yarn so you can knit them in with the stitches.

Even a plain design can look dazzling if you knit in beads or sequins as you go. There is no need to restrict yourself to a pattern specifically for bead knitting. If you want to add beads, say to the yoke of a sweater, mark on the pattern pieces where the beads should go and, using the techniques described in this chapter, turn a day time sweater into an elegant evening version.

Traditional bead knitting

Although very time consuming, the traditional method of knitting with beads was popular in the 18th and 19th centuries. Beautiful examples, such as bonnets and mittens, can be found in many museums, but it was commonly used for small bags and purses and to this day the method is also known as 'purse' knitting.

The bead patterns were abstract or pictorial and the knitters often chose romantic subjects so that the results resembled miniature paintings of pastoral scenes or floral arrangements.

In traditional bead knitting tiny beads in different colours cover the knitted stitches so that no background is visible. The beads are not knitted in with the stitches but lie across the front of the fabric in between the stitches. Reversed stocking stitch is always used for the background.

The yarn, needles and beads are all exceptionally fine and items take a long time to knit which is why the traditional method is seldom used today.

The designs are charted on squared paper and the beads threaded on to the yarn in the correct sequence according to the chart. One bead is allowed for each stitch, with the exception of the last stitch in each row. If one bead is threaded on out of sequence the whole design can be ruined.

Modern bead knitting

Today knitters use a simpler technique, with the beads held on the yarn over a slipped stitch and kept in position by the stitches either side. This means that the beads are more spaced out than in traditional bead

Left: The strong colour contrast of the beads on this navy slipover shows up the diamond pattern.

149

knitting. Pictorial overall designs are not possible but the beads still have to be threaded on to the yarn before knitting. Simple patterns use beads in one colour only, so there is no accurate counting involved. More complex patterns use different coloured beads and these have to be threaded on to the yarn in the correct sequence.

Modern sequin knitting

Sequins are also threaded on to the yarn, in sequence if necessary but, as the sequin is pushed through the stitch as it is knitted, an all-over sequined effect is possible as well as a more random placing.

Preparing to knit with beads

Before you start to knit you have to thread enough beads or sequins on to one ball of yarn to enable you to complete a given area of the pattern. The instructions usually give you an approximate amount of beads. If you find you are running short and still have a lot of yarn left in a ball, simply unravel the ball and thread extra beads or sequins on to the other end of the yarn. If there are too many on the yarn, remove them when you have knitted to the end of the ball and thread them on to the next ball.

Only join in a new ball of yarn at the beginning of a row using a reef knot (page 18), even if knitting in the round. Don't splice the ends of the yarn together as the beads will not slide over the join.

Yarn must be smooth enough for the beads and sequins to slide along it easily – mohair and highly-textured yarns are unsuitable. It must be the right thickness to allow the beads or

Threading beads in sequence for traditional bead knitting

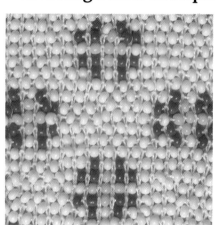

Create your own chart on graph paper to indicate where the beads of each colour should go. (You could borrow a simple Fair Isle design and use an existing chart.) When the beads are knitted in they lie between each stitch so the last stitch in each row does not require a bead.

Lay out the beads on a piece of fabric (they will roll about on a table) to replicate the chart. Thread the beads on to the yarn row by row

Left: A sample of the beautifully delicate traditional bead knitting.

in *reverse* order to the sequence in which they are knitted. In counting rows, it helps to knot a short length of contrasting yarn on to the end of each row before threading on the next row. These can be removed as the beads are knitted in.

As a rough guide half fill each ball of yarn with beads and always thread a complete number of rows on to a ball, so that a new ball of yarn can be joined in at the beginning of a row.

Odd number of rows On a pattern which contains an odd number of

Traditional bead knitting method

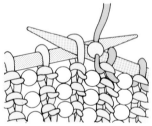 

Purling in beads on right side

Purl the first stitch in the usual way.
*With the yarn at the front of the work push the bead up close to the last purled stitch and leave it at the front of the work.
Purl the next stitch in the usual way.
Repeat from * to the end of the row.

Knitting in beads on wrong side

Knit the first stitch in the usual way.
*With the yarn at the back of the work push the bead up close to the last knitted stitch and leave it at the back of the work.
Knit the next stitch in the usual way.
Repeat from * to the end of the row.

Modern bead knitting method

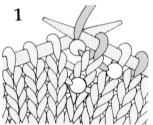 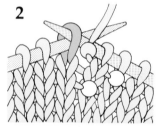

Knit row

Keep the yarn at the back, except when knitting in a bead. Knit the number of plain stitches given in the pattern in the usual way.
1 *Yarn forward between the needles, push the bead up close to the *front* (knit side) of the work.

2 Keep the bead at the front, slip the next stitch in a purlwise direction without working into it, yarn back between the needles.
Repeat from the * every time a bead is knitted in.

sequins to be threaded on to it and firm enough to hold their weight without stretching or sagging.
Beads should be of a size to complement the yarn – too big and they will pull it out of shape, too small and they tend to disappear against the background fabric.
Sequins should have a hole at the top so that when they are knitted in they hang down smoothly against the fabric. Unless the sequins are very small, if they have a central hole they will stick out from the fabric at an angle and catch and break in wear.

Check whether the sequins have a definite right and wrong side. To make sure the right side shows on the knitting all the sequins must be threaded on to the yarn by inserting the sewing needle from the *front* of each sequin.
When knitting in beads or sequins do not place them too close to the edge of the fabric, as this causes difficulty in seaming.

Designs for beads and sequins
The two jerseys given in this chapter are knitted in beaded diamond and

sequin and lace pattern. You can use these patterns to add beads and sequins to a wide variety of designs.
Beaded diamond pattern is worked in just one bead colour but looks most effective against a contrasting background. It can be used as an all-over pattern on a small item, such as a purse, but should be used as vertical panels on a garment.
Sequin and lace pattern is also worked in just one sequin colour against a contrasting or self-coloured background. It forms vertical panels and is also an ideal all-over pattern.

Threading beads or sequins on to yarn

rows, or multiples of an even number of rows plus one extra row to complete the pattern, begin threading on the beads in sequence from the top *left-hand* corner of the chart and finish at the lower right-hand corner.
Even number of rows On a pattern which contains an even number of rows, begin threading on the beads in sequence from the top *right-hand* corner of the chart and finish at the lower right-hand corner. In this way the last bead threaded on to the yarn is the first bead to be knitted.

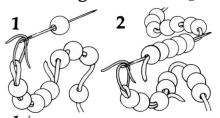

Make sure that the eye of the needle is small enough to pass through the bead or sequin.
Fold a 15cm/6in length of sewing cotton in half and thread both cut ends into the sewing needle from *opposite* directions and push 15cm/

6in of the end of the ball of yarn on to which the beads or sequins are to be threaded through the loop of sewing cotton.
1 Push the bead or sequin on to the needle, slide it down the needle, over the cotton and on to the yarn. Continue until the required number are threaded on to the yarn.
If your beads are already threaded on to a length of thread, transfer them straight on to the yarn.
2 Insert the sewing needle into five or six beads at a time and allow them to slide down on to the yarn.

Modern sequin knitting method

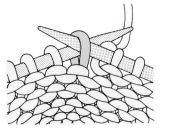 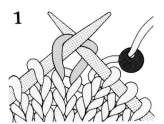 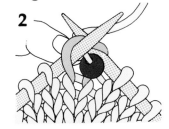 

Purl row
Keep the yarn at the front, except when purling in a bead. Purl the number of plain stitches in usual way.
*Yarn back between the needles, push the bead up close to the *back* (knit side) of the work.
Keep the bead at the back, slip the next stitch in a purlwise direction without working into it, yarn forward between the needles.
Repeat from the * every time a bead is purled in.

Knit row
Keep the yarn at back throughout. Knit the number of plain stitches given in pattern in the usual way.
1 *Insert the right-hand needle into the back loop of the stitch where the sequin is required as if to *knit* it, opening it up with the needle.

2 Push the sequin up close to the back of the work, then push it through the stitch from the back to the front with the forefinger of the left hand. Complete the stitch as for a knit stitch in the usual way and allow it to drop off the left-hand needle.
Repeat from * each time a sequin is knitted in.

Purl row
Keep the yarn at front throughout. Purl the number of plain stitches in usual way.
*Insert the right-hand needle into the back loop of the stitch where sequin is required from left to right, opening it up with the needle.
Push the sequin up close to the front of the work, where the needles cross, then push it through the stitch from the front to the back with the thumb of the left hand at the same time as the stitch is purled. Repeat from *.

Beaded diamond pattern

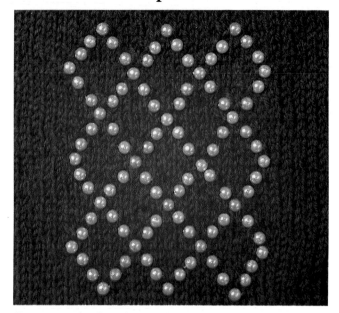

Cast on multiples of 6 sts plus 3 sts, eg 27.
1st row (Rs) K to end.
2nd and every alt row K1, P to last st, K1.
3rd row K4, *sl bead up close to front of work and sl next st – **called bead 1**, K5, rep from * to last 5 sts, bead 1, K4.
5th row K3, *bead 1, K1, bead 1, K3, rep from * to end.
7th row K2, *bead 1, K3, bead 1, K1, rep from * to last st, K1.
9th row K1, *bead 1, K5, rep from * to last 2 sts, bead 1, K1.
11th row As 7th.
13th row As 5th.
14th row as 2nd. Rows 3-14 inclusive form the pattern.

Sequin and lace pattern

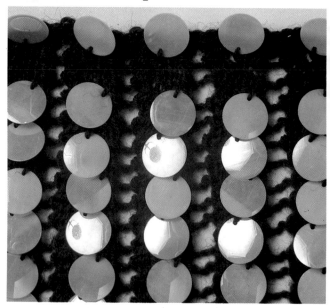

Cast on multiples of 6 sts plus 4 sts, eg 28.
1st row (Rs) K1, *K2, K2 tog, y2rn, K2 tog tbl, rep from * to last 3 sts, K3.
2nd row *P4, P into front then into back of y2rn, rep from * to last 4 sts, P4.
3rd row K1, *K1, sl sequin up close to back of work and K with next st – **called sequin 1**, K2 tog, y2rn, K2 tog tbl, rep from * to last 3 sts, K1, sequin 1, K1.
4th row As 2nd.
5th row As 1st.
6th row As 2nd.
7th row K1, *sequin 1, K1, K2 tog, y2rn, K2 tog tbl, rep from * to last 3 sts, sequin 1, K2.
8th row As 2nd. These 8 rows form the pattern.

Sleeveless slipover for day or evening wear

Two versions of a sleeveless slipover to take you through the day and into the evening. Both have a V neck, and both neck and armholes are trimmed with a dainty picot border.

The evening version is in sequin and lace pattern worked as an all-over fabric. The beaded version features panels of beaded diamond pattern on back and front.

Sizes

To fit 81 [86:91:97]cm/32 [34:36:38]in bust snugly
Length to shoulder, 50 [51:52:53]cm/19¾ [20:20½:20¾]in
The figures in [] refer to the 86/34, 91/36 and 97cm/38in sizes respectively

You will need

4 [5:5:6]×50g balls of Sunbeam 4 ply Pure New Wool (100% wool)

One pair 2¾mm/No 12 needles
One pair 3¼mm/No 10 needles
Set of four 2¾mm/No 12 needles pointed at each end
About 1300 [1300:1400:1400] small beads for the back *and* front
About 1200 [1300:1400:1500] 14mm/½in sequins with hole at top for sequin version

Tension

28 sts and 36 rows to 10cm/4in over plain st st worked on 3¼mm/No 10 needles

Note

Before beginning to knit thread about 350 beads on to 3 [3:3:3] balls of yarn for beaded version, or 400 sequins on to 3 [3:3:3] balls of yarn for sequin version adding more to the other end of the yarn or new ball as required.

Back

With 2¾mm/No 12 needles and unthreaded yarn cast on 112 [118:124:130] sts.
Work 8cm/3¼in K1, P1 rib. Change to 3¼mm/No 10 needles and join in yarn with beads or sequins.

Beaded version only

Next row (Rs) K19 [21:23:25] sts, (bead 1, K5) twice, bead 1, K48 [50:52:54] sts, (bead 1, K5) twice, bead 1, K19 [21:23:25] sts.
Next and every alt row P to end.
Next row K19 [21:23:25] sts, (K1, bead 1, K3, bead 1) twice, K50 [52:54:56] sts, (K1, bead 1, K3, bead

Note: The sequins and beads have been knitted in on the back and front of the slipovers given in this chapter. If you prefer them on the front only remember to use only half the number.

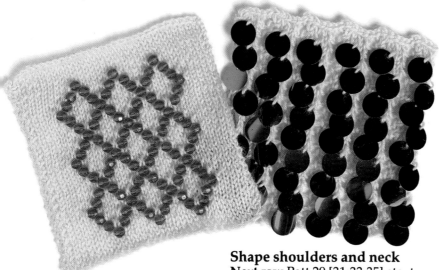

1) twice, K19 [21:23:25] sts.
Next row K19 [21:23:25] sts, (K2, bead 1, K1, bead 1, K1) twice, K50 [52:54:56] sts, (K2, bead 1, K1, bead 1, K1) twice, K19 [21:23:25] sts.
Cont in patt as now set.

Sequin version only
Next row As 1st row for sequins and lace patt.
Next row As 2nd row of sequin and lace patt.
Cont in patt as now set.

Both versions
Cont in patt until work measures 31cm/12¼in from beg, ending with a Ws row.**

Shape armholes
Cast off 8 sts at beg of next 2 rows.
Next row K1, K2 tog, patt to last 3 sts, K2 tog tbl, K1.
Next row Patt to end.
Rep last 2 rows 6 [7:8:9] times more. 82 [86:90:94] sts.
Cont without shaping until armholes measure 19 [20:21:22]cm/ 7½ [7¾:8¼:8¾]in from beg, ending with a Ws row.

Shape shoulders and neck
Next row Patt 29 [31:33:35] sts, turn and leave rem sts on holder.
Complete right shoulder first.
Next row Cast off 3 sts, patt to end.
Next row Cast off 7 [7:8:8] sts, patt to end.
Rep last 2 rows once more, then first of them again. Cast off rem 6 [8:8:10] sts.
With Rs of work facing leave first 24 sts on holder for centre back neck, rejoin yarn to rem sts and patt to end.
Complete to match first side reversing shapings.

Front
Work as given for back to **.

Shape armholes and divide for neck
Next row Cast off 8 sts, patt until there are 48 [51:54:57] sts on needle, turn and leave rem sts on holder.
Next row P1, P2 tog tbl, patt to end.
Next row K1, K2 tog, patt to end.
Next row Patt to end.
Next row K1, K2 tog, patt to last 3 sts, K2 tog tbl, K1.
Cont to dec at armhole edge on every foll alt row 5 [6:7:8] times

more, *at the same time* cont to dec at neck edge on every foll 3rd row until 20 [22:24:26] sts rem.
Cont without shaping until armhole measures same as back to shoulder, ending at armhole edge.

Shape shoulder
Cast off at beg of next and every alt row 7 [7:8:8] sts twice and 6 [8:8:10] sts once.
With Rs of work facing rejoin yarn to rem sts and patt to end.
Complete to match first side reversing all shapings.

Neckband
Join shoulder seams.
With Rs of work facing, set of four 2¾mm/No 12 needles and unthreaded yarn, pick up and K9 sts down right back neck, K across back neck sts on holder, pick up and K9 sts up left back neck and 54 [57:60:63] sts down left front neck, pick up loop lying between sts at centre front and K tbl, then pick up and K54 [57:60:63] sts up right front neck. 151 [157:163:169] sts.
Next round K to 2 sts before centre front picked up st, K2 tog tbl, K centre st, K2 tog, K to end.
Rep last round 4 times more.
Next round (picot round) *K2 tog, yfwd, rep from * to last st, K1, still dec at each side of centre st.
Next round P to one st before centre st, P twice into next st, P centre st, P twice into next st, P to end.
Rep last round 4 times more. Cast off purlwise, still inc each side of centre st.

Armhole borders
With Rs of work facing, 2¾mm/ No 12 needles and unthreaded yarn, pick up and K107 [113:119:125] sts evenly round armhole.
Beg with a P row work 5 rows st st, dec one st at each end of 2nd and 4th rows.
Next row (picot row) *K2 tog, yfwd, rep from * to last st, K1.
Beg with a K row work 5 rows st st, inc one st at each end of 2nd and 4th rows. Cast off.

To make up
Do not press. Join side and armhole border seams. Fold neckband and armhole borders to Ws at picot row and sl st down.

The pattern pieces

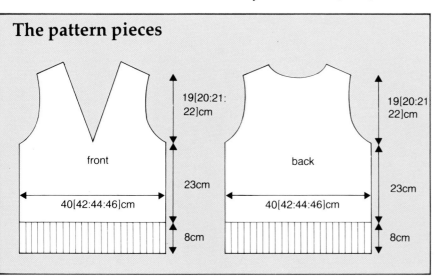

front
19[20:21:22]cm
23cm
40[42:44:46]cm
8cm

back
19[20:21:22]cm
23cm
40[42:44:46]cm
8cm

Lengthening or shortening your knitting

Extend the life of a garment by pulling a thread and re-knitting downwards, adding a contrast stripe or using leftovers of the original wool. You can even anticipate the problem by knitting each piece from the top down and simply unpicking the cast-off edge.

Children grow out of their clothes so fast that it is very useful to know how to lengthen knitted garments or replace worn areas by re-knitting them. To alter a jersey which has been knitted from the lower edge *upwards*, pull out a thread on the row where you want to make the alteration, leaving two sets of exposed stitches. Place the stitches of the main section on to the same-sized needle as was used to knit the jersey in the first place ready to re-knit *downwards*. Do not stretch the stitches by using a needle which is too large.

If possible, refer to the original instructions to check how many stitches were cast on. If you cannot find this, unpick a few stitches at a time and place them on the needle, checking that you have not dropped any. Don't panic if a few stitches begin to run – these can be picked up again with a crochet hook (see page 21).

Alternatively, you can knit a jersey *downwards*, from top to bottom, and it is then a simple matter to unpick the cast off edge and make the alteration required. This chapter includes a pattern which is knitted in this way.

You will obviously need extra yarn to lengthen a garment, but this does not necessarily have to be the same colour as the original, although it must work to the same tension. You can use up oddments of yarn to work stripes or a patterned border above the ribbed welt of a jersey, or above the cuffs on sleeves. By making a colourful focal point of the adjustment you also disguise the join.

Tips for lengthening

When making children's garments which are likely to require adjustments it is always wise to buy one or two extra balls of yarn in the same dye lot as this will look better when knitted up than unravelled yarn.

If you do have to re-knit with unravelled yarn, wash it first according to the washing instructions on the ball band.

Do not attempt to unpick a highly textured yarn which will not unravel easily. This will snag and break, causing unsightly joins in re-knitting.

Do not attempt to unpick a complicated pattern such as lace, where many increased and decreased stitches have been worked in a row. It is difficult to pick these up in sequence.

Take great care when unpicking any seams. Cut the yarn used for sewing, *not* the knitted fabric, otherwise you will find many short ends instead of one continuous length when it is unravelled.

Garments knitted upwards

Because the stitches are the wrong way up when re-knitting downwards, all patterns will be half-a-stitch out of true. This does not show too much in basic patterns such as stocking stitch, garter stitch, etc, but it is noticeable if you go straight into ribbing.

To lengthen the body pull out a thread about two rows above the welt if it is in ribbing. Calculate the extra length required and see how many additional rows you will need to knit, based on the row tension. Remember to count the rows needed to complete a coloured pattern and to allow for re-knitting the welt. Work as given under Lengthening garments knitted upwards.

To lengthen a sleeve pull out a thread about two rows above the cuff and work as given under Lengthening garments knitted upwards.

When re-knitting the sleeve remember to take into account the shaping. If you have unpicked to a point above some of the increases, when knitting downwards you must *decrease* stitches at each end of the rows to arrive at the original number of stitches for the cuff, then continue without shaping for the extra length.

To lengthen a skirt unpick the hem if it is turned under. Pull out a thread about two rows from the hem or two rows above any special knitted edge, such as a picot hem. Work as given under Lengthening garments knitted upwards.

When re-knitting the skirt take into

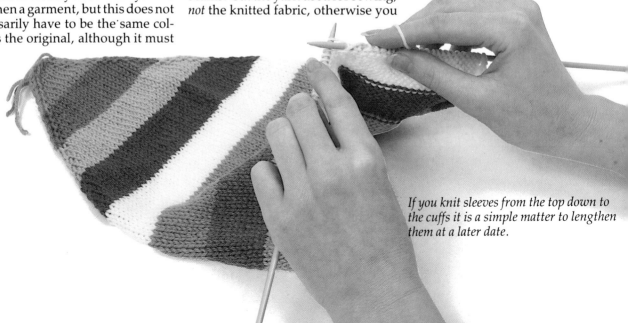

If you knit sleeves from the top down to the cuffs it is a simple matter to lengthen them at a later date.

account any shaping at the sides or in the panels. If you have unpicked to a point above some of the decreases, when knitting downwards you must *increase* stitches as given to arrive at the original number of stitches.
You must then judge whether you need to continue without shaping for the extra length, depending on the final angle of shaping you require.
To shorten the body calculate the number of rows which need to be unravelled to give the shorter length, based on the row tension. Remember to allow for re-knitting the hem or welt.
Mark the position with pins at each end of the row where a thread is to be pulled, keeping two rows clear above any ribbing.
Work as given under Lengthening garments knitted upwards to ** in step 6.
Complete the welt with the original number of rows. Re-join the side seams.
To shorten a sleeve work as given for shortening a body of a garment, pulling out the thread about two rows above the cuff.
Take into account any shaping. If you have unpicked to a point above some of the increases, before working the cuff *decrease* across the row to give the correct number of stitches.
To shorten a skirt work as given for shortening a body of a garment, pulling out a thread just above the hem. There is no need to worry about any shaping.
Complete the hem on the number of stitches which remain. Re-join the side seams. Turn up the hem if required.

Garments knitted downwards

All hems, welts and cuffs on garments knitted downwards have cast-off edges instead of cast-on edges.
To lengthen a garment you just unpick the cast-off edge, unravel any hems or ribbing, and knit an extension in the main patterns or add contrasting stripes or a coloured pattern to give the extra length. If working in the same colour use the original yarn first then join in new yarn. Complete the hem or ribbing again to the length worked before.
To shorten a garment work in the same way, unravelling the number of rows to give the new length and allowing for the depth of hem or ribbing to be re-knitted.

Lengthening garments knitted upwards

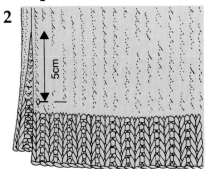

1 With pins, mark the position at each end of the row where a thread is to be pulled so that the minimum of re-knitting is required. Calculate how many additional rows you need to knit, based on the row tension.

2 Prepare the garment by unpicking the sewn side seams to about 5cm/2in above the marked point. This is to allow enough room to manipulate the needles when picking up the stitches.

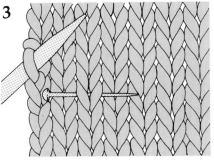

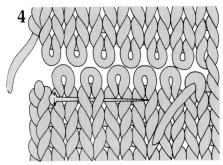

3 With the right side of the work facing, use a knitting needle to pick up a loop at the edge of the knitting on the row above the marked point.

4 Pull this loop up tightly with the needle and cut through the yarn. Carefully part the fabric, exposing two sets of stitches. Pull up the cut end of yarn again and cut it, easing the fabric apart.

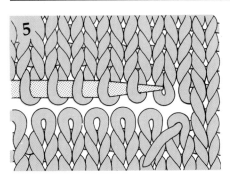

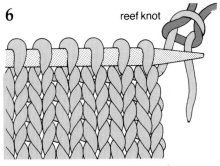

5 When sufficient stitches have been freed, pick them up with a double-pointed knitting needle.
Continue pulling up the cut end of yarn and easing the fabric apart until all the stitches have been placed on the knitting needle. Each stitch must lie in the correct direction without being twisted. Unravel the rest of the yarn and wind it into a ball ready for re-knitting.

6 If working in the same colour throughout, join in the original yarn with a reef knot at the beginning of the row where it was cut, **. If working in a coloured pattern join in the next colour in the same way. Continue until the extra length has been knitted. Complete whatever section of the garment you are knitting. Re-join the seams.

155

V-necked jersey for girl or boy

A jersey which is worn every day often wears out at the elbows or cuffs long before it is outgrown. This pattern is knitted from the top downwards so it is a simple matter to unpick and re-knit it.

Sizes
To fit 71 [76:81:86]cm/28 [30:32:34]in chest
Length from shoulder,
45 [49:53:56]cm/17¾ [19¼:20¾:22]in, adjustable

Below: Knit this classic V-necked, machine washable jersey for your child to wear every day at play or at school. Add a delicate contrasting stripe at the neck and cuffs or knit it completely in one colour.

leeve seam, 36 [39:42:45]cm/
4¼ [15¼:16½:17½]in, adjustable
The figures in [] refer to the 76/30,
1/32 and 86cm/34in sizes
respectively

You will need

- [5:6:6]×50g balls of Robin Reward
  Double Knitting (60% Courtelle,
  40% Bri-nylon) in main colour A
  [1:1:1] ball of same in contrast
  colour B
  One pair 3¼mm/No 10 needles
  One pair 4mm/No 8 needles
  Set of four 3¼mm/No 10 needles
  pointed at both ends

Tension

22 sts and 30 rows to 10cm/4in over
st st worked on 4mm/No 8 needles

Back

With 4mm/No 8 needles and A cast
on 25 [27:29:31] sts and beg at back
neck edge. Beg with a K row work
2 rows st st.
Next row (inc row) K2, pick up loop
lying between needles and K tbl –
called M1, K to last 2 sts, M1, K2.
Next row P.
Rep last 2 rows until there are
73 [79:85:91] sts, ending with a K
row.

Shape underarm
**Cast on 6 sts at beg of next
2 rows. 85 [91:97:103] sts.
Cont in st st without shaping until
work measures 23 [26:28:30]cm/
9 [10¼:11:11¼]in from cast on sts at
underarm, or required length less
4 [4:5:5]cm/1½ [1½:2:2]in, ending
with a P row.
Change to 3¼mm/No 10 needles
Next row K1, *P1, K1, rep from * to
end.
Next row P1, *K1, P1, rep from * to
end.
Rep last 2 rows 5 [5:7:7] times more,
then first of them again. Cast off
loosely in rib.

Front

With 4mm/No 8 needles and A cast
on 2 sts and beg at top of left side.
Beg with a K row work 2 rows st st.
3rd row K1, M1, K1.
4th and every alt row P. **
5th row K1, M1, K2.
7th row K2, M1, K2.
9th row K3, M1, K2.
11th row K2, M1, K to last 2 sts, M1,
K2.

13th row K to last 2 sts, M1, K2.
14th row P.
Rep the last 4 rows until there are
35 [38:41:44] sts, ending on a P row.
Break off yarn and leave sts on a
spare needle.

Right side
Work as given for left side to **.
5th row K2, M1, K to end.
6th row P to end.
Rep last 2 rows until there are 6 sts,
ending with a P row.
11th row K2, M1, K to last 2 sts, M1,
K2.
13th row K2, M1, K to end.
Cont inc in this way until there are
35 [38:41:44] sts, ending on a P row.

Join right and left sides of front
Next row K2, M1, K to end, cast on
one st, K across sts of left side to last
2 sts, M1, K2. 73 [79:85:91] sts.
Complete as given for back from ***
to end.

Sleeves
With 4mm/No 8 needles and A cast
on 7 sts and beg at top. Beg with a K
row work 2 rows st st.
3rd row K2, M1, K to last 2 sts, M1,
K2.
4th row P.
Rep last 2 rows until there are
49 [53:57:61] sts, ending on a P row.
Next row K.
Next row P.
Next row As 3rd.
Next row As 4th. 51 [55:59:63] sts.
Next row K.

Shape underarm
Cast on 6 sts at beg of next 2 rows.

---

63 [67:71:75] sts. Work 9 [11:13:15]
rows st st. Adjust length at this
point.
Next row (dec row) K1, K2 tog, K to
last 3 sts, sl 1, K1, psso, K1.
Beg with a P row work 5 rows st st.
Rep last 6 rows until 37 [39:41:43] sts
rem. Cont without shaping until
sleeve measures 32 [35:37:40]cm/
12½ [13¾:14½:15¾]in from
underarm shaping or required
length less 4 [4:5:5]cm/
1½ [1½:2:2]in, ending with a P row.
Change to 3¼mm/No 10 needles.
Work 4 [4:6:6] rows rib as given for
back.
Cont in rib and work 2 rows B,
2 rows A, 2 rows B and 3 rows A.
Cast off *loosely* in rib.

Neckband

Join raglan seams. With Rs of work
facing, set of four 3¼mm/No 10
needles and A, pick up and
K25 [27:29:31] sts across back neck,
6 sts across left sleeve, 37 [40:43:46]
sts down left front neck, pick up
and K1 from centre front st, pick up
and K37 [40:43:46] sts up right front
neck then 6 sts across right sleeve.
112 [120:128:136] sts.
Next round Work in K1, P1 rib to
2 sts before centre front st, K2 tog,
P1, sl 1, K1, psso, rib to end.
Rep this round working 2 more
rounds in A, 2 rounds in B, and
2 rounds in A. Cast off in rib, still
dec at centre front.

To make up

Press each piece under a dry cloth
with a cool iron. Join side and
sleeve seams. Press seams.

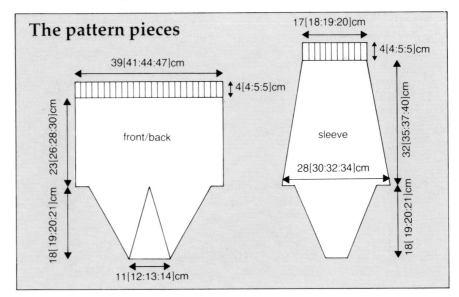

The pattern pieces

39[41:44:47]cm

4[4:5:5]cm

front/back

23[26:28:30]cm

18[19:20:21]cm

11[12:13:14]cm

17[18:19:20]cm

4[4:5:5]cm

sleeve

32[35:37:40]cm

28[30:32:34]cm

18[19:20:21]cm

Adapting a pattern to knit from the top down

You can adapt almost any set of instructions to this method – every time you see the words cast off you must cast on and every time you see the word increase you must decrease.

Read through the instructions and make a note of points to watch. Make sure that the pattern does not have a specific right or wrong way up. A pictorial design knitted from a chart, for example, will have to begin at the *top left-hand* corner or it will be upside down. Some patterns will have to begin with the last pattern row and work back to the first. You will find it easier to begin with a simple pattern in stocking stitch.

Working the back of a jersey
Read through the instructions to the last number of stitches cast off. These may be for one of the shoulders or the back neck. Begin by casting on this number of stitches.
Continue in the pattern given, increasing or casting on for the shoulders instead of decreasing and casting off.
For a set-in armhole, use the row tension to calculate the length you must work before beginning the shaping. Increase and cast on until you have the number of stitches given before the armhole shaping.
A raglan armhole will begin increasing right away and will continue for the depth of the armhole, casting on the final number of stitches to arrive at the number given before the armhole shaping.
Continue knitting the body for the length given, less the hem or welt measurement. Change needle size and work the welt as given. Always cast off very loosely.

Working the front of a jersey
Read through the instructions to the last number of stitches cast off. These will probably be for one of the shoulders. Begin by casting on this number of stitches. When this shoulder has

motifs must be inverted when knitted from the top

select a colour from the motif and lengthen body and sleeves by adding a bold stripe

add extra rows of pattern to a border design

when lengthening a striped jersey remember to keep to the same sequence of colours

been completed, cast on and work the second shoulder.
Work across the first shoulder, cast on the number of front neck stitches given, then work across the second shoulder.
Complete as given for the back of a jersey.

Working the sleeves of a jersey
Read through the instructions to the last number of stitches cast off at the top of the sleeve. Begin by casting on this number of stitches.
Work the top of the sleeve by increasing and casting on, instead of decreasing and casting off, until you have the number of stitches given before shaping the top of the sleeve.
Calculate the length you must work before beginning any sleeve shaping, based on the row tension. Continue in pattern, decreasing at each end of the rows as given instead of increasing, until you have the number of stitches given after the cuff has been worked.
Change needles and work the cuff as given. Cast off loosely.

Making up a garment
Complete as given in the making up section. Neckbands, button, button-hole bands and any additional edges are applied in the usual way.

Enlarging and reducing motifs for knitting

Working out your own motifs gives any basic garment an individual touch and can be great fun. You can use canvaswork or embroidery designs already in chart form or trace over a simple picture and transfer it on to squared paper, enlarging it or reducing it as required.

Knitting becomes really original when you begin to experiment with your own designs. The simplest way to start is to use the instructions for a basic stocking stitch garment and introduce your own coloured motif. The motif can be knitted in as for collage patterns or applied as for Swiss darning.

Choosing a motif

Pick a simple embroidery design with a colour coded chart or a clearly defined coloured illustration of a suitable subject for the motif. It doesn't matter what size it is, as this chapter shows you how to enlarge or reduce a motif to fit it into the number of stitches cast on for the garment. You can use a large motif placed centrally on the front or back of a garment, or a small one just to highlight the shoulder or trim a pocket. Decide on the area you want the motif to fill within the total number of stitches and rows available in the garment, clear of any shaping. Depending on the shape of the design, a large centrally placed motif should take up about half the total number of stitches and rows.

Although the finished design is worked out on graph (squared) paper, knitted stitches are not square. It takes fewer stitches than rows to work a 10cm/4in square as each stitch is wider than it is tall. The knitted version will, therefore, be wider and shallower than the design on the chart. You should allow for this either by choosing a design which is tall and thin, or by adding extra rows to extend the depth when you are filling in the final chart. Take the run-

ning shoe design on the sweater in this chapter for example. It is wider than it is deep so the final depth of the design had to be extended by five rows to compensate.

Enlarging or reducing a motif

A design is enlarged or reduced by using a series of grids. The points of the design are transferred and joined up as you would a child's dot-to-dot picture. The enlarged or reduced design must then be copied on to graph paper – one square represents a stitch and one line of squares a row. Fill in a whole square to the nearest point on the outline – you can't knit half a stitch!

Below: A strong motif with definite outlines reduces well to form a border along the bottom of a jersey.

Enlarging and reducing a design for knitting

You will need

Tracing paper
Graph paper
A soft pencil
A soft rubber
A ruler

To enlarge a design Trace the outline of the design you wish to reproduce, shade over the outlines with a pencil on the back and transfer it to the bottom left-hand corner of a piece of graph paper.
1 Enclose the design in a square or rectangle, extending it to give an even number of complete squares horizontally and vertically. The example shown here has been extended to 20 squares in width, 30 in depth.

Number the squares horizontally and vertically*.
Decide how wide you want the motif to be. In this example it is to be enlarged to 23cm/9in.
2 Mark the corners of the square or rectangle ABCD as shown.
Draw a diagonal line through A/C. Extend the line A/B to give a measurement of 23cm/9in and draw a line at right angles to this point until it cuts the diagonal. This line represents the enlarged height of the motif (34cm/13½in).
Check the number of stitches and rows to 2.5cm/1in given for the tension of the garment you are knitting. If the tension is, say, six stitches and eight rows to 2.5cm/1in, a motif measuring 23cm×34cm/

9in×13½in will take up 54 stitches and 108 rows. On the graph, count off along the bottom the number of squares (stitches) needed for the enlarged motif (in this example, 54) and extend the line A/B to A/E. Draw a line at right angles at this point until it cuts the diagonal. Complete the rectangle AEFG.
3 Transfer the dimensions of the rectangle AEFG to a sheet of tracing paper. Divide this into the same number of squares as the original design and rule up the squares. Copy the enlarged design free-hand, square by square, on to the tracing paper.
If you were to knit the motif from a chart based on the rectangle AEFG it would be foreshortened, as already explained. So now is the

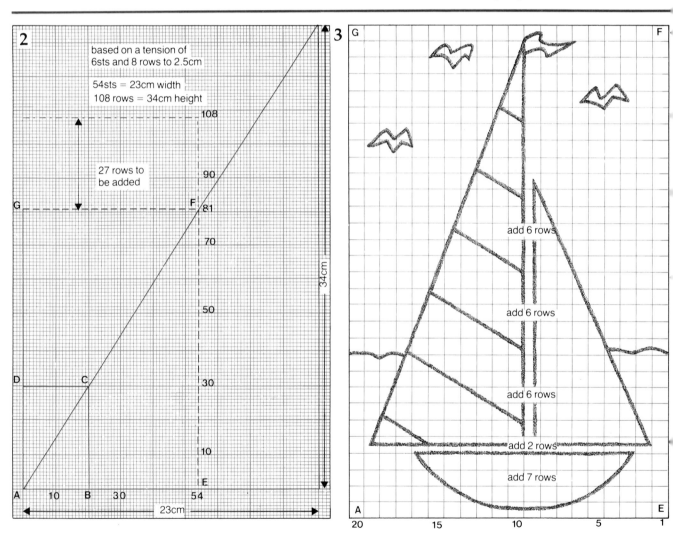

ime to add extra rows to extend the depth. The number of extra rows needed is the difference between the number of squares A/G and the total number of rows needed for a design 34cm/13½in high (as calculated above). Add them in the least complicated parts of the design.

Trace the enlarged design, including the extra rows, on to a fresh piece of graph paper. Colour in the shapes or code each colour with a different symbol, see page 120.

To reduce a design Work as for enlarging a design up to *. Decide on the position of the motif and the number of stitches and rows it is to fill. For example, if the tension is six stitches and eight rows to 2.5cm/

1in, a motif measuring 8cm×9.5cm/ 3¼in×3¾in will fill 20 stitches and 30 rows.

5 On another piece of graph paper draw a rectangle to correspond with the number of squares covered by your design, ABCD. Draw in the diagonal, A/C.

In the corner of the rectangle count the number of squares along the bottom line you wish your design to reduce to. Draw a line at right angles at this point and where it cuts the diagonal draw in the rectangle AEFG.

On the original tracing of the design draw a grid with the same number of squares as in the reduced rectangle. Copy the reduced design freehand, square by square into the smaller rectangle. Colour in the

shapes or code each colour with a different symbol.

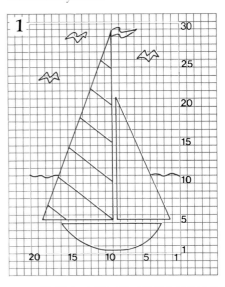

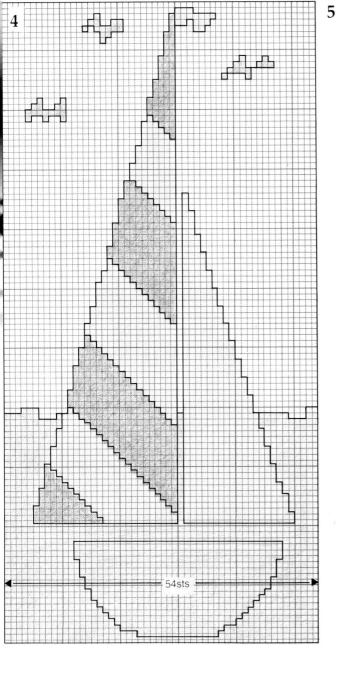

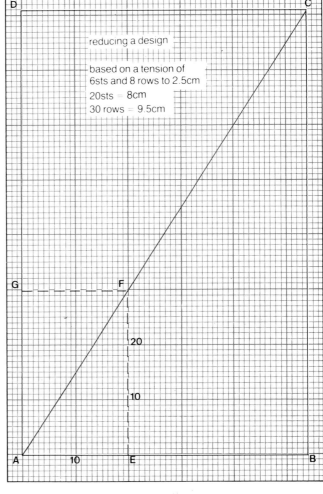

161

Motifs to enlarge

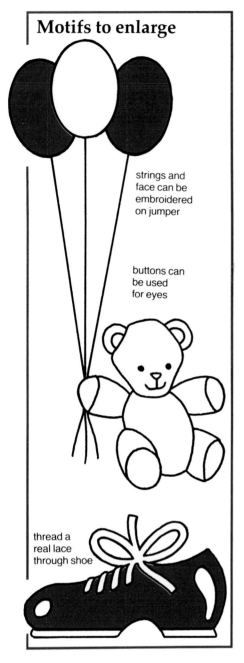

strings and face can be embroidered on jumper

buttons can be used for eyes

thread a real lace through shoe

Jersey with running shoe motif

Enlarge or reduce the running shoe motif as a highlight on the centre front of this sporty jersey. The chart given below will knit up a motif measuring 20cm×8cm/7¾in×3¼in.

Sizes

To fit 71cm/28in chest
Length to shoulder, 46cm/18in
Sleeve seam, 36cm/14in

You will need

5×40g balls of Sirdar Wash 'n' Wear
  Double Crepe (55% nylon,
  45% acrylic) in main colour A
1 ball of same in each of 3 contrast
  colours B, C and D
One pair 3mm/No 11 needles
One pair 3¾mm/No 9 needles
Set of four 3mm/No 11 needles
One boot lace about 30cm/12in long

Tension

24 sts and 32 rows to 10cm/4in over st st worked on 3¾mm/No 9 needles

Note Use separate balls of yarn for each colour on motif, twisting colours together at back of work on every row

Back

With 3mm/No 11 needles and A cast on 91 sts.
1st row (Rs) K1, *P1, K1, rep from * to end.
2nd row P1, *K1, P1, rep from * to end.
Rep these 2 rows for 4cm/1½in, ending with a 2nd row.**
Change to 3¾mm/No 9 needles.
Beg with a K row cont in st st until

work measures 30cm/12in from beg ending with a P row. Adjust length here if required.

Shape armholes

Cast off 6 sts at beg of next 2 rows.
Next row K1, sl 1, K1, psso, K to last 3 sts, K2 tog, K1.
Next row P to end.
Rep last 2 rows until 27 sts rem, ending with a P row. Leave sts on holder for centre back neck.

Front

Work as given for back to **.
Change to 3¾mm/No 9 needles.
Beg with a K row work 50 rows st st
Join in small balls of contrast colours as required and work running shoe motif.
Next row K26 A, 13 B, 10 A, 17 B, K to end with A.
Next row P24 A, 18 B, 10 A, 13 B, P to end with A.
Beg with the 3rd row cont in st st working motif from chart as now set, then cont with A only as given for back until 41 sts rem after armhole shaping, ending with a Ws row.

Shape neck

Next row K1, sl 1, K1, psso, K11 sts, turn and leave rem sts on holder.
Complete left shoulder first.
Next row P to end.
Next row K1, sl 1, K1, psso, K to last 3 sts, sl 1, K1, psso, K1.
Rep last 2 rows 4 times more, then P one row. 3 sts.
Next row K1, sl 1, K1, psso.
Next row P2 tog.

The pattern pieces

4cm
11.25cm
16cm
back/front
26cm
4cm
38cm

3cm
28cm
sleeve
16.25cm
16cm
32cm
4cm

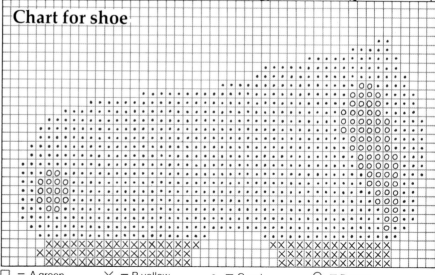

50   40   30   20   10   1

Chart for shoe

☐ = A green   X = B yellow   • = C red   O = D white

162

Fasten off.
With Rs of work facing leave first
13 sts on holder for centre front
neck, rejoin yarn to rem sts.
Next row K to last 3 sts, K2 tog, K1.
Next row P to end.
Next row K1, K2 tog, K to last 3 sts,
K2 tog, K1.
Complete right shoulder to match
first side.

Sleeves

With 3mm/No 11 needles and A cast
on 39 sts. Work 4cm/1½in rib as
given for back, ending with a 2nd
row.
Change to 3¾mm/No 9 needles.
Beg with a K row cont in st st, inc
one st at each end of 5th and every
foll 6th row until there are 67 sts.
Cont without shaping until sleeve
measures 36cm/14in from beg,
ending with a P row. Adjust length
here if required.
Mark each end of last row then
work a further 8 rows. These 8 rows
are set into armhole shaping and
are not included in sleeve seam
measurement.

Shape top
Next row K1, sl 1, K1, psso, K to last
3 sts, K2 tog, K1.
Next row P to end.
Rep these 2 rows until 33 sts rem,
ending with a P row.

Shape centre dart
Next row K1, sl 1, K1, psso, K11,
sl 1, K1, psso, K1, K2 tog, K11, K2
tog, K1.
Cont dec in this way in centre of
every foll 4th row, *at the same time*
cont dec at each end of every alt row
for armhole shaping until 7 sts rem,
ending with a P row. Leave sts on
holder.

Neckband

Join raglan seams, sewing the last
8 rows of sleeve seams to cast off
sts at armholes.
With Rs of work facing, set of four
3mm/No 11 needles and A, K across
sts of back neck and left sleeve K2
tog at seam, pick up and K13 sts
down left front neck, K across front
neck sts, pick up and K13 sts up
right front neck, then K across sts of
right sleeve K last st of sleeve tog
with first st of back neck. 78 sts.
Work 4cm/1½in in rounds of K1, P1
rib. Cast off loosely in rib.

To make up
Press under a dry cloth with a warm
iron. Join side and sleeve seams.
Fold neckband in half to Ws and sl
st down. Press seams. Thread boot
lace along top of motif.

*Above: If preferred you can enlarge the
delightful teddy motif as an alternative
to the running shoe motif shown here.
For the teddy design, tie a ribbon round
his neck or sew on toy eyes or buttons to
put an individual stamp on him.*

Lace background patterns and edgings

The following chapters introduce a variety of lace patterns, big and small and edgings for use as borders or collars. Before making up a garment you might like to try knitting up a few squares in a variety of patterns to make a useful pram cover.

You can make a most attractive cot or pram cover using squares of all of the lace samples that have multiples of the same number of stitches, and mixing there with squares of basic patterns, such as stocking, garter and moss stitches.

Add a lace border using one of the patterns given on pages 174–175. These edgings are knitted sideways across a short pattern row so you can easily calculate the yarn needed and the length to knit.

Cot or pram cover made from lace squares

Calculate the multiples of stitches needed to give the size of square you require. As a guide, the lace stitches that have multiples of 10 stitches plus one stitch, worked in double knitting yarn on 4mm/No 8 needles over 21 stitches will give a square about 9–10cm/3½–4in. Use up oddments of the same yarn in different colours or keep to one colour only for all of the squares. See how many squares you can make out of one ball of yarn to arrive at the total quantity you will need. Allow sufficient to make a lace edging to complete the cover.

The lace patterns are not reversible, so sew all the squares together so that the seams are on the wrong side, then press them lightly as given on the ball band.

Choose the edging you like best and pin it into place around the outer edges as you knit it. Once you are sure you have sufficient length, cast off and join the two short edges together. Keep this seam at one corner of the centre squares and sew the edging into place. Press the seams as before.

Below: Seam the squares together on reverse side using backstitch.

Multiples of stitches in knitting patterns

Stocking stitch and garter stitch are worked over any number of stitches, but even single rib needs multiples of two stitches plus one at the edge if seams are to match exactly. More complicated patterns need larger multiples of stitches. When creating a pattern, the designer must take this into account to ensure that the pattern repeats work out accurately. Sometimes extra stitches are needed at each end of the row so that patterns match up correctly when joined.

The simple lace patterns illustrated below repeat over six stitches. This means that the number of stitches cast on must be a multiple of six, plus one edge stitch. So to begin, you need to cast on a minimum of seven stitches, adding six more for each pattern repeat – 13, 19, 25 and so on.

Instructions for the edge stitches are given at the beginning and end of each row. The multiples of six stitches needed for the pattern are given after the asterisk, *, and are repeated as instructed.

Sample worked in mesh lace.

Sample worked in arrowhead lace.

Sample worked in catkin lace.

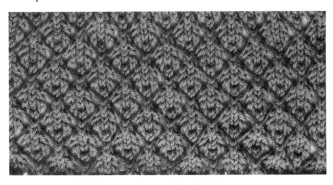

Sample worked in miniature leaf lace.

Mesh lace
1st row K1, *yfwd, sl 1, K1, psso, K1, K2 tog, yfwd, K1, rep from * to end.
2nd and every alt row P to end.
3rd row K1, *yfwd, K1, sl 1, K2 tog, psso, K1, yfwd, K1, rep from * to end.
5th row K1, *K2 tog, yfwd, K1, yfwd, sl 1, K1, psso, K1, rep from * to end.
7th row K2 tog, *(K1, yfwd) twice, K1, sl 1, K2 tog, psso, rep from * to last 5 sts, (K1, yfwd) twice, K1, sl 1, K1, psso.
8th row As 2nd.
These 8 rows form the pattern.

Arrowhead lace
1st row K1, *K2 tog, yfwd, K1, yfwd, sl 1, K1, psso, K1, rep from * to end.
2nd and every alt row P to end.
3rd row K2 tog, *yfwd, K3, yfwd, sl 1, K2 tog, psso, rep from * to last 5 sts, yfwd, K3, yfwd, sl 1, K1, psso.
5th row K1, *yfwd, sl 1, K1, psso, K1, K2 tog, yfwd, K1, rep from * to end.
7th row As 5th.
9th row As 5th.
11th row K2, *yfwd, sl 1, K2 tog, psso, yfwd, K3, rep from * to last 5 sts, yfwd, sl 1, K2 tog, psso, yfwd, K2.
12th row As 2nd.
These 12 rows form the pattern.

Catkin lace
1st row K3, *yfwd, sl 1, K1, psso, K4, rep from * to last 4 sts, yfwd, sl 1, K1, psso, K2.
2nd and every alt row P to end.
3rd row K1, *K2 tog, yfwd, K1, yfwd, sl 1, K1, psso, K1, rep from * to end.
5th row K2 tog, yfwd, *K3, yfwd, sl 1, K2 tog, psso, yfwd, rep from * to last 5 sts, K3, yfwd, sl 1, K1, psso.

7th row K1, *yfwd, sl 1, K1, psso, K1, K2 tog, yfwd, K1, rep from * to end.
9th row As 7th.
10th row As 2nd.
These 10 rows form the pattern.

Miniature leaf lace
1st row K1, *K2 tog, yfwd, K1, yfwd, sl 1, K1, psso, K1, rep from * to end.
2nd and every alt row P to end.
3rd row Sl 1, K1, psso, *yfwd, K3, yfwd, sl 2 tog in knitwise direction, K1, p2sso, rep from * to last 5 sts, yfwd, K3, yfwd, K2 tog.
5th row K1, *yfwd, sl 1, K1, psso, K1, K2 tog, yfwd, K1, rep from * to end.
7th row K2, *yfwd, sl 2, K1, p2sso, yfwd, K3, rep from * to last 5 sts, yfwd, sl 2, K1, p2sso, yfwd, K2.
8th row As 2nd.
These 8 rows form the pattern.

Matinée jacket

These dainty matinée jackets are knitted in one piece to the underarm and you can use any lace pattern in this chapter to work the skirt. The front borders are in moss stitch and the bottom of the skirt and the cuffs have a dainty picot edge. The yoke and sleeves are worked in stocking stitch. Ribbon is slotted through the waist.

Size

To fit 46–48cm/18–19in chest
Length to shoulder, 30cm/11¾in
Sleeve seam, 13cm/5in

You will need

6×20g balls of Wendy Darling
  Double Knitting, 55% Bri-nylon,
  45% Courtelle
One pair 3mm/No 11 needles
One pair 3¾mm/No 9 needles
One 3mm/No 11 circular needle,
  80cm/30in long
One 3¾mm/No 9 circular needle,
  80cm/30in long
3 small buttons
1.5m/1⅝yd of narrow ribbon

Tension

24 sts and 32 rows to 10cm/4in over

The white version features miniature leaf lace for the skirt, and the apricot version opposite, arrowhead lace.

st st worked on 3¾mm/No 9 needles

Jacket (worked in one piece to underarms)
With 3mm/No 11 circular needle cast on 187 sts. Beg with a K row work 4 rows st st.
Next row (picot) Cast on 5 sts for front edge, (K1, P1) twice, K2, * yfwd, K2 tog, rep from * to end.
Next row Cast on 5 sts for front

The skirt of this matinée jacket is knitted in dainty arrowhead lace for a light, yet cosy look.

edge, (K1, P1) twice, K1, P to last 5 sts, (K1, P1) twice, K1.
Next row Work 5 sts in moss st as now set, K to last 5 sts, moss st 5.
Next row Moss st 5, P to last 5 sts, moss st 5.
Rep last 2 rows twice more. Change to 3¾mm/No 9 circular needle.
Next row Moss st 5, work first row of chosen lace patt to last 5 sts, moss st 5.
Cont in patt as now set until work measures 19cm/7½in from picot row ending with a Rs row.
Next row (dec row) Moss st 5, *(P1, P2 tog) 5 times, P2 tog, rep from * to last 5 sts, moss st 5. 131 sts.
Next row (buttonhole and ribbon slotting) K1, P1, yrn, P2 tog, K1, *K2 tog, yfwd, rep from * to last 6 sts, K1, moss st 5.
Next row Moss st 5, P to last 5 sts, moss st 5.

Divide for armholes
Next row Moss st 5, K28 sts, cast off 5, K55 sts, cast off 5, K28 sts, moss st 5.
Cont on last 33 sts for left front:
Next row Moss st 5, P to end.
Keeping moss st edge correct, dec one st at armhole edge on next 4 rows, then on next and every alt row until 25 sts rem. Work 15 rows without shaping, end at front edge.

Shape neck
1st row Moss st 14, P11.
2nd row K11, moss st 14.

3rd row Moss st 6, (yrn, P2 tog, K1, P1) twice, P11.
4th row As 2nd.
5th row Cast off 10 sts in moss st, moss st 4 including st on needle, P to end.
6th row K11, moss st 4.
7th row K1, P1, yrn, P2 tog, P11.
8th row As 6th.
9th row Moss st 4, P11.
10th and 11th rows As 6th and 7th.
12th row Cast off 6, K5, moss st 4.
13th row Moss st 4, P5.
14th row Cast off 5, moss st 4.
Cast off rem 4 sts in moss st.
With Ws of work facing, rejoin yarn to 55 sts for back. Cont in st st dec one st at each end of next 4 rows, then at each end of next and every alt row until 39 sts rem. Cont without shaping until armholes

measure same as left front, ending with a P row.

Shape shoulders and neck
Cast off 6 sts at beg of next 2 rows.
Next row Cast off 5, moss st 17, K5.
Next row Cast off 5, moss st 17.
Next row K1, P1, (yrn, P2 tog, K1, P1) 3 times, yrn, P2 tog, K1.
Work one more row moss st. Cast off in moss st.
With Ws of work facing, rejoin yarn to rem 33 sts for right front. Work to match left front, reversing shaping and making two more buttonholes at intervals of 14 rows.

Sleeves
With 3mm/No 11 needles cast on 33 sts.
Beg with a K row work 4 rows st st.
Next row (picot) K1, *yfwd, K2 tog, rep from * to end.
Beg with a P row work 5 rows st st.
Change to 3¾mm/No 9 needles.
Cont in st st, inc one st at each end of 3rd and every foll 5th row until there are 45 sts. Cont without shaping until sleeve measures 13cm/5in from picot row, ending with a P row.

Shape top
Cast off 3 sts at beg of next 2 rows.
Dec one st at each end of next and every alt row until 19 sts rem, then at each end of every row until 9 sts rem. Cast off.

To make up
Press under a dry cloth with a cool iron. Turn picot hems to Ws and sl st down. Join shoulder seams. Join sleeve seams. Set in sleeves. Press seams. Sew on buttons. Thread ribbon through holes at waist and tie at front.

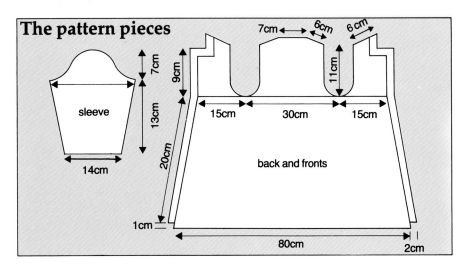

The pattern pieces

sleeve

7cm
9cm
13cm
14cm
20cm
1cm

7cm
6cm
6cm
11cm
15cm
30cm
15cm

back and fronts

80cm
2cm

Lace knitting for beautiful backgrounds

Lace knitting has such a variety of patterns that most beginners are bewildered by the profusion and assume the working methods are complicated. In fact, many small lace patterns are quicker and more interesting to knit than most textured patterns, such as guernseys.

All lace patterns are built up with a sequence of eyelet hole increases, using the yarn forward, over the needle or round the needle methods, see pages 26–28. Stitches must then be decreased in the course of the pattern to compensate for the eyelet increases. The decreases are worked by the normal methods given on pages 30–32. The decreases will not necessarily immediately precede or follow the eyelet increases. In fact, it is the way in which the eyelets are grouped that gives lace knitting its incredible variety – the permutations are almost limitless.

Lace knitting provides for every degree of skill – only a very few patterns are really complicated. To simplify your first attempt, work two vertical panels on the front of a basic stocking stitch jersey, placing them well away from any edges where shaping will take place.

It takes a little practice to tackle shaping in an all-over lace pattern. It is not too difficult if you remember that when decreasing, every time an eyelet hole increase is eliminated from the pattern sequence its cor-

Fan pattern

Cast on multiples of 10 sts plus 1, 21 sts minimum, eg 31.

1st row (Rs) K2 tog, *K3, (yfwd, K1) twice, K2, sl 1, K2 tog, psso, rep from * to last 9 sts, K3, (yfwd, K1) twice, K2, sl 1, K1, psso.

2nd and every alt row P to end.

3rd row K2 tog, *K2, yfwd, K3, yfwd, K2, sl 1, K2 tog, psso, rep from * to last 9 sts, K2, yfwd, K3, yfwd, K2, sl 1, K1, psso.

5th row K2 tog, *(K1, yfwd) twice, sl 1, K2 tog, psso, (yfwd, K1) twice, sl 1, K2 tog, psso, rep from * to last 9 sts, (K1, yfwd) twice, sl 1, K2 tog, psso, (yfwd, K1) twice, sl 1, K1, psso.

7th row K2 tog, *yfwd, K7, yfwd, sl 1, K2 tog, psso, rep from * to last 9 sts, yfwd, K7, yfwd, sl 1, K1, psso.

9th row *K1, (K1, yfwd, sl 1, K2 tog, psso, yfwd) twice, K1, rep from * to last st, K1.

11th row P to end.

12th row K to end.

These 12 rows form the pattern.

Fern leaf pattern

Cast on multiples of 10 sts plus 1, 21 sts minimum, eg 31.

1st row (Rs) K3, *K2 tog, yfwd, K1, yfwd, sl 1, K1, psso, K5, rep from * to last 8 sts, K2 tog, yfwd, K1, yfwd, sl 1, K1, psso, K3.

2nd and every alt row P to end.

3rd row K2, *K2 tog, (K1, yfwd) twice, K1, sl 1, K1, psso, K3, rep from * to last 9 sts, K2 tog, (K1, yfwd) twice, K1, sl 1, K1, psso, K2.

5th row K1, *K2 tog, K2, yfwd, K1, yfwd, K2, sl 1, K1, psso, K1, rep from * to end.

7th row K2 tog, *K3, yfwd, K1, yfwd, K3, sl 1, K2 tog, psso, rep from * to last 9 sts, K3, yfwd, K1, yfwd, K3, sl 1, K1, psso.

9th row K1, *yfwd, sl 1, K1, psso, K5, K2 tog, yfwd, K1, rep from * to end.

11th row K1, *yfwd, K1, sl 1, K1, psso, K3, K2 tog, K1, yfwd, K1, rep from * to end.

13th row K1, *yfwd, K2, sl 1, K1, psso, K1, K2 tog, K2, yfwd, K1, rep from * to end.

15th row K1, *yfwd, K3, sl 1, K2 tog, psso, K3, yfwd, K1, rep from * to end.

16th row As 2nd.

These 16 rows form the pattern.

responding decrease must also be eliminated. Similarly, when increasing, remember that you must not work a new eyelet increase in the pattern sequence until you have also added sufficient stitches to work its corresponding decrease.

Nine different lace patterns are given here. They are all worked over the same multiples of stitches and are, therefore, interchangeable for the jersey pattern given in this chapter.

Fan lace produces groups of eyelets with the decreases forming an inverted fan shape. The pattern is unusual in that it includes a ridge of reversed stocking stitch between each band of lace.

Fern leaf lace is an early English pattern. The decreases form a diamond-shaped outline round the central group of eyelets.

Diamond lace looks good worked as a border or panel against a stocking stitch background. The eyelet holes appear to frame the diamond shapes.

Fir cone lace produces gracefully curved lines because the central decreases draw the stitches out of position in a series of vertical waves. This is a very easy pattern.

Horseshoe lace is one of the basic Shetland lace patterns and is very simple to work. The eyelets form a crescent shape, resembling the print of a horseshoe.

Chevron lace is very simple to work with the eyelets forming rows of chevrons in bands. This pattern is also suitable as a border or panel of lace against a stocking stitch background.

Openwork diamond lace is based on an old Spanish pattern. The pattern is unusual in that it features garter stitch and the eyelet holes are worked on every row.

Falling leaf lace is an undulating pattern, with the eyelets forming a series of deep chevrons.

Mesh lace is a very open pattern which looks best used as an all-over fabric. The pattern does not keep the same number of stitches on every row but the 5th and 7th rows will revert to the original number.

Below: The lacy sections of this jersey have no shaping and so it is easy to substitute the stitch of your choice.

Diamond pattern

Cast on multiples of 10 sts plus 1, 21 sts minimum, eg 31.

1st row (Rs) K2, *K2 tog, (K1, yfwd) twice, K1, sl 1, K1, psso, K3, rep from * to last 9 sts, K2 tog, (K1, yfwd) twice, K1, sl 1, K1, psso, K2.

2nd and every alt row P to end.

3rd row K1, *K2 tog, K1, yfwd, K3, yfwd, K1, sl 1, K1, psso, K1, rep from * to end.

5th row K2 tog, *K1, yfwd, K5, yfwd, K1, sl 1, K2 tog, psso, rep from * to last 9 sts, K1, yfwd, K5, yfwd, K1, sl 1, K1, psso.

7th row K1, *yfwd, K1, sl 1, K1, psso, K3, K2 tog, K1, yfwd, K1, rep from * to end.

9th row K2, *yfwd, K1, sl 1, K1, psso, K1, K2 tog, K1, yfwd, K3, rep from * to last 9 sts, yfwd, K1, sl 1, K1, psso, K1, K2 tog, K1, yfwd, K2.

11th row K3, *yfwd, K1, sl 1, K2 tog, psso, K1, yfwd, K5, rep from * to last 8 sts, yfwd, K1, sl 1, K2 tog, psso, K1, yfwd, K3.

12th row As 2nd.

These 12 rows form the pattern.

Fir cone pattern

Cast on multiples of 10 sts plus 1, 21 sts minimum, eg 31.
1st row (Rs) K1, *yfwd, K3, sl 1, K2 tog, psso, K3, yfwd, K1, rep from * to end.
2nd row P to end.
Rep 1st and 2nd rows 3 times more.
9th row K2 tog, *K3, yfwd, K1, yfwd, K3, sl 1, K2 tog, psso, rep from * to last 9 sts, K3, yfwd, K1, yfwd, K3, sl 1, K1, psso.
10th row P to end.
Rep 9th and 10th rows 3 times more.
These 16 rows form the pattern.

Horseshoe pattern

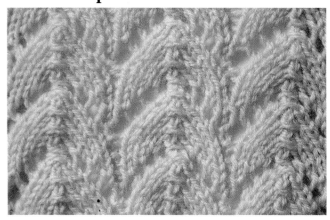

Cast on multiples of 10 sts plus 1, eg 31.
1st row (Rs) P1, *yon, K3, sl 1, K2 tog, psso, K3, yrn, P1, rep from * to end.
2nd and every alt row K1, *P9, K1, rep from * to end.
3rd row P1, *K1, yfwd, K2, sl 1, K2 tog, psso, K2, yfwd, K1, P1, rep from * to end.
5th row P1, *K2, yfwd, K1, sl 1, K2 tog, psso, K1, yfwd, K2, P1, rep from * to end.
7th row P1, *K3, yfwd, sl 1, K2 tog, psso, yfwd, K3, P1, rep from * to end.
8th row As 2nd.
These 8 rows form the pattern.

Chevron pattern

Cast on multiples of 10 sts plus 1, eg 31.
1st row (Rs) *K5, yfwd, sl 1, K1, psso, K3, rep from * to last st, K1.
2nd and every alt row P to end.
3rd row *K3, K2 tog, yfwd, K1, yfwd, sl 1, K1, psso, K2, rep from * to last st, K1.
5th row *K2, K2 tog, yfwd, K3, yfwd, sl 1, K1, psso, K1, rep from * to last st, K1.
7th row *K1, K2 tog, yfwd, K5, yfwd, sl 1, K1, psso, rep from * to last st, K1.
9th row K2 tog, yfwd, K7, *yfwd, sl 1, K2 tog, psso, yfwd, K7, rep from * to last 2 sts, yfwd, sl 1, K1, psso.
10th row As 2nd.
These 10 rows form the pattern.

Openwork diamond pattern

Cast on multiples of 10 sts plus 1, 21 sts minimum, eg 31.
1st row (Rs) K1, *yfwd, sl 1, K1, psso, K5, K2 tog, yfwd, K1, rep from * to end.
2nd row P1, *P1, yrn, P2 tog, K3, P2 tog tbl, yrn, P2, rep from * to end.
3rd row K1, *K2, yfwd, sl 1, K1, psso, K1, K2 tog, yfwd, K3, rep from * to end.
4th row K1, *K2, P1, yrn, P3 tog, yrn, P1, K3, rep from * to end.
5th row K1, *K2, K2 tog, yfwd, K1, yfwd, sl 1, K1, psso, K3, rep from * to end.
6th row K1, *K1, P2 tog tbl, yrn, P3, yrn, P2 tog, K2, rep from * to end.
7th row K1, *K2 tog, yfwd, K5, yfwd, sl 1, K1, psso, K1, rep from * to end.
8th row P2 tog, *yrn, P1, K5, P1, yrn, P3 tog, rep from * to last 9 sts, yrn, P1, K5, P1, yrn, P2 tog.
These 8 rows form the pattern.

Lacy T-top

Choose any of these lacy patterns, all knitted in Wendy Choice DK, to knit up into a simple jersey shape like the T-top on page 18.

For an unusual effect you could knit the back and front in one pattern and the yoke and sleeves in another.

The distortion of the fabric which is caused by the eyelet hole increases and working two together forms a pretty scallop effect along the lower edges.

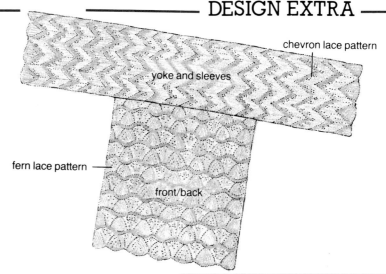

chevron lace pattern

yoke and sleeves

fern lace pattern —

front/back

Front and back

With a tension of 22 sts to 10cm/4in worked on 4mm/No 8 needles, you will need to cast on 111 sts (multiple of 10 plus 1). Work in g st for 2cm/¾in, then work any of the lacy patterns given until the front/back measures 36cm/14¼in from the beginning. Cast off.

Yoke and sleeves

Cast on 51 sts and work 2cm/¾in in g st. Change to another of the lacy patterns and continue until work measures 96cm/37¾in from beg. Work a further 2cm/¾in in g st and cast off.

Right: Sample of scalloped edge.

Falling leaf pattern

Cast on multiples of 10 sts plus 1, 21 sts minimum, eg 31.

1st row (Rs) K1, *yfwd, sl 1, K1, psso, K2 tog, yfwd, K1, rep from * to end.

2nd and every alt row P to end.

3rd row K2, *yfwd, sl 1, K1, psso, K3, K2 tog, yfwd, K3, rep from * to last 9 sts, yfwd, sl 1, K1, psso, K3, K2 tog, yfwd, K2.

5th row K3, *yfwd, sl 1, K1, psso, K1, K2 tog, yfwd, K5, rep from * to last 8 sts, yfwd, sl 1, K1, psso, K1, K2 tog, yfwd, K3.

7th row K4, *yfwd, sl 1, K2 tog, psso, yfwd, K7, rep from * to last 7 sts, yfwd, sl 1, K2 tog, psso, yfwd, K4.

9th, 11th and 13th rows K1, *sl 1, K1, psso, K2, yfwd, K1, yfwd, K2, K2 tog, K1, rep from * to end.

14th row As 2nd.

These 14 rows form the pattern.

Mesh pattern

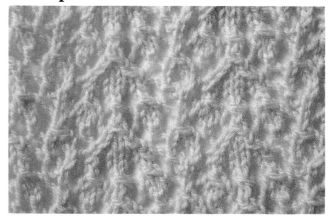

Cast on multiples of 10 sts plus 1, eg 31.

1st row (Rs) K2 tog, *yfwd, K3, yfwd, K into front and back of next st – **called inc 1**, yfwd, K3, yfwd, sl 1, K2 tog, psso, rep from * to last 9 sts, yfwd, K3, yfwd, inc 1, yfwd, K3, yfwd, sl 1, K1, psso.

2nd and every alt row P to end.

3rd row Sl 1, K1, psso, *yfwd, sl 2, K1, p2sso, yfwd, K2 tog, yfwd, sl 1, K1, psso, (yfwd, sl 2, K1, p2sso) twice, rep from * to last 12 sts, yfwd, sl 2, K1, p2sso, yfwd, K2 tog, yfwd, sl1, K1, psso, yfwd, sl 2, K1, p2sso, yfwd, K2 tog.

5th row K2, *K2 tog, yfwd, K3, yfwd, sl 1, K1, psso, K3, rep from * to last 9 sts, K2 tog, yfwd, K3, yfwd, sl 1, K1, psso, K2.

7th row K1, *K2 tog, yfwd, K1 tbl, yfwd, sl 1, K2 tog, psso, yfwd, K1 tbl, yfwd, sl 1, K1, psso, K1, rep from * to end.

8th row As 2nd.

These 8 rows form the pattern.

171

Lace patterned jerseys

Two of a kind for day or evening. The short-sleeved jersey shown earlier is worked in cotton with an openwork diamond pattern – the long-sleeved version opposite is in glitter yarn in the horseshoe pattern.

All of the patterns given in this chapter have the same multiples of stitches so you can knit your own original version of the jersey in the style and pattern of your choice. Remember to adjust the quantity of yarn needed for long or short sleeves.

Sizes

To fit 81 [86:91:97:102]cm/ 32 [34:36:38:40]in bust
Length to shoulder, 59 [60:61:63:64] cm/23[23½:24:24½:25]in
Short sleeve seam, 10cm/4in
Long sleeve seam, 46cm/18in
The figures in [] refer to the 86/34, 91/36, 97/38 and 102cm/40in sizes respectively

You will need

Short-sleeved version
10 [11:12:13:14] × 25g balls of Twilleys Lyscordet No 5 (100% cotton)
Long-sleeved version
16 [17:18:19:20] × 25g balls of Twilleys Goldfingering (80% viscose, 20% metallised polyester)
One pair 3¼mm/No 10 needles
One pair 3mm/No 11 needles
One pair 2¾mm/No 12 needles
Four buttons

Tension

30 sts and 38 rows to 10cm/4in over st st worked on 3¼mm/No 10 needles

Back

With 3mm/No 11 needles cast on 122 [132:142:152:162] sts. Work 3 rows g st.
Next row (inc row) K5 [10:7:8:13] sts, *pick up loop lying between sts and K tbl – **called M1**, K14 [14:16:17:17] sts, rep from * 7 times more, M1, K5 [10:7:8:13] sts. 131 [141:151:161:171] sts.
Change to 3¼mm/No 10 needles.
Cont in openwork diamond patt or horseshoe patt, or any patt of your choice, noting that st and row tension will vary slightly with each patt, until work measures 41cm/ 16¼in from beg, ending with a Ws row. Mark each end of last row as beg of armholes. **
Cont in patt until armholes measure 13 [14:15:17:18]cm/5 [5½:6:6¾:7]in from beg, ending with a Ws row.
Change to 3mm/No 11 needles.
Cont in g st until armholes measure 18 [19:20:22:23:]cm/7 [7½:7¾:8¾:9]in from beg, ending with a Ws row.

Shape shoulders

Cast off at beg of next and every row 9 [10:11:12:13] sts 8 times and 7 sts twice. Leave rem 45 [47:49:51:53] sts on holder for centre back neck.

Front

Work as given for back to **
Divide for front opening
Next row Patt 60 [65:70:75:80] sts, turn.
Complete left shoulder first.
Next row Inc in first st, patt to end. 61 [66:71:76:81] sts.
Cont in patt until work measures

same as back to beg of g st, ending at neck edge. Change to 3mm/No 11 needles.

Shape neck

Cont in g st cast off at beg of next and every alt row 5 sts once, 3 sts twice and 2 sts 3 times. Dec one st at neck edge on next 1 [2:3:4:5] rows. 43 [47:51:55:59] sts.
Cont in g st without shaping until work measures same as back to shoulder, ending at armhole edge.

Shape shoulder

Cast off at beg of next and every alt row 9 [10:11:12:13] sts 4 times and 7 sts once.
With Rs of work facing, sl first 11 sts on to a safety pin and leave for front band, rejoin yarn to rem sts, inc in first st, patt to end.
Complete right shoulder to match left shoulder, reversing all shapings.

Sleeves

With 3mm/No 11 needles cast on 66 [66:71:76:76] sts. Work 3 rows g st.
Next row (inc row) K10 sts, *inc in next st, rep from * to last 11 sts, K11 sts. 111 [111:121:131:131] sts.
Change to 3¼mm/No 10 needles.

Short sleeves

Cont in patt as given for back until work measures 10cm/4in from beg. Cast off.

Long sleeves

Cont in patt as given for back until work measures 46cm/18in from beg. Cast off.

Button band

With 2¾mm/No 12 needles cast on 15 sts. K one row. Cont in g st, sl first st K-wise on every row, until band, when slightly stretched fits along left front edge to beg of neck shaping. Leave sts on holder. Mark positions of buttons, first to come 4 rows above cast-on edge and last to come 4 rows in to neckband, with 2 more evenly spaced between.

Buttonhole band

Slip 11 sts on safety pin on to 2¾mm/No 12 needles.
Next row (inc row) (inc in next st, K2) 3 times, inc in next st, K1. 15 sts.
Work as given for button band,

The pattern pieces

15[16:16:17:18]cm

37[37:40:44:44]cm

18[19:20: 22:23]cm

sleeve

5cm

13[14:15:17: 18]cm

begin armholes

46cm

finish here for short sleeve

10cm

4cm

back/front

40cm

22[22:24:25:25]cm

garter stitch

44[47:50:54:57]cm

1cm

41[44:47:51:54]cm

Above: All shaping is confined to the neat garter stitch yoke.

Right: A change of yarn and stitch pattern gives a totally different look. The jersey can be worn loose or belted.

making buttonholes as markers are reached, as foll:
Next row (buttonhole row) K6, cast off 3, K6.
Next row K to end, casting on 3 sts above those cast off in previous row. Do not break off yarn.

Neckband

Join shoulder seams. With Rs of work facing and 2¾mm/No 12 needles K15 sts of buttonhole band, pick up and K28 [30:32:34:36] sts up right front neck, K across
45 [47:49:51:53] back neck sts on holder, pick up and
K28 [30:32:34:36] sts down left front neck and K15 sts from button band.
131 [137:143:149:155] sts.
Work 2 rows g st.
Next row (dec row)
K16 [19:18:17:20] sts, *K2 tog,
K10 [10:11:12:12] sts, rep from
* 7 times more, K2 tog,
K17 [20:19:18:21] sts.
122 [128:134:140:146] sts.
Work buttonhole on next 2 rows as before. Work 3 rows g st. Cast off.

To make up

Do not press. Sew cast-off edge of sleeves to armholes between markers. Join side and sleeve seams. Sew on front bands, over-lapping buttonhole band over button band at lower edge. Sew on buttons.

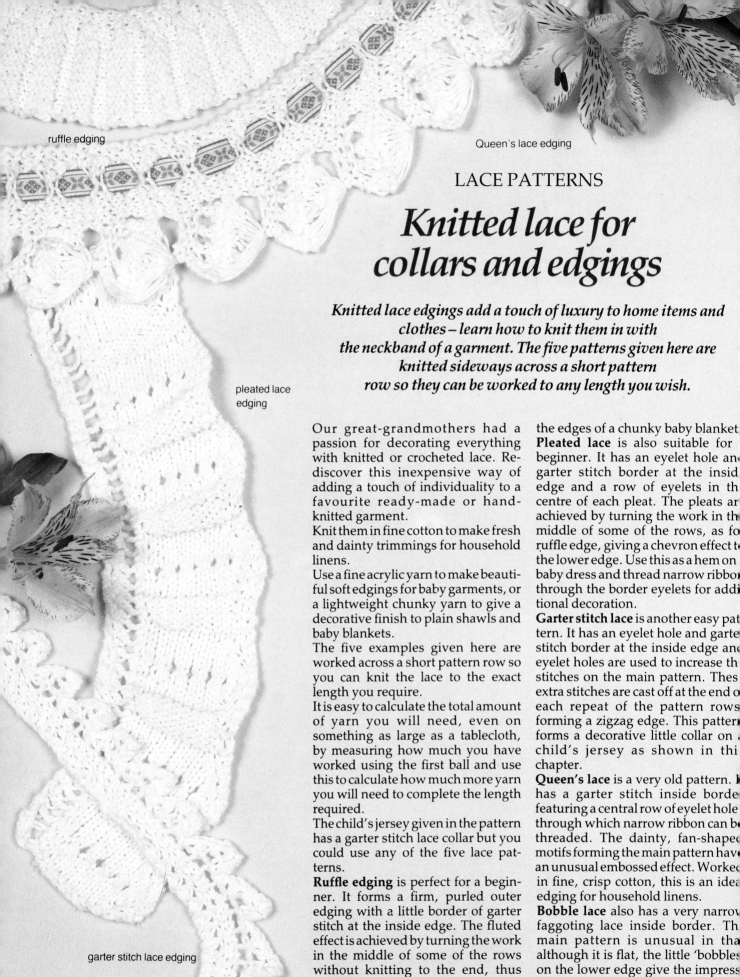

ruffle edging

Queen's lace edging

pleated lace
edging

garter stitch lace edging

LACE PATTERNS

Knitted lace for collars and edgings

Knitted lace edgings add a touch of luxury to home items and clothes – learn how to knit them in with the neckband of a garment. The five patterns given here are knitted sideways across a short pattern row so they can be worked to any length you wish.

Our great-grandmothers had a passion for decorating everything with knitted or crocheted lace. Rediscover this inexpensive way of adding a touch of individuality to a favourite ready-made or hand-knitted garment.

Knit them in fine cotton to make fresh and dainty trimmings for household linens.

Use a fine acrylic yarn to make beautiful soft edgings for baby garments, or a lightweight chunky yarn to give a decorative finish to plain shawls and baby blankets.

The five examples given here are worked across a short pattern row so you can knit the lace to the exact length you require.

It is easy to calculate the total amount of yarn you will need, even on something as large as a tablecloth, by measuring how much you have worked using the first ball and use this to calculate how much more yarn you will need to complete the length required.

The child's jersey given in the pattern has a garter stitch lace collar but you could use any of the five lace patterns.

Ruffle edging is perfect for a beginner. It forms a firm, purled outer edging with a little border of garter stitch at the inside edge. The fluted effect is achieved by turning the work in the middle of some of the rows without knitting to the end, thus making the inside edge shorter than the outside edge. Use this lace round

the edges of a chunky baby blanket **Pleated lace** is also suitable for beginner. It has an eyelet hole an garter stitch border at the insid edge and a row of eyelets in th centre of each pleat. The pleats ar achieved by turning the work in th middle of some of the rows, as fo ruffle edge, giving a chevron effect t the lower edge. Use this as a hem on baby dress and thread narrow ribbo through the border eyelets for addi tional decoration.

Garter stitch lace is another easy pat tern. It has an eyelet hole and garte stitch border at the inside edge and eyelet holes are used to increase th stitches on the main pattern. Thes extra stitches are cast off at the end o each repeat of the pattern rows forming a zigzag edge. This patter forms a decorative little collar on child's jersey as shown in thi chapter.

Queen's lace is a very old pattern. I has a garter stitch inside borde featuring a central row of eyelet hole through which narrow ribbon can b threaded. The dainty, fan-shape motifs forming the main pattern hav an unusual embossed effect. Worke in fine, crisp cotton, this is an idea edging for household linens.

Bobble lace also has a very narro faggoting lace inside border. Th main pattern is unusual in tha although it is flat, the little 'bobbles on the lower edge give the impress ion of Victorian fringing. In cris cotton, this makes a beautiful edging

Knitted lace collars in with the neckband

To work out how long to knit the lace edging, first check how many stitches are to be picked up round the neck for the neckband. For ruffle or pleated edging work this number of rows in the edging and for all the others work double the amount.

With right side of edging facing, pick up and knit one stitch, from the inside edge, from every alternate row end (or every row end for ruffle or pleated edgings) until you have picked up the number that is required for the neckband. Purl one row. Leave stitches for time being.

Join seams of garment as directed and have right side

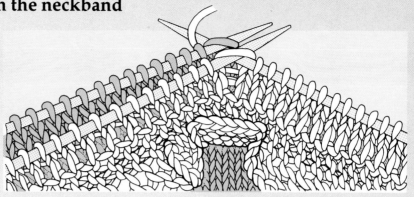

facing. With a 2nd needle pick up and knit the stitches given for the neckband. Place the needle with the collar stitches in front of the neckband stitches and hold both needles together.
Insert the needle into one stitch

from the collar needle and one stitch from the neckband needle, working these two stitches together as one, until all the stitches are on the right-hand needle. Complete neckband as given in instructions.

Ruffle edging

Cast on 13 sts.
1st row (Rs) K.
2nd row P10 sts, turn and K these 10 sts.
3rd row P10 sts, K3.
4th row K3, P10 sts.
5th row K10 sts, turn and P these 10 sts.
6th row K.
These 6 rows form the pattern.

Pleated lace edging

Cast on 16 sts.
1st row (Ws) P.
2nd row K1, sl 1, K1, psso, yfwd and round needle twice to make 2 loops – **called yrn twice**, K2 tog, P8, inc in next st, K2.
3rd row K14, P1, K2
4th row K1, sl 1, K1, psso, yrn twice, K2 tog, P9, inc in next st, K2.
5th row K12, turn, P9, inc in next st, K2.
6th row K16, P1, K2.
7th row K1, sl 1, K1, psso, yrn twice, K2 tog, P1, (yrn, P2 tog) 5 times, P1, K2.
8th row K13, turn, P9, P2 tog, K2.
9th row K15, P1, K2.
10th row K1, sl 1, K1, psso, yrn twice, K2 tog, P9, P2 tog, K2.
11th row As 3rd.
12th row K1, sl 1, K1, psso, yrn twice, K2 tog, P8, P2 tog, K2.
13th row K13, P1, K2.
14th row K1, sl 1, K1, psso, yrn twice, K2 tog, K11.
15th row K2, P8, turn and K10.

16th row As 15th.
17th row K2, P9, K2, P1, K2.
The 2nd to 17th rows inclusive form the pattern.

Garter stitch lace edging

Cast on 6 sts.
1st row (Rs) Yfwd and over needle to inc 1 – **called inc 1**, K2 tog, K2, yfwd, K2. 7 sts.
2nd row K5, yfwd, K2 tog.
3rd row Inc 1, K2 tog, K2, yfwd, K1, yfwd, K2.
4th row K7, yfwd, K2 tog.
5th row Inc 1, K2 tog, K2, (yfwd, K1) 3 times, yfwd, K2. 13 sts.
6th row Cast off 7 sts, K4 including st on needle, yfwd, K2 tog. 6 sts.
These 6 rows form the pattern.

Queen's lace edging

Cast on 13 sts.
1st row (Ws) K.
2nd row Sl 1, K12.
3rd row Sl 1, K1, K2 tog, yfwd and round needle twice to make 2 loops – **called yrn twice**, K2 tog, K7.
4th row Sl 1, K8, P1, K3.
5th and 6th rows Sl 1, K12.
7th row Sl 1, K1, K2 tog, yrn twice, K2 tog, K2, yrn twice, (K1, yrn twice) 3 times, K2.
8th row Sl 1, (K2, P1) 4 times, K4, P1, K3.
9th and 10th rows Sl 1, K20.
11th row Sl 1, K1, K2 tog, yrn twice, K2 tog, K15.
12th row K12 winding yarn 3 times round right-hand needle for each st,

yfwd and round needle 3 times to make 3 loops, K5, P1, K3.
13th row Sl 1, K8, (K1, P1, K1) all into 3 loops, sl rem 12 sts on to right-hand needle dropping the extra loops from needle, sl these 12 long loops back on to the left-hand needle and K12 tog.
The 2nd to 13th rows inclusive form the pattern.

Bobble lace edging

Cast on 13 sts.
1st row (Rs) K.
2nd row K2, yrn, P1, yrn, P2 tog, K5, yfwd, K2 tog, K1.
3rd row K3, yfwd, K2 tog, K2, K2 tog, yfwd, K3, yfwd, K2.
4th row K2, yrn, P1, K3, P1, yrn, P2 tog, K3, yfwd, K2 tog, K1.
5th row K3, yfwd, (K2 tog) twice, yfwd, K7, yfwd, K2.
6th row K2, yrn, P1, K7, P1, yrn, P2 tog, K1, yfwd, K2 tog, K1.
7th row K3, yfwd, K2 tog, K4, with tip of right-hand needle (lift the 2nd st on left-hand needle over the first st and off the needle) 8 times, K1 noting that the last st is the st rem on left-hand needle when all 8 sts have been lifted over it, turn and cast on 3 sts. 13 sts.
The 2nd to 7th rows inclusive form the pattern.

bobble lace edging

Little girl's jersey with lacy collar

This jersey is worked in a pretty eyelet lace pattern with a garter stitch lace collar and neckband in a contrasting colour. The back, front and sleeves are shaped at the armhole into a semi-raglan and all joined into a yoke with back opening.

Sizes

To fit 56 [61:66]cm/22 [24:26]in chest
Length from back neck,
31 [34:37]cm/12¼ [13½:14½]in
Sleeve seam, 21 [23:25]cm/
8¼ [9:9¾]in
The figures in [] refer to the 61/24 and 66cm/26in sizes respectively

You will need

2 [2:3]×50g balls of Wendy Choice 4 ply (65% Courtelle acrylic, 20% wool, 15% Bri-nylon) in main colour A
1 [1:1] ball of same in contrast colour B
One pair 2¾mm/No 12 needles
One pair 3¼mm/No 10 needles
Set of four 3¼mm/No 10 needles pointed at both ends
Three buttons

Tension

28 sts and 36 rows to 10cm/4in over eyelet hole patt worked on 3¼mm/ No 10 needles

Back

With 2¾mm/No 12 needles and A cast on 79 [87:95] sts.
1st row (Rs) K1, *P1, K1, rep from * to end.
2nd row P1, *K1, P1, rep from * to end.
Rep these 2 rows until work measures 4cm/1½in from beg,
ending with a 2nd row and inc one st at end of last row. 80 [88:96] sts.
Change to 3¼mm/No 10 needles. Commence eyelet hole patt.
1st row (Rs) K.
2nd and every alt row P.
3rd row K3, *yfwd, K2 tog, K6, rep from * to last 5 sts, yfwd, K2 tog, K3.
5th row K.
7th row K7, *yfwd, K2 tog, K6, rep from * to last st, K1.
8th row P.
These 8 rows form the patt. Rep patt rows 5 [6:7] times more.

Shape armholes

Keeping patt correct throughout, cast off 3 sts at beg of next 2 rows.
3rd row K2 tog, *K6, yfwd, K2 tog, rep from * to last 8 sts, K6, K2 tog tbl.
4th and every alt row P.
5th row K2 tog, K to last 2 sts, K2 tog tbl.
7th row K2 tog, *yfwd, K2 tog, K6, rep from * to last 4 sts, yfwd, K2 tog, K2 tog tbl.
Keeping eyelet holes in line one above the other as now set cont dec in this way at each end of every alt row until 58 [62:66] sts rem, ending with a Ws row.
Next row K2 tog, K2 [4:6] sts, *yfwd, K2 tog, K6, rep from * to last 6 [8:10] sts, yfwd, K2 tog, K2 [4:6] sts, K2 tog tbl.
Next row P.
Next row K2 tog, K to last 2 sts, K2 tog tbl.
Next row P. 54 [58:62] sts.

3rd size only

Next row K2 tog, K4, *yfwd, K2 tog, K6, rep from * to last 8 sts, yfwd, K2
tog, K4, K2 tog tbl.
Next row P.
Next row K2 tog, K to last 2 sts, K2 tog tbl.
Next row P. 58 sts.

All sizes

Break off yarn. Leave sts on holder.

Front

Work as given for back.

Sleeves

With 2¾mm/No 12 needles and A cast on 47 [47:55] sts. Work 4cm/ 1½in rib as given for back, ending with a 2nd row and inc one st at end of last row. 48 [48:56] sts.
Change to 3¼mm/No 10 needles. Work first 8 patt rows as given for back.
Keeping patt correct throughout, inc one st at each end of next and every foll 8th [4th:6th] row until there are 60 [70:76] sts.
Cont without shaping until 15th [17th:19th] eyelet hole row has been worked from beg, ending with a Ws row.

Shape top

Keeping patt correct throughout, cast off 3 sts at beg of next 2 rows.
Dec one st at each end of next and every alt row until 38 [44:46] sts rem, ending with a Ws row.
Next row K2 tog, K4 [3:4] sts, *yfwd, K2 tog, K6, rep from * until 8 [7:8] sts rem, yfwd, K2 tog, K4 [3:4] sts, K2 tog tbl.
Next row P. 36 [42:44] sts.
Keeping eyelet holes in line one above the other as now set on every 4th row as now set, cont dec one st at each end of next and every alt row until 34 [40:38] sts rem, ending with a Ws row.
Break off yarn. Leave sts on holder.

Yoke

With Rs of back facing, set of four 3¼mm/No 10 needles and A, sl first 29 [31:31] sts on to a spare needle, rejoin yarn to rem sts on left-hand needle, cast on 4 sts for underflap button band at centre back, turn and cont working in rows.

1st size only

1st row K4 button band sts, K1, (K2 tog, K2, yfwd, K2 tog, K2) 3 times,

The pattern pieces

yoke to be worked at top edge

front/back
5 [6:7]cm
13 [15:17]cm
4cm
28 [31:34]cm

sleeve
21 [25:27]cm
5 [6:7]cm
17 [19:21]cm
4cm
17 [17:20]cm

work across first sleeve (K2 tog, K2, yfwd, K2 tog, K2) 4 times, K2 tog tbl, work across front sts (K2, yfwd, K2 tog, K2, K2 tog) 6 times, K2, yfwd, K2 tog, K2, work across 2nd sleeve (K2 tog, K2, yfwd, K2 tog, K2) 4 times, K2 tog tbl, work across right back (K2, yfwd, K2 tog, K2, K2 tog) 3 times, K5. 158 sts.

2nd size only
1st row K4 button band sts, K1, (K2 tog, K2, yfwd, K2 tog, K2) 3 times, K2 tog, work across first sleeve K2 tog, K1, (yfwd, K2 tog, K2, K2 tog, K2) 4 times, yfwd, K2 tog, K1, K2 tog, work across front sts (K2 tog, K2, yfwd, K2 tog, K2) 7 times, K2 tog, work across 2nd sleeve as for first sleeve, work across right back (K2 tog, K2, yfwd, K2 tog, K2) 3 times, K2 tog, K5. 172 sts.

3rd size only
1st row K4 button band sts, work across back sts as given for 2nd size, work across first sleeve (K2, yfwd, K2 tog, K2, K2 tog) 4 times, K2, yfwd, K2 tog, K2, work across front sts as given for 2nd size, work across 2nd sleeve as given for first sleeve, work across right back as given for 2nd size. 172 sts.

All sizes
2nd and every alt row K4, P to last 4 sts, K4.
3rd row K.
5th row (dec row) K4, *K2 tog, K2, yfwd, K2 tog, K1, rep from * to last 7 sts, K2 tog, K5. 135 [148:148] sts.
Rep 2nd to 4th rows once.
9th row (dec and buttonhole row) K3, *K2 tog, K2, yfwd, K2 tog, rep from * to last 7 sts, K2 tog, K1, K2 tog, and yfwd for buttonhole, K2. 114 [124:124] sts.
Rep 2nd to 4th rows once.
13th row (dec row) K4, *K2 tog, yfwd, K2 tog, K1, rep from * to last 5 sts, K2 tog, K3. 92 [100:100] sts.
Rep 2nd to 4th rows once.
17th row (dec row) K5, *yfwd, (K2 tog) twice, yfwd, K2 tog, K2, rep from * 9 [10:10] times more, yfwd, K2 tog, K to end. 82 [89:89] sts.
Beg with a P row work 5 rows st st with g st borders, working buttonhole as before on 2nd row. Leave sts on holder.

Lace collar

With 3¼mm/No 10 needles and B

Above: A pretty eyelet pattern and contrasting lacy collar makes this jersey perfect for a special occasion.

cast on 6 sts. Work 6 rows patt as given for g st lace edging. Rep patt rows until 24 [26:26] patt have been completed. K one row. Cast off.
With Rs of inside edge facing and 3¼mm/No 10 needles, pick up and K74 [81:81] sts along straight edge. P one row. Leave sts for time being.

Neckband

With Rs of work facing, 2¼mm/No 12 needles and A, K4 sts of underflap, drop A and pick up B, with needle holding collar sts in front of needle holding neckband sts, *K1 st from collar and neckband tog, rep from * to last 4 sts, using small separate ball of A, K4 sts of button band. 82 [89:89] sts.
Next row K4 A, using B, P to last 4 sts, dec one st in centre on 1st size only, K4 A. 81 [89:89] sts.
Next row K4 A, using B, work in

K1, P1 rib to last 5 sts, K1, K4 A.
Next row K4 A, using B, work in P1, K1 rib to last 5 sts, P1, K4 A.
Rep last 2 rows once more.
Next row (buttonhole row) K4 A, using B rib to last 4 sts, using A K2 tog, yfwd, K2.
Work 2 more rows as now set. Cast off.

To make up

Press each piece lightly under a dry cloth with a cool iron. Join underarm seams on sleeves. Join side seams. Sew down lower end of button band to back. Press seams. Sew on buttons. Catch down ends of lace collar to button and buttonhole bands.

Exquisite all-over lace patterns

Intricate lace patterns may have as many as forty stitches for each repeat of the pattern, plus edge stitches, and as many rows. Because of these large multiples of stitches, use them as all-over fabrics rather than as panels set against a plain background.

All forms of lace knitting, whether worked in rows or as circular medallions, were very popular in the 18th and 19th centuries. At this time, Vienna and Paris were the acknowledged centres of this type of knitting and countless examples of exquisite beauty and delicacy were produced, imitating pillow and needlepoint lace.

The knitters used the finest lace thread and exceptionally fine knitting 'wires', as the needles were called. The work was very tedious and it must have taken months, if not years, to complete some of the examples we now admire as heirlooms. Perhaps because of this, lace knitting went out of fashion towards the end of the 19th century.

Between the first and second World Wars, new lace patterns began to appear in Germany and Austria bringing about a revival of this beautiful craft and today lace knitting is in vogue again. There are numerous patterns available for working medallions, edgings, baby garments and shawls, using modern yarns and needle sizes.

Working large lace patterns

It requires a great deal of concentration to achieve successful all-over fabrics using large lace patterns – one stitch out of sequence and it is difficult to revert to the original pattern or to unpick the rows.

The principle used is exactly the same as for smaller versions; stitches are decreased at various points within the pattern repeat and replaced with eyelet hole increases. The examples given here are well-worth the effort involved in knitting them and make delightful baby garments and shawls. On all four patterns the multiples of stitches remain the same on all the rows. Either the ogee or ivy leaf patterns can be used in the christening dress pattern.

Cascade pattern looks complicated but is relatively simple to knit as it is made up of four rows which are repeated three times, then alternated. Bell-shaped flowers hang down, each one topped with three sets of leaves.

Ogee pattern forms S-shaped curves on either side of dainty openwork flowers. All four edges of the fabric curve with the shape of the lace.

Candlelight pattern is one of the most popular examples of lace and has more than one variation. This version has a large repeat of the candleflame motif.

Ivy leaf pattern is not as well-known as the other examples and is a version of an old German lace.

Left: The skirt of this dress is worked in one piece to the armholes to eliminate awkward side seams and the yoke has a centre-back opening to make it fit easily over the head. Trim with a braid of your choice and add ribbon in a matching colour.

Ogee pattern

Cast on multiples of 24 sts plus one st, eg 49.

1st row (Rs) *K2, yfwd, K2 tog, K1, K2 tog, K3, yfwd, sl 1, K1, psso, yrn, P1, yon, K2, yfwd, sl 1, K1, psso, (K1, sl 1, K1, psso) twice, yfwd, K1, rep from * to last st, K1.

2nd row P1, *P7, yrn, P2 tog, P5, yrn, P2 tog, P8, rep from * to end.

3rd row *K1, yfwd, K2 tog, K1, K2 tog, K3, yfwd, sl 1, K1, psso, (K1, yfwd) twice, K3, yfwd, (sl 1, K1, psso, K1) twice, sl 1, K1, psso, yfwd, rep from * to last st, K1.

4th row P1, *P6, (yrn, P2 tog, P7) twice, rep from * to end.

5th row *K3, K2 tog, K3, yfwd, sl 1, K1, psso, K1, (yfwd, K3) twice, yfwd, sl 1, K1, psso, K1, sl 1, K1, psso, K2, rep from * to last st, K1.

6th row P1, *P5, yrn, P2 tog, P9, yrn, P2 tog, P6, rep from * to end.

7th row *K2, K2 tog, K3, yfwd, sl 1, K1, psso, K3, yfwd, K1, yfwd, K5, yfwd, (sl 1, K1, psso, K1) twice, rep from * to last st, K1.

8th row P1, *P4, yrn, P2 tog, P11, yrn, P2 tog, P5, rep from * to end.

9th row *K1, K2 tog, K3, yfwd, sl 1, K1, psso, (K3, yfwd) twice, K5, yfwd, sl 1, K1, psso, K1, sl 1, K1, psso, rep from * to last st, K1.

10th row P1, *P3, yrn, P2 tog, P13, yrn, P2 tog, P4, rep from * to end.

11th row Sl 1, K1, psso, *K3, yfwd, sl 1, K1, psso, K1, sl 1, K1, psso, yfwd, K2, yfwd, K1, yfwd, K2, yfwd, K2 tog, K3, yfwd, sl 1, K1, psso, K1, sl 1, K2 tog, psso, rep from * to end, ending last rep with sl 1, K1, psso, instead of sl 1, K2 tog, psso.

12th row P1, *P2, yrn, P2 tog, P15, yrn, P2 tog, P3, rep from * to end.

13th row Sl 1, K1, psso, *K2, yfwd, sl 1, K1, psso, K5, yfwd, K3, yfwd, K7, yfwd, sl 1, K1, psso, sl 1, K2 tog, psso, rep from * to end, ending last rep with sl 1, K1, psso, instead of sl 1, K2 tog, psso.

14th row P1, *P1, yrn, P2 tog, P17, yrn, P2 tog, P1, K1, rep from * to end.

15th row *P1, yon, K2, yfwd, (sl 1, K1, psso, K1) twice, sl 1, K1, psso, yfwd, K3, yfwd, K2 tog, K1, K2 tog, K3, yfwd, sl 1, K1, psso, yrn, rep from * to last st, P1.

16th row As 12th row.

17th row *K1, yfwd, K3, yfwd, (sl 1, K1, psso, K1) twice, sl 1, K1, psso, yfwd, K1, yfwd, K2 tog, K1, K2 tog, K3, yfwd, sl 1, K1, psso, K1, yfwd, rep from * to last st, K1.

18th row As 10th row.

19th row *K2, yfwd, K3, yfwd, sl 1, K1, psso, K1, sl 1, K1, psso, K5, K2 tog, K3, yfwd, sl 1, K1, psso, K1, yfwd, K1, rep from * to last st, K1.

20th row As 8th row.

21st row *K1, yfwd, K5, yfwd, sl 1, K1, psso, K1, sl 1, K1, psso, K3, K2 tog, K3, yfwd, sl 1, K1, psso, K3, yfwd, rep from * to last st, K1.

22nd row As 6th row.

23rd row *K2, yfwd, K5, yfwd, (sl 1, K1, psso, K1) twice, K2 tog, K3, yfwd, sl 1, K1, psso, K3, yfwd, K1, rep from * to last st, K1.

24th row As 4th row.

25th row *K1, yfwd, K2, yfwd, K2 tog, K3, yfwd, sl 1, K1, psso, K1, sl 1, K2 tog, psso, K3, yfwd, sl 1, K1, psso, K1, sl 1, K1, psso, yfwd, K2, yfwd, rep from * to last st, K1.

26th row As 2nd row.

27th row *K2, yfwd, K7, yfwd, sl 1, K1, psso, sl 1, K2 tog, psso, K2, yfwd, sl 1, K1, psso, K5, yfwd, K1, rep from * to last st, K1.

28th row P1, *P8, yrn, P2 tog, P1, K1, P1, yrn, P2 tog, P9, rep from * to end. These 28 rows form the pattern.

Cascade pattern

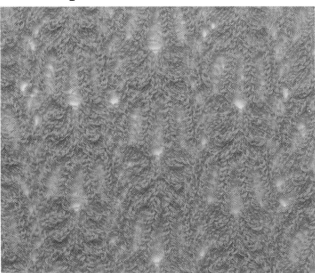

Cast on multiples of 34 sts plus 4 sts, eg 72.

1st row (Rs) K2, *K3, K2 tog, K4 yrn, P2, (K2, yrwd, sl 1, K1, psso) 3 times, P2, yon, K4, sl 1, K1, psso, K3, rep from * to last 2 sts, K2.

2nd row P4, *P2 tog tbl, P4, yrn, P1, K2, (P2, yrn, P2 tog) 3 times, K2, P1, yrn, P4, P2 tog, P4, rep from * to end.

3rd row K3, *K2 tog, K4, yfwd, K2, P2, (K2, yfwd, sl 1, K1, psso) 3 times, P2, K2, yfwd, K4, sl 1, K1, psso, K2, rep from * to last st, K1.

4th row P2, *P2 tog tbl, P4, yrn, P3, K2, (P2, yrn, P2 tog) 3 times, K2, P3, yrn, P4, P2 tog, rep from * to last 2 sts, P2. Rep 1st to 4th rows twice more.

13th row *(K2, yfwd, sl 1, K1, psso) twice, P2, yon, K4, sl 1, K1, psso, K6, K2 tog, K4, yrn, P2, K2, yfwd, sl 1,

K1, psso, rep from * to last 4 sts, K2, yfwd, sl 1, K1, psso.
14th row *(P2, yrn, P2 tog) twice, K2, P1, yrn, P4, P2 tog, P4, P2 tog tbl, P4, yrn, P1, K2, P2, yrn, P2 tog, rep from * to last 4 sts, P2, yrn, P2 tog.
15th row *(K2, yfwd, sl 1, K1, psso) twice, P2, K2, yfwd, K4, sl 1, K1, psso, K2, K2 tog, K4, yfwd, K2, P2, K2, yfwd, sl 1, K1, psso, rep from * to last 4 sts, K2, yfwd, sl 1, K1, psso.
16th row *(P2, yrn, P2 tog) twice, K2, P3, yrn, P4, P2 tog, P2 tog tbl, P4, yrn, P3, K2, P2, yrn, P2 tog, rep from * to last 4 sts, P2, yrn, P2 tog.
Rep 13th to 16th rows twice more.
These 24 rows form the pattern.

Candlelight pattern

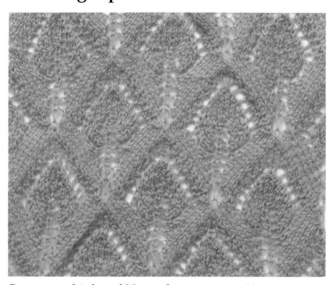

Cast on multiples of 20 sts plus one st, eg 41.
1st and every alt row (Ws) P to end.
2nd row K1, *yfwd, K2 tog, K2, yfwd, K2 tog, K7, sl 1, K1, psso, yfwd, K2, sl 1, K1, psso, yfwd, K1, rep from * to end.
4th row K1, *yfwd, K1, K2 tog, K2, yfwd, K2 tog, K5, sl 1, K1, psso, yfwd, K2, sl 1, K1, psso, K1, yfwd, K1, rep from * to end.
6th row K1, *yfwd, K2, K2 tog, K2, yfwd, K2 tog, K3, sl 1, K1, psso, yfwd, K2, sl 1, K1, psso, K2, yfwd, K1, rep from * to end.
8th row K1, *yfwd, K3, K2 tog, K2, yfwd, K2 tog, K1, sl 1, K1, psso, yfwd, K2, sl 1, K1, psso, K3, yfwd, K1, rep from * to end.
10th row K1, *yfwd, K4, K2 tog, K2, yfwd, sl 1, K2 tog, psso, yfwd, K2, sl 1, K1, psso, K4, yfwd, K1, rep from * to end.
12th row K1, *yfwd, K1, yfwd, sl 1, K1, psso, K2, K2 tog, K5, sl 1, K1, psso, K2, K2 tog, (yfwd, K1) twice, rep from * to end.
14th row K1, *yfwd, K1, K2 tog, yfwd, K3, K2 tog, K3, sl 1, K1, psso, K3, yfwd, sl 1, K1, psso, K1, yfwd, K1, rep from * to end.
16th row K1, *yfwd, K2, K2 tog, yfwd, K3, K2 tog, K1, sl 1, K1, psso, K3, yfwd, sl 1, K1, psso, K2, yfwd, K1, rep from * to end.
18th row K1, *yfwd, K3, K2 tog, yfwd, K3, sl 1, K2 tog, psso, K3, yfwd, sl 1, K1, psso, K3, yfwd, K1, rep from

* to end.
20th row K4, *sl 1, K1, psso, yfwd, K2, sl 1, K1, psso, yfwd, K1, yfwd, K2 tog, K2, yfwd, K2 tog, K7, rep from * to end, ending last rep with K4 instead of K7.
22nd row K3, *sl 1, K1, psso, yfwd, K2, sl 1, K1, psso, (K1, yfwd) twice, K1, K2 tog, K2, yfwd, K2 tog, K5, rep from * to end, ending last rep with K3 instead of K5.
24th row K2, *sl 1, K1, psso, yfwd, K2, sl 1, K1, psso, K2, yfwd, K1, yfwd, K2, K2 tog, K2, yfwd, K2 tog, K3, rep from * to end, ending last rep with K2 instead of K3.
26th row K1, *sl 1, K1, psso, yfwd, K2, sl 1, K1, psso, K3, yfwd, K1, yfwd, K3, K2 tog, K2, yfwd, K2 tog, K1, rep from * to end.
28th row Sl 1, K1, psso, *yfwd, K2, sl 1, K1, psso, K4, yfwd, K1, yfwd, K4, K2 tog, K2, yfwd, sl 1, K2 tog, psso, rep from * to end, ending last rep with K2 tog instead of sl 1, K2 tog, psso.
30th row K3, *sl 1, K1, psso, K2, K2 tog, (yfwd, K1) 3 times, yfwd, sl 1, K1, psso, K2, K2 tog, K5, rep from * to end, ending last rep with K3 instead of K5.
32nd row K2, *sl 1, K1, psso, K3, yfwd, sl 1, K1, psso, (K1, yfwd) twice, K1, K2 tog, yfwd, K3, K2 tog, K3, rep from * to end, ending last rep with K2 instead of K3.
34th row K1, *sl 1, K1, psso, K3, yfwd, sl 1, K1, psso, K2, yfwd, K1, yfwd, K2, K2 tog, yfwd, K3, K2 tog, K1, rep from * to end.
36th row Sl 1, K1, psso, *K3, yfwd, sl 1, K1, psso, K3, yfwd, K1, yfwd, K3, K2 tog, yfwd, K3, sl 1, K2 tog, psso, rep from * to end, ending last rep with K2 tog instead of sl 1, K2 tog, psso. These 36 rows form the pattern.

Ivy leaf pattern

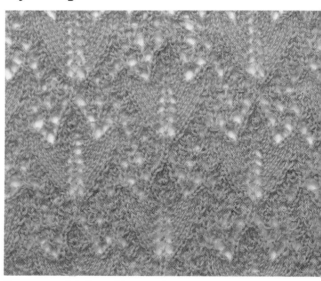

Cast on multiples of 34 sts plus one st, eg 69.
1st row (Ws) P to end.
2nd row K1 tbl, *yfwd, K6, sl 1, K1, psso, K1, K2 tog, yfwd, K1, yfwd, sl 1, K2 tog, psso, yfwd, K3, yfwd, sl 1, K2 tog, psso, yfwd, K1, yfwd, sl 1, K1, psso, K1, K2 tog, K6, yfwd, K1 tbl, rep from * to end.
3rd and every alt row P to end, working K1, P1 into every y2rn of a previous row.
4th row K1 tbl, *yfwd, K2, K2 tog, yfwd, sl 1, K1, psso, K6, yfwd, sl 1, K1, psso, K2 tog, yfwd, K1 tbl, yfwd, sl 1, K1, psso, K2 tog, yfwd, K6, K2 tog, yfwd, sl 1, K1,

180

psso, K2, yfwd, K1 tbl, rep from * to end.
6th row K3, *K2 tog, yfwd, K1, yfwd, sl 1, K1, psso,
K1, K2 tog, y2rn, sl 1, K1, psso, K1, K2 tog, K1, yfwd,
K1 tbl, yfwd, K1, sl 1, K1, psso, K1, K2 tog, y2rn, sl 1,
K1, psso, K1, K2 tog, yfwd, K1, yfwd, sl 1, K1, psso,
K5, rep from * to end, ending last rep with K3 instead
of K5.
8th row K2, *K2 tog, (y2rn, sl 1, K2 tog, psso) twice,
y2rn, sl 1, K1, psso, K1, K2 tog, K2, yfwd, K1 tbl,
yfwd, K2, sl 1, K1, psso, K1, K2 tog, y2rn, (sl 1, K2 tog,
psso, y2rn) twice, sl 1, K1, psso, K3, rep from * to end,
ending last rep with K2 instead of K3.
10th row K1, *K2 tog, yfwd, K6, yfwd, sl 1, K1, psso,
K1, K2 tog, K3, yfwd, K1 tbl, yfwd, K3, sl 1, K1, psso,
K1, K2 tog, yfwd, K6, yfwd, sl 1, K1, psso, K1, rep
from * to end.
12th row K2 tog, *(y2rn, sl 1, K2 tog, psso) twice, y2rn,
sl 1, K1, psso, K1, K2 tog, K4, yfwd, K1 tbl, yfwd, K4,
sl 1, K1, psso, K1, K2 tog, y2rn, (sl 1, K2 tog, psso,
y2rn) twice, sl 1, K2 tog, psso, rep from * to end,
ending last rep with sl 1, K1, psso instead of sl 1, K2
tog, psso.
14th row K7, *yfwd, sl 1, K1, psso, K1, K2 tog, K5,
yfwd, K1 tbl, yfwd, K5, sl 1, K1, psso, K1, K2 tog,
yfwd, K13, rep from * to end, ending last rep with K7
instead of K13.
16th row K2, *yfwd, sl 1, K2 tog, psso, yfwd, K1,

yfwd, sl 1, K1, psso, K1; K2 tog, K6, yfwd, K1 tbl,
yfwd, K6, sl 1, K1, psso, K1, K2 tog, yfwd, K1, yfwd,
sl 1, K2 tog, psso, yfwd, K3, rep from * to end, ending
last rep with K2 instead of K3.
18th row K1 tbl, *yfwd, sl 1, K1, psso, K2 tog, yfwd,
K6, K2 tog, yfwd, sl 1, K1, psso, K2, yfwd, K1 tbl,
yfwd, K2, K2 tog, yfwd, sl 1, K1, psso, K6, yfwd, sl 1,
K1, psso, K2 tog, yfwd, K1 tbl, rep from * to end.
20th row K1 tbl, *yfwd, K1, sl 1, K1, psso, K1, K2 tog,
y2rn, sl 1, K1, psso, K1, K2 tog, yfwd, K1, yfwd, sl 1,
K1, psso, K5, K2 tog, yfwd, K1, yfwd, sl 1, K1, psso,
K1, K2 tog, y2rn, sl 1, K1, psso, K1, K2 tog, K1, yfwd,
K1 tbl, rep from * to end.
22nd row K1 tbl, *yfwd, K2, sl 1, K1, psso, K1, K2 tog,
(y2rn, sl 1, K2 tog, psso) twice, y2rn, sl 1, K1, psso, K3,
K2 tog, y2rn, (sl 1, K2 tog, psso, y2rn) twice, sl 1, K1,
psso, K1, K2 tog, K2, yfwd, K1 tbl, rep from * to end.
24th row K1 tbl, *yfwd, K3, (sl 1, K1, psso, K1, K2 tog,
yfwd, K6, yfwd) twice, sl 1, K1, psso, K1, K2 tog, K3,
yfwd, K1 tbl, rep from * to end.
26th row K1 tbl, *yfwd, K4, sl 1, K1, psso, K1, K2 tog,
(y2rn, sl 1, K2 tog, psso) 5 times, y2rn, sl 1, K1, psso,
K1, K2 tog, K4, yfwd, K1 tbl, rep from * to end.
28th row K1 tbl, *yfwd, K5, sl 1, K1, psso, K1, K2 tog,
yfwd, K13, yfwd, sl 1, K1, psso, K1, K2 tog, K5, yfwd,
K1 tbl, rep from * to end.
These 28 rows form the pattern.

*For the skirt, choose the ogee lace as
shown here, or alternatively, use the ivy
leaf pattern.*

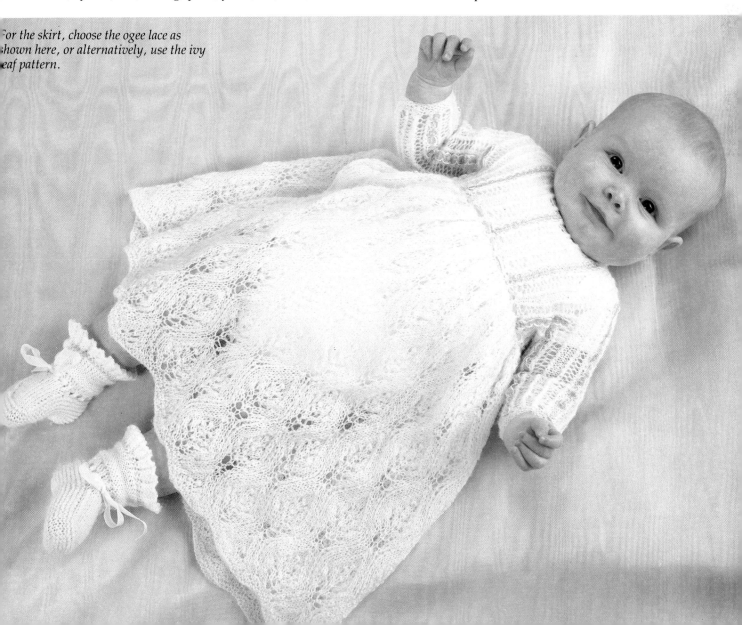

Heirloom christening dress

Knit this beautiful christening dress in white as shown here or choose one of the lovely colours in the same range of fine wool.

Sizes

To fit 41cm/16in chest
Length to shoulder, 42cm/16½in, adjustable
Sleeve seam, 12.5cm/5in

You will need

6×25g balls of Sunbeam Pure New Wool 2 ply (100% wool)
One pair 2¾mm/No 12 needles
One pair 2¼mm/No 13 needles
One 3¼mm/No 10 circular needle, 100cm/40in long
Six buttons
2m/2yd narrow ribbon
3m/3yd narrow trimming, optional

Tension

36 sts and 44 rows to 10cm/4in over st st worked on 2¾mm/No 12 needles

Dress

With 3¼mm/No 10 circular needle cast on 409 sts and work in one piece to underarm. K 5 rows g st. Cont in ogee or ivy leaf patt until work measures 30cm/12in from beg, or required skirt length, ending with a Rs row. Change to 2¾mm/No 12 needles.

Shape bodice

Next row Cast on 6 sts for underflap, K6 sts, (K3 tog) 134 times, K2 tog, K5. 146 sts.
K 2 rows g st.
Next row (eyelet and buttonhole row) K3, (yfwd, K2 tog for buttonhole), K2, *K2 tog, yfwd, rep from * to last 7 sts, K7.
K 3 rows g st. Commence bodice patt.
1st row (Rs) K6, P2, *K2, yfwd, K2 tog, P2, rep from * to last 6 sts, K6.
2nd row K8, *P2, yrn, P2 tog, K2, rep from * to last 6 sts, K6.
Keeping 6 sts at each end in g st and making 4 more buttonholes as before at intervals of 2.5cm/1in, rep last 2 rows until work measures 4cm/1½in from eyelet hole row, ending with a Rs row.

Divide for armholes

Next row K6, patt 28 sts, cast off

8 sts, patt 62 sts, cast off 8 sts, patt 28 sts, K6.
Complete left back first. Cont in patt keeping 6 sts at centre back in g st, working buttonholes as before, *at the same time* dec one st at armhole edge on foll 7 alt rows. 27 sts.
Cont without shaping until armhole measures 7.5cm/3in from beg, ending at armhole edge.

Shape shoulder

Cast off at beg of next and every alt row 4 sts 3 times. Leave rem 15 sts on holder for centre back neck.
With Rs of work facing rejoin yarn to 62 sts for front and patt to end. Dec one st at each end of next and foll 6 alt rows. 48 sts.
Cont without shaping until armholes measure 5cm/2in from beg, ending with a Ws row.

Shape neck

Next row Patt 18 sts, turn.
Complete this side first. Dec one st at neck edge at beg of next and foll 5 alt rows. 12 sts.
Cont without shaping until armhole measures same as back to shoulder, ending at armhole edge.

Shape shoulder

Cast off at beg of next and every alt row 4 sts 3 times.
With Rs of work facing sl first 12 sts on to holder for centre front neck, rejoin yarn to rem sts and patt to end. Complete to match first side, reversing shapings.
With Rs of work facing, rejoin yarn to rem sts and complete right back to match left back, reversing shapings and omitting buttonholes.

Sleeves

With 2¼mm/No 13 needles cast on 30 sts. K 8 rows g st.
Next row (inc row) K1, *K twice into next st, K1, rep from * to last st, K1. 44 sts.
Change to 2¾mm/No 12 needles. Commence patt.
1st row (Rs) P2, *K2, yfwd, K2 tog, P2, rep from * to end.
2nd row K2, *P2, yrn, P2 tog, K2, rep from * to end.
Rep last 2 rows until sleeve measures 12.5cm/5in from beg, ending with a Ws row.

Shape top

Keeping patt correct, cast off 4 sts at beg of next 2 rows. Dec one st at each end of next and foll 6 alt rows, ending with a Ws row. Cast off at beg of every row 2 sts 6 times and 10 sts once.

Neckband

Join shoulder seams. With Rs of work facing and 2¼mm/No 13 needles, K across sts of left back neck, pick up and K12 sts down left front neck, K front neck sts on holder, pick up and K12 sts up right front neck and K across sts of right back neck. 66 sts.
K 7 rows g st, working buttonhole as before on 4th row. Cast off.

To make up

Press each piece lightly under a damp cloth with a warm iron. Join sleeve seams. Set in sleeves. Join centre back seam to within 5cm/2in of eyelet hole row. Press. Thread ribbon through eyelet hole row to tie at centre front. Sew on buttons.
Sew trimming on every alt P2 panel on bodice and sleeves, if required.

The pattern pieces

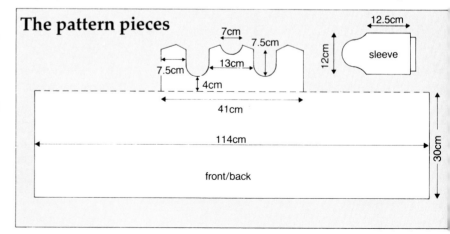

Bobble patterns: some outstanding examples

Small or large bobbles worked against a plain background as all-over patterns form beautiful crunchy fabrics.
The examples given here can also be used as horizontal borders above the welt and cuffs of a plain jersey,
or as central vertical panels on the fronts of a cardigan.

Above: Use a basic stocking stitch jersey shape but work in all-over Trinity or currant pattern – allow extra yarn.

Raised bobble patterns look best worked on to a stocking stitch or reversed stocking stitch surface so that they stand out clearly in relief, rather than on a textured one where they lose impact. Some patterns use stocking stitch bobbles against a reversed stocking stitch background, others reversed stocking stitch bobbles against stocking stitch.

Small or large bobbles can be dotted over the fabric at regular intervals, or grouped together to form different shapes. Other bobble patterns – such as Trinity pattern – produce an all-over fabric and can be used as borders or panels of pattern on an otherwise plain garment. Whatever the final effect, the working methods are simple and produce interesting three-dimensional fabrics.

Small bobbles are made by working more than once into a stitch and compensating for these extra stitches by

Knot pattern

Cast on multiples of 6 sts plus 1, eg 19.
1st row (Rs) K to end.
2nd and every alt row P to end.
3rd row K3, *P into front, back and front of next st, turn and K3 tog, turn and K1 tbl – called MB, K5, rep from * to last 4 sts, MB, K3.
5th row K to end.
7th row K6, *MB, K5, rep from * to last st, K1.
8th row P to end.
These 8 rows form the pattern.

Trinity pattern

Cast on multiples of 4 sts plus 3, eg 23.
1st row (Rs) P to end.
2nd row K1, *(K1, P1, K1) all into next st, P3 tog, rep from * to last 2 sts, (K1, P1, K1) into next st, K1, noting that sts are inc in this row.
3rd row P to end.
4th row K1, *P3 tog, (K1, P1, K1) into next st, rep from * to last 4 sts, P3 tog, K1, noting that sts revert to original number.
These 4 rows form the pattern.

working the next few stitches together.

Large bobbles are made by working more than once into a stitch, or sometimes between stitches, and knitting additional rows over these stitches before decreasing them back to the original number. Because of these working methods, bobble patterns take extra yarn to complete.

If you wish to add bobbles to a basic stocking stitch design, first check that the number of cast-on stitches will give you the correct multiples for the pattern of your choice. It is possible to adjust this by adding or subtracting a few stitches, but do remember to take these into account when shaping. It is also essential to check the tension achieved in the chosen pattern because this will differ from a basic stocking stitch tension. Trinity pattern, for example, needs more stitches to 10cm/4in but fewer rows.

Knot pattern forms a 'pip' in the fabric, adding just a hint of texture to a plain background. Worked in slub or bouclé yarns the knots will vary in size, which adds further interest. A random coloured yarn is not suitable for this pattern because the small knots would be lost.

Trinity pattern, also called blackberry pattern, is used as an all-over fabric or as a border or panel. It looks effective worked in a lightweight yarn on large needles. The name derives from the method of working 'three-in-one and one-in-three'.

Currant pattern is a variation of Trinity pattern. It looks very similar but uses a different working method.

Boxed pattern uses bobbles worked on to a background of five knitted stitches and one purled garter stitch, overstriped with a purl row to give the boxed effect. This looks best worked in a plain, smooth yarn.

Cocoon pattern gives a beautiful texture, with small 'cocoons' of knitting nestling between wavy rib stitches. It is used as an all-over fabric or as a border or panel.

Teardrop pattern forms elongated bobbles in stocking stitch against a reversed stocking stitch background. It can be used as an all-over pattern or the bobbles can be dotted on to the fabric at regular intervals.

Bunches of grapes pattern derives its name from the clusters of tight bobbles in stocking stitch against a reversed stocking stitch background. It can be further embellished by adding embroidered leaves to the top of each cluster of bobbles.

Pussywillow is an unusual, witty pattern. The catkin tails are made by casting on extra stitches then casting them off, leaving them to hang down against the background fabric. Worked in a lightweight, chunky yarn this is a fun pattern for children's garments.

Shaping in bobble patterns is a little difficult. The easiest way is to leave a few stitches at each end of the rows in the background fabric when beginning to increase or decrease. In all shaping and casting off, a bobble counts as one stitch.

Currant pattern

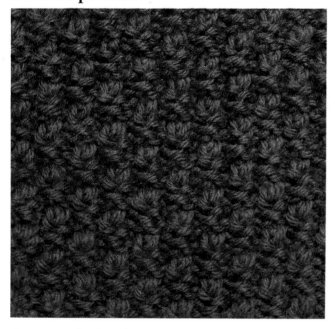

Cast on multiples of 4 sts plus 3, eg 23.
1st row (Rs) P1, *(K1, yfwd, K1) all into next st, P3, rep from * to last 2 sts, (K1, yfwd, K1) into next st, P1, noting that sts are inc in this row.
2nd row K1, *P3 tog, K3, rep from * to last 4 sts, P3 tog, K1, noting that sts revert to original number.
3rd row P3, *(K1, yfwd, K1) into next st, P3, rep from * to end, noting that sts are inc in this row.
4th row K3, *P3 tog, K3, rep from * to end, noting that sts revert to original number.
These 4 rows form the pattern.

Boxed bobble pattern

Cast on multiples of 6 sts plus 1, eg 19.
1st row (Rs) P to end.
2nd and every alt row P to end.
3rd row P1, *K5, P1, rep from * to end.
5th row P1, *K2, (K1, P1, K1) all into next st, turn and K3, turn and P3, use left-hand needle to lift 2nd, and 3rd sts over 1st st and off needle – called MB, K2, P1, rep from * to end.
7th row As 3rd.
8th row P to end.
These 8 rows form the pattern.

Cocoon pattern

Cast on multiples of 8 sts plus 3, eg 27.
1st row (Rs) K1, P1, K1, *P5, K1, P1, K1, rep from * to end.
2nd row P1, K1, P1, *K5, P1, K1, P1, rep from * to end.
3rd row As 1st.
4th row P1, K1 under thread between st just worked and next st, (K1, P1, K1) all into next st, K1 under thread between st just worked and next st – called MB, P1, *P5 tog, P1, MB, P1, rep from * to end, noting that sts are inc in this row.
5th, 7th and 9th rows K1, P5, K1, *P1, K1, P5, K1, rep from * to end.
6th and 8th rows P1, K5, P1, *K1, P1, K5, P1, rep from * to end.
10th row P1, P5 tog, P1, *MB, P1, P5 tog, P1, rep from * to end, noting that sts revert to original number.
11th and 12th rows As 1st and 2nd.
These 12 rows form the pattern.

Pussywillow pattern

Cast on multiples of 4 sts plus 3, eg 23.
1st row (Rs) K to end.
2nd row K to end.
3rd row K3, *insert needle into next st and cast on 6 sts, then cast off these 6 sts – called MB, K3, rep from * to end.
4th row K3, *P1, K3, rep from * to end.
5th and 6th rows K to end.
7th row K1, *MB, K3, rep from * to last 2 sts, MB, K1.
8th row K1, *P1, K3, rep from * to last 2 sts, P1, K1.
These 8 rows form the pattern.

Shaping bobble patterns

Irrespective of the working method or the position of the bobbles, each bobble must be counted as only *one* of the original stitches. Before commencing any shaping it is vital to take note of the multiples of stitches needed to begin each pattern and to check that the number of stitches in each row of the pattern sequence has not altered. When increasing, keep the extra stitches at the ends of each row in stocking stitch until you have added sufficient to work another repeat. When decreasing, it is easier if stitches are cast off at armhole, neck and shoulders in multiples of stitches needed to repeat the pattern. Working stitches together should begin on a row where bobbles are not being worked.

For set-in underarm shaping at each end of the rows on a garment in all-over Trinity pattern, end with a *2nd* row before beginning the shaping.
Next 2 rows Cast off multiples of 4 sts at beg of next 2 rows, eg 4, 8.**
Next row P2 tog, P to last 2 sts, P2 tog tbl.
Next row Patt to end as 4th row.
Repeat last 2 rows as many times as required, noting that 2 sts are dec at each end of every alt row.
For raglan armhole shaping in all-over Trinity pattern, the difference in row tension must be taken into account. Work as for set-in armhole to **.
Work the next 2 dec rows followed by 2 rows without shaping.
Keeping patt correct, cont repeating these 4 rows until about half the

PROFESSIONAL TOUCH

Above: Neat shaping in trinity pattern.

number of sts is dec, then repeat the 2 dec rows only until the total number has been decreased.

Bunches of grapes pattern

Cast on multiples of 8 sts plus 3, eg 27.

1st row (Rs) P to end.

2nd and every alt row K to end, noting that on subsequent rows the MB of previous row should read K1 tbl.

3rd row P2, *P3, (K1, P1, K1, P1, K1) all into next st, turn and P5, turn and K5, use left-hand needle to lift 2nd, 3rd, 4th and 5th sts over 1st st and off needle – called MB, P4, rep from * to last st, P1.

5th row P2, *P2, MB, P1, MB, P3, rep from * to last st, P1.

7th row P2, *P1, (MB, P1) twice, MB, P2, rep from * to last st, P1.

9th and 11th rows P to end.

13th row P1, MB, *P7, MB, rep from * to last st, P1.

15th row P2, *MB, P5, MB, P1, rep from * to last st, P1.

17th row P2, *P1, MB, P3, MB, P1, MB, rep from * to last 9 sts, P1, MB, P3, MB, P3.

19th row P to end.

20th row As 2nd.

These 20 rows form the pattern.

Teardrop pattern

Cast on multiples of 4 sts plus 3, eg 23, noting that this number becomes multiples of 8 plus 3 after the 1st row and varies on the 5th, 7th and 11th rows, reverting to multiples of 8 plus 3 on the 13th row.

1st row (Rs) P3, *(K1, P1, K1, P1, K1) all into next st – called MB, P3, rep from * to end.

2nd and 4th rows K3, *P5, K3, rep from * to end.

3rd row P3, *K5, P3, rep from * to end.

5th row P3, *sl 1, K1, psso, K1, K2 tog, P3, rep from * to end.

6th row K3, *P3, K3, rep from * to end.

7th row P1, MB, P1, *sl 1, K2 tog, psso, P1, MB, P1, rep from * to end.

8th and 10th rows K1, *P5, K3, rep from * to last 6 sts, P5, K1.

9th row P1, *K5, P3, rep from * to last 6 sts, K5, P1.

11th row P1, *sl 1, K1, psso, K1, K2 tog, P3, rep from * to last 6 sts, sl 1, K1, psso, K1, K2 tog, P1.

12th row K1, *P3, K3, rep from * to last 4 sts, P3, K1.

13th row P1, *sl 1, K2 tog, psso, P1, MB, P1, rep from * to last 4 sts, sl 1, K2 tog, psso, P1.

The 2nd to 13th rows form the pattern.

Adapting an existing design

It is a simple matter to experiment with different patterns if you take the time to do a little bit of pre-planning before starting to knit. Begin with a basic design with the minimum of shaping and introduce bands or panels of pattern to enliven an every-day garment. As an example, use some of the bobble patterns given in this chapter as bands on the mohair T-top on page 18.

Back and front

With A cast on 79 sts instead of 78. Work 10 rows g st with A, 16 rows boxed bobble patt with B, 10 rows g st with A, 14 rows teardrop patt with C, 10 rows g st with A, 16 rows Trinity patt with B, (76 rows), and 10 rows g st with A. Cast off. Total of 86 rows.

Yoke and sleeves

With A cast on 37 sts instead of 36. Rep first 76 rows as given for back then first 50 rows again. Work 10 rows g st with A, 16 rows boxed bobble patt with B, 10 rows g st with A, 16 rows Trinity patt with B, 10 rows g st with A, 14 rows teardrop patt with C, 10 rows g st with A, 16 rows boxed bobble patt with B, and 10 rows g st with A, Cast off. Total of 238 rows.

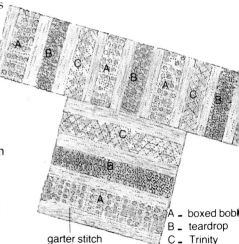

garter stitch

A – boxed bobble
B – teardrop
C – Trinity

Quilt or white knitting

This popular eighteenth-century technique is enjoying a revival today. Triangular and square motifs of any size are knitted in white cotton and sewn together to make beautiful counterpanes and chunky cushion covers. Knitted in mohair they make a lacy shawl.

Quilt knitting was a community activity carried out in rural areas well into the late 1880s. During the long winter evenings, local knitters would congregate in a warm kitchen to share both light and heat. Traditional knitting songs, gossip, and the telling of tales would accompany the furious clicking of needles hence it was often called gossip knitting.

Quilts were made in bleached cottons of various thicknesses. There is a revival of interest in this form of knitting today and suitable yarns range from fine crochet cotton to thick handicraft cotton. Easily-washed synthetic yarns such as nylon, can be used but the fabric needs to be firm. When working in cotton the needle size should be smaller than normal.

This gives a tighter tension that displays the raised patterns effectively and makes it easier to control the shape. Any geometric shape worked flat or by the circular knitting method (see page 60) can be used to build up a quilt. Some of the most interesting examples are made from squares worked on two needles and knitted diagonally from corner to corner. The squares begin with one or two stitches, increasing at the beginning of every row to form a right-angled triangle shape, then decreasing at the beginning of every row to the original number of stitches.

You need triangles as fillers along the sides if the squares are joined in a diamond pattern. To knit a right-angled triangle simply cast off when the diagonal is reached.

The making up is as much a part of quilt knitting as working the pieces. Cotton motifs are crisper if they are dipped in starch before they are blocked and allowed to dry.

It is not advisable to join the motifs with hard seams, such as backstitch. It is much easier to make a loop at the beginning of every row as a selvedge stitch (page 28). These loops can then be crocheted or oversewn together, forming a dainty lattice effect between each square. This method also makes it easier to match row ends exactly.

The following patterns can be used to make cushion covers, counterpanes or lacy shawls.

Lace and garter stitch square is simple to work. Knit it in fine mohair to make a beautiful shawl.

Lace and bobble square looks best worked in a crisp yarn. The squares form attractive pram covers and cushions.

Palm leaf square can be worked in a soft yarn to form shawls and afghans. Work in cotton for a counterpane.

Garden plot square is one of the most popular patterns for quilt knitting and has many variations.

Lace and bobble square

Cast on one st and work first 22 rows as given for lace and garter stitch square (overleaf).
23rd row L1, K1, P to end.
24th row As 2nd.
Rep last 2 rows once more, then 23rd row again.
28th row As 23rd.
29th row As 2nd. 31 sts.
30th row L1, *P1, yrn, P2 tog, rep from * to last st, K1.
31st row As 2nd.
32nd row As 23rd. 34 sts.
Rep 23rd to 27th rows once more. 39 sts.
Rep 2nd row 10 times more. 49 sts.
48th row (centre bobble row) L1, K3, *(yfwd, K1) 3 times into next st, turn and P6, turn and sl 1 purlwise, K5, turn and sl 1 knitwise, P5, turn and sl 1 purlwise, K5, turn and (P2 tog) 3 times, turn and sl 1, K2 tog, psso – **called MB**, K5, rep from * to last 4 sts, MB, K3. 50 sts.
49th row L1, K3 tog, K to end.
Rep last row 9 times more. 40 sts.
59th row L1, K3 tog, P to end.
60th row L1, K3 tog, K1, yfwd, K2 tog, *K2, yfwd, K2 tog, rep from * to last st, K1. 38 sts.
61st row As 59th.
62nd row L1, K3 tog, *K2, yfwd, K2 tog, rep from * to last 2 sts, K2.
63rd row As 59th.
64th row L1, K3 tog, K1, *K2, yfwd, K2 tog, rep from * to last 3 sts, K3.
65th row As 59th. 33 sts.
66th row L1, K3 tog, K2, *K2, yfwd, K2 tog; rep from * to last 4 sts, K4.
67th row As 59th.
Rep 60th to 63rd rows once more. 27 sts.
Rep 49th row until 3 sts rem. K3 tog and fasten off.

Lace and garter stitch square

Cast on one st.
1st row Loop the yarn right round the right-hand needle to inc 1 – **called L1**, K into front and back of cast-on st. 3 sts.
2nd row L1, K to end.
Rep 2nd row 20 times more. 24 sts.
23rd, 25th, 27th, 29th, 31st and 33rd rows L1, K1, P to end.
24th, 28th and 32nd rows L1, *K2, yfwd, K2 tog, rep from * to last st, K1.
26th, 30th and 34th rows As 2nd.
Rep 2nd row 7 times more. 43 sts.
42nd row (centre row) L1, K2 tog, K to end.
43rd row As 42nd.
44th row L1, K3 tog, K to end. 42 sts.
Rep 44th row 6 times more. 36 sts.
51st, 53rd, 55th, 57th, 59th and 61st rows L1, K3 tog, P to end.
52nd, 56th and 60th rows L1, K3 tog, K1, yfwd, K2 tog, *K2, yfwd, K2 tog, rep from * to last st, K1.
54th, 58th and 62nd rows As 44th.
Rep 44th row 21 times more.
84th row K3 tog. Fasten off.

Garden plot squares and lace borders

Garden plot is a popular pattern for quilts. Four squares make up one complete motif and several together create a beautiful bedspread. Choose from four border patterns to make a decorative edging. They are all knitted sideways, so accurate measuring is made easy.

Embossed leaves and bobbles are an integral part of many of the patterns used in quilt knitting and give it its characteristic look.

One of the most popular of all the traditional squares used for quilt knitting is known as garden plot. This delightful design has been known to knitters for more than 200 years. It has a large leaf in one corner, followed by ridged patterns and a row of smaller leaves across the diagonal of the square. The pattern is larger than the other examples given on pages 187, 188 and 192 and cannot be halved in the same way to form two right-angled triangles, but must be worked as a full square. Four of these squares joined together, with the leaves of each square to the centre, form the complete pattern.

Border patterns

If you are making a counterpane it needs to be finished with a border and several examples are given here. They are all knitted across a short row to give the required depth of border.

The knitting is continued until it is of sufficient length to go right round the quilt. Allow extra to enable the border to be eased into place round the corners. Making a loop along the top edge of the border produces a lattice effect when the border is sewn in place.

The four borders described can also be used round the edge of cushions.

Garter stitch border looks well when combined with lace and garter stitch squares.

Ring lace border combines well with lace and garter stitch and palm leaf squares.

Serrated border looks particularly effective when combined with lace and bobble squares.

Leaf border combines well with any of the squares. It is most effective when used with garden plot squares.

Opposite: A variation of the garden plot square has been used for this superb example of a traditional quilt and single garden plot squares are used for each of the cushions. Use the patterns given here to create your own heirloom.

Garden plot square

Cast on and work first 26 rows as given for palm leaf square, see page 192.
27th row L1, K1, P to end.
28th row L1, K to end.
Rep last 2 rows once more.
31st row As 28th.
32nd row As 27th.
Rep last 2 rows once more.
Rep last 8 rows 4 times more, then first 4 rows again. 73 sts.
71st row L1, K4, *(yfwd, K1, yfwd), P6*, rep from * to * 3 times, (yfwd, K1, yfwd), P7, rep from * to * 4 times, (yfwd, K1, yfwd), K4.
72nd row L1, K4, *(P3), K6*, rep from * to * 3 times, (P3), K7, rep from * to * 4 times, (P3), K5.
73rd row L1, K5, *(K1, yfwd, K1, yfwd, K1), P6*, rep from * to * 3 times, (K1, yfwd, K1, yfwd, K1), P7, rep from * to * 4 times, (K1, yfwd, K1, yfwd, K1), K5.
74th row L1, K5, *(P5), K6*, rep from * to * 3 times, (P5), K7, rep from * to * 4 times, (P5), K6.
75th row L1, K6, *(K2, yfwd, K1, yfwd, K2), P6*, rep from * to * 3 times, (K2, yfwd, K1, yfwd, K2), P7, rep from * to * 4 times, (K2, yfwd, K1, yfwd, K2), K6.

76th row L1, K6, *(P7), K6*, rep from * to * 3 times, (P7), K7, rep from * to * 4 times, (P7), K7.
77th row L1, K7, *(K3, yfwd, K1, yfwd, K3), P6*, rep from * to * 3 times, (K3, yfwd, K1, yfwd, K3), P7, rep from * to * 4 times, (K3, yfwd, K1, yfwd, K3), K7.
78th row L1, K7, *(P9), K6*, rep from * to * 3 times, (P9), K7, rep from * to * 4 times, (P9), K8.
79th row L1, K3 tog, K5, *(sl 1, K1, psso, K5, K2 tog), K6*, rep from * to * 3 times, (sl 1, K1, psso, K5, K2 tog), K7, rep from * to * 4 times, (sl 1, K1, psso, K5, K2 tog), K to end.
80th row L1, K3 tog, K5, *(P7), K6*, rep from * to * 3 times, (P7), K7, rep from * to * 4 times, (P7), K to end.
81st row L1, K3 tog, K4, *(sl 1, K1, psso, K3, K2 tog), P6*, rep from * to * 3 times, (sl 1, K1, psso, K3, K2 tog), P7, rep from * to * 4 times, (sl 1, K1, psso, K3, K2 tog), K to end.
82nd row L1, K3 tog, K4, *(P5), K6*, rep from * to * 3 times, (P5), K7, rep from * to * 4 times, (P5), K to end.
83rd row L1, K3 tog, K3, *(sl 1, K1, psso, K1, K2 tog), P6*, rep from * to * 3 times, (sl 1, K1, psso, K1, K2 tog), P7, rep from * to * 4 times, (sl 1, K1, psso, K1, K2 tog), K to end.
84th row L1, K3 tog, K3, *(P3), K6*, rep from * to * 3 times, (P3), K7, rep from * to * 4 times, (P3), K to end.
85th row L1, K3 tog, K2, *(sl 2, K1,

Garter stitch border

Cast on 17 sts noting that this number varies from row to row. K one row.
1st row (Beg at inside edge) Yarn right round right-hand needle to inc 1 – **called L1**, K2 tog, K2, (yarn round needle twice – **called y2rn**, K2 tog) twice, K6, y2rn, K2 tog, K1.
2nd row K2, K into front of loop then P into same loop – **called K1P**, K7, (K1P, K1) twice, K3.
3rd row L1, K2 tog, K to end.
4th row K to end.
5th row L1, K2 tog, K2, (y2rn, K2 tog) twice, K7, (y2rn, K2 tog) twice, K1.
6th row K2, (K1P, K1) twice, K7, (K1P, K1) twice, K3.
7th row L1, K2 tog, K to end.
8th row K to end.
9th row L1, K2 tog, K2, (y2rn, K2 tog) twice, (y2rn, sl 1, K2 tog, psso) 5 times, K1.
10th row K2, (K1P, K1) 7 times, K3.
11th row L1, K2 tog, K to end.
12th row Cast off 9 sts, K to end.
These 12 rows form the pattern.

Ring lace border

Cast on 28 sts noting that this number varies from row to row. K one row.
1st row (Beg at outside edge) L1 as 1st row of garter stitch border, (K2 tog) twice, K1, yfwd, K2 tog, K5, K2 tog, yfwd, K2 tog, K9, yfwd, K2 tog, K1.
2nd row Sl 1 in a purlwise direction – **called sl 1P**, K2, yfwd, K2 tog, K1, (K2 tog, yfwd) twice, K2 tog, K2, yfwd, K2 tog, K3, K2 tog, yfwd, K5.
3rd row L1, K2 tog, yfwd, K4, yfwd, K2 tog, K1, K2 tog, yfwd, K11, yfwd, K2 tog, K1.
4th row Sl 1P, K2, yfwd, K2 tog, K3, (yfwd, K2 tog) twice, K3, yfwd, K3 tog, yfwd, K8.
5th row L1, K2 tog, yfwd, K1, K2 tog, y2rn as 1st row of garter stitch border, K18, yfwd, K2 tog, K1.
6th row Sl 1P, K2, yfwd, K2 tog, K4, (yfwd, K2 tog) twice, K8, K1P as 2nd row of garter stitch border, K5.
7th row L1, K2 tog, K1, K2 tog, (y2rn, K2 tog) twice, K16, yfwd, K2 tog, K1.
8th row Sl 1P, K2, yfwd, K2 tog, K5, (yfwd, K2 tog) twice, K6, (K1P, K1) twice, K3.
9th row L1, (K2 tog) twice, K1, K2 tog, y2rn, K2 tog, K3, yfwd, K1, yfwd, K2 tog, K11, yfwd, K2 tog, K1.
10th row Sl 1P, K2, yfwd, K2 tog, K3, K2 tog, yfwd, K2 tog, (yfwd, K3) twice, yfwd, K2 tog, K2, K1P, K2 tog, K3.
11th row L1, (K2 tog) twice, K3, K2 tog, yfwd, K5, yfwd, K2 tog, K10, yfwd, K2 tog, K1.
12th row Sl 1P, K2, yfwd, K2 tog, K2, (K2 tog, yfwd) twice, K3, yfwd, K7, yfwd, K2 tog, K1, K2 tog, K2.
These 12 rows form the pattern.

p2sso), P6*, rep from * to * 3 times,
(sl 2, K1, p2sso), P7, rep from * to * 4
times, (sl 2, K1, p2sso), K to end.
86th row L1, K3 tog, K2, *(P1), K6*,
rep from * to * 3 times, (P1), K7, rep
from * to * 4 times, (P1), K to end.
87th row L1, K3 tog, P to end.
88th row L1, K3 tog, K to end.
89th row As 87th.
Rep 60th to 69th rows as given for
palm leaf square (see overleaf), 6
times in all. K3 tog and fasten off.

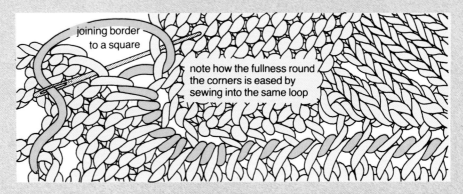

joining border
to a square

note how the fullness round
the corners is eased by
sewing into the same loop

Serrated border

Cast on 9 sts noting that this number varies from row
to row.
1st row (Beg at inside edge) L1 as 1st row of garter st
border, K2 tog, K to last 2 sts, K into front and back of
next st – **called inc 1**, K1.
2nd row K1 tbl, K1, (yfwd, sl 1, K1, psso, K1) twice,
K2.
3rd row L1, K2 tog, K to end, turn and cast on 3 sts.
4th row K1 tbl, inc 1, K2, (yfwd, sl 1, K1, psso, K1)
twice, yfwd, K3.
5th row L1, K2 tog, K to last 2 sts, inc 1, K1.
6th row K1 tbl, inc 1, K2, (yfwd, sl 1, K1, psso, K1) 3
times, K3.
7th row L1, K2 tog, K to last 3 sts, K2 tog, K1.
8th row K1 tbl, sl 1, K1, psso, sl 1, K1, psso, K3, (yfwd,
sl 1, K1, psso, K1) twice, K2.
9th row L1, K2 tog, K to last 3 sts, K2 tog, K1.
10th row Cast off 3 sts loosely, then K2, (3 sts on
needle), yfwd, sl 1, K1, psso, K1, yfwd, sl 1, K1, psso,
K2.
The 3rd to 10th rows inclusive form the pattern.

Leaf border

Cast on 10 sts noting that this number varies from row
to row.
1st row (Beg at inside edge) L1 as 1st row of garter st
border, K2 tog, K5, yfwd, K1, yfwd, K2.
2nd row P6, K into front and back of next st – **called inc
1**, K5.
3rd row L1, K2 tog, K4, P1, K2, yfwd, K1, yfwd, K3.
4th row P8, inc 1, K6.
5th row L1, K2 tog, K4, P2, K3, yfwd, K1, yfwd, K4.
6th row P10, inc 1, K7.
7th row L1, K2 tog, K4, P3, K4, yfwd, K1, yfwd, K5.
8th row P12, inc 1, K8.
9th row L1, K2 tog, K4, P4, sl 1, K1, psso, K7, K2 tog,
K1.
10th row P10, inc 1, K9.
11th row L1, K2 tog, K4, P5, sl 1, K1, psso, K5, K2 tog,
K1.
12th row P8, inc 1, K2, P1, K7.
13th row L1, K2 tog, K4, P1, K1, P4, sl 1, K1, psso, K3,
K2 tog, K1.
14th row P6, inc 1, K3, P1, K7.
15th row L1, K2 tog, K4, P1, K1, P5, sl 1, K1, psso, K1,
K2 tog, K1.
16th row P4, inc 1, K4, P1, K7.
17th row L1, K2 tog, K4, P1, K1, P6, sl 1, K2 tog, psso,
K1.
18th row P2 tog, cast off next 5 sts using P2 tog to cast
off first st, P3, K6.
These 18 rows form the pattern.

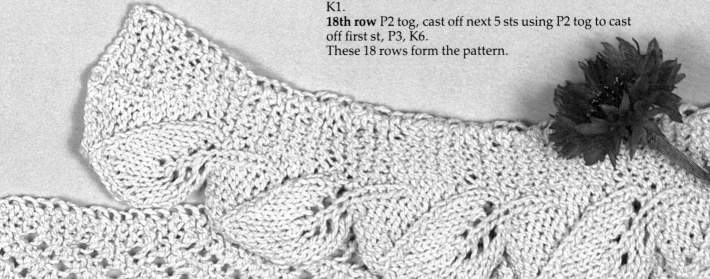

leaf border

serrated border

Palm leaf square

Cast on 3 sts.

1st and 2nd rows Loop the yarn right round the right-hand needle to inc 1 – **called L1**, K to end.

3rd row L1, K2, (yfwd, K1, yfwd), K2.

4th row L1, K2, (P3), K3.

5th row L1, K3, (K1, yfwd, K1, yfwd, K1), K3.

6th row L1, K3, (P5), K4.

7th row L1, K4, (K2, yfwd, K1, yfwd, K2), K4.

8th row L1, K4, (P7), K5.

9th row L1, K5, (K3, yfwd, K1, yfwd, K3), K5.

10th row L1, K5, (P9), K6.

11th row L1, K6, (K4, yfwd, K1, yfwd, K4), K6.

12th row L1, K6, (P11), K7.

13th row L1, K7, (K5, yfwd, K1, yfwd, K5), K7.

14th row L1, K7, (P13), K8.

15th row L1, K8, (sl 1, K1, psso, K9, K2 tog), K8.

16th row L1, K8, (P11), K9.

17th row L1, K9, (sl 1, K1, psso, K7, K2 tog), K9.

18th row L1, K9, (P9), K10.

19th row L1, K10, (sl 1, K1, psso, K5, K2 tog), K10.

20th row L1, K10, (P7), K11.

21st row L1, K11, (sl 1, K1, psso, K3, K2 tog), K11.

22nd row L1, K11, (P5), K12.

23rd row L1, K12, (sl 1, K1, psso, K1, K2 tog), K12.

24th row L1, K12, (P3), K13.

25th row L1, K13, (sl 2, K1, p2sso), K13.

26th row L1, K1, P to end.

27th row L1, *K2, yfwd, K2 tog, rep from * to last st, K1.

28th, 30th, 32nd and 34th rows L1, K1, P to end.

29th row L1, K1, yfwd, K2 tog, *K2, yfwd, K2 tog, rep from * to end.

31st row L1, K2, *K2, yfwd, K2 tog, rep from * to last 3 sts, K3.

33rd row L1, K1, *K2, yfwd, K2 tog, rep from * to last 2 sts, K2.

35th row L1, K to end.

Rep last row 11 times more. 49 sts.

47th row (centre bobble row) As 48th row of lace and bobble square.

48th row L1, K3 tog, K to end.

Rep last row 11 times more. 38 sts.

60th row L1, K3 tog, P to end.

61st row L1, K3 tog, K to end.

Rep last 2 rows once more, then 60th row again.

65th row As 60th.

66th row As 61st. 31 sts.

67th row L1, K3 tog, *P1, yrn, P2 tog, rep from * to last st, K1.

68th row As 61st.

69th row As 60th. 28 sts.

Rep 60th to 66th rows once more.

77th row L1, K3 tog, *yrn, P2 tog, P1, rep from * to end.

78th and 79th rows As 68th and 69th.

Rep 60th to 66th rows once more.

87th row L1, K3 tog, P1, *P1, yrn, P2 tog, rep from * to last st, K1.

88th and 89th rows As 68th and 69th.

Rep 60th to 64th rows once more. K3 tog and fasten off.

Feather-light mohair shawl

Make a beautiful feather-light shawl in fine kid mohair using lace and garter stitch squares. Add a lavish fringe of long double lengths of the yarn to give it that extra special look.

Size

96cm/37¾in square

You will need

7 × 20g balls of Twilleys Wisper (80% kid mohair, 20% nylon)
One pair 3¾mm/No 9 needles

Tension

A square measures about 16cm/6¼in worked on 3¾mm/No 9 needles

Shawl

Make 36 lace and garter stitch squares.

To make up

Join 6 squares to form first row alternating the direction of the knitted stitches, as illustrated. Join a total of 6 rows.

Cut rem yarn into 30cm/11¾in lengths. Take 2 strands at a time and knot into each loop round edges.

Far right: Although very fine, the kid mohair used for this shawl makes it extremely warm to wear. Right: Detail of fringing in another colourway.

Travelling stitches which twist and cross

Knitting a stitch out of sequence – with or without a cable needle – gives some interesting twisted cables, lattice and chevron patterns and fancy ribs. Choose one of the six patterns given here to make a classic V-necked jumper with short sleeves.

Travelling stitches are carried across the knitting and are used to outline a pattern, form twisted lines and geometric designs. The stitch always shows as a knit stitch on the front of the fabric, whether it is moved on a right-side or a wrong-side row. The stitches show up best against a background of reversed stocking stitch, moss stitch or small eyelet patterns. There are two methods of working travelling stitches – one involves the use of a cable needle.

Twisted stitches

Two knit stitches, as seen from the right side of the fabric, twisted together, are the simplest to work. A single stitch knitted one stitch out of sequence to right or left at the same place in each row forms vertical lines of twisted stitches. The way in which the stitches are worked determines whether they twist to the right or the left. Twisted rib, mock cable, ears of wheat and window pane patterns all use twisted stitches.

Twisted rib pattern is simple to work and looks most effective in place of a normal wide rib on welt or cuffs.
Mock cable pattern has tiny twisted cables which are ideal as an all-over pattern for baby clothes.
Ears of wheat pattern is an unusual design ideal for bulky sweaters. It is also effective worked as a panel against plain stocking stitch.
Window pane pattern is used in the jumper shown opposite. The twisted stitches form chevron outlines on panels of faggoting, suggesting a gable window. This pattern could be added above the welt and cuffs of a plain jersey by working the pattern rows once only.

Crossed stitches

These require the use of a cable needle to cross the first stitch on the left-hand needle round the second stitch. Use this method to transfer one knit stitch round a purl stitch, or purl stitch round a knit stitch. Diagonal lines of crossed stitches slanting in both directions form dia-

Twisted stitches

1

2

1
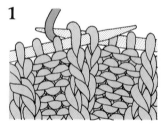

2

Twisting two knit stitches to the right
1 Pass the right-hand needle in *front* of the first st on the left-hand needle and K into the front loop of the next st. Leave this st on the left-hand needle.

2 Go back and K the first st on the left-hand needle in the usual way. Slip both sts off the left-hand needle tog.
This is abbreviated as tw2F.

Twisting two knit stitches to the left
1 Pass the right-hand needle *behind* the first st on the left-hand needle and K into the back loop of the next st. Leave this st on the left-hand needle.

2 Go back and K the first st on the left-hand needle in the usual way. Slip both sts off the left-hand needle tog.
This is abbreviated as tw2B.

Crossed stitches

1
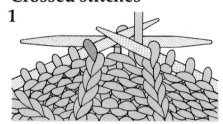

2
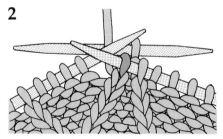

3
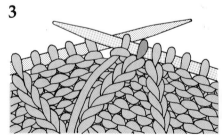

Crossing one knit stitch to the right on a purl background.
1 Slip the P st before the travelling st on to a cable needle and hold this at the *back* of the work.

2 Knit the next st on the left-hand needle in the usual way and leave it on the right-hand needle.

3 Go back and P the st on the cable needle in the usual way and leave it on the right-hand needle.
The knit stitch has now changed places with the purl stitch. This is abbreviated as cr2R.

...nond or chevron patterns and the ...cuteness of the angle is varied by ...noving a stitch every row or every ...lternate row.

...able needles are very short and ...ointed at both ends. Slip a stitch ...rom the left-hand needle on to the ...eft-hand point of the cable needle to ...old it while the next stitch is knitted. ...ring the stitch on the cable needle ...ack into the work and knit it from ...he right-hand point of the needle. ...he cable needle is held at the front or ...he back of the work depending on ...whether the stitch is crossing to the ...ight or the left.

...attice pattern and faggoting cable ...attern both use the crossed stitch ...method.

...attice pattern effect looks best ...gainst a reversed stocking stitch ...ackground as an all-over pattern.

...aggoting cable is very easy to work ...nd uses the cross stitch method on ...ust one row of the pattern repeat.

Right: Jersey knitted in the twisted stitch known as windowpane pattern.

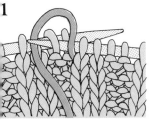

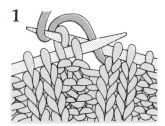

Twisting two purl stitches to the right to give a knit twist to the right on the front of the work.
1 Pass the right-hand needle in *front* of the first st on the left-hand needle and P the next. Leave

this st on the left-hand needle.
2 Go back and P the first st on the left-hand needle in the usual way. Slip both sts off the left-hand needle tog.
This is abbreviated as tw2PF.

Twisting two purl stitches to the left to give a knit twist to the left on the front of the work.
1 Pass the right-hand needle *behind* the first st on the left-hand needle and P into the back loop of the next st from the

left to the right. Leave this st on left-hand needle.
2 Go back and P the first st on the left-hand needle in the usual way. Slip both sts off the left-hand needle tog.
This is abbreviated as tw2PB.

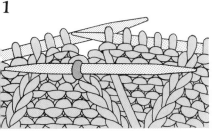
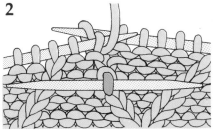

Crossing one knit stitch to the left on a purl background.
1 Slip the next st, (the travelling st), on to a cable needle and hold this at the *front* of the work.

2 Purl the next st on the left-hand needle through the back of the loop, (this tightens up the st), and leave it on the right-hand needle.

3 Go back and K the st on the cable needle in the usual way and leave it on the right-hand needle.
The knit stitch has now changed places with the purl stitch.
This is abbreviated as cr2L.

Mock cable pattern

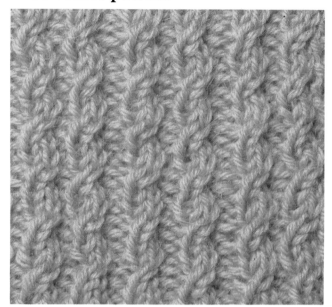

Cast on multiples of 4 sts plus 2 sts, eg 26.
1st row (Rs) P2, *K2, P2, rep from * to end.
2nd row K2, *P2, K2, rep from * to end.
3rd row P2, *tw2F, P2, rep from * to end.
4th row As 2nd.
These 4 rows form the pattern.

Twisted rib pattern

Cast on multiples of 8 sts plus 4 sts, eg 28.
1st row (Rs) P4, *(tw2F) twice, P4, rep from * to end.
2nd row K4, *P4, K4, rep from * to end.
3rd row P4, *(tw2B) twice, P4, rep from * to end.
4th row As 2nd.
These 4 rows form the pattern.

Ears of wheat pattern

Cast on multiples of 10 sts plus one st, eg 31.
1st row (Ws) P1, *K2, P5, K2, P1, rep from * to end.
2nd row K1 tbl, *P2, tw2F, K1, tw2B, P2, K1 tbl, rep from * to end.
Rep these 2 rows 4 times more.
11th row P3, *K2, P1, K2, P5, rep from * to last 8 sts, K2, P1, K2, P3.
12th row K1, *tw2B, P2, K1 tbl, P2, tw2F, K1, rep from * to end.
Rep these 2 rows 4 times more.
These 20 rows form the pattern.

Faggoting cable

Cast on multiples of 5 sts plus 2 sts, eg 22.
1st row (Rs) P2, *K1 tbl, yfwd and over needle to inc 1, K2 tog tbl, P2, rep from * to end.
2nd row K2, *P1, yrn to inc 1, P2 tog, K2, rep from * to end.
Rep these 2 rows twice more.
7th row P2, *sl next st on to cable needle and hold at front of work, K2 tog tbl from left-hand needle, yfwd and over needle to inc 1, K1 tbl from cable needle, P2, rep from * to end.
8th row As 2nd.
These 8 rows form the pattern.

Windowpane pattern

Cast on multiples of 10 sts plus 2 sts, eg 22.

1st row (Rs) K4, *tw2F noting that on subsequent reps of this row the first st worked is a P st, tw2B noting that on subsequent reps of this row the 2nd st worked is a P st, K1, sl 1, K1, psso, yfwd, K3, rep from * to last 8 sts, tw2F, tw2B, K1, sl 1, K1, psso, yfwd, K1.

2nd row P9, *P2 tog, yrn, P8, rep from * to last 3 sts, P2 tog, yrn, P1.

3rd row K3, *tw2F, K2, tw2B, K4, rep from * to last 9 sts, tw2F, K2, tw2B, K3.

4th row P to end.

5th row K2, *tw2F, K4, tw2B, K2, rep from * to end.

6th row P4, *P2 tog, yrn, P8, rep from * to last 8 sts, P2 tog, yrn, P6.

7th row K1, *tw2F, K1, sl 1, K1, psso, yfwd, K3, tw2B, rep from * to last st, K1.

8th, 10th, 12th and 14th rows K2, *P2, P2 tog, yrn, P4, K2, rep from * to end.

9th, 11th and 13th rows P2, *K2, sl 1, K1, psso, yfwd, K4, P2, rep from * to end.

15th row K1, *tw2B noting that 2nd st worked is a P st, K1, sl 1, K1, psso, yfwd, K3, tw2F noting that first st worked is a P st, rep from * to last st, K1.

16th row As 6th.

17th row K2, *tw2B, K4, tw2F, K2, rep from * to end.

18th row As 4th.

19th row K3, *tw2B, K2, tw2F, K4, rep from * to last 9 sts, tw2B, K2, tw2F, K3.

20th row As 2nd.

21st row K4, *tw2B, tw2F, K1, sl 1, K1, psso, yfwd, K3, rep from * to last 8 sts, tw2B, tw2F, K1, sl 1, K1, psso, yfwd, K1.

22nd, 24th, 26th and 28th rows P5, *K2, P2, P2 tog, yrn, P4, rep from * to last 7 sts, K2, P2, P2 tog, yrn, P1.

23rd, 25th and 27th rows K5, *P2, K2, sl 1, K1, psso, yfwd, K4, rep from * to last 7 sts, P2, K2, sl 1, K1, psso, yfwd, K1.

These 28 rows form the pattern.

Lattice pattern

Cast on multiples of 8 sts plus 2 sts, eg 26.

1st row (Ws) K4, *P2, K6, rep from * to last 6 sts, P2, K4.

2nd row P3, *cr2R, cr2L, P4, rep from * to last 7 sts, cr2R, cr2L, P3.

3rd row K3, *P1, K2, P1, K4, rep from * to last 7 sts, P1, K2, P1, K3.

4th row P2, *cr2R, P2, cr2L, P2, rep from * to end.

5th row K2, *P1, K4, P1, K2, rep from * to end.

6th row P1, *cr2R, P4, cr2L, rep from * to last st, P1.

7th row K1, *P1, K6, P1, rep from * to last st, K1.

8th row P1, K1, *P6, miss the first st on left-hand needle and K into the front of the 2nd st, then K the first st tbl and sl both sts off needle tog – **called cr2KR**, rep from * to last 8 sts, P6, K1, P1.

9th row As 7th.

10th row P1, *cr2L, P4, cr2R, rep from * to last st, P1.

11th row As 5th.

12th row P2, *cr2L, P2, cr2R, P2, rep from * to end.

13th row As 3rd.

14th row P3, *cr2L, cr2R, P4, rep from * to last 7 sts, cr2L, cr2R, P3.

15th row As 1st.

16th row P4, *cr2KR, P6, rep from * to last 6 sts, cr2KR, P4.

These 16 rows form the pattern.

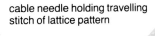

cable needle holding travelling
stitch of lattice pattern

Close-fitting short-sleeved jerseys

The two jerseys shown here – one in faggoting cable pattern and the other in windowpane pattern – have a welt, cuffs and neckband in twisted rib. You can, if you wish, use any of the other patterns given in this chapter to knit the main body pieces, but remember to adjust the number of stitches cast on to give the correct multiples for the pattern you have chosen.

Below: Knitted in fine yarn these lacy jerseys have a timeless appeal. The short-sleeved, V-necked classic shape is slim fitting and flattering.

Sizes

To fit 81 [89:97]cm/32 [35:38]in bust
Length to shoulder, 56 [57:58]cm/
22 [22½:22¾]in
Sleeve seam, 13cm/5in
The figures in [] refer to the 89/35
and 97cm/38in sizes respectively

You will need

9 [10:11]×25g balls of Sunbeam
  Pure New wool 3 ply (100% wool)
One pair 2¼mm/No 13 needles
One pair 3mm/No 11 needles
One cable needle
Set of four 2¼mm/No 13 needles
  pointed at both ends

Tension

30 sts and 40 rows to 10cm/4in over
st st worked on 3mm/No 11 needles

Back

With 2¼mm/No 13 needles cast on
130 [142:150] sts.
1st row (Rs) P2, *put needle behind
first st on left-hand needle and K
next st tbl, K first st and sl both sts
off needle tog, P2, rep from * to end.
2nd row K2, *P2, K2, rep from * to
end.
Rep these 2 rows for 8cm/3¼in,
ending with a 2nd row and inc one
st at each end of last row on 1st and
3rd sizes only if working in
faggoting cable or windowpane
patt. (Adjust sts at this point to give
correct multiples for patt of your
choice.) 132 [142:152] sts.
Change to 3mm/No 11 needles.
Cont in faggoting cable or
windowpane patt until work
measures 38cm/15in from beg,
ending with a Ws row.

Shape armholes

Keeping patt correct throughout,
(remembering to take sts into
account if working in any other
patt), cast off at beg of next and
every row 6 sts twice and 2 sts 4
times. Dec one st at each end of next
and foll 4 alt rows. 102 [112:122] sts.
Cont without shaping until
armholes measure 18 [19:20]cm/
7 [7½:7¾]in from beg, ending with
a Ws row.

Shape shoulders

Cast off at beg of next and every
row 7 [8:9] sts 6 times and
8 [9:10] sts twice. Leave rem
44 [46:48] sts on holder for centre
back neck.

Front

Work as given for back to armholes,
ending with a Ws row.

Shape armholes and divide for neck

1st row Cast off 6, patt 60 [65:70] sts,
turn and leave rem 66 [71:76] sts on
holder.
Complete left shoulder first.
2nd row Patt to end.
3rd row Cast off 2 sts, patt to last
2 sts, K2 tog.
4th row Patt to end.
5th row Cast off 2 sts, patt to end.
6th row P2 tog, patt to end.
Dec one st at armhole edge on next
and foll 4 alt rows, *at the same time*
cont dec one st at neck edge on
every foll 3rd row until 29 [33:37] sts
rem.
Cont without shaping until armhole
measures same as back to shoulder,
ending at armhole edge.

Shape shoulder

Cast off at beg of next and every
alt row 7 [8:9] sts 3 times and
8 [9:10] sts once.
With Rs of work facing, rejoin yarn
to rem sts and patt to end.
Complete to match first side,
reversing all shapings and dec by
working sts tog tbl.

Sleeves

With 2¼mm/No 13 needles cast on
82 [86:90] sts. Work 4cm/1½in
twisted rib as given for back, ending
with a 2nd row and inc 10 [16:12] sts
evenly in last row, (or number
required to give correct multiples
of sts for patt of your choice).
92 [102:102] sts.
Change to 3mm/No 11 needles.

Cont in patt as given for back until
sleeve measures 13cm/5in from beg,
ending with a Ws row.

Shape top

Keeping patt correct throughout,
(remembering to take sts into
account if working in any other
patt), cast off 6 sts at beg of next 2
rows. Dec one st at each end of next
and foll 14 [16:18] alt rows, ending
with a Ws row. 50 [56:52] sts. Cast
off at beg of next and every row
2 sts 8 [10:10] times, 3 sts 4 times
and 22 [24:20] sts once.

Neckband

Join shoulder seams. With Rs of
work facing and set of four 2¼mm/
No 13 needles, K across back neck
sts on holder, pick up and K61
[64:67] sts down left front neck, pick
up loop between sts at centre front
and K tbl, pick up and K61 [64:67] sts
up right front neck. 167 [175:183] sts.
K1 [2:3] sts, mark this point and beg
round from here.
1st round (P2, K2) to 4 sts before
centre front st, P2, K2 tog tbl, K1,
K2 tog, (P2, K2) to end.
2nd round (P2, twist 2 as given for
back) to 3 sts before centre front st,
P1, K2 tog tbl, K1, K2 tog, P1, twist
2, (P2, twist 2) to end.
Cont in twisted rib as now set, dec
each side of centre front st on every
round for 3cm/1¼in, ending with a
2nd round. Cast off in rib, still dec
at centre front.

To make up

Press each piece under a damp cloth
with a warm iron. Sew in sleeves.
Join side and sleeve seams. Press
seams.

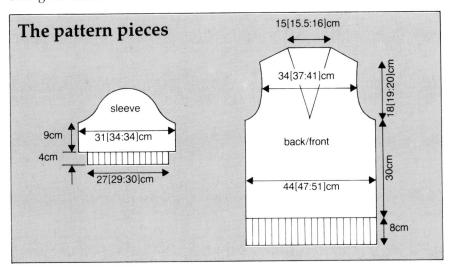

The pattern pieces

sleeve

9cm
4cm
31[34:34]cm
27[29:30]cm

15[15.5:16]cm
34[37:41]cm
18[19:20]cm
back/front
30cm
44[47:51]cm
8cm

Stitches with surface detail

*One of the easiest ways of adding interest to basic back-
grounds is the use of self-coloured surface
detail. By stranding the yarn across the front of the work,
or wrapping it round groups of stitches, you
can produce fabrics of unusual density and texture.*

Surface texture patterns in knitting are created by using the working yarn in various ways. This chapter deals with two surface decoration techniques.

Carrying the yarn across the front of the work produces a woven appear-ance and the fabric is double the thickness of ordinary knitting. The first and last edge stitches need to be worked very firmly on these patterns to avoid a fluted effect. It takes two rows of knitting to complete one pat-tern row.

Alternatively, wrap the yarn around a group of stitches held on a cable needle to add surface embellish-ments to the knitting. This produces a single thickness fabric and the pat-tern takes the same number of rows to complete as ordinary knitting.

The seven patterns given here need plain backgrounds, such as stocking stitch, so that the surface detail shows up clearly in relief, but varia-tions in ribbing can also be effective for the smocking patterns.

Woven cluster pattern is most effec-tive used as a border or panel of pat-tern, as in the cardigan shown here.

Woven diagonal pattern adds just a touch of surface interest to a stocking stitch background. Worked in a soft,

lightweight yarn, it is ideal for baby garments where extra warmth with-out weight is required.

Woven ladder pattern has the look of basketweave. Use it as an all-over pattern in a tweedy yarn.

Woven bar pattern forms a firm fabric suitable for outer garments. Add in-terest by working the first two rows of the pattern in one colour and the next two rows in a contrasting colour and repeating throughout.

Woven smocking pattern is self-col-oured, but gives the appearance of smocking. It is knitted in by taking the yarn round groups of stitches, and can be worked over variations of ribbing to form a yoke on a toddler's dress, or to gather up the cuffs on a jersey.

Woven zigzag pattern forms vertical chevron patterns of yarn in relief against a stocking stitch background. This is a highly-textured all-over pat-tern suitable for chunky jackets.

Woven butterfly pattern catches up the strands of yarn on the surface of the fabric to form dainty butterfly wings. It is an ideal all-over pattern for children's garments.

Right: An example of an all-over texture using woven clusters and cable.

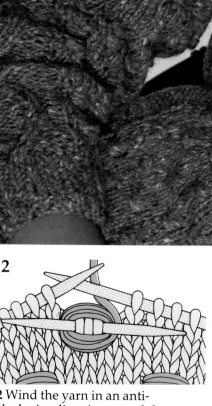

Working a cluster

The yarn must not be wound round the stitches on the cable needle too tightly or the fabric will be distorted, or so loosely that the cluster does not lie neatly on the fabric. Knit up a sample of this pattern to practise the technique.

You can make the clusters smaller or larger by putting fewer or more stitches on to the cable needle – the number should not exceed five or the fabric will pucker. You can also alter the chunkiness of the cluster by winding the yarn round the group of stitches fewer or more times.

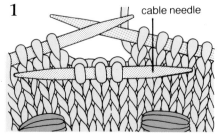

1 Knit the given number of stitches, keep the yarn at the back and slip the given number of stitches on to a cable needle and hold at the front of the work.

2 Wind the yarn in an anti-clockwise direction round the stitches on the cable needle and take the yarn back between the needles.

Knit the stitches from the cable needle to complete the cluster.

Woven cluster pattern

Cast on multiples of 8 sts plus 5 sts, eg 29.

1st row (Rs) K to end.

2nd row P to end.

3rd row *K5, sl next 3 sts on to cable needle and hold at front of work, take the yarn across the back of these sts and right round them 6 times then to back between needles, sl the 3 sts from cable needle back on to left-hand needle and K them – **called CL**, rep from * to last 5 sts, K5.

4th row P to end.

Rep 1st and 2nd rows once more.

7th row *K1, CL, K4, rep from * to last 5 sts, K1, CL, K1.

8th row P to end.

These 8 rows form the pattern.

Woven diagonal pattern

Cast on multiples of 4 sts plus 2 sts, eg 26.
1st row (Rs) K2, *yarn forward between needles –
called yfwd, sl 2 purlwise, yarn back between needles
– **called ybk**, K2, rep from * to end.
2nd row and every alt row K1, P to last st, K1.
3rd row Yfwd, sl 1 purlwise, ybk, *K2, yfwd, sl 2
purlwise, ybk, rep from * to last st, K1.
5th row Yfwd, sl 2 purlwise, ybk, *K2, yfwd, sl 2
purlwise, ybk, rep from * to end.
7th row K1, yfwd, sl 2 purlwise, ybk, *K2, yfwd, sl 2
purlwise, ybk, rep from * to last 3 sts, K2, yfwd, sl 1
purlwise, ybk.
8th row As 2nd.
These 8 rows form the pattern.

Woven ladder pattern

Cast on multiples of 8 sts, plus one, eg 25.
1st row (Rs) *K5, yarn forward between needles –
called yfwd, sl 3 purlwise, yarn back between needles
– **called ybk**, rep from * to last st, K1.
2nd row K1, *ybk, sl 3 purlwise, yfwd, P5, rep from *
to end, ending last rep with K1.
3rd row As 1st.
4th row K1, P to last st, K1.
5th row K1, *yfwd, sl 3 purlwise, ybk, K5, rep from * to
end.
6th row K1, *P4, ybk, sl 3 purlwise, yfwd, P1, rep from
* to end, ending last rep with K1.
7th row As 5th.
8th row As 4th. These 8 rows form the pattern.

Woven zigzag pattern

Cast on multiples of 5 sts, eg 30.
1st row (Rs) *K1, yarn forward between needles –
called yfwd, sl 3 purlwise, yarn back between needles
– **called ybk**, K1, rep from * to end.
2nd row *Ybk, sl 3 purlwise, yfwd, P2, rep from * to
end, ending last rep with K1.
3rd row Yfwd, *sl 1 purlwise, ybk, K2, yfwd, sl 2
purlwise, rep from * to end.
4th row Yfwd, *sl 1 purlwise, keep yfwd and P2, ybk,
sl 2 purlwise, rep from * to end, ending with sl 1, K1.
5th row *Yfwd, sl 3 purlwise, ybk, K2, rep from * to
end.
6th row *P1, ybk, sl 3 purlwise, yfwd, P1, rep from * to
end.
7th row As 5th.
8th row As 4th.
9th row As 3rd.
10th row As 2nd.
These 10 rows form the pattern.

Woven bar pattern

Cast on multiples of 2 sts plus 2 sts, eg 26.
1st row (Rs) K1, *yarn forward between needles –
called yfwd, sl 2 purlwise, yarn back between needles
– **called ybk**, K2, rep from * to last st, K1.
2nd row K1, *P2, keep yarn at front and sl 2 purlwise,
rep from * to last st, K1.
3rd row K3, *yfwd, sl 2 purlwise, ybk, K2, rep from * to
last 3 sts, yfwd, sl 2 purlwise, ybk, K1.
4th row K1, yfwd, *sl 2 purlwise, keep yarn at front
and P2, rep from * to last st, ybk, K1.
These 4 rows form the pattern.

Woven smocking pattern

Cast on multiples of 6 sts, eg 30.
1st row (Rs) K1, *K1, P2, rep from * to last 2 sts, K2.
2nd row K1, *P1, K2, rep from * to last 2 sts, P1, K1.
3rd row K1, *keep yarn at back of work, sl next 4 sts on
to cable needle and hold at front of work, take yarn
round these 4 sts from right to left twice then to back
between needles, K1, P2, K1 from cable needle – **called
smock 4**, P2, rep from * to last 5 sts, smock 4, K1.
4th row As 2nd.
5th row As 1st.
6th row As 2nd.
7th row K2, P2, *smock 4, P2, rep from * to last 2 sts,
K2.
8th row As 2nd. These 8 rows form the pattern.

Woven butterfly pattern

Cast on multiples of 10 sts plus 7 sts, eg 37.
1st row (Rs) K6, *yarn forward between needles –
called yfwd, sl 5 purlwise, yarn back between needles
– **called ybk**, K5, rep from * to last st, K1.
2nd row K1, P to last st, K1.
Rep 1st and 2nd rows 3 times more.
9th row K8, *insert right-hand needle under the 4
loops stranded across the front, yarn round needle and
draw a loop through, keep this st on the right-hand
needle and K the next st from the left-hand needle, lift
the first st over the last st – **called LK1**, K9, rep from *
to last 9 sts, LK1, K8.
10th row As 2nd.
11th row K1, yfwd, sl 5 purlwise, ybk, *K5, yfwd, sl 5
purlwise, ybk, rep from * to last st, K1.
12th row As 2nd.
Rep 11th and 12th rows 3 times more.
19th row K3, LK1, *K9, LK1, rep from * to last 3 sts, K3.
20th row As 2nd.
These 20 rows form the pattern.

Tweed cardigan with woven clusters

The main fabric of this tweed cardigan is covered with woven clusters, worked using the technique given in this chapter. There are also panels of cables decorated with woven clusters similar to the woven smocking pattern.

Sizes

To fit 86 [94]cm/34 [37]in bust loosely
Length to shoulder, 64 [66]cm/ 25¼ [26]in
Sleeve seam, 46cm/18in
The figures in [] refer to the 94cm/ 37in size only

You will need

19 [21]×50g balls of Sunbeam Aran Tweed (100% wool)
One pair 3¾mm/No 9 needles
One pair 4½mm/No 7 needles
One cable needle
Seven buttons

Tension

20 sts and 28 rows to 10cm/4in over st st worked on 4½mm/No 7 needles

Back

With 3¾mm/No 9 needles cast on 103 [111] sts.
1st row P1, *K1, P1, rep from * to end.
2nd row K1, *P1, K1, rep from * to end.
Rep these 2 rows for 8cm/3¼in, ending with a 1st row.
Change to 4½mm/No 7 needles.
Next row (set position of patts) K6, P21 [25] sts, K4, (P4, K4) twice, P1, K7, P1, K4, (P4, K4) twice, P21 [25] sts, K6.
Commence cluster and cable patt.
1st row (Rs) P6, K21 [25] sts, P4, sl next 2 sts on to cable needle and

hold at back of work, K2, K2 from cable needle – **called C4B**, P4, sl next 2 sts on to cable needle and hold at front of work, K2, K2 from cable needle – **called C4F**, P4, K1, P7, K1, P4, C4B, P4, C4F, P4, K21 [25] sts, P6.
2nd row K6, P21 [25] sts, K4, (P4, K4) twice, P1, K7, P1, K4, (P4, K4) twice, P21 [25] sts, K6.
3rd row P6, K5 [1], (sl next 3 sts on to cable needle and hold at front of work, wind yarn across back and round front of these 3 sts 6 times then back between needles, sl 3 sts back on to left-hand needle and K them – **called cl 3**, K5) 2 [3] times, P3, (sl next st on to cable needle and hold at back of work, K2, P1 from cable needle – **called cr3R**, sl next 2 sts on to cable needle and hold at front of work, P1, K2 from cable needle – **called cr3L**, P2) twice, P1, K1, P7, K1, P3, (cr3R, cr3L, P2) twice, P1, K5 [1], (cl 3, K5) 2 [3] times, P6.
4th row K6, P21 [25] sts, K3, (P2, K2) 4 times, K1, P1, K7, P1, K3, (P2, K2) 4 times, K1, P21 [25] sts, K6.
5th row P6, K21 [25] sts, P2, (cr3R, P2, cr3L) twice, P2, K1, P7, K1, P2, (cr3R, P2, cr3L) twice, P2, K21 [25] sts, P6.
6th row K6, P21 [25] sts, K2, P2, K4, P4, K4, P2, K2, P1, K7, P1, K2, P2, K4, P4, K4, P2, K2, P21 [25] sts, K6.
7th row P6, K1 [5], (cl 3, K5) twice, cl 3, K1, P2, K2, P4, C4B, P4, K2, P2, K1, P7, K1, P2, K2, P4, C4B, P4, K2, P2, K1 [5], (cl 3, K5) twice, cl 3, K1, P6.
8th row As 6th.
9th row P6, K21 [25] sts, P2, K2, P4, K4, P4, K2, P2, K1, P7, K1, P2, K2, P4, K4, P4, K2, P2, K21 [25] sts, P6.
10th row As 6th.

11th row P6, K5 [1], (cl 3, K5) 2 [3] times, P2, K2, P4, C4B, P4, K2, P2, K1, P7, K1, P2, K2, P4, C4B, P4, K2, P2, K5 [1], (cl 3, K5) 2 [3] times, P6.
12th row As 6th.
13th row P6, K21 [25] sts, P2, (cr3L, P2, cr3R) twice, P2, K1, P7, K1, P2, (cr3L, P2, cr3R) twice, P2, K21 [25] sts, P6.
14th row As 4th.
15th row P6, K1 [5], (cl 3, K5) twice, cl 3, K1, P3, (cr3L, cr3R, P2) twice, P1, K1, P7, K1, P3, (cr3L, cr3R, P2) twice, P1, K1 [5], (cl 3, K5) twice, cl 3, K1, P6.
16th row As 2nd.
17th row As 1st.
18th row As 2nd.
19th row As 3rd.
20th row As 4th.
21st row P6, K21 [25] sts, P3, (K2, P2) twice, K2, sl the last 6 sts just worked on to cable needle and hold at front of work, wind yarn across front and round to back 4 times, sl 6 sts back on to right-hand needle – **called cl 6**, P2, K2, P3, K1, P7, K1, P3, (K2, P2) twice, K2, cl 6, P2, K2, P3, K21 [25] sts, P6.
22nd row As 4th.
23rd row As 15th.
24th row As 2nd.
These 24 rows form patt and are rep throughout.
Cont in patt until work measures 42cm/16½in from beg, ending with a Ws row.

Shape armholes

Cast off 6 sts at beg of next 2 rows. 91 [99] sts.
Cont without shaping until armholes measure 22 [24]cm/ 8¾ [9½]in from beg, ending with a Ws row.

Shape shoulders

Cast off at beg of next and every row 6 sts 4 times and 5 [7] sts 4 times.
Leave rem 47 sts on holder for centre back neck.

Left front

With 3¾mm/No 9 needles cast on 49 [53] sts. Work 8cm/3¼in rib as given for back, ending with a 1st row.
Change to 4½mm/No 7 needles.**
Next row (set position of patts) K1, P1, K4, (P4, K4) twice, P21 [25] sts, K6.
Commence cluster and cable patt.

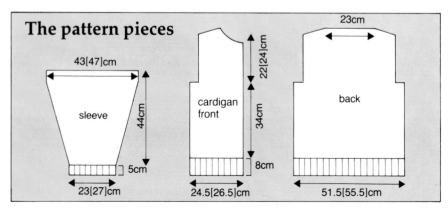

The pattern pieces

43[47]cm
sleeve
44cm
5cm
23[27]cm

22[24]cm
cardigan front
34cm
8cm
24.5[26.5]cm

23cm
back
51.5[55.5]cm

204

1st row (Rs) P6, K21 [25] sts, P4, C4B, P4, C4F, P4, K1, P1.
2nd row K1, P1, K4, (P4, K4) twice, P21 [25] sts, K6.
Cont in patt as now set until work measures same as back to underarm, ending with the same patt row.

Shape armhole
Cast off 6 sts at beg of next row. 43 [47] sts.
Cont without shaping until armhole measures 16 [18]cm/6¼ [7]in from beg, ending with a Rs row.

Shape neck
Cast off at beg of next and every alt row 9 sts once, 3 sts once, 2 sts 3 times, then dec one st at same edge on foll 3 alt rows. 22 [26] sts.
Cont if necessary without shaping until armhole measures same as back to shoulder, ending at armhole edge.

Shape shoulder
Cast off at beg of next and every alt row 6 sts twice and 5 [7] sts twice.

Right front
Work as given for left front to **.

Above: This casual, long-line cardigan is knitted in a warm tweedy yarn. It buttons up to a round neck, and the neckband is folded over to the right side and stitched neatly into place.

Next row (set position of patts) K6, P21 [25] sts, K4, (P4, K4) twice, P1, K1.
Commence cluster and cable patt.
1st row (Rs) P1, K1, P4, C4B, P4, C4F, P4, K21 [25] sts, P6.
Cont in patt as now set and complete to match left front, reversing all shapings.

Sleeves
With 3¾mm/No 9 needles cast on 41 [45] sts. Work 5cm/2in rib as given for back, ending with a 1st row and inc 5 [9] sts evenly in last row. 46 [54] sts.
Change to 4½mm/No 7 needles.
Next row (set position of patts) P13 [17] sts, K4, (P4, K4) twice, P13 [17] sts.
Commence cluster and cable patt.
1st row (Rs) K13 [17] sts, P4, C4B, P4, C4F, P4, K to end.
2nd row P13 [17] sts, K4, (P4, K4) twice, P to end.
3rd row K5 [1], (cl 3, K5) 1 [2] times,

P3, (cr3R, cr3L, P2) twice, P1, (K5, cl 3) 1 [2] times, K5 [1].
Cont in patt as now set, inc one st at each end of 7th and every foll 6th row, working the extra sts into cluster patt, until there are 21 [25] sts in each cluster panel, then work inc sts into reverse st st until there are 86 [94] sts.
Cont without shaping until sleeve measures 49cm/19¼in, or 3cm/1¼in more than required length to underarm, ending with a Ws row.
Cast off very loosely.

Right front band
With 3¾mm/No 9 needles and Rs of work facing, pick up and K124 [130] sts evenly up right front edge.
Next row *K1, P1, rep from * to end.
Work 2 more rows in rib as now set.
Next row (buttonhole row) Rib 7 sts, (cast of 3 sts, rib 17 [18] sts) 5 times, cast off 3 sts, rib 14 [15] sts.
Next row Rib to end, casting on 3 sts above those cast off in previous row.
Work 3 more rows in rib. Cast off in rib.

Left front band
Work to match right front band, noting that 1st row will read *P1, K1, rep from * to end, and omitting buttonholes.

Neckband
Join shoulder seams. With 3¾mm/ No 9 needles and Rs of work facing, pick up and K33 sts up right front neck, K across back neck sts and pick up and K33 sts down left front neck. 113 [113] sts.
Next row P1, *K1, P1, rep from * to end.
Work 2 more rows in rib as now set.
Next row (Buttonhole row) Rib 3 sts, cast off 3 sts, rib to end.
Next row Rib to end, casting on 3 sts above those cast off in previous row.
Cont in rib for 5cm/2in, then rep the 2 buttonhole rows. Work a further 4 rows in rib. Cast off very loosely.

To make up
Do not press as this will flatten the patt. Set in sleeves, sewing last 3cm/1¼in to cast off sts at underarm on body. Join side and sleeve seams. Fold neckband in half to outside and sl st in place, sewing round double buttonhole. Sew on buttons.

Learn the ropes with cables

*Cable patterns are one of the simplest methods of achieving
a textured look on knitting. They can
be spaced out in panels or worked as an all-over fabric.
The eight patterns given here are just a
selection from the scores of possible variations.*

Cables add an interesting feature to a garment and are easy to knit. They can be worked in a variety of patterns and sizes ranging from chunky rope-like cables on husky sportswear to intricate braid effects for panels and dainty miniature twists on baby garments.

The stitches which are twisted to form the cables are usually worked in stocking stitch against a reversed stocking stitch or moss stitch background which makes them stand out.

How to work a cable

A cable is formed by a number of stitches changing places with an adjacent number of stitches. The groups of stitches can be moved to the right or to the left or alternately right and left to give different patterns. No more than twelve stitches should be used in a single cable or the fabric will be pulled out of shape.

Use a cable needle to hold the stitches being moved from one place to another in a row (see page 194). If it is not possible to find a cable needle of the same size as the main needles, use a finer gauge. A cable needle thicker than the main needles will stretch the stitches out of shape.

The abbreviations used for cable patterns are always preceded by full working instructions, either at the beginning of the pattern or the first time a particular cable is used in the pattern. From then on only the abbreviation is given.

As a general guide, the letter C stands for cable. The figure after this represents the *total* number of stitches to be used in a cable twist. This number is divided in half to make the two parts which twist over or under each other. This is followed by the letter B for back or F for front, depending on whether the cable will twist to the right or the left.

The working methods for simple cables are given below.

*Right: The knitter holds four stitches at
the back on a cable needle.*

Working a cable twist from right to left

For a single cable worked over 6 knit stitches against a purl background, cast on 18 sts.
1st row (Rs) P6, K6, P6.
2nd row K6, P6, K6.
Rep these 2 rows once more.
5th row P6, sl next 3 sts on to a cable needle and hold at the front of the work, ybk to K the next 3 sts from the left-hand needle, then K3 sts from cable needle – **called C6F**, P6.
6th row As 2nd.
7th row As 1st.
8th row As 2nd.
These 8 rows form the pattern.

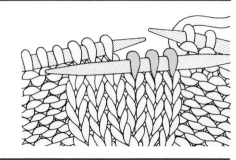

Working a cable twist from left to right

For a single cable worked over 6 knit stitches against a purl background, cast on 18 sts.
1st row (Rs) P6, K6, P6.
2nd row K6, P6, K6.
Rep these 2 rows once more.
5th row P6, sl next 3 sts on to a cable needle and hold at the back of the work, ybk to K the next 3 sts from the left-hand needle, then K3 sts from cable needle – **called C6B**, P6.
6th row As 2nd.
7th row As 1st.
8th row As 2nd.
These 8 rows form the pattern.

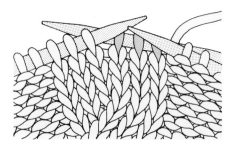

*Cast on 100 sts to make this double
thickness scarf in DK wool. Work any
of the cable patterns on one side of
the scarf, and then fold it in half
and seam down the side edges.*

Cabling stitches with a crochet hook

If you do not have a suitable cable needle use a crochet hook to move stitches from one place to another in a row.

Crochet hooks come in the same range of sizes as knitting needles so it is possible to match the size of the main needle exactly. This will ensure that the stitches do not become stretched. It is particularly important not to spoil the appearance of the fabric when using fine yarns and needles.

Use the hooked end of the crochet needle to lift the stitches off and hold them on the shank until they are required.

Knit the stitches from the left-hand needle and then the stitches on the hook from the rounded end.

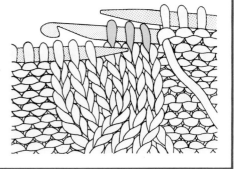

Alternating cables

Cast on multiples of 12 sts plus 6 sts, eg 30.
1st row (Rs), P6, *K6, P6, rep from * to end.
2nd row K6, *P6, K6, rep from * to end.
Rep 1st and 2nd rows once more.
5th row P6, *C6F, P6, rep from * to end.
6th row As 2nd.
Rep 1st and 2nd rows 3 times more.
13th row P6, *C6B, P6, rep from * to end.
14th row As 2nd.
Rep 1st and 2nd rows once more.
These 16 rows form the pattern.

Braid cables

Cast on multiples of 10 sts plus 2 sts, eg 32.
1st row (Rs) P2, *K8, P2, rep from * to end.
2nd row K2, *P8, K2, rep from * to end.
3rd row P2, *(sl next 2 sts on to a cable needle and hold
at back of work, ybk and K2 from left-hand needle,
then K2 from cable needle – **called C4B**) twice, P2, rep
from * to end.
4th row As 2nd.
5th row P2, *K2, sl next 2 sts on to a cable needle and
hold at front of work, ybk and K2 from left-hand
needle, then K2 from cable needle – **called C4F**, K2, P2,
rep from * to end. The 2nd to 5th rows incl form patt.

Honeycomb cables

Cast on multiples of 18 sts plus 6 sts, eg 42.
1st row (Rs), P6, *K12, P6, rep from * to end.
2nd row K6, *P12, K6, rep from * to end.
Rep 1st and 2nd rows once more.
5th row P6, *C6B, C6F, P6, rep from * to end.
6th row As 2nd.
Rep 1st and 2nd rows twice more.
11th row P6, *C6F, C6B, P6, rep from * to end.
12th row As 2nd.
These 12 rows form the pattern.

Single plaited cables

Cast on multiples of 9 sts plus 3 sts, eg 30.
1st row (Rs) P3, *K6, P3, rep from * to end.
2nd row K3, *P6, K3, rep from * to end.
3rd row P3, *sl next 2 sts on to a cable needle and hold
at back of work, ybk and K2 from left-hand needle,
then K2 from cable needle – **called C4B**, K2, P3, rep
from * to end.
4th row As 2nd.
5th row P3, *K2, sl next 2 sts on to a cable needle
and hold at front of work, K2 from left-hand needle,
then K2 from cable needle – **called C4F**, P3, rep from
* to end.
6th row As 2nd.
The 3rd to 6th rows inclusive form the pattern.

Crossed rib cables

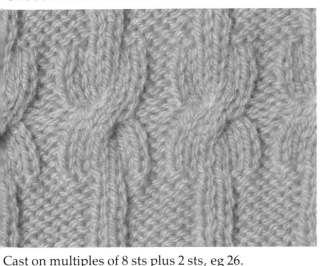

Cast on multiples of 8 sts plus 2 sts, eg 26.
1st row (Rs) P2, *K6, P2, rep from * to end.
2nd row K2, *P6, K2, rep from * to end.
Rep 1st and 2nd rows twice more.
7th row P2, *C6B, P2, rep from * to end.
8th row As 2nd.
Rep 1st and 2nd rows twice more.
13th row *P4, K2, P2, rep from * to last 2 sts, P2.
14th row *K4, P2, K2, rep from * to last 2 sts, K2.
Rep 13th and 14th rows 3 times more.
These 20 rows form the pattern.

Double cables

Cast on multiples of 10 sts plus 2 sts, eg 32.
1st row (Rs) P2, *K8, P2, rep from * to end.
2nd row K2, *P8, K2, rep from * to end.
3rd row P2, *sl next 2 sts on to a cable needle and hold
at back of work, ybk and K2 from left-hand needle,
then K2 from cable needle – **called C4B**, sl next 2 sts on
to a cable needle and hold at front of work, ybk and K2
from left-hand needle, then K2 from cable needle –
called C4F, P2, rep from * to end.
4th row As 2nd.
Rep 1st and 2nd rows twice more.
These 8 rows form the pattern.

Double plaited cables

Cast on multiples of 24 sts plus 6 sts, eg 54.
1st row (Rs) P6, *K18, P6, rep from * to end.
2nd row K6, *P18, K6, rep from * to end.
3rd row P6, *(C6B) 3 times, P6, rep from * to end.
4th row As 2nd.
Rep 1st and 2nd rows once more.
7th row P6, *K3, (C6F) twice, K3, P6, rep from * to end.
8th row As 2nd.
These 8 rows form the pattern.

Link cables

Cast on multiples of 18 sts plus 6 sts, eg 42.
1st row (Rs) P6, *K12, P6, rep from * to end.
2nd row K6, *P12, K6, rep from * to end.
Rep 1st and 2nd rows twice more.
7th row P6, *C6F, C6B, P6, rep from * to end.
8th row As 2nd.
These 8 rows form the pattern.

Chunky knit coat with link cables

This slimline coat has panels of inverted link cables on the back and front worked against a reversed stocking stitch background. These cables are the same as those given in the pattern sample for link cable on the previous page but in this design they have been turned upside down. To make a jacket from this pattern simply omit the pockets and adjust the length to suit. You will, of course, need less yarn.

Sizes

To fit 81 [86:91]cm/32 [34:36]in bust loosely
Length to shoulder, 115cm/45¼in, adjustable
Sleeve seam, 55cm/21¾in, including cuff
The figures in [] refer to the 86/34 and 91cm/36in sizes respectively

You will need

20 [20:21]×100g balls of 3 Suisses Cortina (45% viscose, 30% acrylic, 25% wool)
One pair 7mm/No 2 needles
One 7mm/No 2 circular Twin Pin, 100cm/40in long
One cable needle
Five buttons

Tension

11 sts and 15 rows to 10cm/4in over st st worked on 7mm/No 2 needles

Back

With 7mm/No 2 needles cast on 70 [74:78] sts.
1st row (Rs) K2, *P2, K2, rep from * to end.
2nd row P2, *K2, P2, rep from * to end.
Rep these 2 rows for 8cm/3¼in, ending with a 1st row.
Next row (inc row for cable) Rib 15 [16:17] sts, pick up loop lying between needles and K tbl – **called M1**, (rib 3 sts, M1) 3 times, rib to last 24 [25:26] sts, (M1, rib 3 sts) 3 times, M1, rib to end. 78 [82:86] sts.
Commence patt.
1st row (Rs) K13 [14:15] sts, P3, K12,

Left: Simple cable twists are used against reversed stocking stitch to highlight the long lines of this coat.

P3, K16 [18:20] sts, P3, K12, P3, K to end.
2nd row P13 [14:15] sts, K3, P12, K3, K16 [18:20] sts, K3, P12, K3, P to end.
3rd row K13 [14:15] sts, P3, sl next 3 sts on to cable needle and hold at back of work, K3, then K3 from cable needle – **called C6B**, sl next 3 sts on to cable needle and hold at front of work, K3, then K3 from cable needle – **called C6F**, P3, K16 [18:20] sts, P3, C6B, C6F, P3, K to end.
4th row As 2nd.
5th row As 1st.
Rep last 2 rows 3 times more.
12th row As 2nd.
The 3rd to 12th rows form the patt and are rep throughout. Cont in patt as now set, dec one st at each end of every foll 12th row until 66 [70:74] sts rem. Cont without shaping until work measures 115cm/45¼in from beg, or required length to shoulder, ending with a Ws row.

Shape shoulders

Cast off 24 [25:26] sts at beg of next 2 rows. Leave rem 18 [20:22] sts on holder for centre back neck.

Left front

With 7mm/No 2 needles cast on 22 sts for pocket lining.
Beg with a K row work 11cm/4¼in st st, ending with a P row. Leave sts on holder.
With 7mm/No 2 needles cast on 34 [36:38] sts for main body. Work 8cm/3¼in rib as given for back, noting that on 2nd size the rib will be K2, P2 to end, and ending with a 1st row.**
Next row (inc row for cable) Rib 9 [10:11] sts, (M1, rib 4) twice, M1, rib to end. 37 [39:41] sts.
Commence patt.
1st row (Rs) K13 [14:15] sts, P3, K12, P3, K to end.
2nd row P6 [7:8] sts, K3, P12, K3, P to end.
3rd row K13 [14:15] sts, P3, C6B, C6F, P3, K to end.
Cont in patt as now set, working cables on every foll 10th row as given for back, *at the same time* dec one st at end of 24th and every foll 12th row until 31 [33:35] sts rem. Cont in patt without shaping until work measures 58cm/22¾in from beg, ending with a Ws row.

Place pocket

Next row K4 [5:6] sts, sl next 22 sts on to holder, K across sts of pocket lining, K to end.
Cont in patt until work measures same as back to shoulder, ending with a Ws row.

Shape shoulder

Next row Cast off 24 [25:26] sts, K to end.
Leave rem 7 [8:9] sts on holder.

Right front

Work as given for left front to **, reversing rib as beg of 2nd size.
Next row (inc row for cable) Rib 17 [18:19] sts, (M1, rib 4) twice, M1, rib to end. 37 [39:41] sts.
Commence patt.
1st row (Rs) K6 [7:8] sts, P3, K12, P3, K to end.
2nd row P13 [14:15] sts, K3, P12, K3, P to end.
Complete as given for left front, reversing position of pocket and all shapings.

Sleeves

With 7mm/No 2 needles cast on 50 sts. Work 20cm/8in rib as given for back, ending with a 2nd row and inc 2 sts evenly in last row. 52 sts.
Beg with a K row cont in st st until work measures 55cm/21¾in from beg, ending with a P row. Cast off loosely.

Collar

Join shoulder seams. With Rs of work facing and 7mm/No 2 needles, beg with P2 and work in K2, P2 rib across 7 [8:9] sts of right front, 18 [20:22] sts of back neck inc 2 sts evenly across them and 7 [8:9] sts of left front. 34 [38:42] sts.
Work 17cm/6¾in rib. Cast off *very* loosely.

Buttonhole band

With Rs of work facing and 7mm/No 2 circular needle, pick up and K150 sts evenly up right front edge and edge of collar. Beg with P2, work 4 rows K2, P2 rib.
Next row (buttonhole row) Rib 48 sts, (cast off 2 sts, rib 10) 4 times, cast off 2 sts, rib to end.
Next row Rib to end, casting on 2 sts above those cast off in previous row.
Work 4 more rows rib. Cast off loosely in rib.

Button band

Work as given for buttonhole band, omitting buttonholes.

Pocket tops

With Rs of work facing, sl pocket top sts on to 7mm/No 2 needle, rejoin yarn and beg with P2, work 10 rows K2, P2 rib.
Cast off in rib.

To make up

Do not press. Place a marker on side seams about 24cm/9½in down from shoulders. Sew in sleeves between markers. Join side and sleeve seams. Sew down pocket tops and pocket linings. Sew on buttons.

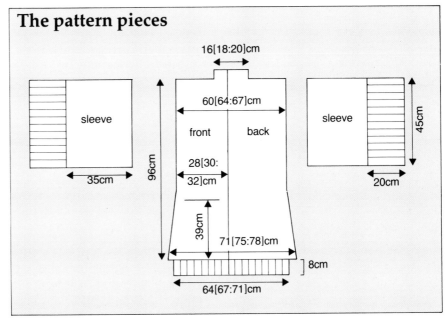

The pattern pieces

sleeve 35cm

16[18:20]cm

60[64:67]cm

front back

96cm

28[30:32]cm

39cm

71[75:78]cm

64[67:71]cm

8cm

sleeve 20cm

45cm

Cable patterns used for panels and borders

If you find working all-over cable patterns too complicated, try using one or two vertical panels to highlight a basic stocking stitch jersey. Or use the cables as a single band across the width of the fabric above the welt and cuffs of a plain garment.

For many centuries men and women in small fishing ports experimented with the fascinating twists and turns of cable patterns.

Today, cables are mainly associated with Aran designs but you do not have to work them in conjunction with other Aran patterns or as an all-over pattern. You could position just one or two vertical cable panels on the left or right-hand side of a jersey or cardigan knitted in a basic stitch or add one repeat of the pattern rows as a cable border above the welt or cuffs of a garment.

The main pattern of the garment should not be too highly textured or it will detract from the effect of the cables. If adding cables to a complex stitch pattern, add two or three stitches in reversed stocking stitch or moss stitch either side of the cables to define them and show them off to

their best advantage on a garment.

For a border, keep the same number of stitches in reversed stocking stitch between each repeat of the pattern across the row. Make sure that the multiples of stitches will fit into the total number of stitches given in the pattern, working any extra stitches at each end in reversed stocking stitch. This chapter includes seven more cable patterns. Five have been knitted as panels and two are more suitable as borders. The lover's cable, shown as a panel, also looks good as a border.

The jersey has been worked entirely in reversed stocking stitch and has a double line of simple cables down the left side which incorporate a lacy pattern at intervals. Any of the cable panels could be substituted provided you start the pattern at the same point on the first cable pattern row.

PROFESSIONAL TOUCH

Positioning the vertical cable panel

You can use any of the cable patterns shown here for the vertical panel on the front of the jersey given in this chapter.

To make sure the panel is off centre, you must first work out how many stitches to knit either side in reversed stocking stitch.

Begin by deducting the number of stitches used for the panel from the total. As an example, to feature the tied cluster cable, deduct the 20 stitches for the panel from the total of 110 stitches (1st size), leaving 90 stitches.

Divide the remaining stitches by four, to the nearest number. Knit one quarter of the number (ie 23 stitches) in reversed stocking stitch at the beginning of the row, then

the 20 stitches for the cable and finally continue in reversed stocking stitch with the remaining (67) stitches at the end of the row.

Left: Close up of seeded trellis cable.

Staghorn cable

Worked as a panel of 20 stitches against a reversed stocking stitch background.
1st row (Ws) K2, P16, K2.
2nd row P2, K4, sl next 2 sts on to cable needle and hold at back of work, K2 from left-hand needle, then K2 from cable needle – **called C4B**, sl next 2 sts on to cable needle and hold at front of work, K2 from left-hand needle, then K2 from cable needle – **called C4F**, K4, P2.
3rd row As 1st.
4th row P2, K2, C4B, K4, C4F, K2, P2.
5th row As 1st.
6th row P2, C4B, K8, C4F, P2.
These 6 rows form the pattern.

Twisted rib cable

Worked as a panel of 15 stitches against a reversed stocking stitch background.
1st row (Rs) P4 sts, K next st tbl, *P1, K next st tbl, rep from * twice more, P4 sts.
2nd row K4 sts, P next st tbl, *K1, P next st tbl, rep from * twice more, K4 sts.
3rd to 6th rows Rep 1st and 2nd rows twice more.
7th row P4 sts, sl next 3 sts on to cable needle and hold at front of work, (K next st tbl, P1) twice then from cable needle K next st tbl, P1, K next st tbl, P4 sts.
8th row As 2nd.
9th to 12th rows Rep 1st and 2nd rows twice more.
These 12 rows form the pattern.

Seeded wishbone cable

Worked as a panel of 17 stitches against a reversed stocking stitch background.
1st row (Ws) K6, P2, K1, P2, K6.
2nd row P6, sl next 3 sts on to cable needle and hold at back of work, K2 from left-hand needle, sl the P st from cable needle back on to the left-hand needle and P this st, then K2 from cable needle, P6.
3rd row As 1st.
4th row P5, sl next st on to cable needle and hold at back of work, K2 from left-hand needle, then P1 from cable needle – **called C3B**, K1, sl next 2 sts on to cable needle and hold at front of work, P1 from left-hand needle, then K2 from cable needle – **called C3F**, P5.
5th and every alt row K all the K sts facing you and P all the P sts facing you.
6th row P4, C3B, K1, P1, K1, C3F, P4.
8th row P3, C3B, (K1, P1) twice, K1, C3F, P3.
10th row P2, C3B, (K1, P1) 3 times, K1, C3F, P2.
12th row P1, C3B, (K1, P1) 4 times, K1, C3F, P1.
14th row K3, P3, K2, P1, K2, P3, K3.
These 14 rows form the pattern.

Lover's cable

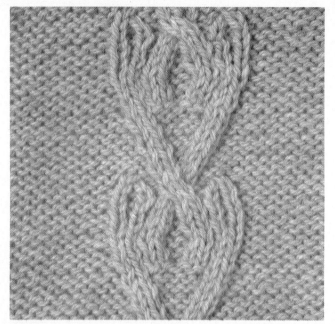

Worked as a panel of 18 stitches against a reversed stocking stitch background.

1st row (Ws) K7, P4, K7.

2nd row P7, sl next 2 sts on to cable needle and hold at front of work, K2 from left-hand needle, then K2 from cable needle, P7.

3rd row As 1st.

4th row P6, sl next st on to cable needle and hold at back of work, K2 from left-hand needle, then P1 from cable needle – **called C3B**, sl next 2 sts on to cable needle and hold at front of work, P1 from left-hand needle, then K2 from cable needle – **called C3F**, P6.

5th row K6, P2, K2, P2, K6.

6th row P5, C3B, P2, C3F, P5.

7th row K5, P2, K4, P2, K5.

8th row P4, C3B, P4, C3F, P4.

9th row K4, P2, K6, P2, K4.

10th row P3, (C3B) twice, (C3F) twice, P3.

11th row K3, P2, K1, P2, K2, P2, K1, P2, K3.

12th row P2, (C3B) twice, P2, (C3F) twice, P2.

13th row K2, P2, K1, P2, K4, P2, K1, P2, K2.

14th row P2, K1, sl next st on to cable needle and hold at front of work, P1 from left-hand needle, then K1 from cable needle – **called C2F**, C3F, P2, C3B, sl next st on to cable needle and hold at back of work, K1 from left-hand needle, then P1 from cable needle – **called C2B**, K1, P2.

15th row K2, (P1, K1) twice, P2, K2, P2, (K1, P1) twice, K2.

16th row P2, K1, P1, C2F, C3F, C3B, C2B, P1, K1, P2.

17th row (K2, P1) twice, K1, P4, K1, (P1, K2) twice.

18th row P2, C2F, C2B, P1, sl next 2 sts on to cable needle and hold at front of work, K2 from left-hand needle, then K2 from cable needle, P1, C2F, C2B, P2.

19th row K3, sl next st on to cable needle and hold at back of work, K1 from left-hand needle, then K1 from cable needle, K2, P4, K2, sl next st on to cable needle and hold at front of work, K1 from left-hand needle, then K1 from cable needle, K3.

The 4th to 19th rows inclusive form the pattern.

Seeded trellis cable

Worked as a panel of 25 stitches against a reversed stocking stitch background.

1st row (Ws) P2, K6, P4, (K1, P1) 3 times, P4, K3.

2nd row P2, sl next st on to cable needle and hold at back of work, K2 from left-hand needle, then P1 from cable needle – **called C3BP**, sl next 2 sts on to cable needle and hold at front of work, P1 from left-hand needle, then K2 from cable needle – **called C3FP**, (K1, P1) twice, C3BP, sl next 2 sts on to cable needle and hold at front of work, K1 from left-hand needle, then K2 from cable needle – **called C3FK**, P4, C3BP.

3rd and every alt row K all K sts facing you and P all P sts facing you.

4th row P1, C3BP, P2, C3FP, K1, P1, C3BP, K1, P1, C3FK, P2, C3BP, P1.

6th row C3BP, P4, C3FP, C3BP, (K1, P1) twice, C3FK, C3BP, P2.

8th row K2, P6, sl next 2 sts on to cable needle and hold at back of work, K2 from left-hand needle, then K2 from cable needle – **called C4BK**, (K1, P1) 3 times, C4BK, P3.

10th row C3FP, P4, C3BP, C3FK, (K1, P1) twice, C3BP, C3FP, P2.

12th row P1, C3FP, P2, C3BP, K1, P1, C3FK, K1, P1, C3BP, P2, C3FP, P1.

14th row P2, C3FP, C3BP, (K1, P1) twice, C3FK, C3BP, P4, C3FP.

16th row P3, sl next 2 sts on to cable needle and hold at front of work, K2 from left-hand needle, then K2 from cable needle – **called C4FK**, (K1, P1) 3 times, C4FK, P6, K2.

These 16 rows form the pattern.

Tied cluster cable

Round seeded cable

Worked as a panel of 20 stitches against a reversed stocking stitch background.

1st row (Ws) K4, (P4, K4) twice.

2nd row P4, sl next 2 sts on to cable needle and hold at back of work, K2 from left-hand needle, then K2 from cable needle – **called C4B**, P4, sl next 2 sts on to cable needle and hold at front of work, K2 from left-hand needle, then K2 from cable needle – **called C4F**, P4.

3rd row As 1st.

4th row P3, sl next st on to cable needle and hold at back of work, K2 from left-hand needle, then P1 from cable needle – **called C3B**, sl next 2 sts on to cable needle and hold at front of work, P1 from left-hand needle, then K2 from cable needle – **called C3F**, P2, C3B, C3F, P3.

5th and every alt row K all the K sts facing you and P all the P sts facing you.

6th row P2, (C3B, P2, C3F) twice, P2.

8th row P2, K2, P4, C4B, P4, K2, P2.

10th row P2, K2, P4, K4, P4, K2, P2.

12th row As 8th.

14th row P2, (C3F, P2, C3B) twice, P2.

16th row P3, C3F, C3B, P2, C3F, C3B, P3.

18th row As 2nd.

20th row As 4th.

22nd row P3, (K2, P2) twice, K2, sl the last 6 sts worked on to a cable needle, wrap the yarn 4 times round these 6 sts in an anti-clockwise direction then sl them all on to the right-hand needle again, P2, K2, P3.

24th row As 16th.

These 24 rows form the pattern.

Worked as a panel of 12 stitches against a reversed stocking stitch background.

1st row (Ws) K4, P4, K4.

2nd row P4, K4, P4.

3rd row K4, P1, keeping yarn at front of work sl next 2 sts in a purlwise direction, P1, K4.

4th row P2, sl next 3 sts on to cable needle and hold at back of work, K1 from left-hand needle, then (P1, K1, P1) from cable needle, sl next st on to cable needle and hold at front of work, (K1, P1, K1) from left-hand needle, then K1 from cable needle, P2.

5th, 7th and 9th rows K2, (P1, K1) 3 times, P2, K2.

6th, 8th and 10th rows P2, (K1, P1) 3 times, K2, P2.

11th row K2, keeping yarn at front of work sl next st in a purlwise direction, (K1, P1) 3 times, keeping yarn at front sl next st in a purlwise direction, K2.

12th row P2, sl next st on to cable needle and hold at front of work, (P2, K1) from left-hand needle, then K1 from cable needle, sl next 3 sts on to cable needle and hold at back of work, K1 from left-hand needle, then (K1, P2) from cable needle, P2.

13th row As 1st.

14th row As 2nd.

These 14 rows form the pattern.

staghorn cable

Cable panelled jersey

The rather unusual lace and cable pattern panel on this jersey is fairly simple to work as it avoids any shaping until it reaches the neck. The back and sleeves are worked in plain reverse stocking stitch.

Sizes

To fit 86 [91:97]cm/34 [36:38]in bust
Length to shoulder, 56 [57:58]cm/ 22 [22½:22¾]in
Sleeve seam, 44cm/17¼in
The figures in [] refer to the 91/36 and 97cm/38in sizes respectively

You will need

8 [9:9]×50g balls of Wendy Shetland Double Knitting (100% wool)
One pair 3mm/No 11 needles
One pair 3¾mm/No 9 needles
One cable needle

Tension

24 sts and 32 rows to 10cm/4in over st st worked on 3¾mm/No 9 needles

Back

With 3mm/No 11 needles cast on 101 [107:113] sts.
1st row (Rs) K1, *P1, K1, rep from * to end.
2nd row P1, *K1, P1, rep from * to end.
Rep these 2 rows for 10cm/4in, ending with a Rs row.
Next row (inc row) Rib 6 [9:12] sts, *pick up loop lying between needles and K tbl – **called M1**, rib 11 sts, rep from * 7 times more, M1, rib 7 [10:13] sts. 110 [116:122] sts.**
Change to 3¾mm/No 9 needles.
Beg with a P row cont in reversed st st until work measures 35cm/13¾in from beg, ending with a K row.

Shape armholes

Cast off at beg of next and every row 6 sts twice and 2 sts twice. Dec one st at each end of next and foll 4 [5:6] alt rows. 84 [88:92] sts. Cont without shaping until armholes measure 21 [22:23]cm/ 8¼ [8¾:9]in from beg, ending with a K row.

Shape shoulders

Cast off at beg of next and every row 6 sts 6 times, 6 [7:8] sts twice and 36 [38:40] sts once.

Front

Work as given for back to **.
Change to 3¾mm/No 9 needles.
Commence cable patt.
1st row (Rs) P23 [25:27] sts, K7, P8, K7, P to end.
2nd row K65 [69:73] sts, P7, K8, P7, K to end.
3rd row P23 [25:27] sts, sl next 4 sts on to cable needle and hold at back of work, K3, then K4 from cable needle – **called C7B**, P8, C7B, P to end.
4th row As 2nd.
5th row P23 [25:27] sts, K7, P6, K3 tog, yfwd, K1, yfwd, K2 tog, yfwd, (K1, yfwd) twice, sl 1, K2 tog, psso, P to end.
6th row K63 [67:71] sts, P11, K6, P7, K to end.
7th row P23 [25:27] sts, K7, P5, (K2 tog, yfwd) 3 times, K1 tbl, (yfwd, sl 1, K1, psso) 3 times, P to end.
8th row K62 [66:70] sts, P13, K5, P7, K to end.
9th row P23 [25:27] sts, K7, P3, K3 tog, yfwd, (K2 tog, yfwd) twice, K1 tbl, yfwd, K1, yfwd, K1 tbl, (yfwd, sl 1, K1, psso) twice, yfwd, K2 tog, psso, P to end.

10th row K60 [64:68] sts, P17, K3, P7, K to end.
11th row P23 [25:27] sts, C7B, P4, (K2 tog, yfwd) 3 times, K1 tbl, K1, K1 tbl, (yfwd, sl 1, K1, psso) 3 times, P to end.
12th row K61 [65:69] sts, P15, K4, P7, K to end.
13th row P23 [25:27] sts, K7, P5, (K2 tog, yfwd) twice, K1 tbl, K3, K1 tbl, (yfwd, sl 1, K1, psso) twice, P to end.
14th row K62 [66:70] sts, P13, K5, P7, K to end.
15th row P23 [25:27] sts, K7, P6, K2 tog, yfwd, K1 tbl, K5, K1 tbl, yfwd, sl 1, K1, psso, P to end.
16th row K63 [67:71] sts, P11, K6, P7, K to end.
17th to 20th rows As 1st to 4th rows.
21st row P21 [23:25] sts, K3 tog, yfwd, K1, yfwd, K2 tog, yfwd, (K1, yfwd) twice, sl 1, K2 tog, psso, P6, K7, P to end.
22nd row K65 [69:73] sts, P7, K6, P11, K to end.
23rd row P20 [22:24] sts, (K2 tog, yfwd) 3 times, K1 tbl, (yfwd, sl 1, K1, psso) 3 times, P5, K7, P to end.
24th row K65 [69:73] sts, P7, K5, P13, K to end.
25th row P18 [20:22] sts, K3 tog, yfwd, (K2 tog, yfwd) twice, K1 tbl, yfwd, K1, yfwd, K1 tbl, (yfwd, sl 1, K1, psso) twice, yfwd, sl 1, K2 tog, psso, P3, K7, P to end.
26th row K65 [69:73] sts, P7, K3, P17, K to end.
27th row P19 [21:23] sts, (K2 tog, yfwd) 3 times, K1 tbl, K1, K1 tbl, (yfwd, sl 1, K1, psso) 3 times, P4, C7B, P to end.
28th row K65 [69:73] sts, P7, K4, P15, K to end.
29th row P20 [22:24] sts, (K2 tog, yfwd) twice, K1 tbl, K3, K1 tbl, (yfwd, sl 1, K1, psso) twice, P5, K7, P to end.
30th row K65 [69:73] sts, P7, K5, P13, K to end.
31st row P21 [23:25] sts, K2 tog, yfwd, K1 tbl, K5, K1 tbl, yfwd, sl 1, K1, psso, P6, K7, P to end.
32nd row K65 [69:73] sts, P7, K6, P11, K to end.
These 32 rows form cable patt and are rep throughout. Cont until work measures same as back to underarms, ending with a Ws row.

Shape armholes

Keeping patt correct, work as given for back.

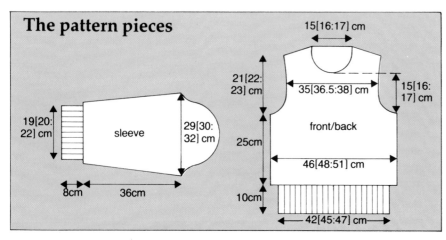

The pattern pieces

19[20:22] cm

sleeve

29[30:32] cm

8cm   36cm

15[16:17] cm

21[22:23] cm

35[36.5:38] cm

15[16:17] cm

25cm

front/back

46[48:51] cm

10cm

42[45:47] cm

Cont without shaping until armholes measure 15 [16:17]cm/ 6 [6¼:6¾]in from beg, ending with a Ws row.

Shape neck
Next row Patt 30 [31:32] sts, turn and leave rem sts on holder. Complete left side first.
Dec one st at neck edge on next 6 rows, then cont without shaping until armhole measures same as back to shoulder, ending at armhole edge.

Shape shoulder
Cast off at beg of next and every alt row 6 sts 3 times and 6 [7:8] sts once. With Rs of work facing rejoin yarn to rem sts, cast off first 24 [26:28] sts, P to end.
Complete to match first side.

Sleeves
With 3mm/No 11 needles cast on 45 [49:53] sts. Work 8cm/3¼in rib as given for back, ending with a 1st row.
Next row (inc row) Rib 5 [7:9] sts, *M1, rib 5 sts, rep from * 6 times more, M1, rib 5 [7:9] sts. 53 [57:61] sts.
Change to 3¾mm/No 9 needles. Beg with a P row cont in reversed st st, inc one st at each end of 11th and every foll 12th row until there are 69 [73:77] sts. Cont without shaping until sleeve measures 44cm/17¼in from beg, ending with a K row.

Shape top
Cast off 6 sts at beg of next 2 rows. Dec one st at each end of next and every foll 3rd row until 21 [23:25] sts rem, ending with a K row. Cast off.

Collar
With 3mm/No 11 needles cast on 81 [85:89] sts and work in rib as given for back, inc one st at each end of 3rd and every alt row until there are 113 [117:121] sts. Work one row. Cast off loosely in rib.

To make up
Press each piece under a damp cloth with a warm iron. Join shoulder seams. Sew in sleeves. Join side and sleeve seams. Sew cast on edge of collar to neck, beginning and ending at centre front. Press seams.

Right: Rounding off the corners gives a neat shape to the ribbed collar.

These casual windcheaters are not only
extremely stylish but very warm and
practical. The chunky thermal yarn
chosen for these designs is so lightweight
that it provides maximum warmth with
minimum weight and bulk.

Brioche patterns for warmth

This family of patterns produces thick but surprisingly light fabrics that retain body heat very well – which makes them particularly good choices for husky outdoor garments. Try them out on the his and her windcheaters in this chapter, ready for a country weekend.

Basic brioche pattern uses a travelling thread, subsequently knitted in with a stitch. It is formed by a 'yarn

Below: Knitted in thermal yarn this windcheater is ideal for outdoor sports giving warmth with freedom of movement. The open-ended zip makes the front opening easily adjustable – see the Professional Touch for insertion instructions.

over', 'yarn forward' or 'yarn round needle' movement and is always preceded or followed by a slipped stitch. Because this method uses slipped stitches in each or alternate rows it takes more rows than normal to work a given depth.

Brioche patterns in use Basic brioche forms a loose ribbed fabric. This is ideal where warmth without weight is required. Turkish brioche reverses

the position of the ribs and broken brioche alternates rows of basic and Turkish to give a basket stitch effect. All three patterns are reversible. Double brioche forms a loose honeycomb fabric; worked in fine yarn it has a delicate mesh-like appearance. This pattern is not reversible.

Shaping in brioche patterns Because extra rows are needed to work a given depth, increasing and decreasing takes place at each end of every 4th row, instead of every alternate row. Keep the continuity of pattern correct.

working the preparation row

Casting on

Use the two-needle method of casting on and one size larger needles than for the actual knitting. All of the patterns given here begin with an odd number of stitches. The number of cast-on stitches is increased in the first preparation row – this does not form part of the pattern sequence and is not repeated. The made stitches in the rows do not count as pattern stitches.

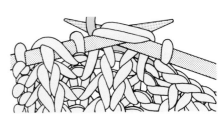

Casting off

Use one size larger needle than for the actual knitting.

The continuity of pattern must be maintained throughout. Whether casting off on a right side or a wrong side row, the yarn forward, yarn over needle and yarn round needle stitches must be made, then cast off as part of the pattern sequence. Slipped stitches must also be slipped and stitches worked together before casting them off as part of the pattern sequence.

Basic brioche pattern

Preparation row K1, *yfwd, sl 1 in a purlwise direction, take yarn over the top of the right-hand needle and K1, rep from * to end.
1st row (Rs) K1, K2 tog, *yfwd, sl 1 purlwise, yon and K tog the yfwd and sl 1 of previous row, rep from * to last st, K1.
2nd row K1, *yfwd, sl 1 purlwise, yon and K tog the yfwd and sl 1 of previous row, rep from * to last 2 sts, yfwd, sl 1 purlwise, yon, K1.
These 2 rows form the pattern. End with a 2nd row before shaping.

Broken brioche pattern

Preparation, 1st and 2nd rows As given for basic brioche pattern.
Rep 1st and 2nd rows twice more.
7th row As 2nd row of Turkish brioche pattern.
8th row As 1st row of Turkish brioche pattern.
Rep 7th and 8th rows twice more.
These 12 rows form the pattern. End with a 6th or 12th row before shaping.

Double brioche pattern

Preparation row K1, *yfwd, sl 1 in a purlwise direction, take yarn over the top of the right-hand needle and K1, rep from * to end.
1st row (Rs) K1, P2 tog, * sl 1 purlwise, take yarn over and round between needles to front again, P tog the yrn and sl 1 of previous row, rep from * to last st, ybk, K1.
2nd row K1, P1, *sl the yrn purlwise, P2, rep from * to last st, ybk, K1.
3rd row K1, yfwd between needles, *sl 1 purlwise, yrn, P tog the next st and yrn of the 1st row, rep from * to last 2 sts, sl 1, yon, K1.
4th row K1, yfwd between needles, *sl the yrn purlwise, P2, rep from * to last 3 sts, sl the yrn purlwise, P1, K1.
5th row K1, P tog next st and yrn of 3rd row, *sl 1 purlwise, yrn, P tog next st and yrn of 3rd row, rep from * to last st, ybk, K1.
The 2nd to 5th rows inclusive form the pattern. End with a 2nd or 4th row before shaping.

Turkish brioche pattern

Preparation row K1, P1, *sl 1 in a purlwise direction, yrn, P1, rep from * to last st, K1.
1st row (Rs) K1, yfwd between needles, *sl 1 purlwise, take yarn over and round between needles to front again, P tog the yrn and sl 1 of previous row, rep from * to last 2 sts, sl 1 purlwise, yon, K1.
2nd row K1, yfwd between needles, *P tog yrn and sl 1 of previous row, sl 1 purlwise, yrn, rep from * to last 3 sts, P2 tog, K1.
These 2 rows form the pattern. End with a 2nd row before shaping.

Increasing and decreasing in basic brioche pattern

decreasing

increasing

To decrease

End with a 2nd row before beginning decreasing.

1st row (dec row) K1, P tog the yfwd and next 2 sts – **called P3 tog**, yon and K tog yfwd and sl 1 of previous row, now work as 1st patt row from * to last 4 sts, P3 tog, yon, K1.

2nd row Work as 1st patt row.

3rd row Work as 2nd patt row.

4th row Work as 1st patt row.

5th row (dec row) K1, K tog the next st, yfwd and the next st – **called K3 tog**, * yfwd, sl 1 purlwise, now work as 2nd patt row to last 4 sts, yon, K3 tog, K1.

6th row Work as 2nd patt row.

7th row Work as 1st patt row.

8th row Work as 2nd patt row.

Rep these 8 rows as required, thus decreasing one st at each end of every 4th row.

To increase

End with a 2nd row before beginning increasing.

1st row (inc row) K twice into first st, K2 tog, now work as 1st patt row from * to last st, K twice into last st.

2nd row K2, *yfwd, sl 1 purlwise, now work as 2nd patt row to last 3 sts, yfwd, sl 1 purlwise, yon, K2.

3rd row Work as 2nd patt row.

4th row Work as 1st patt row.

5th row (inc row) K twice into first st, *yfwd, sl 1 purlwise, now work as 2nd patt row to last 2 sts, yfwd, sl 1 purlwise, yon, K twice into last st.

6th row Work as 2nd patt row.

7th row Work as 1st patt row.

8th row Work as 2nd patt row.

Rep these 8 rows as required, thus increasing one st at each end of every 4th row.

PROFESSIONAL TOUCH

Setting in a zip fastener

How well the zip is set in marks the difference between a cobbled home-made and a professional hand-made garment.

The zip should be eased in to place without stretching the knitted edges – so it is better to have one which is slightly too short for the opening rather than one which is too long and consequently bulges out in an unsightly way when closed.

Use an ordinary sewing needle and a double strand of sewing thread in a matching colour.

Closed zip

Keep the zip closed and begin at the top, pinning it in to the opening along both sides.

With the right side of the work facing and beginning at the top left-hand edge of the zip (right-hand side of garment), sew it in place with a firm backstitch, one or two stitches in from the edge of the knitting, depending on the thickness of the fabric. The further in you set the zip the less the teeth will show when closed. Work a few extra stitches across the bottom ends of the zip to secure them. Continue up the right-hand side, making sure that the row ends match on either side of the zip.

Turn the garment to the wrong side. Tuck in the top ends of the zip and secure them with a few stitches. Lightly sew the edges of the zip to the knitting, making sure that the sewing does not show on the right side of the garment.

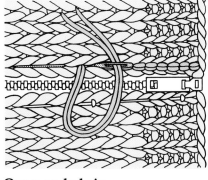

Open-ended zip

Keep the zip closed and work as given for a closed zip but beginning at the bottom left-hand edge of the zip (right front of garment). Fasten off securely at the top.

Begin at the bottom right-hand edge and work up this side in the same way.

Complete as for a closed zip.

His and hers zipped windcheaters

Use basic brioche or double brioche patterns for these lightweight windcheaters, knitted in thermal yarn for extra warmth and protection.

An open-ended zip is set in to the fronts so that they can be left completely open like a cardigan, if you wish. The useful slit pockets are surprisingly roomy.

Sizes

To fit 81 [86:91:97:102:107]cm/ 32 [34:36:38:40:42]in bust/chest
Length to shoulder, 58 [60:62:64:66:68]cm/ 22¾ [23½:24½:25¼:26:26¾]in
The figures in [] refer to the 86/34, 91/36, 97/38, 102/40 and 107cm/42in sizes respectively

You will need

5 [6:7:7:8:9]×50g balls of Robin Thermospun Chunky (48% acrylic, 32% nylon, 20% polypropylene)
One pair 5mm/No 6 needles
One pair 6mm/No 4 needles
One 55 [55:60:60:65:65]cm/ 22 [22:24:24:25:25]in open-ended zip

Tension

12 sts and 28 rows to 10cm/4in over patt worked on 6mm/No 4 needles

Back

With 5mm/No 6 needles and a length of contrast yarn cast on 26 [28:30:32:34:36] sts for the invisible method. Break off contrast yarn. Join in main yarn.
1st row K1, *yfwd, K1, rep from * to end. 51 [55:59:63:67:71] sts.
2nd row K1, *yfwd, sl 1 purlwise, ybk, K1, rep from * to end.
3rd row *Sl 1 purlwise, ybk, K1, yfwd, rep from * to last st, sl 1 purlwise.
Rep 2nd and 3rd rows once more.
6th row (Ws) K1, *P1, K1, rep from * to end.
7th row P1, *K1, P1, rep from * to end.
Rep 6th and 7th rows until work measures 8cm/3¼in from beg, ending with a 7th row. Take out contrast yarn from cast-on edge. Change to 6mm/No 4 needles.
Next row (preparation row) K1, *yfwd, sl 1 purlwise, yon, K1, rep from * to end.**
Cont in basic or double brioche patt until work measures 38 [39:40:41:42:43]cm/ 15 [15¼:15¾:16¼:16½:17]in from beg, ending with a Ws row.

Shape armholes

Keeping patt correct throughout cast off 4 sts in patt at beg of next 2 rows, then work 2 rows. Cast off 2 sts at beg of next 2 rows then work 2 rows.
Rep last 4 rows 1 [1:2:2:3:3] times more. 35 [39:39:43:43:47] sts.
Cont without shaping until armholes measure 20 [21:22:23:24:25]cm/ 7¾ [8¼:8¾:9:9½:9¾]in from beg, ending with a Ws row.

Shape shoulders

Cast off 8 [10:10:11:11:13] sts in patt at beg of next 2 rows. Leave rem 19 [19:19:21:21:21] sts on holder for centre back neck.

Pocket linings (make 2)

With 6mm/No 4 needles and main yarn cast on 13 [13:13:15:15:15] sts.
1st row K1, *yfwd, sl 1 purlwise, yon, K1, rep from * to end.
Cont in basic or double brioche patt and work 16 rows. Break off yarn and leave sts on holder.

Left front

With 5mm/No 6 needles and contrast yarn cast on 13 [14:15:16:17:18] sts. Work as given for back to **.
25 [27:29:31:33:35] sts.
Cont in basic or double brioche patt and work 16 rows.***

Place pocket

Next row Patt 8 [8:10:10:12:12] sts, then patt across sts of pocket lining and leave rem sts on holder.
Cont on these 21 [21:23:25:27:27] sts. Work 31 [31:31:35:35:35] more rows, ending with a Ws row.
Next row Patt 8 [8:10:10:12:12] sts, cast off rem 13 [13:13:15:15:15] sts in patt. Break off yarn and leave these sts for time being.
With Rs of work facing rejoin yarn to rem 17 [19:19:21:21:23] sts on holder and work 33 [33:33:37:37:37] rows in patt, ending with a Rs row.
Next row Patt to end then patt across the other 8 [8:10:10:12:12] sts.
Cont in patt until work measures same as back to underarm, ending with a Ws row.

Shape armhole

Keeping patt correct throughout cast off 4 sts at beg of next row then work 3 rows.
Cast off 2 sts at beg of next row then work 3 rows. Rep last 4 rows 1 [1:2:2:3:3] times more. 17 [19:19:21:21:23] sts.
Cont without shaping until armhole measures 16 [17:18:19:21:23] cm/ 6¼ [6¾:7:7½:8¼:9]in from beg, ending with a Ws row.

Right: The yarn is so soft and light that the windcheater looks very appealing worn over a pretty dress to give extra warmth on chilly summer days.

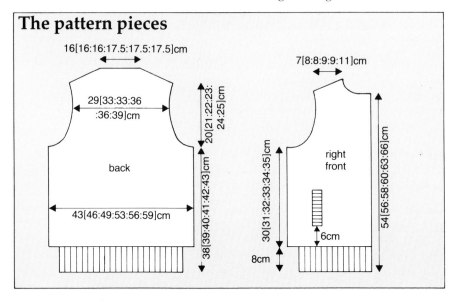

The pattern pieces

16[16:16:17.5:17.5:17.5]cm

29[33:33:36 :36:39]cm

20[21:22:23: 24:25]cm

back

38[39:40:41:42:43]cm

43[46:49:53:56:59]cm

7[8:8:9:9:11]cm

right front

30[31:32:33:34:35]cm

54[56:58:60:63:66]cm

6cm

8cm

Shape neck

Next row Patt 12 [14:14:15:15:17] sts, turn and leave rem 5 [5:5:6:6:6] sts on safety pin for centre front neck. Work 2 rows, ending at neck edge. Cast off 2 sts at beg of next and foll 4th row. Cont without shaping until armhole measures same as back to shoulder, ending with a Ws row. Cast off in patt.

Right front

Work as given for left front to ***

Place pocket

Next row Patt 17 [19:19:21:21:23] sts, turn.
Work 33 [33:33:37:37:37] rows in patt, ending at inside edge. Leave sts on holder.
With Rs of work facing rejoin yarn to sts of pocket lining and patt across these sts then patt across rem 8 [8:10:10:12:12] sts of front.
Work 31 [31:31:35:35:35] more rows.

Next row Cast off 13 [13:13:15:15:15] sts in patt, patt to end.
Next row Patt 8 [8:10:10:12:12] sts then patt across 17 [19:19:21:21:23] sts on holder. Complete to match left front, reversing all shapings.

Neckband

Join shoulder seams. With Rs of work facing and 5mm/No 6 needles work in P1, K1 rib across 5 [5:5:6:6:6] front neck sts on safety pin, pick up and K14 sts up front neck, K across back neck sts on holder, pick up and K14 down front neck then rib rem 5 [5:5:6:6:6] sts on safety pin. 57 [57:57:61:61:61] sts. Beg and end 1st row with K1, work 3cm/1¼in K1, P1 rib. Cast off in rib.

Armbands

With Rs of work facing and 5mm/No 6 needles pick up and K69 [73:77:81:85:89] sts round armhole. Beg and end 1st row with K1, work 3cm/1¼in K1, P1 rib. Cast off in rib.

Front edges

With Rs of work facing and 5mm/No 6 needles pick up and K one st for every 2 rows along front edge. Cast off knitwise.

Pocket edges

With Rs of work facing and 5mm/No 6 needles pick up and K21 [21:21:25:25:25] sts along pocket opening edge. Beg and end 1st row with K1, work 3cm/1¼in K1, P1 rib. Cast off in rib.

To make up

Do not press. Join side seams. Sew down pocket edges. Sew in pocket linings. Sew in zip to come to top of neckband. (See Professional Touch on previous page.)

Gloves and mittens

Hand-knitted gloves and mittens can be fun fashion accessories and being washable, they are also practical. Use up oddments of yarn to make a colourful striped pair or work a traditional Norwegian design and all the patterns can be knitted on two or four needles.

For many centuries Spain was the main centre for hand knitted gloves made in silk. The finest examples were produced for the church and they still remain part of a bishop's regalia.

From about the 15th century, knitted gloves became a fashion accessory and were worn as an indication of wealth and position. Gauntlets were very much the vogue – the larger the gauntlet the more powerful the wearer. The gauntlets and the hands of the gloves would often be lined with silk and embellished with gold thread.

During the 17th century, long cotton gloves, knitted in lace patterns, were the mode for ladies and long, silk, fingerless mittens were still being worn at the end of the 19th century. Today, gloves have to be more practical but the methods for making them are still the same.

Choosing the right yarn for gloves is very important. Bulky fashion yarns may look very attractive but will not prove hard-wearing. Pure wool strengthened with about 40% nylon will provide warmth and durability and, if the yarn is machine-washable, so much the better.

Fingers and thumbs are fiddly to knit, so the yarn must not be too thick and clumsy. A four-ply crêpe yarn is ideal as it has extra strength.

Mittens do not need such intricate shaping and so allow for a wider choice of thickness of yarn, such as double knitting, but the blend of fibres must still provide for wear and tear.

The needles should be finer than normally used for the yarn, giving a close firm fabric. Choose between knitting in rows or rounds.

Two needles are easier to manipulate, particularly when working fingers, but you must then seam the gloves along the sides of the palms and each finger. This hard edge can be uncomfortable, particularly on children's gloves.

You need four or five needles to knit gloves and mittens in the round. On gloves, the tops of the fingers are shaped, then drawn together and fastened off.

When working mittens, whether on two or four needles, the shaped edges at the top should be grafted together, see pages 45–47.

Measure the hand before beginning to knit. Most instructions give the sizes to fit an average hand and although knitting stretches, you may need to adjust the length of palm, thumb and fingers to fit.

Tight-fitting gloves or mittens will restrict the circulation, defeating the whole objective of warmth. Add a few extra stitches at the beginning if you think they will be too tight and, on gloves, take these into account when dividing the stitches for the thumb and fingers, or on the top shaping of mittens.

alternative colourway for Fair Isle gloves

Knitting gloves and mittens

Start at the cuff and knit upwards to the top of the hand, stopping when you have completed each section to check the measurements.

Cuffs

These should be long enough to fully cover the wrist and tuck up comfortably underneath a coat sleeve.

The wrist

The short section between the top of the cuff and the beginning of the thumb shaping. Work about 2.5cm/1in before beginning any shaping to ensure a snug fit.

Thumbs

Extra stitches are gradually increased in a triangular shape to give the final number. The increase triangle can be placed in three different positions on both gloves and mittens.

Straight thumb The increase is set into the side of the palm and back of the glove, exactly in the centre. Both gloves will fit either hand, avoiding undue wear and tear on one glove.

Left or right thumb The increase is placed on the palm just a few stitches in from the side of the glove or mitten. This means that one glove will be worked to fit the right hand and the other to fit the left hand.

Palm thumb Positioning the increase on the palm of the hand is the simple method to use when knitting Scandinavian-type patterns. One glove fits the right hand, and one the left. Alter the number of rows worked between the increase rows to suit the length of the thumb.

Thumb gussets

Cast on extra stitches at the division of the thumb and the hand. Use these stitches to join the thumb into a circle. There is no gusset on a palm thumb.

Forchettes

These are the extra stitches cast on or picked up to form a gusset between each finger. These stitches join the fingers into circles.

Fingers

Work each finger separately – instructions usually refer to the forefinger as the first finger; the middle finger as the second finger; the ring finger as the third finger and the little finger as the fourth finger.

Knitting thumbs on four needles in stocking stitch

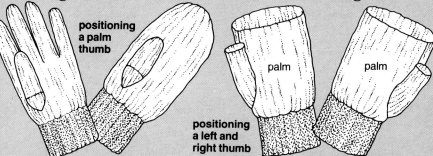

positioning a palm thumb

palm   palm

positioning a left and right thumb

Complete the cuff, wrist and thumb shaping to the required length for the division of the thumb.

Positioning a palm thumb
On an adult glove for the right hand with a total of 64 stitches at this point divide for the thumb as follows, noting that the stitches are reversed for the left hand.

Next round K34 sts, with a separate length of contrast yarn K13 sts for the thumb. Carry the main yarn loosely behind these sts and K17 to end of round.
Complete palm and fingers then return to the 13 thumb stitches. Remove the contrast yarn from these stitches, pick up all of the exposed loops at the top and bottom (26 in all). Continue in rounds for the length of the thumb to the lower edge of the thumbnail, then decrease evenly in the next few rounds to shape the top.

Positioning a left or right thumb
On an adult glove for a right hand, with a total of 78 stitches at this point, divide for the thumb as follows, noting that the stitches are reversed for the left hand.
Next round K31 sts and slip these on to a length of yarn, K21 sts for thumb, turn and cast on 3 sts, leaving rem 26 sts on another length of yarn.
Join thumb stitches into a round and complete as for palm thumb.

Knitting thumbs on two needles in stocking stitch

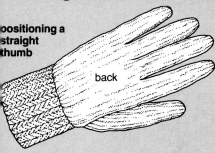

positioning a straight thumb

back

Complete the cuff, wrist and thumb shaping to the required length for the division of the thumb, ending with a purl row.

Positioning a straight thumb
On an adult glove for the right hand, with a total of 64 stitches at this point, divide for the thumb as follows, (both gloves are the same).

Next row K40 sts, turn and leave rem sts on holder.
Next row Cast on 3 sts, P these 3 sts and next 16 sts and leave rem 24 sts on another holder. 19 sts.
Continue in rows of st st for the length of thumb to the lower edge of the thumbnail, then decrease evenly in the next few rows to shape the top.

Working fingers on four needles in stocking stitch

Work the palm and back of the hand to the division of the fingers.
On an adult glove for the right hand, with a total of 64 stitches, divide for the fingers as follows (stitches are reversed for the left hand).

First finger
Knit the first 24 stitches of the round for the back and leave them on a separate length of thread. Knit the next 19 stitches of the round, noting that this is 10 stitches from the back and 9 stitches from the palm, and arrange them on three needles.
Leave the remaining 21 stitches of the palm on another separate thread. Cast on 2 stitches for the forchette. Join into a round, making 21 stitches. Knit the finger until it comes to the lower edge of the finger nail. Decrease evenly in next few rounds to shape top.
Break off the yarn, thread it into a blunt-ended sewing needle, pass through the remaining stitches, draw up and fasten off to complete.

Second finger
Slip the first 8 stitches of the back on the thread on to a needle, pick up and knit 2 stitches from base of first finger, knit the first 7 stitches of the palm on the thread, turn and cast on 2 stitches. Arrange on three needles and join into a round. 19 stitches.
Complete as given for first finger.

Third finger
Work as given for second finger.

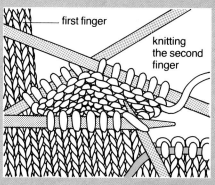

first finger

knitting the second finger

Fourth finger
Arrange the remaining 15 stitches on three needles, pick up and knit 2 stitches from base of third finger.
Join into a round. 17 stitches.
Complete as given for first finger.

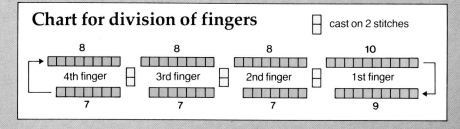

Chart for division of fingers

cast on 2 stitches

8   8   8   10

4th finger   3rd finger   2nd finger   1st finger

7   7   7   9

Working fingers on two needles in stocking stitch

Work the palm and back of the hand to the division of the fingers. On an adult glove for the right hand, with a total of 64 stitches, divide for the fingers as follows (stitches are reversed for the left hand).

First finger

Next row K43 sts, turn and leave remaining 21 sts on a holder for the palm.
Next row P19 sts, turn and cast on 2 sts, leave remaining 24 sts on a holder for the back. 21 sts for finger. Complete as given for first finger worked on four needles, then join the side seam of the finger.

Second finger

Next row Pick up and knit 2 sts from base of first finger, K7 sts from palm, turn, P17 sts, turn and cast on 2 sts. 19 sts for finger.
Complete as given for first finger.

Third finger

Work as given for second finger.

Fourth finger

Next row Pick up and K2 sts from base of third finger, K7 sts, turn and P17 sts.
Complete as given for first finger, joining finger and side seam of glove.

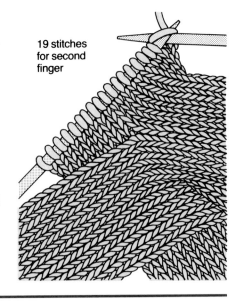

19 stitches for second finger

Gloves and mittens

Here is a choice of three patterns to knit. The first is for Fair Isle gloves worked on four needles with a traditional pattern on the back and palm of the gloves. The second is for fingerless gloves worked on four needles in narrow stripes with one of the colours picked out for the cuff. Finally, there is a pattern for a pair of mittens worked in a thicker yarn on two needles. One colour is used for the hand section and a contrast colour for the cuff and thumb but you can work them all in one colour.

Below: The Fair Isle gloves are knitted using the palm thumb technique.

Chart for right glove

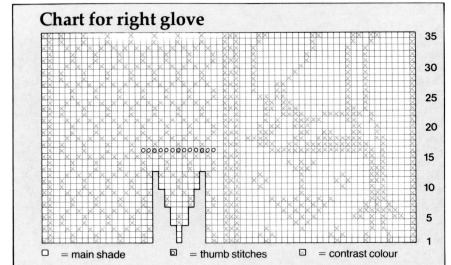

□ = main shade   ▣ = thumb stitches   ▢ = contrast colour

Sizes

To fit an average woman's size
Length, about 23cm/9in

You will need

Fair Isle gloves 1 × 40g ball of Sirdar Wash 'n' Wear 4 ply (55% Bri-nylon, 45% acrylic) in main colour A
1 ball of same in contrast colour B
Set of four 2¼mm/No 13 needles pointed at both ends
Striped fingerless gloves 1 × 40g ball of Sirdar Wash 'n' Wear 4 ply in each of 5 colours, A, B, C, D and E
Set of four 2¼mm/No 13 needles pointed at both ends
Mittens 1 × 40g ball of Sirdar Wash 'n' Wear Double Crêpe (55% Bri-nylon, 45% acrylic) in main colour A
1 ball of same in contrast colour B, optional
One pair 3mm/No 11 needles
One pair 3¾mm/No 9 needles

Tension

Fair Isle and fingerless gloves 34 sts and 44 rows to 10cm/4in over plain st st worked on 2¼mm/No 13 needles
Mittens 24 sts and 32 rows to 10cm/4in over st st worked on 3¾mm/No 9 needles

Fair Isle gloves

With set of four 2¼mm/No 13 needles and A cast on 56 sts. Work in rounds of K1, P1 rib for 5cm/2in. K one round, then join in B and cont in rounds of st st, working first 3 rounds of patt from chart.** Complete right glove first.

Shape right thumb

Next round Keeping patt correct, K36 sts, pick up loop lying between sts and K tbl – **called M1**, K1, M1, K19 sts.
Keeping patt correct, work 2 rounds.

Next round K36 sts, M1, K3, M1, K19 sts.
Work 2 rounds.
Next round K36 sts, M1, K5, M1, K19 sts.
Work 2 rounds.
Next round K36 sts, M1, K7, M1, K19 sts. 64 sts.
Work 3 rounds.

Position thumb
Next round K34 sts, using a length of different coloured yarn K13 sts for thumb, using the 2 main yarns for glove, patt 17 sts, noting that the 2 yarns of the glove are carried loosely behind the 13 thumb sts and that the contrast yarn will be removed to knit the thumb.
Cont in patt over all sts without shaping until 35 rounds of chart have been completed, ending at the end of the round. Break off B and cont with A.

First finger
Next round K24 sts and leave these on a thread for back of hand, K19 sts for finger, leave rem 21 sts on another thread for palm.
Cast on 2 sts, join these 21 sts into a round and cont in rounds of st st for 7cm/2¾in.

Shape top
Next round *K1, K2 tog, rep from * to end.
K one round.
Next round *K2 tog, rep from * to end.
Break off yarn, thread through rem 7 sts, draw up and fasten off.

Second finger
Sl 8 sts from back of hand on to needle, pick up and K2 sts from 2 cast-on sts at base of first finger, K7 sts from palm, then cast on 2 sts

and join into a round. 19 sts.
Cont in rounds of st st for 8cm/3¼in.

Shape top
Next round *K1, K2 tog, rep from * to last st, K1.
K one round.
Next round *K2 tog, rep from * to last st, K1.
Break off yarn and complete as first finger.

Third finger
Work as given for second finger but making length 7cm/2¾in.

Fourth finger
Sl rem 15 sts on to needles, pick up and K2 sts from base of third finger. 17 sts.
Cont in rounds of st st for 5cm/2in.

Shape top
Next round *K1, K2 tog, rep from * to last 2 sts, K2.
K one round.
Next round *K2 tog, rep from * to end.
Break off yarn and complete as for first finger.

Thumb
Remove contrast yarn from 13 sts, sl all 26 loops on to needles, join in A and cont in rounds of st st for 4cm/1½in.

Shape top
Work as given for fourth finger.

Left glove
Work as given for right glove to **.

Shape left thumb
Next round K19 sts, M1, K1, M1, K36 sts.
Complete as given for right glove noting that division for thumb will

be K17 sts, K13 sts with contrast yarn, K36 sts in patt and division for first finger will be K21 sts and leave for palm, K19 sts, leave rem 24 sts for back of hand.

Striped fingerless gloves
With set of four 2¼mm/No 13 needles and A cast on 56 sts. Work in rounds of K1, P1 rib for 5cm/2in, inc 4 sts evenly in last round. 60 sts.
Cont in rounds of st st working in stripes of 2 rounds B, C, D, E and A throughout, *at the same time* shape thumb gusset when 4 rounds have been worked. **

Shape right thumb
Next round K32 sts, pick up loop lying between needles and K tbl – **called M1**, K1, M1, K27 sts.
K one round.
Next round K32 sts, M1, K3, M1, K27 sts.
Cont inc in this way on every alt round until there are 78 sts, then K three rounds.

Divide for thumb
Next round K31 sts and sl these on to a length of thread, K21 sts for thumb, leave rem 26 sts on another thread.
Cast on 3 sts, join into a round. 24 sts.
Using A, work 3 rounds K1, P1 rib. Cast off loosely in rib.
Sl the first 31 sts back on to needle, using correct colour for striped patt, pick up and K3 sts from base of thumb, then K rem 26 sts. 60 sts.
Cont in rounds of st st until work measures 16cm/6¼in from beg, ending at the end of a round. Break off yarn.

First finger
Sl the first 21 sts on to a thread,

Below: Use the left or right thumb shaping method on the fingerless gloves and the straight thumb method on the mittens.

using B, K18 sts for first finger, leave rem 21 sts on another thread. Using B, cast on 2 sts and join into a round. 20 sts. Work 3 rounds K1, P1 rib. Cast off loosely in rib.

Second finger

Using C, cast on 2 sts, K7 sts from back of hand, pick up and K2 sts from base of first finger, then K7 sts from palm. 18 sts.
Complete as given for first finger.

Third finger

Using D, work as second finger.

Fourth finger

Using E, K14 rem sts, pick up and K2 sts from base of third finger. 16 sts. Complete as given for first finger.

Left glove

Work as given for right glove to **.

Shape left thumb

Next round K27 sts, M1, K1, M1, K32 sts.
Complete as given for right glove, reversing all shapings.

Mittens (both alike)

With 3mm/No 11 needles and B, (or A if working in one colour), cast on 39 sts.
1st row (Rs) K1, *P1, K1, rep from * to end.
2nd row P1, *K1, P1, rep from * to end.
Rep these 2 rows for 5cm/2in ending with a 1st row.
Next row (inc row) Rib 4 sts, *pick up loop lying between needles and K tbl – **called M1**, rib 10, rep from * twice more, M1, rib 5 sts. 43 sts.
Cont using A only. Change to 3¾mm/No 9 needles. Beg with a K row work 6 rows st st.

Shape thumb

Next row K21, M1, K1, M1, K to end.
Next row P to end.
Next row K21, M1, K3, M1, K to end.
Cont inc in this way on every alt row until there are 55 sts, then work 5 rows.

Divide for thumb

Next row K34, turn and leave rem sts on holder.
Next row Using B, (or A), cast on 3 sts, P these 3 sts and next 13 sts,

turn and leave rem 21 sts on another holder.
Cont on thumb sts for 5cm/2in, ending with a P row.
Next row (K2 tog) to end.
Break off yarn, thread through rem sts, draw up and fasten off. Join thumb seam.
With Rs of work facing, sl first 21 sts on to needle, join in A, pick up and K2 sts from base of thumb, K rem 21 sts. 44 sts.
Cont in st st until work measures 19cm/7½in from beg, or required length less about 5cm/2in, ending with a P row.

Shape top

Next row K1, (sl 1, K1, psso, K17, K2 tog) twice, K1.
Next row P to end.
Next row K1, (sl 1, K1, psso, K15, K2 tog) twice, K1.
Cont dec in this way on every alt row 5 times more, ending with a K row.
Next row P8, turn, fold work in half and graft sts.

To make up

Join side seams. Press seams lightly under a dry cloth with a cool iron.

DESIGN EXTRA

Mitten puppets

A pair of children's plain mittens can be transformed into colourful puppet characters by adding features and trimmings. The mittens can be bought ready knitted or hand knitted but should be in double knitting yarn. You can use up oddments of the same thickness of yarn to create your own original designs. Centralize the features of the clown shown here over 15 stitches and the Red Indian over 19 stitches, positioned on the back of each mitten.

Clown puppet

Swiss darn the features given on the chart. Sew on round wooden bead as nose.

	clown puppet	Indian puppet
□ = main shade		
⊠ = red		
⊠ = yellow		
⊡ = white		
⊞ = black		
◩ = blue		
◪ = turquoise		
■ = bead for nose		

To make the hair With 3¼mm/No 10 needles cast on 35 sts.
With 8mm/No 0 needles K one row, winding the yarn twice round right-hand needle for each st. With 3¼mm/No 10 needles cast off, K each pair of loops tog as one st. Sew round top of mitten.

Indian puppet

Swiss darn the features given on the chart.
To make the hair Plait 24 strands of black yarn, long enough to go round top of mitten and hang down at each side. Sew in place.

Plain and patterned socks in all sizes

Socks are knitted in the round to avoid hard seams which are uncomfortable to wear. Start at the ribbed top and learn how to turn the heel, work a gusset and shape the toe for a perfect pair of hand-made socks knitted in stocking stitch or with a decorative cable.

The art of knitting socks and stockings with well-shaped heels and toes has been known for thousands of years. Fourth century sandal-socks which have a separate division for the big toe, show a remarkable degree of skill. The heels were turned and the gusset worked in rows just as we do today.

By the 16th century there was a thriving hosiery industry throughout Europe. The rich wore costly hand knitted silk stockings which were

Add stripes to the top of the men's socks for an individual look, or a cable panel each side of the women's.

mostly made in Spain, and the term stocking stitch was used to describe the smooth fabric.

In England, Queen Elizabeth I was presented with a pair of delicate black silk stockings and was so delighted with them that a whole industry grew up making hand-knitted stockings for the court.

During the late 16th century a modest English clergyman, the Reverend William Lee, invented a knitting machine to produce machine-made stockings. It is said that he was exasperated at seeing his wife forever knitting and set about inventing a quicker mechanical method! In doing so, this remarkable man altered the social and industrial history of Britain long before the start of the industrial revolution.

Traditionally, socks are knitted on four, double pointed needles, working the ribbing on one size smaller needles than for the main fabric. They can be knitted on two needles but this means they have to be seamed down the back of the leg and under the foot which can be uncomfortable to wear.

Four patterns for socks are given in this chapter. The children's ankle length socks are knitted in stocking stitch and there is a choice of toe. A flat toe is most suitable for children and adults where the sock is to be worn with shoes. A round toe is used for babies' socks. The toe is knitted in stocking stitch for comfort in wear and to add strength to the fabric. The three-quarter length socks for men are also knitted in stocking stitch. For women there is a choice between a pair of knee length socks with cables up the sides and a gaily striped pair.

Knitting socks

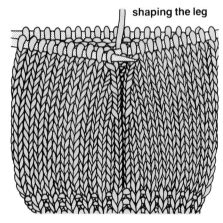

shaping the leg

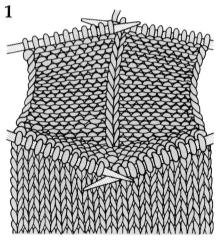

1

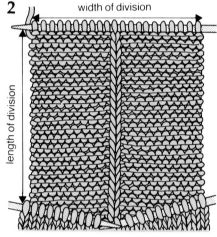

2 width of division

length of division

Start at the top leg end and cast on the required number of stitches. Work in rounds of ribbing to give a snug fit at the top and prevent it from rolling over.

The depth of the ribbing for socks without a turn down top is about 2.5cm/1in. For socks with turn down tops allow about 10cm/4in for adults and 7cm/3in for children's ankle socks.

After ribbing, adjust the number of stitches, if necessary, to suit the stitch pattern and continue in rounds down the leg. Work a mock seam stitch at the end of each round to divide the fabric down the back of the leg and provide a guide for shaping and turning the heel. Do this by working a purl stitch on every round for stocking stitch and a plain stitch on every round for rib.

Shaping the leg
Depending on the thickness of the calf, between a quarter and a fifth of the total number of stitches need to be decreased. Begin about 3cm/1¼in below the ribbing and end just below the calf.

Depending on the length of the leg, work between four and six plain rounds between each decrease round.

Divide for the heel and instep
Leave the instep stitches divided equally on two needles until later. The same number of stitches in each section makes for well-fitting hosiery but if you have an odd number of stitches or exact multiples of stitches are needed to

continue the pattern down the instep, adjust them to give more on the instep section rather than less.
1 Keeping the centre stitch of the heel as a purl stitch, continue in rows of stocking stitch.
2 Continue knitting the heel until the length from the division equals the width at the division.

Below: Pick up stitches along the side of the heel ready to work in the round again for the foot.

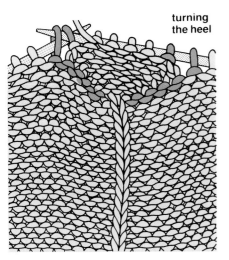

turning
the heel

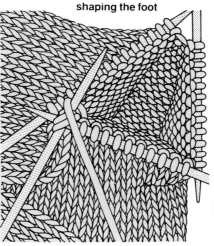

shaping the foot

Above: Shape the socks to form either a flat toe (top) for an adult or child, or a round toe (bottom) for a baby.

Turn the heel, dividing the stitches into three equal sections and, knitting in rows across the central heel section only, decrease one stitch from each of the side gusset sections on every row. The middle section can be reinforced by knitting in a matching silk sewing thread with the yarn.

When all the side gusset stitches have been decreased, leave the central heel stitches on a needle and pick up and knit stitches along one side of the heel and across half the central heel stitches from the needle. With another needle, knit across the remaining central heel stitches and pick up and knit stitches along the other side of the heel. Bring in the instep stitches and continue knitting in the round.

Shape the foot
Decrease one stitch each side of the instep until the correct width is reached to give a triangular shaping. Continue knitting the foot in rounds, keeping the instep in pattern if there is one, until the division of the toes is reached, ending at the end of a round.
Shape a flat toe by decreasing two stitches either side to reduce the width by about one third. Knit the stitches from the first needle on to the third needle and graft stitches together to complete (pages 46–47).
Shape a round toe by dividing the remaining stitches into sections and then working two stitches together at the end of each section. The rounded effect is obtained by gradually decreasing the number of

rounds worked between the shaping rounds. Only three or four stitches remain at the end, break off the yarn, thread it through these stitches, draw it up and fasten off.

Plain and patterned socks

Knit socks for your whole family to keep them warm all winter long. The children's and the men's socks are knitted in plain stocking stitch and the women's are in a choice of a pretty cable pattern or three colour stripes. Experiment by adding stripes at the top of the socks, or for fun just work the toe in a different colour.

Sizes
Child's socks, Leg to base of heel 22cm/8¾in
Foot length, 15cm/6in, adjustable
Men's socks, leg to base of heel 33cm/13in
Foot length, 26cm/10¼in, adjustable
Women's socks, leg to base of heel 40cm/15¾in
Foot length, 22cm/8¾in, adjustable

You will need
Child's socks 1 × 50g ball of Emu Superwash 4 ply (100% wool)
Men's socks 3 × 50g balls of same
Women's cable socks 3 × 50g balls of same
Women's striped socks 1 × 50g ball of same in each of 3 colours A, B and C
Set of four 2¾mm/No 12 needles pointed at both ends
Cable needle for socks with cables

Tension
32 sts and 40 rows to 10cm/4in over st st worked on 2¾mm/No 12 needles

Child's plain socks
With set of four 2¾mm/No 12 needles cast on 54 sts. Work in rounds of K1, P1 rib for 2cm/¾in,

ending at the end of a round, and inc one st at end of last round. 55 sts.
Keep the inc st as a P st to denote a seam and cont in rounds of st st until work measures 5cm/2in from beg, ending at the end of a round.

Shape leg
Next round On the first needle, sl 1, K1, psso, K to end; on the 2nd needle K to end; on the 3rd needle K to last 3 sts, K2 tog, P1.
Cont dec in this way on every fourth round until 41 sts rem. Cont without shaping until work measures 16cm/6¼in from beg, ending at the end of a round.

Divide for heel
Next row K10, turn and slip last

11 sts of round on to the other end of this same needle. 21 sts.
Divide rem 20 sts on 2 needles and leave for instep.
Cont in rows of st st on heel sts for 6cm/2¼in ending with a P row and dec one st in centre of last row. 20 sts.

Turn heel

Next row K12, sl 1, K1, psso, turn.
Next row P5, P2 tog, turn.
Next row K5, sl 1, K1, psso, turn.
Rep last 2 rows 5 times more, then first of them again. 6 sts.
Next row K3.
This completes the heel. Sl the instep sts back on to one needle.
Next round With first needle K next 3 sts of heel pick up and K17 sts along side of heel, with 2nd needle K instep sts, with 3rd needle pick up and K17 along side of heel, then K3. 60 sts.
Next round K to end.
Next round On first needle K to last 2 sts, K2 tog; on 2nd needle K to end; on 3rd needle sl 1, K1, psso, K to end.
Rep last 2 rounds until 40 sts rem.
Cont without shaping until foot measures 12cm/4¾in from back of heel, or 3cm/1¼in less than required foot length, ending at end of round.

Shape flat toe

Next round On first needle K to last 3 sts, K2 tog, K1; on 2nd needle K1, sl 1, K1, psso, K to last 3 sts, K2 tog, K1; on 3rd needle K1, sl 1, K1, psso, K to end.
Next round K to end.
Rep last 2 rounds until 16 sts rem, ending with a dec round, then K sts from first needle on to 3rd needle and graft sts tog.

Shape round toe

Next round *K6, K2 tog, rep from * to end. 35 sts.
Next and every alt round K to end.
Next round *K5, K2 tog, rep from * to end. 30 sts.
Next round *K4, K2 tog, rep from * to end. 25 sts.
Next round *K3, K2 tog, rep from * to end. 20 sts.
Next round *K2, K2 tog, rep from * to end. 15 sts.
Next round *K1, K2 tog, rep from * to end. 10 sts.
Break off yarn, thread through

remaining stitches, draw up and fasten off.

Men's plain socks

With set of four 2¾mm/No 12 needles cast on 70 sts. Work in rounds of K1, P1 rib for 7cm/2¾in, ending at the end of a round.
Cont in rounds of st st until work measures 14cm/5½in from beg, ending at the end of a round.

Shape leg

Next round Sl 1, K1, psso, K to last 3 sts, K2 tog, K1.
Cont dec in this way on every 8th round until 60 sts rem. Cont without shaping until work measures 25cm/9¾in from beg, ending at the end of a round.

Divide for heel

Next row K14, turn and sl last 15 sts of round on to the other end of this same needle. 29 sts.
Divide rem 31 sts on 2 needles and leave for instep.
Cont in st st on heel sts for 8cm/3¼in, ending with a P row.

Turn heel

Next row K18, sl 1, K1, psso, turn.
Next row P8, P2 tog, turn.
Next row K8, sl 1, K1, psso, turn.
Rep last 2 rows 8 times more, then first of them again. 9 sts.
Next row K4.
This completes the heel. Sl the instep sts back on to one needle.
Next round With the first needle K5, pick up and K25 sts along side of heel, with the 2nd needle K across instep sts, with the 3rd needle pick up and K25 sts along side of heel, then K4. 90 sts.
Next round K to end.
Next round On first needle K to last 2 sts, K2 tog; on 2nd needle K to end; on 3rd needle sl 1, K1, psso, K to end.
Rep last 2 rounds until 62 sts rem.
Cont without shaping until foot measures 21cm/8¼in from back of heel, or 5cm/2in less than required foot length, ending at the end of a round.

Shape toe

Next round On first needle K to last 3 sts, K2 tog, K1; on 2nd needle K1, sl 1, K1, psso, K to last 3 sts, K2 tog, K1; on 3rd needle K1, sl 1, K1, psso, K to end.

Next round K to end.
Rep last 2 rounds until 26 sts rem, then K sts from first needle on to 3rd needle and graft sts tog.

Women's striped socks

With set of four 2¾mm/No 12 needles and A cast on 74 sts. Work in rounds of K1, P1 rib for 3cm/1¼in, ending at the end of a round.
Commence leg patt.
Join in B and C and work in rounds of st st, working 2 rounds each B, C and A throughout until work measures 10cm/4in from beg, ending at the end of a round and noting that yarns are twisted neatly on inside at each change of colour.

Shape leg

Next round Sl 1, K1, psso, K to last 3 sts, K2 tog, K1.
Cont dec in this way on every 8th round until 58 sts rem. Cont without shaping until work measures 33cm/13in from beg, ending with 2 rounds in C.
Break off B and C.

**Divide for heel

Next row Using A, K13, turn and sl last 14 sts of round on to other end of this same needle. 27 sts.
Divide rem 31 sts on 2 needles and leave for instep.
Cont in st st on heel sts for 7cm/2¾in, ending with a P row.

Turn heel

Next row K17, sl 1, K1, psso, turn.
Next row Sl 1, P7, P2 tog, turn.
Next row Sl 1, K8, sl 1, K1, psso, turn.
Next row Sl 1, P9, P2 tog, turn.
Cont to work one more st on every row in this way until all sts are worked, ending with a P row. 17 sts.
Next row K9.
This completes the heel. Sl the instep sts back on to one needle.
Next round With first needle and A, K8, pick up and K21 sts along side of heel, with the 2nd needle K across instep sts, with the 3rd needle pick up and K21 sts along side of heel, then K9. 90 sts.
Next round With A, K to end.
Next round With B, on first needle K to last 2 sts, K2 tog; on 2nd needle K to end; on 3rd needle sl 1, K1, psso, K to end.
Working throughout in stripes as

before, rep last 2 rounds until 62 sts rem.

Cont without shaping until foot measures 17cm/6¾in from back of heel, or 5cm/2in less than required foot length, ending at the end of a round. Break off B and C. Cont in A only.

Shape toe

Next round On first needle K to last 3 sts, K2 tog, K1; on 2nd needle K1, sl 1, K1, psso, K to last 3 sts, K2 tog, K1; on 3rd needle K1, sl 1, K1, psso, K to end.

Next round K to end.

Rep last 2 rounds until 18 sts rem, then K sts from first needle on to 3rd needle and graft sts tog.

Women's cable socks

Cast on and work rib as given for striped socks. Commence patt.

1st round K17, *P twice into next st, K8, P twice into next st, *, K20, rep from * to *, K18. 78 sts.

2nd round K17, *P2, K8, P2, *, K20, rep from * to *, K17.

3rd round K17, *P2, sl next 2 sts on to cable needle and hold at back of work, K2, K2 from cable needle – **called C4B**, sl next 2 sts on to cable needle and hold at front of work, K2, K2 from cable needle – **called C4F**, P2, *, K20, rep from * to *, K17.

4th, 5th and 6th rounds As 2nd.

7th round K17, *P2, C4F, C4B, P2, *, K20, rep from * to *, K17.

8th and 9th rounds As 2nd.

The 2nd to 9th rounds inclusive form the patt and are rep throughout legs. Cont in patt until work measures 10cm/4in from beg, ending at the end of a round.

Shape leg

Next round Sl 1, K1, psso, patt to last 3 sts, K2 tog, K1.

Cont dec in this way on every 8th round until 62 sts rem. Cont without shaping until work measures about 33cm/13in from beg, ending with a 4th or 8th round.

Next round K9, *P2 tog, K8, P2 tog, *, K20, rep from * to *, K9. 58 sts.

Working in one colour throughout, complete as given for striped socks from ** to end.

Right: Knit the women's socks in three colour stripes as shown here or knit completely plain as given for the child's socks.

Knitting pattern abbreviations

alt	alternate(ly)
approx	approximate(ly)
beg	begin(ning)
ch	chain(s)
cm	centimetre(s)
cont	continu(e)(ing)
cr2L	cross 1 knit st to left
cr2R	cross 1 knit st to right
dec	decreas(e)(ing)
foll	follow(ing)
g st	garter stitch
g	gramme(s)
inc	increas(e)(ing) by working twice into a stitch
K	knit
K up	pick up and knit, as round neck edge
K-wise	knitwise direction
m	metre(s)
MB	make bobble, as specified
mm	millimetre(s)
M1	make one by picking up loop lying between needles and knit through back of loop to increase one
patt	pattern
psso	pass slipped stitch over
p2sso	pass 2 slipped stitches over
P	purl
P up	pick up and purl
P-wise	purlwise direction
rem	remain(ing)
rep	repeat(ing)
Rs	right side of fabric
sl	slip
sl st	slip stitch(es)
st(s)	stitch(es)
st st	stocking stitch
tog	together
tw2B	twist 2 knit stitches to left
tw2F	twist 2 knit stitches to right
tw2PB	twist 2 purl stitches to left
tw2PF	twist 2 purl stitches to right
Ws	wrong side of fabric
ybk	yarn back between needles
yfwd	yarn forward between needles
yon	yarn over needle
yrn	yarn around needle

Pattern symbols

An asterisk, *, in a pattern row denotes that the stitches after this sign must be repeated from that point to the end of the row, or to the last number of stitches given.

Instructions shown in round brackets (), denote that this section of the pattern is to be worked for all sizes. Instructions shown in square brackets, [], denote larger sizes.

Choosing the right yarn

Every effort has been made to ensure that the colours and qualities shown in the knitting patterns are available at the time of publication. However, the spinners (yarn manufacturers) introduce new ranges each year and reserve the right to withdraw colours in each range, or a complete range, at any time entirely at their discretion. They assess each range at regular intervals and change the yarns according to fashions and sales. When possible, it is wise to use the yarn recommended for each design featured in this book but do remember that many of the yarns are unique and will not be interchangeable without adjusting the pattern. If you have difficulty in obtaining the correct yarn, contact the spinner at the address shown below or use the mail order address if there is one given. The yarns used in this book are given alphabetically under each spinner together with the manufacturer's recommended tension and aftercare advice. If the recommended yarn is unobtainable, make a note of the number of stitches and rows to a 10cm/4in square and look for another yarn with the same tension. If a yarn is near to this size, you could use a coarser or finer needle to achieve the required tension, check by knitting a tension square. Remember also, that if you substitute one yarn for another, the texture may not be the same as the original and the quantities and aftercare may vary.

Chat Botte

UK: Groves of Thame Ltd, Lupton Road, Industrial Estate, Thame, Oxfordshire, OX9 3PR.

Kid Mohair
(p96)
Recommended tension 24 sts and 34 rows to 10cm/4in over st st worked on 3mm/No 11 needles.
Aftercare Hand or machine wash (35°C), dry clean Ⓕ, do not iron or bleach.

D.M.C.

UK: Dunlicraft Ltd, Pullman Road, Wigston, Leicestershire LE8 2DY.
Mail order: The Needlewoman of Chingford, 15 Station Road, London E4.
Australia: Olivier (Australia) PTY Ltd, 47–57 Collins Street, Alexandria, New South Wales 2015.
S. Africa: S. African Threads & Cottons Ltd, 56 Barrack Street, Cape Town 8001.

Pearl Cotton No 4
(p138)
Recommended tension 26 sts and 34 rows to 10cm/4in over st st worked on 3¼mm/No 10 needles.
Aftercare Warm hand wash, cold rinse, dry flat, dry clean Ⓐ, warm iron under a damp cloth.

Emu Wools

UK: Leeds Road, Greengate, Bradford, West Yorkshire.
Australia: The Needlewoman, Karingal, Grove, Tasmania 7106.
S. Africa: Patons & Baldwins S. Africa Ltd, PO Box 33, Randfontein 1760, Transvaal.

Guernsey
(p76)
Recommended tension 28 sts and 36 rows to 10cm/4in over st st worked on 3mm/No 11 needles.
Aftercare Hand wash only (40°C), dry flat, do not wring, dry clean Ⓟ, warm iron.

Superwash
4 ply (p231)
Recommended tension 28 sts and 36 rows to 10cm/4in over st st worked on 3¼mm/No 10 needles.
Aftercare Hand wash (40°C), machine wash (5), dry clean Ⓟ, cool iron.

Hayfield

UK: Hayfield Textiles Ltd, Hayfield Mills, Glusburn, Keighley, West Yorkshire BD20 8QP.
Australia: Panda Yarns (International) PTY Ltd, 17–27 Brunswick Rd, E. Brunswick, Victoria 3057.
S. Africa: A & H Agencies, 392 Commissioner St, Fairview, Johannesburg 2094.

Brig Double Knitting
(p72)
Recommended tension 22 sts and 30 rows to 10cm/4in over st st worked on 4mm/No 8 needles.
Aftercare Handwash only (40°C), warm iron.

Grampian Double Knitting
(p107)
Recommended tension 24 sts and 32 rows to 10cm/4in over st st worked on 3¾mm/No 9 needles.
Aftercare Hand or machine wash (40°C), cool iron.

Jaeger

UK: Jaeger Hand Knitting Ltd, Alloa FK10 1EG, Clackmannanshire, Scotland.
Mail order: Woolfayre, 120 High Street, Northallerton, Yorkshire.
Australia: Coats Patons (Australia) Ltd, 321–355 Ferntree Gulley Road, PO Box 110, Mount Waverley, Victoria 3149.
S. Africa: Patons Baldwin S. Africa Ltd, PO Box 33, Randfontein, 1760, Transvaal.

Luxury Spun Double Knitting
(p24)
Recommended tension 22 sts and 30 rows to 10cm/4in over st st worked on 4mm/No 8 needles.
Aftercare Hand wash only, dry clean Ⓐ, warm iron.

Mohair Spun
(pp15,18)
Recommended tension 16 sts and 21 rows to 10cm/4in over st st worked on 5½mm/No 5 needles.
Aftercare Hand wash only, dry clean Ⓐ, do not iron or bleach.

3 ply
(p24)
Recommended tension 32 sts and 40 rows to 10cm/4in over st st worked on 3mm/No 11 needles.
Aftercare Hand wash only, dry clean Ⓐ, warm iron.

Wool/Silk
(p87)
Recommended tension 28 sts and 36 rows to 10cm/4in over st st worked on 3¼mm/No 10 needles.

Lister-Lee

UK: George Lee & Sons Ltd, Whiteoak Mills, PO Box 37, Wakefield WF2 9SF, Yorkshire.
Australia: M J Shaw, Butterfield Holding PTY Ltd, PO Box 518, Manuka, ACT 2603.

Richmond Double Knitting
(p125)
Recommended tension 22 sts and 28 rows to 10cm/4in over st st worked on 4mm/No 8 needles.
Aftercare Hand wash (40°C), machine wash (6), dry clean ℗, cool iron under a dry cloth.

Richmond Fair Isle Effect
(p125)
Recommended tension 22 sts and 28 rows to 10cm/4in over st st worked on 4mm/No 8 needles.
Aftercare Hand wash (40°C), machine wash (6), dry clean ℗, cool iron under a dry cloth.

Patons and Baldwins Ltd

UK: Alloa FK10 1EG, Clackmannanshire, Scotland.
Mail order: Woolfayre, 120 High Street, Northallerton, Yorkshire.
Australia: Coats Patons (Australia) Ltd, 321–355 Ferntree Gulley Road, PO Box 110, Mount Waverley, Victoria, 3149.
S. Africa: Patons Baldwin S. Africa Ltd, PO Box 33, Randfontein, 1760, Transvaal.

Clansman
4 ply (p122)
Recommended tension 28 sts and 36 rows to 10cm/4in over st st worked on 3¼mm/No 10 needles.
Aftercare Hand wash (40°C), machine wash (5), dry clean Ⓐ, warm iron, do not bleach.

Fairytale Double Knitting
(p28)
Recommended tension 22 sts and 30 rows to 10cm/4in over st st worked on 4mm/No 8 needles.
Aftercare Hand wash (40°C), machine wash (6), dry clean Ⓐ, warm iron under dry cloth.

Flair Double Knitting
(p34)
Recommended tension 22 sts and 30 rows to 10cm/4in over st st worked on 4mm/No 8 needles.
Aftercare Hand wash (40°C), machine wash (6), dry clean Ⓐ, do not iron.

Robin Wools Ltd

UK: Robin Mills, Idle, Bradford, West Yorkshire.
Australia: Mrs Rosemary Mallet, The Needlewoman, Karingal, Grove, Huon, Tasmania.
S. Africa: E Brasch and Son, 57 La Rochelle Rd, Trojan, Johannesburg.

Columbine Double Knitting
(p134)
Recommended tension 22 sts and 28 rows to 10cm/4in over st st worked on 4mm/No 8 needles.
Aftercare Hand or machine wash (40°C), dry clean ℗, cool iron.

Reward Double Knitting
(p156)
Recommended tension 22 sts and 30 rows to 10cm/4in over st st worked on 4mm/No 8 needles.
Aftercare Hand or machine wash (40°C), dry clean ℗, cool iron.

Thermospun Chunky
(p222)
Recommended tension 12 sts and 20 rows to 10cm/4in over st st worked on 6mm/No 4 needles.
Aftercare Hand or machine wash (40°C), cold rinse, short spin, dry flat. Do not dry clean or iron.

Scheepjeswol

UK: Aero Needles Group plc (Scheepjeswol), Box 2, Edward Street, Redditch, Worcs.
Australia: Thorobred Scheepjeswol MPTY Ltd, 726 High Street, East Kew, Melbourne, Victoria 3102.
S. Africa: Woolcraft Agencies MPTY Ltd, PO Box 17657, 2038 Hillbrow, Johannesburg.

Superwash Zermatt
(p102)
Recommended tension 21 sts and 28 rows to 10cm/4in over st st worked on 4mm/No 8 needles.
Aftercare Hand or machine wash (30°C), do not dry clean, warm iron.

Luzern
(p130)
Recommended tension 20 sts and 26 rows to 10cm/4in over st st worked on 4½mm/No 7 needles.
Aftercare Hand or machine wash (30°C), dry clean Ⓐ, do not iron.

Sirdar Ltd

UK: Flanshaw Lane, Alverthorpe, Wakefield, Yorkshire WF2 9ND.
Mail order: The Best Woolshop, 26–28 Frenchgate, Doncaster, South Yorkshire.
Australia: David L Rowl, Sirdar (Australia) PTY Ltd, PO Box 110, Mount Waverley, Victoria 3149.
S. Africa: Patons Baldwins S. Africa Ltd, PO Box 33, Randfontein 1760, Transvaal.

Country Style Double Knitting
(Tweed) (pp82, 92, 99)
Recommended tension 24 sts and 30

rows to 10cm/4in over st st worked on 3¾mm/No 9 needles.
Aftercare Hand wash (40°C), dry clean, medium iron.

Terry Look
(p112)
Recommended tension 28 sts and 36 rows to 10cm/4in over st st worked on 3¼mm/No 10 needles.
Aftercare Hand or machine wash, do not iron.

Wash 'n' Wear
4 ply (p226)
Recommended tension 28 sts and 36 rows to 10cm/4in over st st worked on 3¼mm/No 10 needles.
Aftercare Hand or machine wash (40°C), dry clean Ⓐ, warm iron under a dry cloth.

Wash 'n' Wear Double Crêpe
(pp162, 226)
Recommended tension 24 sts and 30 rows to 10cm/4in over st st worked on 4mm/No 8 needles.
Aftercare Hand or machine wash (40°C), dry clean Ⓐ, warm iron under a dry cloth.

3 Suisses

UK: Filature de l'Espierres, Marlborough House, 38 Welford Road, Leicester LE2 7AA.

Cortina
(p210)
Recommended tension 12 sts and 16 rows to 10cm/4in over st st worked on 7mm/No 2 needles.
Aftercare Hand or machine wash (40°C), ℗, do not iron.

Sunbeam

UK: Richard Ingham & Co. Ltd, Crawshaw Mills, Pudsey, Yorkshire.
Mail order: Woolfayre, 120 High Street, Northallerton, Yorkshire.

Aran Tweed
(p204)
Recommended tension 20 sts and 28 rows to 10cm/4in over st st worked on 4½mm/No 7 needles.
Aftercare Hand wash (30°C).

Mohair
(p62)
Recommended tension 16 sts and 21 rows to 10cm/4in over st st worked on 5½mm/No 5 needles.
Aftercare Hand wash, dry clean Ⓐ, cool iron, do not bleach.

Pure New Wool
4 ply (p152)
Recommended tension 28 sts and 36 rows to 10cm/4in over st st worked on

3¼mm/No 10 needles.
Afterware Hand wash (40°C), machine wash (6), dry clean Ⓟ, warm iron.

Pure New Wool
3 ply (p199)
Recommended tension 32 sts and 40 rows to 10cm/4in over st st worked on 3mm/No 11 needles.
Aftercare Hand wash (40°C), machine wash (7), dry clean Ⓟ, warm iron.

Pure New Wool
2 ply (p182)
Recommended tension 36 sts and 44 rows to 10cm/4in over st st worked on 2¾mm/No 12 needles.
Aftercare Hand wash (40°C), machine wash (5), dry clean Ⓟ, cool iron.

Trophy Double Knitting
(p42)
Recommended tension 24 sts and 30 rows to 10cm/4in over st st worked on 4mm/No 8 needles.
Aftercare Hand wash only, warm iron.

Twilleys

UK: H G Twilley Ltd, Roman Mill, Stamford. Lincoln PE9 1BG.
Mail order: Ries Wools, 243 High Holborn, London WC1.
Australia: Panda Yarn, 17–27 Brunswick Road, East Brunswick, 3057 Victoria.
S. Africa: S W Nyman, PO Box 292, Durban 4000.

Goldfingering
(p172)
Recommended tension 30 sts and 48

rows to 10cm/4in over st st worked on 2¾mm/No 12 needles.
Aftercare Hand wash only, dry flat.

Lyscordet No 5
(p172)
Recommended tension 30 sts and 48 rows to 10cm/4in over st st worked on 2¾mm/No 12 needles.
Aftercare Hand wash only, dry flat.

Stalite
(pp67, 146)
Recommended tension 28 sts and 36 rows to 10cm/4in over st st worked on 3¼mm/No 10 needles.
Aftercare Warm hand wash, cold rinse, dry flat away from sun, dry clean Ⓐ, warm iron under a damp cloth.

Wisper
(p192)
Recommended tension 30 sts and 36 rows to 10cm/4in over st st worked on 3¼mm/No 10 needles.
Aftercare Hand wash only, short spin, dry flat, do not press.

Wendy

UK: Carter and Parker Ltd, Gordon Mills, Guiseley, West Yorkshire.
Australia: Craft Warehouse, 30 Guess Avenue, Arncliff, New South Wales, 2205.
S. Africa: Woolcraft Agencies, PO Box 17657, 2038 Hillbrow, Johannesburg.

Choice Double Knitting
(p171)
Recommended tension 24 sts and 32

rows to 10cm/4in over st st worked on 4mm/No 8 needles.
Aftercare Hand or machine wash (40°C), cool iron under a dry cloth.

Choice
4 ply (p176)
Recommended tension 28 sts and 36 rows to 10cm/4in over st st worked on 3¼mm/No 10 needles.
Aftercare Hand wash (40°C), machine wash (6), cool dry iron.

Courtellon Double Knitting
(pp58, 116)
Recommended tension 24 sts and 32 rows to 10cm/4in over st st worked on 4mm/No 8 needles.
Aftercare Hand or machine wash (40°C), cool iron under a dry cloth.

Darling Double Knitting
(pp166)
Recommended tension 24 sts and 32 rows to 10cm/4in over st st worked on 4mm/No 8 needles.
Aftercare Hand or machine wash (40°C), cool iron under a dry cloth.

Shetland Double Knitting
(pp48, 216)
Recommended tension 24 sts and 32 rows to 10cm/4in over st st worked on 4mm/No 8 needles.
Aftercare Hand wash (40°C), machine wash (7), warm iron.

Index